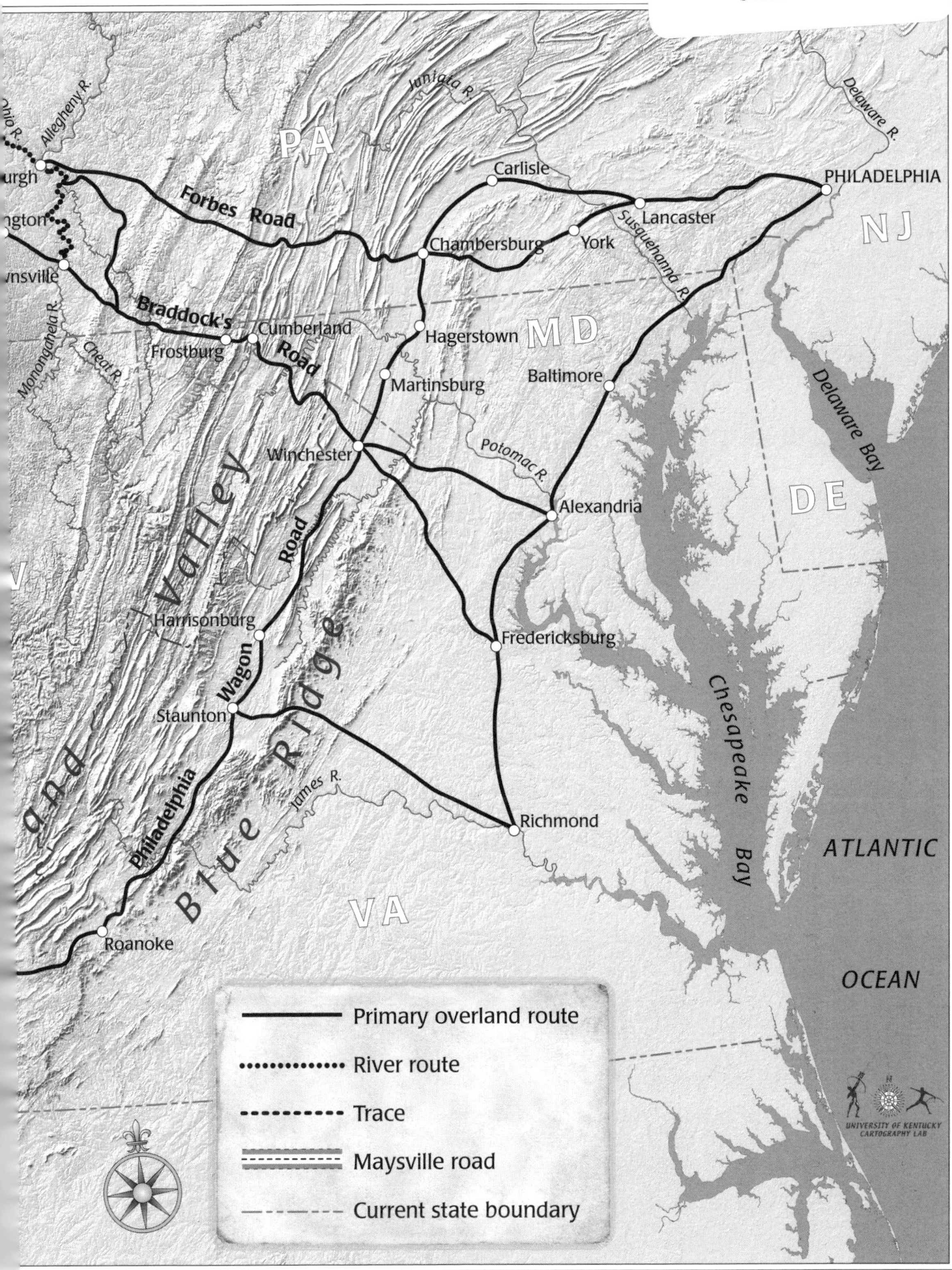

PA
MD
NJ
DE
VA
PHILADELPHIA
Carlisle
Lancaster
York
Chambersburg
Hagerstown
Cumberland
Frostburg
Martinsburg
Baltimore
Winchester
Alexandria
Harrisonburg
Fredericksburg
Staunton
Richmond
Roanoke
Forbes Road
Braddock's Road
Valley Road
Wagon
Philadelphia
Blue Ridge
Allegheny R.
Juniata R.
Delaware R.
Susquehanna R.
Monongahela R.
Cheat R.
Potomac R.
James R.
Delaware Bay
Chesapeake Bay
ATLANTIC OCEAN
Primary overland route
River route
Trace
Maysville road
Current state boundary
UNIVERSITY OF KENTUCKY CARTOGRAPHY LAB

Kentucky's Frontier Highway

Kentucky's Frontier Highway

Historical Landscapes along the Maysville Road

Karl Raitz
and
Nancy O'Malley

Cartographic Design and Production by Dick Gilbreath,
Gyula Pauer Center for Cartography and GIS

University Press of Kentucky

Scholarly publisher for the Commonwealth,
serving Bellarmine University, Berea College, Centre College of Kentucky, Eastern Kentucky University, The Filson Historical Society, Georgetown College, Kentucky Historical Society, Kentucky State University, Morehead State University, Murray State University, Northern Kentucky University, Transylvania University, University of Kentucky, University of Louisville, and Western Kentucky University.

Editorial and Sales Offices: The University Press of Kentucky
663 South Limestone Street, Lexington, Kentucky 40508-4008
www.kentuckypress.com

Unless otherwise noted, photographs were taken by Karl Raitz between 2005 and 2007.

16 15 14 13 12 5 4 3 2 1

Library of Congress Cataloging-in-Publication Data

Raitz, Karl B.
Kentucky's frontier highway : historical landscapes along the Maysville Road / Karl Raitz and Nancy O'Malley.
pages cm
Includes bibliographical references and index.
ISBN 978-0-8131-3664-6 (hardcover : acid-free paper) —
ISBN 978-0-8131-3666-0 (pdf) (print) -- ISBN 978-0-8131-4069-8 (epub) (print)
1. Historic sites—Kentucky—Maysville Region. 2. Landscapes—Kentucky—Maysville Region. 3. Trails—Kentucky—Maysville Region—History. 4. Roads—Kentucky—Maysville Region—History. 5. Maysville Region (Ky.)—History, Local. 6. Maysville Region (Ky.)—Description and travel. 7. Frontier and pioneer life—Kentucky—Maysville Region. 8. Maysville Region (Ky.)—History. I. O'Malley, Nancy. II. Title.
F459.M47R35 2012
976.9'323—dc23 2012032833

This book is printed on acid-free paper meeting the requirements of the American National Standard for Permanence in Paper for Printed Library Materials.

∞

Manufactured in the United States of America.

Member of the Association of
American University Presses

Contents

Maps and Illustrations

Maps

Illustrations

Part I

Introduction

As Carl G. Fisher wrote in 1912: "The highways of America are built chiefly of politics, whereas the proper material is crushed rock, or concrete."

—George R. Stewart,
U.S. 40: Cross Section of the United States of America

1

Reading America's Roads

The twenty-first-century road, whether in Kentucky or elsewhere in America, is sufficiently ubiquitous that its commonness may lull drivers into assuming its presence and passable condition. We tend to speed along, ignoring the road's distinctive qualities, until a construction detour, accumulating snow, an outsize sign touting an outlet mall, or a highway patrol car's flashing red and blue lights remind us that the road is a place of intersection, in both a literal and metaphorical sense, for a host of different actors, interests, and priorities all interacting through time. The product is a linear place that is at once part of a larger network of linear places that are linked together but comprise particularistic parts—a bridge, a quarter-mile section of road, a freeway interchange, a curb cut that opens to an abandoned building foundation—that are always changing, adjusting, in flux. Neither the road—as a whole or a part—nor the people or institutions that build, maintain, or use it are static or stable.[1] The road, its companion roadside, and the society that builds and uses it are always changing, adjusting, and becoming something new and different.[2] Some changes have long historical trajectories that are technology-dependent, such as a road's cross-sectional form and its configuration in relation to topographic surfaces. Other changes occur within much shorter temporal windows, such as the weathering of smooth, black asphalt into a checked surface, sun-bleached and oxidized to a whitish gray. Just so, the roadside is in continual adjustment as businesses are established and fail, or as changes in travel technology—from stagecoach to interurban rail to private automobile—render nineteenth-century taverns anachronistic or motivate construction of a fast-food franchise restaurant.

Such change does not necessarily obliterate established landscape elements such as road sections, bridges, townhouses, taverns, or gas stations. Some elements recede from view when engineers make minor road realignments that bypass them; others stolidly remain standing along the road, but people convert them to new uses. The historical composite road-roadside landscape is therefore a complex palimpsest of structures and land uses that represent a host of incommensurable yet intersecting engineering technologies, legal edicts, political imbroglios, societal milieus, and economic conditions. Acknowledging that a road landscape is exceptionally complicated signals frustration because its very complexity implies that not even the best-informed

Now orphaned by the realignment of the road, the Ellis Tavern at Ellisville in Nicholas County once stood directly next to the thoroughfare, convenient to the passing traveler in need of libations, a hot meal, stabling and feed for a horse, or a night's accommodation. The massive stone construction promised sanctuary within, and visitors found solid respectability in the person of James Ellis, proprietor, who also built a log courthouse, jail, and a pen for stray livestock near the tavern when Ellisville served as the county seat.

person can begin to enumerate, never mind understand, all the interrelated factors that create and reside in a single mile of road. On the other hand, by its very nature as a public thoroughfare, the road is always open to our inspection, our questions and musings, as long as we remain open to serious engagement with its surfaces, signs, structures, and situations.

The metaphor of road-as-intersection acknowledges the road's position as a node within any number of knowledge networks or systems that range from the abstract to the concrete, from the theoretical to the functional, from the historic to the current.[3] For example, three technical knowledge networks intersect at the road-roadside; science, technology, and engineering. Before World War I engineers constructed roads on the basis of empirically derived understandings of nature and knowledge gained from "cut-and-try" techniques and the practical experience of observing what worked best in actual applications. The Federal Office of Public Roads did not use the term *research* to describe its laboratory and field investigations work until 1916.[4]

A little more than a mile west of the Maysville Road in southwest Mason County, an old road said by some to follow a historical buffalo trace cuts across a farm pasture entrenched into the land surface by iron-shod horses' hooves and iron-rimmed wagon wheels. Some abandoned roadways are marked today by linear depressions across farm fields and pastures; others continue in use as farm driveways or field access roads.

The applications, processes, and tools of road-construction technology remained embedded in traditional folkways—axes and brush hooks, picks and pry bars, shovels and wheelbarrows—until the 1870s, largely without the benefit of considered engineering or the application of scientific investigation.[5] The best nineteenth-century roads in Kentucky were built from hand-broken stone laid and packed into a hard surface according to principles developed by the Scottish engineers John McAdam and Thomas Telford. Innovations in road construction technology or engineering, whether in Kentucky or elsewhere, were stimulated not by an absence of roads and bridges across minimally developed areas but by a bustling regional economy that was served by an overtaxed and dysfunctional road network.[6] Laborers constructed the nation's first brick-surfaced pavement of annealed shale-clay brick in Charleston, West Virginia, about 1870. By the 1890s brick road technology was in common use in Pennsylvania, Ohio, Indiana, and Illinois, where construction crews converted the National Road and other major thoroughfares from McAdam's stone to brick surfacing. Although some Kentucky towns and cities employed brick as a street-covering material, it never became a common road surface in the state.[7]

The twentieth century's first two decades brought a host of revolutionary changes to road-building technology and engineering practices. Portland cement, invented in the 1870s, was first used to produce concrete street surfacing in Bellefontaine, Ohio, in 1891. In 1909 the Association of American Portland Cement Manufacturers offered prizes for the best articles on the increasing importance of concrete for road construction; *Good Roads Magazine* published the winning essays. By the 1910s concrete was coming into general use for road construction in the Northeast and Midwest, especially in urban areas.[8] Engineers completed Kentucky's first concrete road in 1915, a steep, two-mile section of the Covington-Lexington Road in Kenton County near the Ohio River.[9] This road section was one of the state's busiest, and its traditional rock-covered macadam structure failed repeatedly under heavy traffic loads. That the state legislature placed a high priority on rebuilding this road with resilient, albeit expensive, concrete was an affirmation of the principle that road construction innovation is stimulated by the failure of existing roads to serve the demands placed on them.[10]

The rapidly escalating market for large-scale farm machinery on California's Central Valley bonanza wheat farms after the Civil War stimulated the development of track-type tractors. The crawler tractor's arrival paralleled that of the gasoline engine, which, when petroleum fuels became available and engine electrical systems had been perfected, led to the manufacture of a gasoline engine–powered crawler tractor by a Stockton, California, machinery manufacturer in 1906. Soon thereafter road-construction contractors had access to track-type Caterpillar tractors equipped with bulldozer blades that allowed engineers to design and build roads that required moving large volumes of earth and rock to reduce grades by hill cuts and valley fills or embankments.[11]

A different though parallel string of technology innovations began with a 1903 adaptation of a wagonlike box to what was by then a traditional passenger-car chassis to create the truck. By the 1910s trucks were increasingly displacing horse-drawn wagons for common dray work, thereby extending hauling and delivery-service distances fivefold or more. Trucking companies proliferated rapidly, eclipsing the horse-and-wagon lines with multiple, often unanticipated branching effects. As urban horse populations declined, for example, livery owners tore down their central-city stables, thus vacating large blocks of land for alternative development. Once in active use, heavily loaded trucks pounded and pulverized old macadam roads with catastrophic results. By 1918 road failure had become sufficiently pervasive that Prevost Hubbard of the Federal Bureau of Public Roads was moved to observe: "These failures were not only sudden but complete, and almost overnight an excellent surface might become impassable. A very large proportion of the failures have been characterized by an almost simultaneous destruction of the entire road structure, and not merely the disintegration of the wearing course or pavement proper."[12] Contemplating the potential disruption to commerce and the cost of road replacement, states began to consider imposing weight and speed limits on trucks.[13]

These and many other science, engineering, and technology object lessons illustrate

During the Great Depression, circa 1934, WPA work crews improved some of central Kentucky's rural farm-service roads, such as Squires Road in Fayette County, south of Lexington. A track-type tractor tows a leaning-wheel blade grader manufactured by J. D. Adams & Company of Indianapolis. The grader fills ruts and levels the road surface in preparation for the application of a thin layer of crushed stone. The roller-packer on the distant hillside compacts and levels the new stone surface. In the 1970s and 1980s farmland here was converted into subdivisions and Squires Road became a city street. (Courtesy of the University of Kentucky Library Special Collections, Goodman-Paxton WPA Collection, PA64M1-5381)

that the parentage of road-related knowledge networks must, perforce, include legal, political, economic, and social dimensions that also intersected at the road and roadside. The Kentucky legislature passed a road law in 1797, five years after attaining statehood, a statute that essentially copied Virginia's road law, itself an adaptation of centuries-old English road law.[14] Thereafter, however, state-level legislative oversight of road construction was limited largely to concerns for a few major baseline roads, as they were termed, that connected the larger towns. Nineteenth-century roads in Kentucky and many other eastern and Atlantic coast states, especially local-scale roads that connected the rural countryside to a county seat or a cross-state thoroughfare, were built and maintained as toll roads not by governmental agencies but by local people guided only by practical knowledge and a few vague legislative edicts.[15] When Kentucky's U.S. representatives sought to obtain federal support for the construction of a proper macadam road from Maysville to Lexington in 1830, President Andrew Jackson vetoed the proposed legislation, arguing that the Constitution prohibited expending federal funds for projects of "purely local character."[16] The state, for its part, expedited plans to underwrite Maysville Road improvements internally by chartering the Maysville and Washington Turnpike Road Company and providing limited financing for road construction through the sale of shares in the company and tolls collected from road users.[17]

By the 1830s most state political leaders and businesspeople were becoming increasingly concerned that local and regional accessibility to East Coast ports and urban centers be enhanced through what were termed *internal improvements*—constructing harbors and canals, improving river navigation, and building long-distance roads. Kentucky's legislature created the state Board of Internal Improvement, whose chief engineer began issuing detailed guidelines for road construction, although the state continued to insist that roads be financed and built by the people who used the roads.[18] The Board of Internal Improvement lacked legal authorization to oversee or enforce state-level directives other than in the most elementary way. Board members, therefore, could only voice displeasure when local turnpike company officers hired immigrant road builders who were unable or unwilling to comply with directives of which they were unaware or lacked sufficient capital with which to conform. The abstract idealism of Kentucky's early road law was dramatically attenuated, however; the divide between the legislative action that produced road law and the earth-and-rock reality of road building was chasmal. Furthermore, few state-level public officials were willing to acknowledge that the age-old traditionalist maxim that roads served local constituents and communities was anachronistic and that construction of roads and the establishment of planned road networks would require direction, oversight, and financing from a central governmental authority. This shortsighted perspective necessarily placed responsibility for road construction and maintenance in the hands of landowners, a logic that represented a failure to discern the potential economic and social value of trans-county, trans-state, and trans-regional roads. Local communities, never mind the few shareholders in a turnpike company, could never muster the large-scale financing and system management required to transform thousands of short, badly maintained road segments into a highway network characterized by

A rare Maysville Road iron turnpike mile marker is bolted to the road frontage fence in front of Daniel Drake's home in Mayslick, Mason County. Embossed hands point north to Zanesville, Ohio, and Maysville, and south to Lexington, Nashville, Tennessee, and Florence, Alabama. Though Andrew Jackson in 1830 famously vetoed legislation to provide federal monies to build the turnpike on the grounds that the improved road would serve only Kentucky, he also traveled this road between his home in Nashville and Washington, D.C., and so personally experienced its regional character.

connectivity, standardization, and reliability. If Kentucky governmental representatives were slow to grasp the import of their well-informed and adequately funded participation in large-scale internal improvement projects, the federal government was similarly vacuous and could offer little in the way of an object lesson in appropriate management techniques for road network development and oversight.

Kentucky and the rest of America exited the nineteenth century acceding to public demands for free roads; most roadside tollhouses were closed, and newly written state legislation enabled local governments to purchase and maintain the old pikes as free public ways. Between 1890 and 1930 inventor-entrepreneurs created multiple technological advances that were concomitant and intersecting and which manufacturers applied to vehicular construction—synthetic rubber and balloon tires, hydraulic presses and high-strength steels, petroleum refining and gasoline engines, storage batteries and electric ignition systems. The rush of transport-related innovations yielded an awkward imbalance between road-using vehicles that rapidly increased in number and capability, and road-building technology, governmental enfranchisement of construction finance, and engineering oversight; each of these sectors lagged annoyingly. Identifying and evaluating such lags is important in understanding the uneven evolution of road and society linkages. A useful concept for identifying technology-society system lags is that of "reverse salient"—literally a reentrant angle in a star-shaped fortification wall or a sagging section in an advancing weather front—which is a metaphorical reference to a component of an expanding system that does not advance harmoniously with other components. A reverse salient will present critical problems that will hamper or thwart the growth of an entire enterprise and begs for concerted action through technical inventions and procedural innovations if expansion is to proceed.[19]

In the twentieth century's first three decades, state and federal governments, spurred by automobile manufacturers and owners who instigated the Good Roads Movement, and by a rapidly increasing cohort of bicyclists, reluctantly accepted responsibility for and control over road construction and maintenance. The movement was perhaps the most visible and well-documented response to the reverse salient of lagging governmental participation in the large-scale management of road construction technology and finance.[20] From 1915 to 1920 Kentucky's commissioner of public roads oversaw construction of some eight hundred miles of state-aid roads that were, according to statute, to be maintained by the counties the roads traversed. When, for lack of funds to purchase equipment or to hire trained engineers and laborers, counties failed to maintain their new roads, the state in 1918 passed additional legislation permitting the government to redirect to road maintenance those state aid funds intended for county general fund expenditures. The state subsequently found, to its rather profound embarrassment, one might imagine, that it had neither the funds nor the equipment required to maintain the roads its state-aid program had built. To refine road jurisdiction, the Kentucky legislature passed a new road law in 1920 that designated a primary road system of some four thousand miles to be constructed and maintained by the Department of State Roads and Highways. The statute designated the Maysville Road a state road.[21] The department organized a maintenance division in 1921 under the direction of an engineer who had supervisory control over the division's labor crews. The state's dearth of construction equipment was finally addressed when the federal government released surplus materiel from World War I, including trucks, tractors, and small tools sufficient to outfit state labor crews almost entirely.[22]

For its part, the federal government passed its initial road act in 1916, followed by another in 1921. Though both acts allocated funds to state legislatures to repair old roads and build new ones, neither conceived of a planned, coherent nationwide road network. Furthermore, instead of initially focusing on upgrading primary intercity and intercounty roads, local county politics often siphoned off funds for small neighborhood roads used by limited but influential constituents. The concept of a road network that maximized traffic flow for trucks and automobiles over long distances lay beyond federal grasp. Instead, funds and labor were expended on unconnected local road segments; cross-country roads with sharp curves, steep hills, at-grade intersections, and narrow, shoulderless roadbeds were largely ignored.[23] In 1914 the American Association of State Highway Officials (AASHO) formed to advocate for federal support for road construction and quickly became one of the most influential lobbying groups in Washington, D.C. Working with the federal Bureau of Public Roads, AASHO helped bring order to the chaos of route designations by eliminating traditional road names and devising a uniform system of road numbers and standardized road signage. East-west roads received even numbers, north-south roads odd numbers. In 1926 the Maysville Road became part of U.S. 68, a trans-regional highway that linked Findlay, Ohio, and Paducah, Kentucky.[24] The process of creating a systematically numbered national road network was initially a mapping exercise that in many cases pieced together long roads from short fragments, but the net effect was to institutionalize or render permanent a master highway pattern that still obtains nearly ninety years later. Though the generalized routeways gained some measure of permanence, the technologies of vehicle construction and road and bridge engineering, and the interplay of legal statutes, tax-based financing, business and political priorities, were set into a gyre of continuous flux whereby changes in one segment necessarily unbalanced others.

As governmental organization and regulation of roadway construction became systematized and road quality improved, traffic volume increased geometrically, leading to congestion on cross-country roads and city streets, a rapidly accelerating accident rate, and a demonstrated need to bring discipline to roadway travel by instituting a variety of traffic-control regulations and creating special road police to provide enforcement. The first highway centerline formally dividing a hard-surface highway into two traffic lanes was painted on a Michigan highway in 1917. At-grade highway railroad crossings were particularly treacherous, and federal legislation in the mid-1930s allocated more than $600 million to states for highway safety and road improvement programs especially targeted at separating at-grade railroad crossings.[25] During the 1930s most states created a highway-oriented police force to assist motorists who had breakdowns or accidents and enforce state traffic laws. Kentucky's Highway Patrol formed in 1936 and was reorganized into the State Police force in 1948.

An active accompaniment to this complex interplay of technical, economic, political,

Three different Maysville Road alignments lie in close proximity at the front of Eaglestone Farm north of Millersburg in Nicholas County. The oldest track, possibly the original pre-turnpike route, crosses the pasture to the far left. The first-generation engineered road is now a short access road to the immediate left. The modern road, established in 1948, cut through a sidehill of limestone bedrock on the right to straighten a dangerously tight curve. Between the two roads is a small island of rock and earth left behind by the 1948 cut-through. Excavated into the hillside to the far right, and camouflaged by trees, is an old roadside quarry that was likely a source of macadam stone for nineteenth-century road builders.

and legal processes is the dynamic social world of all those whose lives and livelihoods were intertwined with the roads and vehicles that enabled discretionary movement. For rural people, access to the automobile presented a resolution to the isolation of remote farmsteads. But as rural residents took up the automobile and truck, their long-standing networks of social relations and socially created places based on horse and buggy travel were necessarily distorted and distressed. The car's speed and long range threatened the viability of rural schools and churches. Improved roads and vehicles meant that children could attend consolidated schools in the county seat; a wider selection of religious philosophies was now within a Sunday morning's driving range.[26] The frequency of visiting distant relatives increased, and the acquaintance pool from which one might draw a marriage partner expanded significantly. Farmers driving trucks had relatively easy access to mills and blacksmith shops in town; the trip via packhorse to the nearest creek-side gristmill in the countryside now became a quaint

The twelve-and-one-half-mile section of the Maysville Road–U.S. 68 between Lexington and Paris follows an 1830s turnpike alignment and has long been known as Paris Pike. Engineers reconfigured the narrow, two-lane highway into a four-lane parkway in 2003. The parkway now crosses North Elkhorn Creek on twin concrete-and-steel bridges in front of Elmendorf Farm. The turnpike's original track crossed the creek where the left-hand bridge now stands and traced straight across the hill in the distance, where it splices into the right-hand, or northbound, lanes.

experience. Urban residents could drive to work and shopping and enjoy a ubiquity of areal access far greater than was possible when a person's movements were dependent on the now derogated trolley car and interurban rail. State governments and city boosters promoted auto-borne tourism, and Sunday drivers began to clog rural highways and city streets. The spate of road traffic recatalyzed the roadside as a venue for potential businesses that served travelers. And people, through their purchase preferences and use patterns, influenced how motor vehicles were built and used and how governmental priorities for road construction and maintenance were established.

From the Ohio River's south-bank landing site at Maysville south to Lexington, the Maysville Road's length is less than seventy miles. Yet along its corridor is a grand tableau of varied physical environments on which people from many cultures, deploying varied technologies, have pursued life and made a living. The engaged pathway traveler, whether auto-borne or armchaired, is aware of countryside and community

Many eighteenth-century overland roads originated at important water-land connecting points, be they ocean or river ports. Maysville—originally named Limestone—is sited at the riverboat landing on the Ohio's south bank near the mouth of Limestone Creek. Ferryboats connected Kentucky and Ohio at this point until 1931, when engineers completed the Simon Kenton Memorial Bridge. Maysville's residential streets step down the Ohio River valley's south bluff to the river's edge. In this view of the Maysville skyline, a cruciform roof and twin bell towers identify St. Patrick Church on Third Street; the spire just to the left marks the Episcopal church.

along the highway and the subtle evidences of past and current lives. Perceptive travel requires locally scaled information on geography and history to confirm suspicions or spark revelations. The traveler should seek more insights than the declarative historic plaque at the roadside that offers a sliver of information, more often about powerful men than common people who created the landscape through which the road traverses. But that landscape is also a kind of historic plaque that, with great frequency, records the actions of the common folk who used the land and built the structures and incorporated them into their lives. No landscape biography could record every building, street, or landscape detail. Rather, the traveler should pay keen attention to the corridor along which the road passes and try to recognize the sites that represent the great processes of human agency that stand like felicitous scaffolding behind the making of the road's landscape. Historic events and important individuals play a significant role in landscape making, but we need to place them within the larger landscape of common people and common artifacts, among sites both celebrated and commonplace. Both kinds of places are part of the language of landscape interpretation, meaning, and understanding.

Travel along an old road such as the Maysville Road can be much more than an invitation to daydream to the accompaniment of satellite-broadcast radio music. Rather, the modern roadway offers the curious traveler an opportunity to engage the road as a tableau of historical geography, to see, perhaps to read, in its routeway and roadside buildings the layers and bundles of human agency that it incorporates.

2

Traveling the Road

Purposeful travelers have a common goal: to depart a starting point and reach safely a destination. But what of the experience that links a journey's beginning and end? Travel is a multidimensional process that blends predictable and unpredictable events. The transport mode (stagecoach or automobile), trip length, and date or season of travel are largely predictable. Weather, traveling companions (chosen or voluntary), and road quality are marginally predictable. And many of the trip's events and perhaps much of its scenery are wholly unanticipated, and therein, for some travelers at least, resides the pleasure of the journey, the joy of experiencing the new, the unexpected.[1] Other travelers find the unpredictable aspects of a journey discomforting and seek to increase their comfort by increasing predictability. They do this by maintaining their conveyance, traveling in good weather, and staying overnight at inns or hotels where they have stayed before or they know by reputation to offer peerless accommodation.

The earliest historic travelers on the Limestone Trace walked or rode on horseback along a trail that was muddy and slick in wet weather, dusty in dry weather, and rutted all year round. And *mud* is a rather one-dimensional term for a variety of conditions, depending on location. Where the road crossed river floodplains, for example, the silty soils turned into a carbon-colored ooze when wet, creating a seemingly bottomless mire the consistency of thick porridge. The sickly yellow-blue-green mud on an Eden Shale hillside might be slick, even slimy, and a gangue of rock and clay. The Bluegrass limestone lands entrained high levels of organic material yet drained rapidly; the reddish-brown muds here were often thickly viscous.

In the early years of historic settlement, the Limestone Trace was the last leg of a long journey that had already tallied weeks of anxious and exhausting travel aboard a wagon or on a flatboat or keelboat drifting with the current down the Ohio River. When a group of settlers finally tied up at the Limestone landing (now Maysville), they may have been relieved that they no longer had to worry about capsizing and drowning, but hazards of a different kind remained and the trials of travel were far from over. Few early travelers stayed at the Limestone landing because of its exposed position and lack of amenities. Joel Watkins did have a salutary experience when he passed through Limestone in 1789, largely because he was fortunate to stay with his former tutor, Thomas Brooks. Brooks entertained him "with the greatest civility,"

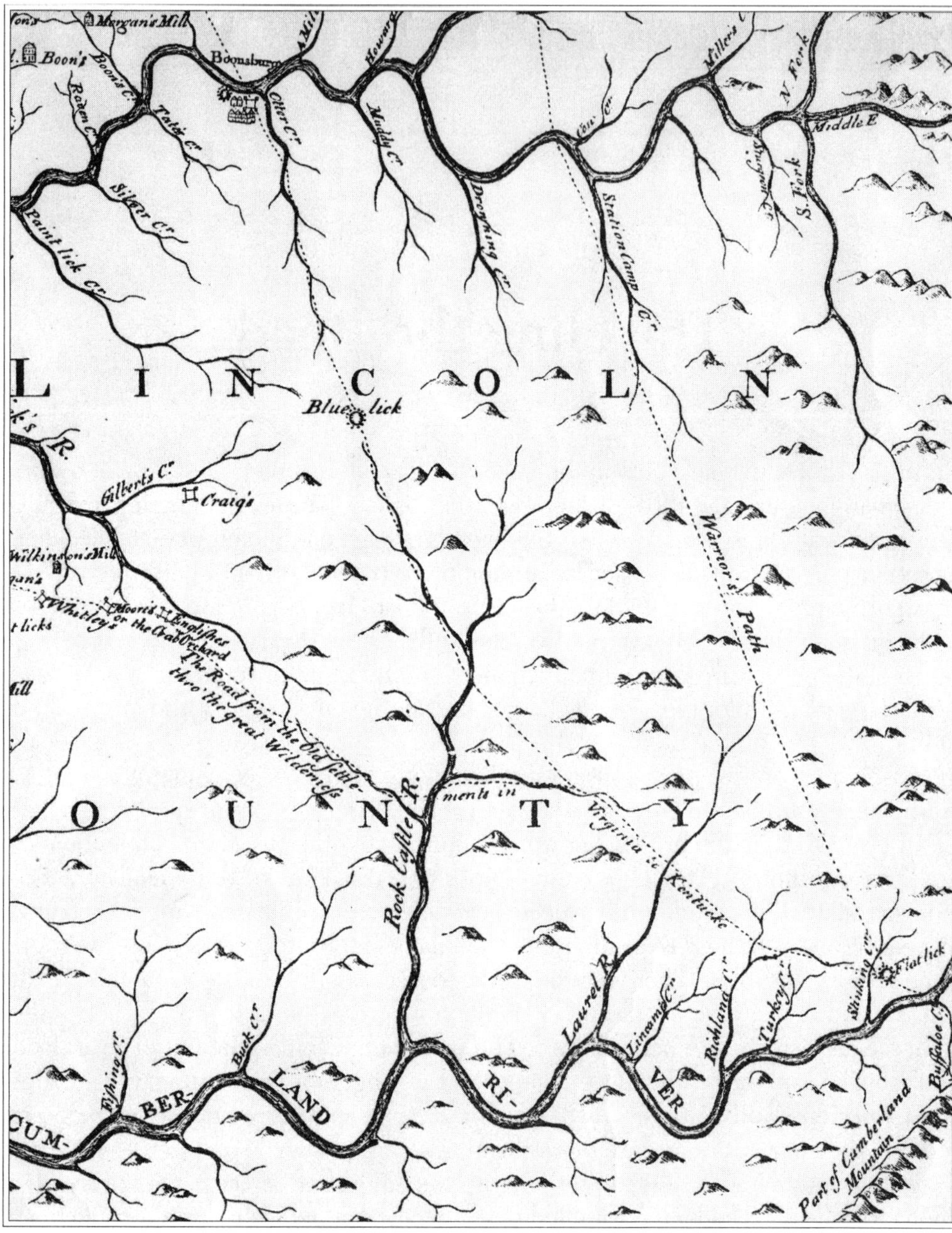

John Filson's *Kentucke*—Cumberland Gap to Boonesborough. John Filson, a schoolteacher, surveyor, cartographer, and land speculator from Pennsylvania, came to the Kentucky frontier in 1783. The following year he published a book entitled *The Discovery, Settlement, and Present State of Kentucke,* with an accompanying map simply entitled *Kentucke.* Filson used fine dashed lines to depict generalized trail routes, and this map segment portrays southeastern Kentucky, including Cumberland Mountain, and the Warrior's Path, Daniel Boone's Trace, and the Wilderness Road. Filson's cartography uses "mole hills" to represent topography, but these symbols only hint at the rugged mountain land that these narrow paths traversed. At Flat Lick, just north of the Cumberland River, Boone's Trace—labeled "Virginia to Kentucke"—angles north- northwest to Boonsburg (Boonesborough) on the Kentucky River. The Wilderness insisted on his "tarrying some time with him in town," and gave him a "very agreeable breakfast" and the opportunity to shave, take a nap, and explore the settlement. Watkins then spent the night where he had the satisfaction of being able to sleep in a bed "with my Breeches off" for the second night in a row.[2] Needham Parry, traveling to Limestone five years later, in 1794, was unimpressed with the people he encountered. He saw the potential for a "flourishing little place" at Limestone, but only if "it was but settled with people of any principle: which I think they are the clearest of, of any set I ever saw."[3]

Most settlers who traveled to the region via Limestone headed inland from the river toward the Inner Bluegrass, where settlement was denser, quality land could be found, and, because of strength in numbers, conditions were safer, although the threat of Indian attack persisted until the close of the Revolutionary War. Along the corridor into Kentucky's Bluegrass country, travelers on the Limestone Trace experienced widely variable conditions in the fundamental comforts available at roadside; food, drink, and acceptable beds.

Proceeding from the riverside landing at Limestone, travelers ascended the steep south bluff and made their way four miles inland to the village of Washington. By 1784, the year before Washington was formally surveyed, the place included only a few very crude buildings. Ned Darnaby described the place as he encountered it in October of that year: "I noticed several houses commenced but not finished—bodies not covered. I don't know whether there were any persons living there."[4] Compared to his treatment at Brooks's residence in Limestone, Joel Watkins's experience in Washington was a disagreeable contrast. He encountered houses erected with hewn logs of very "indifferent" construction, and he could find no feed for his horse.

These examples at the Ohio River end of the Limestone Trace were typical of conditions in the 1780s, but matters improved as emigration increased and people established villages and rural communities along the road. As the increasingly preferred route into Kentucky, the Limestone Trace became the Limestone Road and later the Maysville-to-Lexington Turnpike. Although it was a direct route of only some sixty miles into the coveted Inner Bluegrass country, variable road quality dramatically dampened travel speed to the extent that one might require three or even four days to reach Lexington. Travelers needed sustenance to complete the trip, and over time their options for accommodations expanded as local residents established roadside businesses offering food, drink, overnight lodging, and stabling and feed for their horses. To describe such places of sanctuary, the lexicon of the day included a variety of terms including inn, tavern, ordinary, place of entertainment, tippling house, hotel, and resort. Some terms were interchangeable; others implied availability of specific types of services and amenities—or the lack thereof. Travelers brought their own conceptions of what qualities such roadside businesses should have, and their

Road crosses the Rock Castle River heading northwest toward Crab Orchard and Whitley's Station. Though thousands of migrants traveled the Wilderness Road and Boone's Trace to reach the Bluegrass Region, most traveled on horseback or on foot leading packhorses. These legendary mountain tracks were not made suitable for heavy wagon traffic until after the Civil War. (Courtesy of the University Press of Kentucky and the Kentucky Geological Survey)

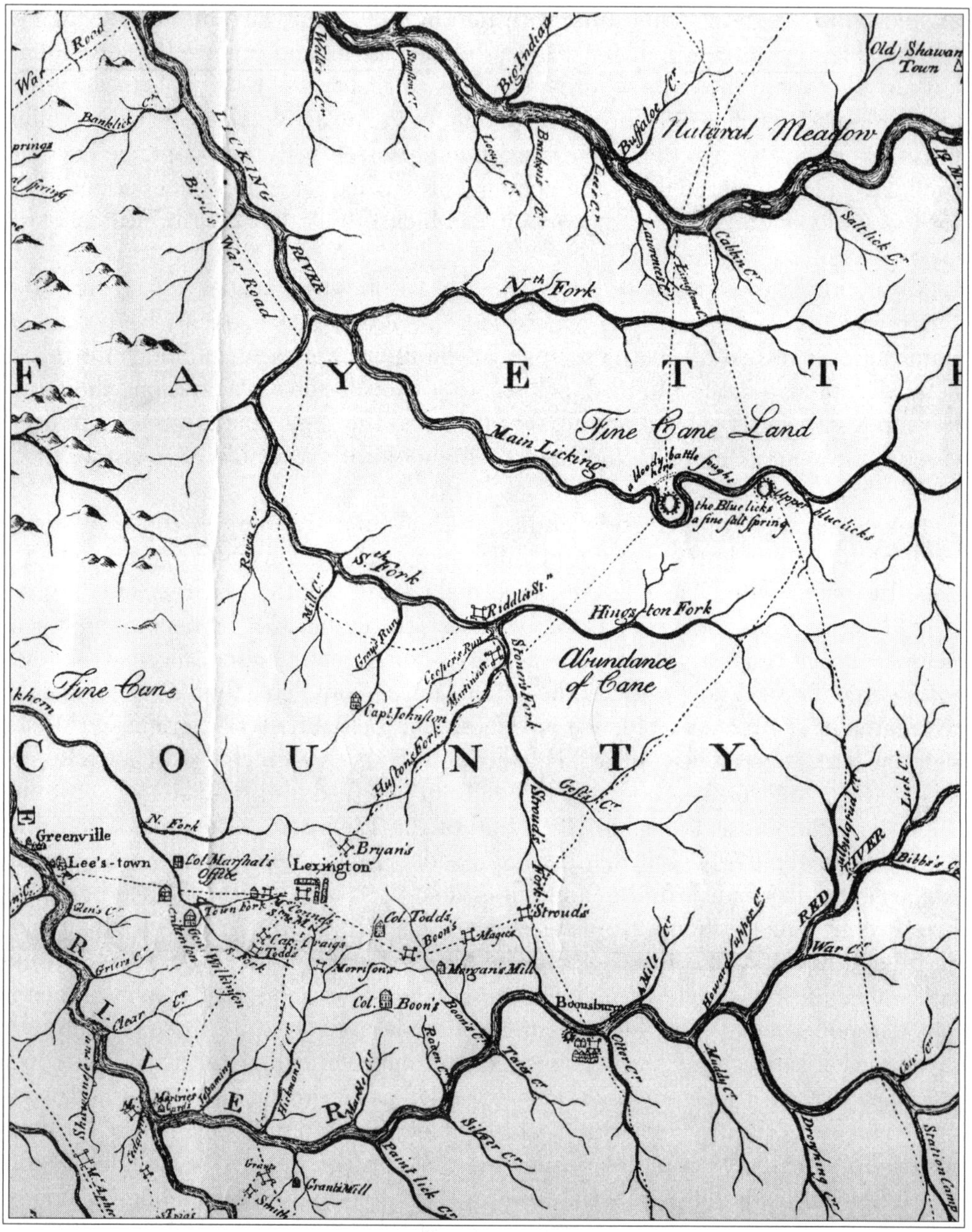

John Filson's *Kentucke*—Ohio River to Lexington. This segment of John Filson's map depicts the northeast section of the Bluegrass Region extending from the Ohio River in the north to the Kentucky River in the southwest. At the point where Limestone Creek joins the Ohio River (Maysville), Smith's Waggon Road, later known as the Maysville Road, leads south to the Blue Licks on the Licking River. From there the track turns southwest to Hingston Fork (Hinkston Creek and Millersburg), Stoner's Fork (Paris), Bryan's Station, and Lexington. Filson's Maysville Road corridor seems topographically benign, marked only by an imagined harmonic sinuosity of its streams and "Fine Cane Land." Settlers associated cane with fertile soils and found that their cattle would readily feed on the luxuriant plant. (Courtesy of the University Press of Kentucky and the Kentucky Geological Survey)

expectations were not always matched by the reality they encountered. Consequently, traveler's observations recorded the verities, as they saw them, from high praise to dismayed criticism, often expressed during a single trip.

An example from 1795–1796: Thomas Chapman, an Englishman who intended to emigrate to the United States, traveled from Newport, Kentucky, east to Virginia via the Limestone Trace to Lexington and the Wilderness Road from Danville, Kentucky, with side trips to Harrodsburg and Frankfort. His experiences are illustrative of what a traveler could expect in Kentucky in the 1790s. From Newport to Washington, his party slept two nights in log cabins, all sharing one bed, where they received "civil usage although the fare was Homely." The first tavern he encountered was at Mayslick, where Isaac Drake, a New Jersey man, offered travelers respite. This tavern elicited no special comment, but Eve's Tavern (probably Thomas Eades's establishment) in Paris earned the unfavorable rating of "a very dirty uncomfortable House."[5]

Conditions were better at more populous towns, Chapman found. At McNair's Tavern in Lexington, he pronounced the proprietor "a civil, well behaved Irishman." Mr. Wissengar's Tavern in Frankfort was, in Chapman's opinion, "the best in the Town, and a very good one it is," attributing its quality to the presence of state legislators and other members of government who stayed there. Chapman stayed at a small log tavern on his way to Harrodsburg, an experience that passed without criticism. He then returned to Lexington, where he again stayed with McNair and was again impressed, calling him "a much civiler Landlord than are commonly to be met with in this part of the World."

That Chapman would affirm McNair's business persona so positively is all the more remarkable because the prevailing attitude toward Irishmen at the time was decidedly negative. Irish emigrants encountered an unambiguous disapproving attitude from other settlers, often expressed in offhand comments later recorded by such chroniclers as John Dabney Shane and Lyman Draper. Writers expressed similar prejudice toward those of German or Dutch descent. The difference in McNair's case may relate to his ethnic background; his surname suggests he was a Scot whose family may have moved to Ireland before his birth.

On his return east through the Wilderness of southeastern Kentucky, Chapman found quality accommodations scarce, if not nonexistent. From Danville southeast toward the Cumberland River, he found no taverns at all, and at Crab Orchard he had to resort to spreading his blankets on the floor of a house belonging to a poor farmer named Pembleton. Leaving Crab Orchard, Chapman stayed at another farmhouse where he was obliged to leave his horses tied to a rail near the door all night. Heading for Rockcastle, deeper into the Wilderness, he spent a night in a rock shelter. Over the next few nights matters did not improve—the only accommodations were dirty cabin floors on which to sleep. Chapman's sole positive experience during this part of the trip was a "comfortable breakfast" given him by a Mrs. Goodwin, "a very clean nice Woman." Finally, after leaving Kentucky via the Cumberland Gap and proceeding east across the Clinch River, Chapman's party stayed at Mr. Craigies's Tavern, where they "found ourselves exceedingly comfortable . . . , besides getting each of us a good Bed and clean Sheets, things we had not seen since leaving Kentucky."[6]

Chapman's commentary on Kentucky taverns offers clues to his expectations; his idea of a good tavern included a "good Bed," that is, one that preferably was not shared and whose sheets were clean, decent food for himself and feed for his horse, and amiable, "civil" company. Though not stated explicitly, Chapman's attitude was that of someone whose self-worth suggested a sense of superiority over the average Kentuckian, who, he implies, was frequently dirty, ate "homely" food, and on the whole lacked refinement. His was a common opinion, and others expressed themselves much more forcefully. An unidentified traveler in 1791 wrote, "the Taverns are generally wretched . . . and you are charged extravagantly for the worst fare; should a man go to Kentuckey, who could eat neither milk nor bacon, his case would be pitiable."[7]

Though many travelers found much to criticize about Kentucky's frontier accommodations, conditions improved rapidly as settlement density increased. One traveler, whose anonymous account was published in 1834, attributed the disparity in roadside business quality to differentials in the geography of roads.[8] Tavern presence and quality, he observed, corresponded directly to the importance of the road being traveled. Main roads connecting important points attracted more travelers and generally had more places to stay. A little advance planning was all that was needed for people moving along these routes to identify the "best houses," with palatable food and comfortable lodgings. He distinguished "regular hotels" and taverns from "houses of entertainment," the latter kept by farmers who did not hold liquor licenses or sell liquor but simply offered food and lodging to infrequent travelers. "The addition of a spare room, with two or three neat beds for strangers, is usually the only preparation made by those who engage in this business, and although the fare is sometimes very coarse, the traveler often finds more comfort at these places, than at better furnished hotels." The traveler perceptively recognized that people who supplied such minimal services were simply local people who were not obliged to serve the public but were essentially doing travelers a favor. He described the process by which the practice arose:

> When a road begins to be traveled, through an entirely new country, there are no taverns, and the travelers are obliged to seek shelter and food at the houses of the farmers, who entertain them gratuitously—but the number [of travelers] at length increases, so as to render that kind of hospitality burthensome, and the farmers request some one of their number, to relieve them from such calls, by making the reception of strangers a matter of business; or some one whose house is so situated as to be more exposed than others to the visits of travelers, determines to receive pay for that which his hospitable nature will not permit him to refuse, and which he cannot afford to bestow gratuitously. He agrees therefore to feed the horse of the traveler, and to furnish him with such accommodations as his house affords, for a trifling compensation—but he makes no contract to do any more—and, as the whole arrangement is the result of an accommodating spirit, and is made for the benefit of the stranger, and the public convenience, it is justly considered that the advantage is mutual, and that the party is really receiving a civility, which a person of a correct mode of thinking would consider enhanced by being permitted to pay for it.[9]

In this way, roadside residents, be they farmers in the open countryside or villagers, found early on that they could supplement their modest incomes by expanding their homes and taking in travelers for cash.

Discerning travelers soon recognized that accommodation quality varied according to the clients served, and whether such places operated as a business dedicated to serving the traveling public or as a convenience provided by a farmer impressed to do so by plaintive travelers. The Kentucky General Assembly recognized only two types of roadside places for public accommodations: taverns and tippling houses. Legislators sought to regulate the former while restraining the latter. The Assembly approved an act on December 19, 1793, amending two earlier Virginia laws adopted before Kentucky had attained statehood.[10] This act equated the terms *tavern* and *house of entertainment* and required that such establishments be licensed yearly upon petition to the county court. The key distinction between a tavern or inn and a tippling house was that the tippling house was essentially a bar where liquor was sold, and the law made such businesses illegal. The court had the discretion to refuse a tavern license to any person "of bad character" who did not keep an orderly house. The licensee also had to have the financial wherewithal to file a bond for one hundred dollars. The law further required tavern keepers to provide "good, wholesome, cleanly lodging and diet for travelers" as well as "stableage, provender or pasturage for horses." The license prohibited gambling and enjoined the tavern keeper to prevent his patrons from drinking "more than is necessary" or indulging in scandalous or disorderly behavior.

The act further imposed on tavern keepers the requirement that they charge standardized rates and prices that county court justices established, and to display prominently in each tavern's public entertaining room a schedule of rates and prices. Clearly, the act's provisions were intended to prevent price gouging; it was enforced through penalties levied on those who failed to comply. Aggrieved travelers could bring charges against an offending tavern keeper at the county court, although the law also permitted appeals.

Tippling houses, where drinking alcoholic beverages was the primary activity, with the potential for drunkenness and disorderly behavior this implied, were subject to more stringent regulation and higher penalties for noncompliance. The 1793 act prohibited all attempts to sell by retail wine, beer, brandy, cider, whiskey, rum, or other liquors, directly or indirectly, in any house, booth, arbor, stall, boat, or other place without a license. The penalty for the first offense was a fine of three pounds; a second offense cost double that amount and prompted seizure of the liquor, which the court then sold, the proceeds being applied to relief of the poor. In 1823 a revision removed cider and beer from the licensed liquor list, but the rest of the law remained in force for many years.[11] Laws whose express purpose was regulating alcoholic beverage sales by licensing were also a means of controlling social behavior, whether or not they generated revenue from license fees or taxes.

If the Kentucky General Assembly sought to control public drunkenness and protect the consumer, those who operated higher-quality "houses of entertainment" took their cue from their patrons and managed their establishments so as to attract people of quality and exclude commoners. By the late 1790s the "hotel" emerged as a new building form that was dramatically different in size and quality—the building was larger, the furnishings were more refined, even elegant, and sleeping quarters were private. In time, changes in the law stripped the county courts of their authority to establish standardized tavern and hotel prices and rates. Lifting price controls, however, permitted hotels or "houses" such as the Thurston House in Paris and Travellers Hall in Lexington to exclude working-class patrons by pricing room costs beyond their financial reach. Such houses thus positioned themselves as the proper places for mannerly drinking and upper-class social interaction.[12] The distinction between taverns of quality and lower-class establishments such as drovers' inns and wagon yards was further differentiated when businesspeople established stagecoach routes along major roads. Stagecoaches carried mail and passengers, and post offices were routinely established at local inns. By negotiating a service relationship with local stage line companies, shrewd innkeepers increased their clientele and, thereby, their profits. In addition, the inn offered amenities to local community residents, who frequented the place to pick up their mail, hear the latest news and gossip, attend public meetings, or transact other business in the salutary atmosphere of a well-run house.

If the high prices at large roadside houses and inns excluded lower-class people, where could they stay? Common folk—the drovers who herded livestock to market, or the wagoners who hauled loads of farm commodities and merchandise—were not encouraged to stay at the respectable inns or taverns even if they could afford the prices. Drovers' first concerns were to obtain water and pasturage for their large herds—beef cattle, sheep, hogs, and mules—and a place where they could overnight, such as at a "stockstand" outside a town or on a roadside farm, paying the farmer on whose land they stopped for the privilege. Wagoners stayed at common taverns that had public scales to weigh their loads and open sheds under which they parked their wagons. The White Horse wagon stand outside Maysville provided these amenities.[13] These establishments may not have sold liquor other than beer or cider, although they were free to do so after 1823. Common taverns and stockstands were made ordinary by their comparison to the high-quality hotels, the sharp distinction a physical reminder of the parallel differences in class consciousness and social exclusivity that increasingly typified Bluegrass society in the postfrontier era.[14]

Increasing traffic on the Limestone Road, and later on the Lexington-Maysville Turnpike, was a powerful enticement for local people to establish businesses at the roadside. By the 1790s the better-quality roadside establishments were concentrated in the towns—Washington, Mayslick, Millersburg, Paris, and Lexington—but between these emerging urban places rural locales such as Peyton's Tavern near Forest Retreat, the home of General Thomas Metcalfe in Nicholas County, Ellis Tavern at Ellisville, and Bedinger's Inn at Blue Licks also offered quality accommodations.

When James Darnaby and William Ellis surveyed the road from Lexington to Maysville in 1827 in preparation for establishing the turnpike route, they recorded eighteen "inns." Their map did not include the inns or taverns in Lexington, Paris, Millersburg, Mayslick, Washington, or Maysville since their concern was to refine the road alignment between these places. Even allowing for the exclusion of the inns in towns, the density of inns was one per three and one-half miles, although they were

Washington's Paxton Inn is thought to have been built in 1810. This romanticized view of the inn is probably a composite of historic periods. Stagecoach arrivals were important events in road towns such as Washington. A "modern" coach, circa the 1830s, has just pulled to a stop. Luggage is piled atop its roof, and it is likely that the rear leather boot holds luggage and mail. A local boy in a buckskin shirt and coonskin cap stops to watch two well-dressed travelers alight from the coach. A hunter wearing a fringed buckskin coat has tied his horse to a hitching rail, while a local resident or inn guest lounges on the walk near the inn's front door, at which stands a woman servant wearing an apron. (Courtesy of the Kentucky Gateway Museum Center)

not spaced regularly along the road. Heading north from Lexington, the first inn, E. H. Herndon's, was nearly nine miles from town. Some twelve miles from Lexington, William Moreland and Benjamin Halleck operated inns within one-half mile of one another. There followed a gap of another six miles to Ryan's Tavern, just outside Paris. Various accommodations were available in Paris, and the first inn beyond Paris, Eli Current's, was three miles along the road. Three inns, T. Champ's, H. Martin's, and J. S. Hill's, stood in close proximity about five miles north of Paris. Approaching Millersburg, a traveler could stop at Talbott's Inn about a mile from town or venture

The tavern at Forest Retreat still stands as a private residence along the Maysville Road near the junction of SR 32, formerly Carlisle Pike. This country tavern was a popular stagecoach stop and also served as a post office. Thomas Metcalfe, a stonemason, built the tavern's limestone foundation in 1806. A large single room, built with poplar logs and a limestone chimney, served as the public space, and a three-room wing to the right provided sleeping space for guests. One gained access to a loft by an outside ladder. Historic photographs from the 1920s show an additional room and chimney attached to the right, or foreground, end of the sleeping-room wing. That room has since been removed. In 1816 Metcalfe built a home for himself, called Forest Retreat, atop a hill across the road from the tavern. Thomas Metcalfe was active in politics. He served as a state representative (1812–16); U.S. representative (1819–28); governor (1828–32); and as president of the Kentucky Board of Internal Improvement (1840–48), during which time he strongly advocated for construction of high-quality roads through science-based engineering. He also supported using state funds to underwrite construction of the Maysville-to-Lexington Turnpike. Restoration work on the tavern began in 1976. (J. Winston Coleman Jr. Photographic Collection, Transylvania University Library)

farther to Shurral's Inn on the town's outskirts. Between Millersburg and Ellisville only three inns operated, J. Throckmorton's, Holladay's, and Arnett's. And all were within seven miles of Millersburg. By 1827 the stone house that had earlier operated as Ellis's Tavern still stood but no longer functioned as an inn. The fledgling resort at Blue Licks attracted a cluster of inns; Bedinger, Moor, Throckmorton, and Boolingal all provided accommodations, venturing correctly that foul-smelling sulfurous water would attract customers. Only Lacy's Inn served the twelve-mile stretch between Blue Licks and Mayslick. Similarly, Kirk's Inn was the lone accommodation along the seven miles between Mayslick and Washington.

Irregular inn distribution along the road was probably the product of several different considerations. The Blue Licks mineral springs drew visitors seeking the water's supposed beneficial medicinal qualities, so the site was obviously attractive as an inn location. The dearth of inns between Blue Licks and Maysville, on the other hand,

The springs at Lower Blue Licks, adjacent to the Licking River, were once the haunt of buffalo, elk, and other animals. White settlers boiled the mineralized water to obtain salt. The Maysville Road passed by the springs, and in 1794 a tavern here served travelers. In 1816 a store and post office also occupied the site. By the 1840s the mineral springs had attracted investors who intended to build resort hotels. The outsize three-hundred-room Arlington Hotel was in operation by the early 1860s. The main hotel's three stories, shown here in a view attributed to Seth Eastman, were lined with long, covered galleries. Accommodations included a large dining room, a ballroom, and three elegant parlors. The Arlington burned in 1862. Smaller hotels were built in 1870 and 1877, but by the 1880s the springs failed and the resort businesses went into steep decline. (From Lewis Collins, *History of Kentucky*, 2 vols. [orig. 1797; this ed. 1847, repr. Lexington, Ky.: Henry Clay Press, 1968])

may relate to lower population densities in the road's Eden Shale Hills section; it is likely that farmers on these hardscrabble lands had little surplus income to invest in adding travelers' rooms to their modest homes, never mind building a large, multi-room inn. Knowledgeable travelers avoided the accommodation desert of the Shale and broke their trip in the larger towns. The number of inns increased dramatically south of Ellisville as one approached the Inner Bluegrass: twelve of the road's eighteen inns were strung out along the next thirty-five miles.

Facile explanations are wanting as to why Champ, Martin, and Hill clustered their inns, or why Halleck and Moreland chose to build their inns so close together. As to accommodation quality, the Halleck and Moreland inns were probably equivalent. When turnpike builders completed the relocated pike between Lexington and Paris, Moreland moved his inn to the new road, where it functioned as a hotel, stagecoach stop, and post office. In addition to short-stay travelers, his clientele included permanent boarders. The new turnpike effectively bypassed the Halleck Inn; thereafter, the family moved into Paris, where they opened the Thurston House, which operated for many years as a high-quality hotel. Extant records reveal little detail about the quality of the inns managed by Champ, Martin, and Hill. Inn accommodation and quality differences were probably reflected in the prices for beds, food, and drink. Mindful that this period quite possibly marks the era when roadside entrepreneurs were inventing workable and profitable business practices, it is likely that inns serving different visitor classes may have functioned profitably near other inns because they were not competing for the same customers. Such complementary business clusters actually reinforced one another, attracting more customers, not fewer, a business location principle that would later be discovered by Main Street store and shop proprietors. If, furthermore, an innkeeper chose a crossroads location, the potential clientele pool would increase, as it would if farmsteads thickly populated rural neighborhoods. Local people often frequented nearby inns to read newspapers, glean news from passengers and stage drivers, or eat and drink, thereby supplementing the income an innkeeper derived from travelers. Alternatively, inns that catered to the same clientele may have opened as competitors to lure customers away from their neighbors or with the intent or promise of a stage-line post office contract. Some inn owners may not have actively pursued customers but simply took advantage of their roadside location to charge the occasional visitor for room, board, and animal care. Furthermore, operating an inn proximate to other inns might not have been a competitive disadvantage if the innkeeper considered the business a sideline, a supplement to a farm or blacksmithing shop.

By the early 1830s, when road builders completed rebuilding and surfacing the entire Maysville-to-Lexington Turnpike, the distribution of inns and taverns along the improved road began to change. The road's new resilient stone surface significantly decreased travel time, which thereby changed travel dynamics. Stagecoach lines altered their schedules. The slow stage line from Lexington to Maysville began at Brennann's Hotel and stopped at William Moreland's 10-Mile House, Charles Talbott's hotel in Paris, James Bassell's in Millersburg, Mrs. Pryor's at Blue Licks, and Mrs. Goddard's at Maysville; the trip took about eight and one-half hours. At each stop the stage driver delivered mail and changed horses, and passengers could unload to stretch and converse with locals. The larger road towns and roadside communities added residents and stores that in turn attracted more commercial travelers, especially salesmen. Inns and hotels in these places could operate as full-time commercial establishments. Small taverns in the open country between the major towns began to lose customers unless the stage lines patronized them. Many such taverns reverted to private homes in the 1840s and 1850s.

When completed, the railroad between Maysville and Lexington drew business away from the road's stagecoach lines as travelers opted to patronize the faster and more comfortable transport medium. Given the vicissitudes of construction and corporate mergers, however, railroad construction along this corridor was not a focused process. The Maysville & Lexington Railroad Company completed the eighteen-mile section from Lexington to Paris in late 1854. Not until nearly two decades later, in 1873, did the M & L Railroad's Northern Division complete a single-track line from

Paris to Maysville. Two years later the Kentucky Central Railroad Company acquired the Maysville line.[15] When rail service did commence, stage lines found their business increasingly siphoned off by the railway, and many roadside commercial accommodations closed or moved their businesses into the major towns. By 1861 no taverns or hotels remained along the road's rural sections between Lexington, Paris, and Millersburg.[16] North of Millersburg, the railroad route diverted east to Carlisle and then turned north toward Maysville. North of Carlisle the railroad maintained a route parallel to the Maysville Road, two to five miles east. In contrast to the Lexington-to-Millersburg section, where the railroad built few open-country stations—Hutchison and Elmendorf being notable exceptions—from Carlisle north to the Ohio River the railroad established several stations or trackside warehouses. Ewing, east of the Maysville Road hamlet of Fairview, was the largest of the railroad station settlements, its population about six hundred. Ewing's clapboard hotel stood only a short distance from the railroad depot.

Business gazetteers chronicle the shift in hotel accommodations from the country roadsides to the towns. By 1865 hostlers operated three hotels in Paris: the Bourbon House, run by Mrs. R. Thurston and her son; the Paris Hotel, operated by Mrs. C. Talbott; and John Griffith's Western Hotel.[17] In 1879–1880 a hotel operated in Millersburg that had an attached livery stable and also catered to railroad passengers.[18] The Bourbon House was still in business in Paris, as was the Thurston House. By 1883–1884 the Purnell House had opened in Millersburg. Henry Turney operated Paris's Bourbon House and advertised it as "the leading hotel in the city and headquarters for commercial travelers [with] sample rooms on ground floor [and] bus and baggage transfer in connection with every train."[19] By 1896 Millersburg had two hotels, both run by women. The Conway House solicited the transient trade and featured "everything new and first rate." Mrs. Mary Beeding offered accommodations at the Hotel Beeding for two dollars per day as well as "First-Class Livery." In Paris the Windsor (formerly the Bourbon House), Fordham, and St. Charles hotels competed for the traveler's patronage.[20] Following the model of big-city hotels, these establishments offered amenities at one central location: barbershops, excellent dining, stylish rooms, and luggage transfer to and from the train station. Their proprietors often were women, a practice that harkened back to the turnpike era, when widows operated taverns after their husbands' deaths. Before 1827, for example, Benjamin Halleck operated a tavern on the old Limestone Trace. After his death, his wife, Polly, and daughter Rachel became the tavern's proprietors. When the new turnpike rerouted traffic, bypassing the tavern, road-borne trade withered. The family moved into Paris, where Polly and Rachel opened the Bourbon House. Rachel married Ezekiel Thurston about 1847, but she did not relinquish her proprietorship of the hotel to her husband. When he died in 1849, he left his entire estate, without conditions, to his wife. In an era when most middle-class white women were expected to stay at home and run the household, managing a hotel was one of the few occupations that women could engage in without encountering the sullen whispers of community social disapproval. Rachel Thurston sold the hotel to Redmon, Talbott, and Thompson in January 1866.[21] The Turney family later acquired the property and managed it for the remainder of the nineteenth century. By 1896 the owners changed the Thurston's name to the Windsor, and its clientele regarded it as one of the finest hotels in the area. Fire consumed the building in 1945; the Fordham Hotel had burned in 1932, a misfortune shared by many large-city hotels.

The twentieth century's first two decades marked a peak in the popularity of the fancy, central-city hotel. Every sizable community on the railroad offered hotel accommodations, usually close to the depot or adjacent to the old road, which, after 1926, may have been designated a state or federal highway. Traveling salesmen were a particularly important part of the hotel trade, although hotels also catered to customers who traveled for pleasure. Because a hotel often operated a town's best restaurant, local patrons who preferred hotel victuals, and could afford them, bolstered the profit margin. As automobile travel accelerated rapidly between 1915 and 1920, road travelers seeking overnight accommodations had little or no alternative to the central-city hotel. Roadside campgrounds and cabin camps appeared along major highways by the late 1920s.[22] Meanwhile, many auto-borne visitors patronized the established city hotels that were conveniently positioned near the point where the through highway bisected the business district. Rail-side hotels away from the central city, adjacent to the noise, smoke, and general commotion of the rail yard, often declined into seediness as railroad passengers sought better-quality accommodations or stopped in larger cities.

Automotive travel increased after World War II, and highway builders responded to the rapid increase in horrifying roadway accidents by widening roads, constructing bypasses, and performing other engineering wizardry. All these changes in basic travel geography conspired to disadvantage the old central-city hotel, which now lost clientele to the new roadside motels that were conveniently situated at city gateway sites. By the 1960s railroad passenger travel had declined to unsustainable levels, which truncated the traditional customer demographic for in-town hotels, especially those that had been rail-dependent. In larger cities a few historic hotels have been rehabilitated through extensive remodeling and reopened as luxury accommodations, alluring to travelers nostalgic for the grand old days of sumptuous hotel living or those on corporate expense accounts. Many central-city hotels in the Maysville Road towns have closed, although some have been converted into low-cost apartments for local residents. Others still stand but no longer fulfill their original function. In Paris, for example, the Baldwin and the St. Charles hotels have been transformed into offices and a day-care center.

Roads and travelers cannot thrive in isolation. Rather, they enable and reinforce one another. Cross-country travelers establish the initial trail connecting one place with another. Farmers whose houses stand proximate to the trail can elect to provide food and accommodations to travelers as a courtesy or as a considered business. This essential service supports additional travel, which in turn stimulates further roadside entrepreneurship that creates a new, specialized category of business that is dependent on the road for income and profit while simultaneously fostering road travel. Isolated roadside settlements may grow into communities that offer an increasing diversity of services to travelers and their own residents. Growing commercial road traffic helps these communities become self-sustaining. Increasing traffic degrades the unimproved trail, which brings demands for quality road construction. Traditional road-building practices, though tacitly regulated by legal statutes, cannot answer the demand and roads come under the purview of formal legal and engineering practices funded by state government and local investors. The stone-surfaced turnpike is the result. As road quality improves, travel, be it by private phaeton, freight wagon, or stagecoach, becomes much more efficient, which encourages even more travel. All this demonstrates that the relationship between the road and the traveler is reciprocal. Improvements in the mode of travel lead to refinements of the travel venue, the road.

Part II

Overland Roads and the Epic of Kentucky's Settlement

Roads no longer merely lead to places; they *are* places. And as always they serve two important roles: as promoters of growth and dispersion, and as magnets around which new kinds of development can cluster. In the modern landscape, no other space has been so versatile.

—J. B. Jackson,
A Sense of Place, a Sense of Time, 1994

3

Coming to Kentucky

For more than three decades before Kentucky separated from Virginia in 1792 to become a state, explorers, hunters, surveyors, and settlers moved west across the Appalachian Plateau and associated mountain ranges in search of open land and social betterment. Their laudatory observations about the exceptional fertility of Kentucky's lands west of the mountains passed back to the residents of Virginia, Maryland, Pennsylvania, and the other Atlantic coast settlements, promulgating the region's reputation as the "Eden of the West." Two routes permitted access, albeit challenging, to the Kentucky country that lay west of the great Appalachian topographic barrier: a mountainous southern track via Virginia's Great Valley, the Cumberland Gap, and the Wilderness Road or Boone's Trace, and a northern route across western Maryland and southwest Pennsylvania to Brownsville (known earlier as Red Stone) on the Monongahela River. From Brownsville, the Monongahela flowed north to join the Allegheny at Pittsburgh, where the two streams formed the Ohio River. At Brownsville, travelers could transfer from overland wagon to river raft or flatboat and proceed north, or downstream, to Pittsburgh, where, moving with the current, they could continue their trip down the Ohio to northeastern Kentucky, where they disembarked at Limestone, a small landing site at the mouth of Limestone Creek. From there travelers followed an overland trace southwest into the Bluegrass country. Increasing traffic—be it wagons, carriages, coaches, driven livestock, or people moving by foot or horseback—beat the old path into a road. It is the road's status as a key link in the first mail or post road to connect Zanesville, Ohio, to Florence, Alabama, and as the West's first stone-surfaced macadam road, as well as its age, that give this road pride of place as the nation's first highway in the trans-Appalachian west.

Many literate travelers from Europe and the East Coast states made their way to Kentucky in the period from statehood to the 1840s, often recording what they saw in diaries or published tracts. In 1793, for example, the Reverend Harry Toulmin traveled from Lancashire, England, to America seeking lands suitable for his parishioners. The following year Toulmin wrote a letter to a friend residing in Virginia's Shenandoah Valley, then regarded as that state's most agriculturally promising region. "The luxuriance of the soil," in Kentucky, he said, "exceeds everything to be met with in eastern America, whilst it is a stranger to the cold winters and the sickly falls of the

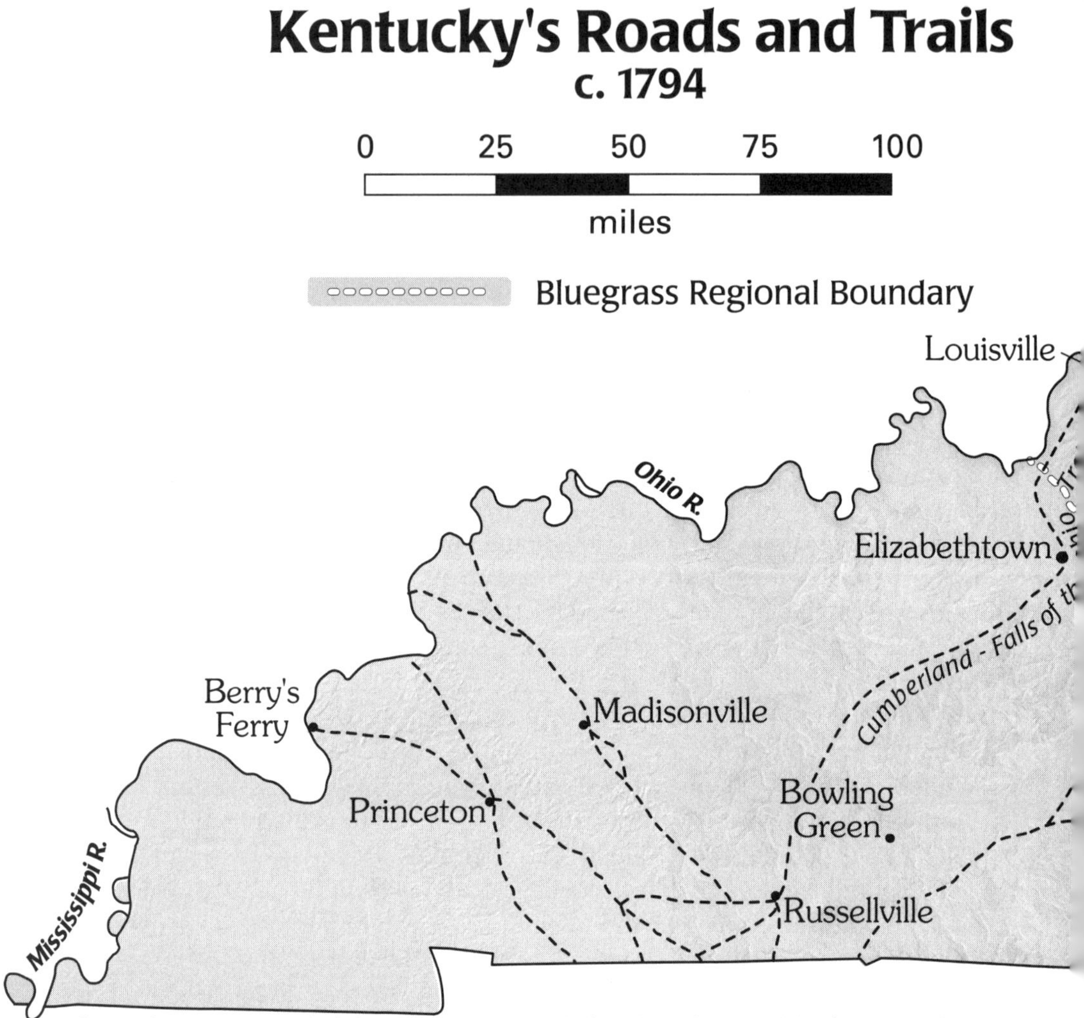

After Thomas P. Field, *Kentucky and the Southwest Territory 1794*, 1965.

Genesee Country [in New York]. The produce of an acre is double that of the Shenandoah Valley, and you can send it to market for less money."[1] Some twelve years later, the Philadelphia cartographer John Melish, widely respected for his keen observation and exceptionally well-crafted engraved maps, said of central Kentucky that it was "the most beautiful tract of land I ever saw."[2]

Following a colonial Virginia law dating to 1705 that allowed residents to claim uninhabited frontier land, or directives made to surveyors by Royal Governor Lord Dunmore to demarcate Kentucky lands according to military warrants, land surveys proceeded with some urgency across central Kentucky's most coveted lands before the American Revolution. By 1780 the largest proportion of high-quality land north and east of the Kentucky River, and within a fifty-mile radius of the frontier settlement

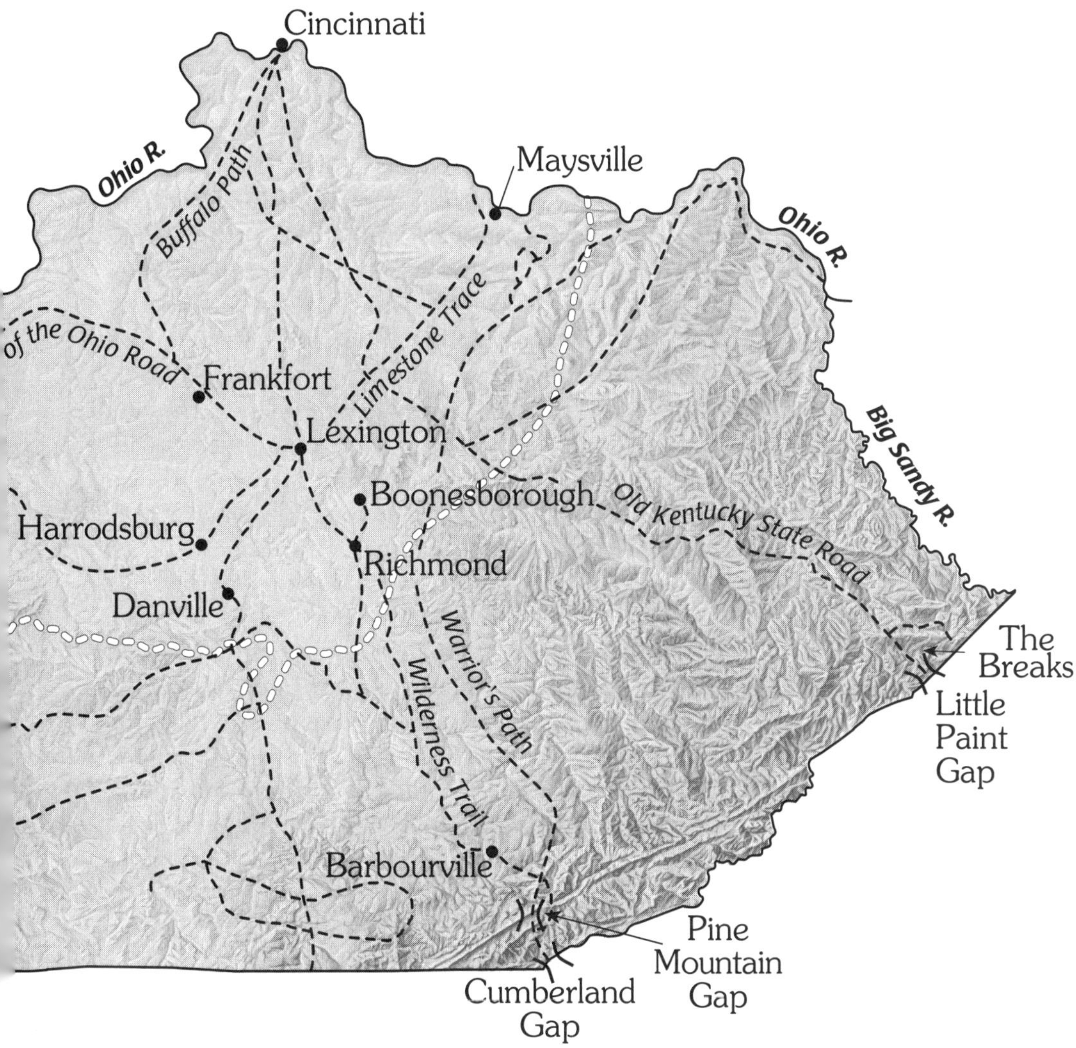

of Lexington, was taken up by claims and warrants. Additional land claims lined the major trans-regional overland routes—the Limestone Road linking the Ohio River port at Limestone Creek with Washington, Paris, and Lexington; the route linking Frankfort on the Kentucky River to Louisville at the Falls of the Ohio; and the route from Bardstown to Louisville. Within this circumscribed area lay the state's best farmland, many of its salt springs, and the most geographically favored town sites. Early on, surveyors and land claimants assiduously avoided hilly, hardscrabble lands, be they in central Kentucky or in the eastern mountains. Notably, early settlers made no land claims along the Wilderness Road between Cumberland Gap and Dicks (Dix) River near present-day Brodhead.[3]

Though conflicting land claims resulting from careless surveys, multiple land grants on the same property, or outright fraud were not fully resolved in the courts for decades, emigrants from the eastern states and Europe moved into Kentucky's fat lands in rapidly increasing numbers. The first federal census in 1790 recorded Kentucky's population at just over 77,000. Most people lived on farms in the countryside; census takers counted only five towns of consequence. Lexington and Washington, the villages that stood at or near either end of the Limestone Road, were the two largest urban places, with 834 and 462 inhabitants, respectively. Bardstown (216) and Louisville (200) were less than half Washington's size, and Danville at 150 was only a third as large. By 1800 Kentucky's population had nearly tripled to about 221,000; whites constituted 81 percent of the total, and about 19 percent were slaves or free blacks. Over the next decade the state's population nearly doubled: the 1810 census recorded about 407,000, 20 percent of whom were slaves or free blacks.

This book is about the Maysville Road, which, because of the political policy it fomented, the economic development that followed its way, the innovative road-building technology it demonstrated, and the cultural landscapes it prompted, was one of the most important roads in postcolonial America. The road linked Lexington, the largest urban center in Kentucky's fabled Bluegrass country, to Limestone, an eighteenth-century port town on the Ohio River. Limestone was renamed Maysville after John May, an early surveyor and landowner. The Maysville Road has been known by many names. From the 1770s early settlers referred to the track as Smith's Waggon Road and the Limestone Trace. In 1827 the road became the Maysville, Washington, Paris, and Lexington Turnpike. When the turnpike or toll-road era ended in 1896, the road became known as the Maysville Road if one lived in Lexington, or the Lexington Road if one lived in Maysville. The section from Lexington to Paris has been known as Paris Pike for more than a century. In 1926 federal policy created a standardized numbering system for federally subsidized highways, and the road became a combination of U.S. highways 68, 62, and 27. Vestiges of the old road's nomenclature can be seen in the towns whose growth it fostered, especially in Lexington, where one of the major north-south streets is still named Limestone.

Whatever its name or numerical designation, this overland route has played a foundational role in fostering Kentucky's historic population growth and economic development.[4] Though Lexington was Kentucky's largest city in 1820, with 5,279 people—compared to Louisville's 4,012—the city was landlocked, located well away from large, navigable rivers. Nevertheless, the people of Lexington and central Kentucky managed to obtain supplies from and export farm and industrial products to the Ohio River via the Maysville Road. The Ohio River, 981 miles in length from Pittsburgh to its junction with the Mississippi, flows west-southwest toward the continent's heart, theater of the westward-moving frontier, and the same direction as the general movement of people migrating west. Once settlers had established farms in the Bluegrass country, they exported surplus produce by way of roads or the Kentucky River to the Ohio, and thence downstream to New Orleans for reshipment to markets in East Coast cities such as Baltimore, Philadelphia, and New York, or to Europe.

The first steam-powered boat to navigate the Ohio upstream managed the New Orleans–Louisville trip in 1816. By 1820 the river was "alive with steamboats (sixty by

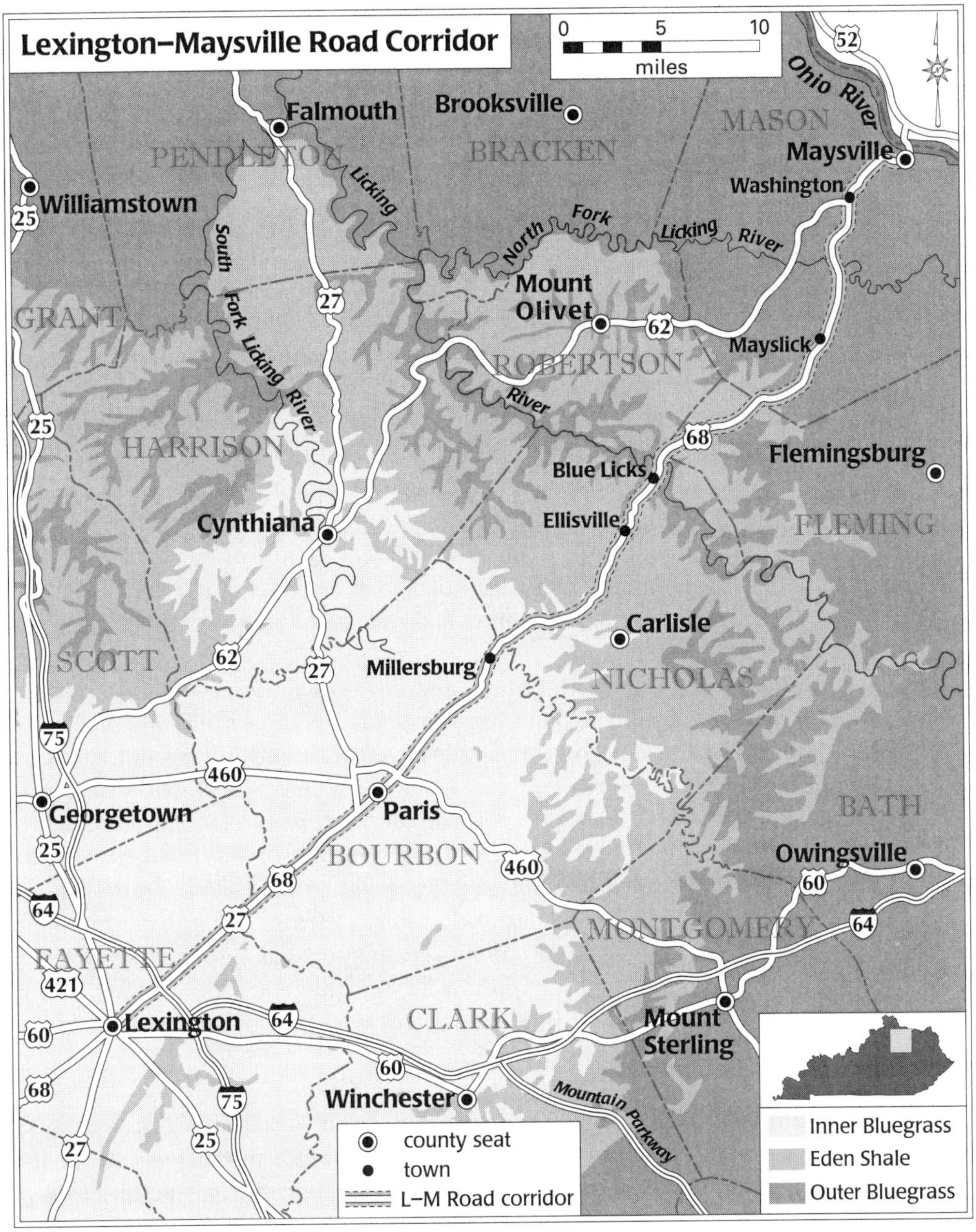

that year), barges, schooner boats, keelboats, flatboats, Kentucky and New Orleans boats, skiffs, rowboats, and ordinary rafts."[5] As steamboats gained in reliability and number during the 1820s and 1830s, Ohio River towns such as Louisville gained a decided geographic advantage in fostering trade and commerce. By 1830 Louisville's population reached 10,341, while Lexington's increased at a more modest rate to 6,026. Although central Kentucky's rich Bluegrass lands continued to produce hemp, tobacco, cattle, mules, and other agricultural products, those products did not become commodities until they were transported to a market or factory where they were manufactured into goods demanded by farmers and townspeople. The primary transportation mode that energized the central Kentucky economy early on was the road and the overland freight or road wagons, as they were called, that followed its track.[6]

When the Pennsylvania Mainline Canal and connecting Allegheny Portage Railroad opened in March 1834, the first shipment of goods west from Philadelphia reached Pittsburgh in thirteen days, and three days later the shipment arrived in Maysville. From there the goods were reloaded into six-horse road wagons packed with seven tons each for the trip along the road south to Lexington, where they arrived two or three days later.[7] Increasing sophistication of Ohio River riverboat technology and a rapidly growing volume of boat traffic, abetted by long-distance linkages to Ohio and New York canals and early trans-Appalachian railroads, helped foster continued use of the Maysville Road, even advancing the expansion of its functions from that of migration route and mail or post road to an avenue for commerce.

In 1846 Thomas Metcalfe, president of Kentucky's Board of Internal Improvement, expounded on the fundamental relationship between road and riverine transportation and the state's potential for economic development and progress:

> An examination of the map of the State, and of her position in regard to her own commerce . . . will fully explain the whole matter of her difficulties. For a distance of more than nine hundred miles, the Ohio and Mississippi rivers skirt one of her borders; and these two rivers are now, and will probably be for generations to come, *the fixed basis of nearly all the commercial operations of the State.* Each of the different sections of the state has or will connect itself with this line of navigation *at the most contiguous accessible point.* There will, in all time to come, be as many roads or other lines of travel and transportation to and from this grand basis of our commercial pursuits, as there are sections of country to accommodate. Our exports will seek this navigation, no matter whether to go up or down or across it. In like manner, our imports are to come from above, below, or across this channel.[8]

Metcalfe's commentary on transportation drew from five decades of state economic growth and development in the context of revolutionary advances in steam and related transport technologies. Any astute observer could encounter examples to support Metcalfe's contentions in all sections of the state, but especially in the Bluegrass and along the Maysville Road. Lexington's early start as an important regional urban place and rural service center, for example, was directly attributable to its access to the Ohio River via the Maysville Road. The Bluegrass country surrounding the city was fertile and productive almost beyond imagination. Some of Virginia's and Maryland's wealthiest individuals migrated to Kentucky to establish large farms and estates that became centers of agricultural innovation—including importing and breeding blooded cattle, horses, and sheep. Eastern markets demanded central Kentucky's

Seth Eastman was a nineteenth-century U.S. Army topographic artist and one of the nation's foremost artists of American Indian culture. He recorded this Ohio River valley view from an overlook downstream from Maysville sometime before 1847. The town site was centered at the point where Limestone Creek passes through a gap in the river's south bluff to flow into the river. Steamboats navigate the river; two side-wheel steamboats head downstream, and one works against the current while two more are at anchor along the city's riverfront landing. The Maysville-to-Lexington road tracks up the bluff unseen behind the first hill on the right. (From Lewis Collins, *History of Kentucky*, 2 vols. [orig. 1797; this ed. 1847, repr. Lexington, Ky.: Henry Clay Press, 1968])

tobacco and hemp products, and Maysville had become a tobacco warehouse inspection site by 1787.

The road also linked north by ferry across the Ohio River to Zanes Trace, which transected southeastern Ohio and connected directly to the National Road at Zanesville. As America's first federally funded highway, the National Road was intended to connect Baltimore and Washington, D.C., to the Northwest Territory. National Road construction crews bridged the Appalachians and reached Wheeling and the Ohio River in 1818. Kentucky travelers such as Henry Clay were frequent patrons of the Maysville and National roads. In 1830 Clay, a strong proponent of internal improvements, proposed that the federal government subscribe funds to purchase stock in the Maysville, Washington, Paris, and Lexington Turnpike, thereby underwriting road construction costs. The advantages of a high-quality Kentucky road that was linked north to Zanes Trace and the National Road were obvious to many: it provided the primary overland connections between the Ohio Valley and the Atlantic Seaboard; it had already established interior connections to Louisville and Nashville; and it offered the potential of new linkages to cities in the Tennessee River valley such as Knoxville. President Andrew Jackson did not acknowledge the merits of Clay's argument and vetoed the bill because the turnpike, as he saw it, would serve only Kentucky and, therefore, did not merit federal subsidy. Ironically, Jackson was a frequent traveler of the Maysville Road, which was a key connection between his home in Nashville and Washington, D.C. Critics saw in Jackson's decision a profound ignorance of emerging Ohio Valley economies and the transportation requirements inherent in regional development. Further, his action reinforced a federal policy of denying support for road construction that would continue for almost ninety years thereafter.[9]

4

Regional Context

Kentucky's territory is neatly demarcated into sharply contrasting regions by emphatic changes in bedrock, surface topography, and concomitant variation in soils and natural vegetation. Though scientists would eventually explain the rationale for these regional divisions, and their implications for resources—salt for food preservation, iron for tools and utensils, and fertile soils for farming—immigrant folk knowledge of one section's advantages over another for economic development was couched in practical experience gained in other climes.

The state's entire topographic surface is underlain by sedimentary rocks, largely sandstones, limestones, and shales, and there are extensive coal measures in the eastern and western sections. The eastern quarter is part of the Appalachian Plateau, a high-elevation, stream-dissected upland that is the headwaters for major streams that flow northwest toward the Ohio River—the Big Sandy, the Licking, the North, Middle, and South Forks of the Kentucky, and the Cumberland rivers. Though the region was rich in coal and iron deposits, the first explorers and settlers did not deem its steep slopes and nearly impenetrable hardwood forests attractive for agriculture-based settlement. Traveling through the Cumberland Gap to central Kentucky in 1796, the mining entrepreneur Moses Austin observed that the eastern Kentucky wilderness was "a Disagreeable broken Mountain Country but some good lands, and will be in time Sufficiently settled to furnish Travellers, but can Never be a desirable Country."[1]

Whether immigrants traveled from the southeast by way of the Cumberland Gap–Wilderness Road, or the northeast and the Ohio River–Maysville Road, in their minds Kentucky was synonymous with the central limestone plains, the region that became known as the Bluegrass. Most early travelers, whether they were prospective settlers scouting for new business or social opportunities or scientists intent on examining the natural environment for scholarly publications, found that the Bluegrass plain was not a uniform place. Rather, its topographical attributes differed dramatically from one section to another. Needham Parry, seeking settlement opportunities in Kentucky in 1794, traveled down the Ohio River to Limestone. At Washington, four miles south of the river, Parry noted that the land there was "quite as rich as I expected, but not so level, nor any good water, it being in Mason County."[2] Proceeding south along the road toward the Licking River, he "came to thinner land, which got worse and worse untill we came to the Blue Lick, where it was as poor and as stony as the pine barrens. At this place there is a Salt Spring, and salt works just erecting. This Salt Spring smells strong of sulphur or gun-powder, and looks as black as the blackest swamp water." South of the salt spring, Parry crossed "about 3 miles through stony, poor land."[3] The next day Parry found that four to five miles south of Blue Licks the land began to improve. At Millersburg on Hinkston Creek, he found "the land here being excellent, and timbered with Walnut, Honey Locust, Buckeye, and Cherry trees."[4] By listing walnut and locust trees first, Parry may have been acknowledging a long-standing folk tradition of associating these species with naturally high-fertility soils. At Paris, in Bourbon County, Parry found "the land adjacent to this place is as good as it can well be."[5]

An English farmer, William Faux, traveling the Maysville Road in 1819, thought the area adjacent to the Ohio "a fine country," but farther south he "rode over an extent of hills, 20 miles, so flinty and barren, that the plough never could and never will touch it. The hogs that grunt and roam over it look lean, hungry, and starved. The few inhabitants live by hunting."[6] At Lexington, though Faux thought the city proper "filthy, neglected, and in ruins, particularly the court-house, the temple of justice" he found that the surrounding land was "rich, cultivated, cleared, and . . . looks much like the best districts of Old England, only the soil of Kentucky is better."[7]

The French botanist André Michaux traversed this same country in 1793, as did his son, the naturalist François André Michaux, in 1802. Though they were trained as scientific observers, their assessments of Bluegrass land quality were similar to those of other travelers. South of Mayslick, François Michaux found the land "dry and sandy; the road . . . covered with immense flat chalky stones, of a blueish cast inside, the edges of which are round." The white oak and hickory trees that he saw there were stunted: their "wretched appearance clearly indicated the sterility of the soil."[8] Lexington, on the other hand, impressed Michaux as one of the "most wealthy [cities] of the three new western states." He reasoned that its prosperity and rapid population growth could be attributed to "its situation in the centre of one of the most fertile parts of the country, comprised of a kind of semi-circle, formed by the Kentucky river."[9]

The lands described by those who saw central Kentucky in the eighteenth and early nineteenth centuries were part of what today is known as the Bluegrass Region, an area comprising roughly one-fifth of the state. The Bluegrass in outline is annular, its north boundary circumscribed by the Ohio River's great northwest-southwest arc, while hilly knob lands demarcate its east, south, and west edges. (See the map "Kentucky's Roads and Trails, circa 1794" in chapter 3.) The region draws its distinct topographic character and soils from its bedrock—400-million-year-old Ordovician-age limestones and shales, for the most part. Because Kentucky's sedimentary rocks formed through deposition in ancient shallow seas, the normal position of those rocks today would be horizontal. Central Kentucky, however, has been uplifted by tectonic forces to form a broad arch, which caused the bedrock strata to pitch gently upward toward the region's center. The arch's crest is near Lexington, as suggested by drainage divides and streams that flow away from that point in all directions. Surface streams have eroded the top portion of the arch, and the region's horizontally bedded rocks

The most difficult topography to traverse along the Lexington-to-Maysville corridor is the Eden Shale Hills in Fleming County, where hard limestones are interbedded with very soft shales. The shale readily erodes, undermining the limestone and producing a dendritic maze of steep-sided hills and narrow valleys. The hills typically exhibit compound slopes with a convex crown at the top, which transitions to a concave slope near the bottom. At or near the hillcrests erosion of soil and rock is relatively slow, although rainwater does infiltrate the soil and rock. Downhill the slope steepens and erosion increases as soil either creeps slowly down the slope or moves rapidly in the wash of a heavy rain. Near the valley bottoms soil and rock from the upper slope accumulate, creating a concave lower slope profile. The Licking River valley, a short distance south of this scene, provides a local base level that lies 250 feet lower than the Eden Shale ridgetops. The elevation difference gives the river and its tributary streams a considerable mechanical advantage in fostering erosion.

are now exposed as a series of concentric rings, rather like cutting the top third off of an outsized onion and exposing the different layers as a pattern of irregular rings from center to edge. The oldest Bluegrass limestones lie near the region's center. They contain phosphates and other minerals that are released through erosion by rainwater and groundwater to form fertile soils. This distinctive area is the Inner Bluegrass. The youngest limestones—Ordovician and Silurian—rim the region's perimeter, and while not as rich in minerals as the older rocks, they nevertheless break down to yield productive soils. This roughly circular topographic zone is the Outer Bluegrass. Between the Inner and Outer Bluegrass lies a ring of mixed rocks, shales and limestones. Upon exposure to water, the shales readily disintegrate into a green-gray paste that dissolves into fine silts, which rain runoff carries into the nearest creek bottom. This topographic zone is the Eden Shale Hills; stream erosion has sliced its surface into a maze of sharply creased ridges and narrow valley bottoms.[10] Soils formed on this surface are tight yellow-orange clays that form sour, unproductive soils. When wet, shale soils resemble a sticky ooze; when baked by the hot summer sun, they take on the consistency of crockery.

The eighteenth- and nineteenth-century travelers Parry, Faux, and Michaux—among many others—readily identified these three distinctive topographic zones and noted their signature characteristics. Edward Harris, writing to a friend in New Hampshire in 1797 about his impressions of the rich Kentucky Bluegrass lands, said of the soil that it was "free from sand and gravel; when you take it between your fingers you cannot perceive any more grit than in butter; it is what is called the rich land it looks as black as the bottom of your dung heaps; the under strata is Clay of different complexions but generally inclined to a redish." Harris concluded that the area comprised "the richest & best poor mans Country in the World."[11] People settling the Bluegrass country's contrasting lands quickly recognized their merits for farming or commercial enterprise. Land values varied from one zone to another according to both distance from suitable town markets and inherent land quality. William Faux found Outer Bluegrass land near Washington valued at forty to fifty dollars per acre in 1819—a year of considerable financial distress nationwide. A few years earlier, John Melish recorded the price of Inner Bluegrass land near Lexington as fifty to two hundred dollars per acre, depending on location.[12] The Maysville Road traversed all three zones and the towns and farm settlements that evolved along the road's corridor reflected the opportunities presented by these contrasting lands.

5

Road Evolution

America's modern roads conform to many technical and operational standards—bed and surface material, grade, sight lines, curve radii, banking or super elevation, signage, driving rules and regulations, and surveillance. Adherence to such standards yields roads that permit safe and predictable travel. Perhaps standards and predictability also tempt an amnesiac public into an ambivalent attitude toward roads. It is easy for today's traveler to accept the unproblematic view that roads simply follow logical tracks that represent the shortest distance between important places. That is, we tend to think of roads as without origins, ahistorical and ageographical; they simply exist as background landscape without acknowledgment of their obscure origins and enigmatic evolution. Yet a careful review of the Maysville Road's two-hundred-year geographical history confirms that roads are anything but static in form or specific in route. Nor are roads innocent of influence in the creation of human landscapes. Most roads, in fact, began as organic tracks—people called them natural roads—created when people crossed a space repeatedly to reach some common destination. Organic roads are not constructed with tools. Rather, they form through gradual, additive accumulation—animal trails, human footpaths, and vehicular tracks conforming to the earth's topographic surface. Organic roads ford streams rather than bridge them; go around hills rather than cutting through them; cross rough land via ridgetops or valley bottoms, not along embankments, viaducts, or tunnels. By the 1830s, as the organic road was increasingly disciplined by imposed conventions such as the engineer's metrics and the legislator's statutes, its path or way was increasingly removed—depending on the technology of the day—from the varied disposition of natural topographies such as stream breadth and volume of flow, or degree of hillside slope.

Eventually, improvements in transportation technology—as when the lightly built farm wagon was superseded by the cleverly designed Conestoga freight wagon that, in turn, was replaced by the engine-powered, rubber-tired truck in the 1920s—led to a pervasive foregrounding of those technologies in people's everyday lives. An expensive albeit heavy-duty freight wagon was not put to its full potential use—it was not economical—unless the roads on which it traveled were capable of supporting its weight and allowing it to move at efficient speeds. Having encountered new transport technologies that promised significantly greater efficiencies, the traveling public escalated

A derelict Conestoga wagon stands beside a stone outbuilding on a central Kentucky farm circa 1930. The Conestoga was a distinctive heavy-duty freight wagon built in Lancaster, Pennsylvania, from about 1750 to 1855. Ostensibly named for the Conestoga River, which flows through Lancaster, this was the wagon of choice for teamsters moving freight, especially on the great roads that connected coastal ports at Philadelphia and Baltimore with the interior lands west of the Appalachians. Much heavier than and configured quite differently from common farm wagons, the Conestoga was capable of hauling ten thousand pounds, or a "hundred-hundred," when pulled by six heavy horses. Building the wagon required several skilled tradesmen, including carpenters, wood turners, blacksmiths, wheelwrights, and harness makers. The wagon's distinctive design featured several innovations: front and rear end gates to facilitate loading and unloading; a convex floor that sloped up to the back and the front to help contain boxes and barrels on grades or rough roads and reduce the weight on the end gates; a rear-wheel brake; a toolbox mounted on the left side between the front and rear wheels; and wooden hoops attached to the box braces supporting a canvas top that provided an all-weather cover for the contents. The wagon had no seat. The driver often rode astride the left rear horse or sat on a "lazy board" that extended from the left side ahead of the rear wheel. Conestoga builders typically painted their wagons Prussian blue with red axles, wheels, and undercarriage. (J. Winston Coleman Jr. Photographic Collection, Transylvania University Library)

their demands for resilient, all-weather roads. But large-scale road improvement was beyond the capabilities of individuals, neighborhoods, or even county-level governments. Only a state- or national-level government could muster the financial and engineering resources to promote generalized road improvement. Accordingly, elected officials had usurped roads from private landowners or turnpike companies through legislative statutes by the late 1890s. Political oversight included creating state engineering standards and methods for funding road construction and repair. Improved roads invited transport vehicle manufacturers to refine their products. Vehicular travel speed and carrying capacity increased. By the 1920s and 1930s engineers were rerouting and rebuilding organic tracks that twisted through rough land to straighten alignments, easing abrupt right-angle turns and rebuilding roads at stream crossing points to align them with newly constructed bridges. Improved road quality led to increased use by people who had intentionally sited themselves along the road to take advantage of the accessibility the road provided. High-quality roads drew local travelers from the surrounding countryside who would rather travel to the county seat for church or shopping by way of a good road—even if it meant traveling a greater distance—than endure the nuisance of mud, ruts, rocks, or dust on old organic roads.

As road improvements accumulate and new road alignments succeed their predecessors, the older tracks often remain in place; sections of one may become the bed for the new road, some tracks are abandoned or orphaned, others are converted to local "access roads." The result is a tangled skein of roughly parallel routes following a general corridor but not the same track. This process has a peculiar effect on landscapes and structures built according to an understanding of road routes and discernment of the "rules" that govern them during a given era. As road builders change road alignments, they disassociate roadside taverns, hotels, stagecoach stops, farmsteads, even entire towns from their established proprietary position at the roadside. A new road thereby creates a host of new, locationally advantaged sites along its right-of-way, while old sites are cut from their sustaining umbilical and left to retrograde on now-neglected, orphaned road fragments. Some people may relocate to sites along the new route, others may choose to remain in place and find ways to deal with their unsolicited isolation.

Roads, then, are not simply convenient access routes across the countryside. They are dynamic, even formative landscape elements in their own right that often enable and direct community development and change. The first path, track, or road across an open, unsettled country tends to be transductive in that its establishment and use are likely to direct a sequence of newer roads along the same corridor. Whether an initial path was established by buffalo, American Indians, or early pioneers, alignment choices were straightforward although topographically sensitive—the most resilient surface; the lowest gradient; the shallowest river crossing; the shortest practical distance between two important locations. As time passed and transportation technology advanced, new transport routes tended to bundle together along the same general alignment as the original route. Villages grew up along the road to serve travelers and to provide a commercial link between the thoroughfare and local townspeople and farmers. The villages and their businesses and industries then became magnets for future road alignments. Improved road-building technology came first to the main roads, which attracted freight wagon, stagecoach, and, finally, automobile and truck traffic. When major through roads became choked with traffic, they were widened and straightened, and engineers often redirected them to bypass the very villages that spawned their use. But, as the term *bypass* implies, engineers reattached the improved road to the initial alignment, again cleaving faithfully to the original route. Rarely are major through roads closed or relocated a substantial distance from the historical primary way.

To some degree railroad routes were influenced by existing roads in that railroad construction engineers often sought to direct their rail beds to the same ports, towns, and cities that had oriented themselves to rivers and early roadways. As countryside railroad use for freight shipments and passenger travel increased, roadside business often declined, illustrating another source of road corridor instability: the arrival of competing transport technologies.

An old road such as the Maysville Road invites many questions about the process of place creation and the countryside to which it relates—the rationale for the original route and how and why that route changed through time; communities connected and communities bypassed; the nature of the roadside and how it developed; the road's role in creating or responding to local and regional economies; the clientele the road served and how that patron group changed through time. Why did different road sections develop differently, including one section—the Paris Pike from Lexington to Paris—that has become one of the most beautiful and expensive four-lane parkways in the nation? In short, how does a country road become a road across the country? Put another way, how over two centuries does a buffalo trace and wagon track become the first major highway west of the Appalachians? How does that road become part of a federal trans-regional highway and to what effect? Our Maysville Road narrative begins by reviewing the road's evolution—from frontier track to modern highway.

6

Indian Paths and Buffalo Traces

The establishment of early paths and "roads" across central Kentucky cannot be attributed solely to buffalo, elk, or deer, though this is a common assumption that oversimplifies the process of road creation.[1] The paths that became the Limestone Trace, as well as other regional trails, were probably used by members of prehistoric societies. Archaeologists have unearthed abundant evidence that records the presence of humans in Kentucky for at least 12,000 years before settlers of European and African origins entered the trans-Appalachian west. Prehistoric hunters and gatherers and, later, horticulturists moved across the landscape, following game animals and exploiting seasonal wild plants. Although modern buffalo (*Bison bison*) are credited with the creation of many of Kentucky's early trails, the species was a latecomer to the region, expanding from their western Great Plains homeland into Kentucky shortly before historic settlement began. Many paths that pioneers identified as buffalo traces—they also described these paths as "roads" or "streets"—may have originated during the Pleistocene Ice Age, when now-extinct bison species traveled between Kentucky's salt licks. Humans and animals continued to use these paths as the climate warmed and Pleistocene fauna were gradually replaced by modern species.

New World settlement by Europeans introduced a surfeit of consequences, such as decimating diseases and population dislocation and redistribution that advanced inland from the initial contact points on the East Coast and reached native peoples living in the Ohio Valley years in advance of formal settlement. Archaeologists identify the late prehistoric horticulturists resident in the region as members of the Fort Ancient culture, who lived much like the historic tribes encountered by the settlers and were probably antecedent to them. The Fort Ancient people left no irrefutable evidence to link them unambiguously to the Shawnee, Cherokee, or other groups that used Kentucky's lands and resources. Settlers entering central Kentucky misperceived the land as uninhabited by native peoples and, therefore, free for the taking. Rather, geopolitical turmoil associated with English and French competition for land along the eastern seaboard and for control of the lucrative inland fur trade displaced many native tribes, who moved their primary villages north of the Ohio River, which the 1768 Treaty of Fort Stanwix had established as the boundary between Indian lands to the north and English lands to the south. Tribes continued to occupy winter hunting camps in Kentucky and visit salt licks to process the water for salt, setting the scene for the myth of Kentucky as a "dark and bloody ground."[2] Although the Shawnee, in particular, claimed Kentucky as their own, they allowed the Cherokee also to hunt there. Incoming European settlers were unfamiliar with how the tribes viewed land ownership and concluded that their right to the land was equally valid.

Eighteenth-century travelers moving overland through north central Kentucky encountered an elaborate network of what they identified as bison or buffalo traces. The buffalo range in the eastern United States extended to the Atlantic and south into Florida and the Gulf states. In their peripatetic migrations bison traveled from grazing areas to salt licks, often moving in file and eventually creating broad paths or traces across the countryside.[3] Buffalo paths were not through roads in the sense of modern point-oriented highways that link towns and cities but, rather, focused at salt springs, where the animals licked salt deposits in the soil, suggesting to early explorers and hunters the term *lick* for such sites.[4] From the licks multiple buffalo paths extended across the country, some linked to other lick sites, others splayed out into the animals' grazing range. Of the nine major salt lick sites in the Bluegrass Region, five occurred on or a short distance from the Licking River, which flows northwest from the eastern mountains to a confluence with the Ohio at Covington-Newport. Beginning upstream in Bath County, these licks were Mud Lick (Olympia Springs), Upper Blue Licks, Lower Blue Licks, Mays Lick (Mayslick), and Grants Lick. The Maysville Road crossed the Licking River at Lower Blue Licks. Simon Kenton, a frontiersman, explored the area near Maysville about 1773 and in "the vicinity of May's Lick . . . fell in with the great buffalo trace, which in a few hours brought [him] to the Lower Blue Lick."[5] Traveling this same route south from Maysville a decade later, James Smith reached the Lower Blue Licks and described the unusual landscape created by the buffalo:

> The amazing resort of buffalo to the Licks in former times . . . [formed] . . . roads of an amazing size, in all directions, [that] unite at the Licks, as their common center. Here immense herds of buffalo used formerly to meet and with their fighting, scraping, etc., have worn away the ground to what it is at present. The Salt Spring at this place rises in a flat ground near the river Licking, and affords a great deal of water. The water is brackish with a touch of sulphur, and has a bluish appearance, which is the reason of its being called the Blue Licks. We left the Lick and pursued our journey to Lexington following one of the old buffalo roads, which I suppose was generally 200 feet wide.[6]

In 1784 the surveyor and cartographer John Filson recorded his impression of the salt licks and buffalo roads. "The amazing herds of Buffaloes which resort [to the lick], by their size and number, fill the traveller with amazement and terror, especially when he beholds the prodigious roads they have made from all quarters, as if leading to some populous city."[7] By 1807 the last buffalo in central Kentucky had been killed or driven off, but their legacy of cross-country trails remained in folk memory, and some were incorporated into pioneer roads.[8] By the 1820s the buffalo roads were still visible, but as land clearing and cultivation expanded in subsequent decades, their imprint began to fade.[9] Along the Maysville Road, few identifiable buffalo road remnants remain today. In Blue Licks State Park a sign identifies a small trace segment, and a county road commemorated as Buffalo Trace Road leads north from the village of Headquarters, about two and one-half miles west of the Maysville Road in Nicholas County.

7

Pioneer Road

A Virginia planter, David Meade, moved his family to Kentucky in 1796, leaving behind his plantation in Prince George County on the James River in eastern Virginia. Meade's objective was to reach the three-hundred-acre farm near Lexington that he had purchased.[1] His traveling company included family members, slaves, and twenty-one horses drawing passenger coaches and baggage wagons bearing their belongings. He departed his Virginia property on June 8 and arrived via two houseboats at Limestone in Kentucky on July 4 after an exhausting trek across the Appalachians. Meade's account of the trip from Limestone to Lexington is illustrative of cross-country travel conditions along this route near the close of the pioneer era. Once ashore at Limestone, which he called a "trifling Hamlet," Meade set out with "very poor horses and tattered Carriages," but he could find only one local wagon to rent to haul baggage and had to leave the rest of the family belongings behind in storage.[2]

The party's first encounter with the road to Lexington was the steep ascent up the river bluff above Limestone to reach the Outer Bluegrass plain, some three hundred feet above the river. The difficult climb and the comparatively short four-mile ride into Washington over "natural" dirt roads required several hours. Washington consisted of one long street with log and stone buildings on both sides. Here the Meades found "very good quarters . . . in a two-story log tavern."[3] The next day the family "proceeded on our journey and without meeting with any but petty disasters of the minor class we got that night to a mean Cabbin on Johnsons fork of the Licking where our horses found much better than we did."[4] The distance by road from Washington to Johnsons Fork was about twelve miles. On the third day, July 6, the party advanced south past the Blue Licks and found accommodations at a roadside "Cabbin within six miles of Paris" where "the lodging this night was much worse than the night before, for it was the filthiest Cabbin we had heretofore been in."[5] On the morning of July 7 the group arrived in Paris for breakfast. They found "this village very thriving & well built, more of Brick & Stone than of Wood—of the former are several large well-looking houses."[6] They continued on to Lexington and arrived before sunset, covering about twenty-four miles on their fourth day out from the Ohio landing at Limestone.

David Meade did not record the practical problems his party experienced in moving from the Ohio River landing to Lexington along a rutted dirt trail across varied topography. Depending on the exact track he followed, his party probably crossed more than twenty streams; the Licking River at Blue Licks, Hinkston Creek at Millersburg, Stoner Creek at Paris, Houston Creek south of Paris, and North Elkhorn Creek north of Lexington all offered substantial barriers if the water was high. Where bridges did exist, they were little more than tree trunks placed across a steam and perhaps covered with earth or smaller half logs, or "corduroy," laid crosswise.[7] Without a bridge, a stream crossing might require an awkward ford down steep banks and across a rocky creek bottom, or a fatiguing slog through deep mud and high, swiftly moving water.

Many early travelers complained bitterly about poor road conditions; their bad experiences usually correlated with wet weather. The first trial began at Maysville, with the exhausting climb up a very steep grade to gain the upland. People did develop alternative routes up the bluff, including a wagon road that followed the Limestone Creek valley on the town's east side. This route, called the Hill City Road, led southeast. Once on the plain above the river, this route angled south and approached Washington from the east. Travelers moving toward Lexington across the Outer Bluegrass surface found that the road followed a broad ridge for a distance before descending into a valley to cross a creek. When the route followed lowlands near streams, boggy conditions made for heavy going through deep mud. In the Eden Shale Hills, steep slopes meant moving through a gauntlet of sharp, difficult climbs and descents, or switchback curves. Travelers also discovered an unexpected incongruence between road quality and land fertility—the best, most fertile land seemed associated with the worse roads. In 1793 Harry Toulmin traversed the Maysville Road in wet weather and noted: "The soil being much richer, . . . [the roads] are rendered much worse by rain than the roads in other parts of America. The roads are adapted for carriages, but they proceed with great difficulty in bad weather, owing to the richness of the soil."[8] Nearly three decades later, the English traveler William Blane bought a horse in Maysville and planned to ride to Lexington because poor road conditions made carriage or coach travel impractical. But even this adjustment did not suffice, as his vituperative prose suggests, because he found that

> the road was beyond all comparison the worst I had ever seen. It was full of holes, and in many places nearly up to my horse's knees, in mud intermixed with large stones and pieces of rock, which seemed as if put there on purpose to annoy equestrians. Moreover, the road is a *natural* one, that is to say, it is a track left open and cleared, but which has never had a single cart load of gravel or stones thrown upon it. Add to this, a great many heavily laden wagons are obliged to travel over it, when carrying goods to Lexington. The natural roads are . . . worse than usual, if, as was the case here, the country through which they run is fertile. . . . My journey was impeded by several creeks and rivers of no inconsiderable depth. On coming to one of them after a fall of rain, the traveler is obliged either to halt or to swim; for in the whole distance between Maysville and Lexington, there are only two bridges."[9]

Whether following elementary tracks beaten overland without a cleared or leveled right-of-way, drainage, bridges, or hard surfacing, or navigating rivers before snag clearance, dams, locks, canals, or constructed landings, migrants moving to Kentucky's frontier experienced one of the considerable ironies of cross-country travel in an era of movement by way of organic or natural routes. Because travel via the Maysville Road necessitated intermodal movement by way of both river flatboats and overland wagons, migrants found themselves in need of rain when they moved by river craft and longing for dry weather when moving overland, be it traversing Pennsylvania's ridges and plateaus or the sidling hills of Kentucky's Bluegrass Region. Though prolonged summer dry spells made for rough but steady travel overland, sparse rainfall left the Monongahela and Ohio rivers too low for navigation and subjected travelers to long waits in port or the frustration of sticking fast on a shallow river bar, where they were forced to await the rain and higher water to lift them off.[10]

Establishing the road initially involved little more than clearing underbrush and using carts and wagons to beat a path through the woodland. To the traveler the countryside still appeared as endless ranges of woods, grassy openings, and cane (*Arundinaria gigantea*) brakes. Roads tended to follow uplands, be they expansive levels or spatulate ridges, wherever possible.[11] As settlers cleared their farmland of trees and brush and opened pastures to grazing by cattle and other livestock, a parkland savanna emerged, punctuated by groves of ancient hardwood trees—oaks, ashes, hickories, walnuts, cherries—with an understory of cane, clover, grasses, pea vines, and forbs.[12] By the end of the eighteenth century the native vegetative cover had been radically modified, although one could still travel the Maysville Road through dense cane stands ten to twelve feet in height.[13] Settlements remained relatively sparse; modest farmsteads or roadside neighborhoods were separated by several miles of open country. Early emigrants, drovers, teamsters, and travelers sought overnight roadside accommodations at frontier stations or fortified houses, or, by the 1790s, roadside taverns and drovers' yards.[14] Yet by 1800 only six roadside inns between Maysville and Lexington provided reputable lodgings and fairly priced feed for draft animals.[15]

Although the road surface was poor, streams lacked bridging, and roadside accommodations were elementary, traffic along the Maysville Road was only minimally deterred, as a steady stream of migrants sought out the fecund lands of the Inner Bluegrass countryside. Towns and rural settlements were rapidly evolving into strong markets for foodstuffs and manufactured goods imported from Atlantic coast cities. Travel time for goods moving along the combined overland wagon and Ohio River flatboat route from Philadelphia to Maysville was five to six weeks. Freight wagons made frequent trips from Maysville to Lexington and back—the round-trip required six days if the road was in good condition.[16] A Lexington store proprietor, John Moylan, for example, carried a wide range of dry goods, spirits, and groceries. His ledger for 1792 lists for sale household items such as cutlery, cooking vessels, bed linens, soaps, carpets, and sewing supplies; construction materials and tools, including locks and latches, doorknobs, and specialized woodworking tools; clothing and yard goods such as shoes, silk handkerchiefs, and worsted hosiery; foodstuffs and spirits, including

Lisbon wine, port, sherry, spices, and Chinese teas; and a wide assortment of other goods. Most of Moylan's store stock arrived from Philadelphia or other East Coast sources by way of Ohio River flatboats and Maysville Road freight wagons.[17] By the early 1800s most manufactured goods imported into Kentucky came from England by way of Philadelphia merchants. Drapery and fine earthenware and fabrics came from India, and sugar and coffee arrived from the Caribbean. From France, Lexington shops obtained silk fabrics and liquors.[18] As Lexington and other towns established manufacturing businesses such as ropewalks, cotton, wool, and paper mills, and even coach and carriage makers, their products faced competition from imports because "the whole country [was] inundated by the importation of British goods."[19]

The late eighteenth- and early nineteenth-century overland transport connection from central Kentucky to East Coast cities and ports was tortuous and expensive, so merchants and freighters sought the shortest, most direct routes. Philadelphia and southeastern Pennsylvania enjoyed a longitudinal position that placed the Delaware Valley closer geographically to the Ohio Valley than was New York City. The Philadelphia region also stood approximate to several gaps in the Appalachian Mountains, a happy coincidence that invited a focus of overland routes at the Delaware River waterfront. The Delaware estuary provided a convenient deepwater port for waterborne commerce. Additionally, Philadelphia and the Delaware Valley began to attract manufacturers who wished to build industrial plants at the waterpower sites along the several rivers that tumbled across the rocky splice between the Piedmont and the Coastal Plain. Drawing on these geographic advantages, Philadelphia developed into a major manufacturing center; its primary colonial industries included woolen textiles, leather tanning, papermaking, printing, and sugar refining, although numerous craft industries also flourished. Kentucky merchants therefore found Philadelphia an important source of finished goods. That Kentucky's businesses were also successful in arranging credit with Philadelphia banks and wholesalers was a financial convenience that reinforced the trade linkage between the two places.[20]

During the pioneer decades, though wagon freighters, emigrants, travelers, and local residents daily demonstrated an increasing demand for passable roads, the state's interests in road improvements remained oddly positioned in the archaic traditions of Virginia and England, which placed responsibility for internal improvements such as roads with the people, not the state.[21] Kentucky's 1797 road law was a near copy of Virginia road laws dating from 1785, 1748, and 1658—the principles therein derived from English feudal customs that held that the purpose of roads was to serve the local community, not the larger state, and therefore road-building and maintenance responsibilities resided with local parishes and counties. The law's fundamental principles of community-scale access and usufruct-based right-of-way were seated in a tradition of local self-sufficiency, wherein travel for exchange of commodities was local, and roads, where they existed, led to a parish center or market town. Long-distance overland travel was the obligation of armies or the privilege of royalty and the upper classes. Therefore, the early state found no practical necessity in building regional or national road networks. As a consequence, the archetypal local road was a natural track beaten across the country by farmers' draft animals and wagon wheels; it was not constructed.

A road's purpose was to serve the local community's daily needs and in the process help preserve its traditions and culture.[22]

Embracing the continuity of English and Virginian feudal traditions, Kentucky's 1797 road law placed the responsibility for roads with the county court. Local residents could petition a county court to open a new road or alter an existing road, provided that the road led "to their county courthouse, a public warehouse, a landing, ferry, mill, lead or iron-works, or the seat of government."[23] The law presented no directives to create a systematic road network that connected farms and towns or promoted long-distance travel. Nor did the law create or underwrite professional road builders or engineers; rather, roads were conceived as a local service to be laid out and maintained by local people, whatever their qualifications and resources might be. People whose lands were compromised in some way by the establishment of new roads were entitled to damages that would be tallied by court-appointed surveyors and paid by the county through tax levies. The responsibility for road maintenance lay, again, with court-appointed precinct-level surveyors who were required to keep roads cleared and in good repair. To this end, precinct labor crews or militias made up of locally impressed citizens were obligated to contribute their time and tools—wagons, draft animals and harnesses, and drivers—to road clearing and maintenance. All this was a form of statute labor tax and was conducted under penalty of a fine for noncompliance.[24]

The road law provided no innovative guidance for road construction and maintenance but, rather, offered vague direction or adhered to traditional folk practice in creating "natural" roads. Road surveyors were charged with keeping roads cleared and smoothed to a width of thirty feet and with erecting at forks and crossroads a stone or sign that carried an informative inscription noting the place where each road would lead. Bridges and causeways were to be at least twelve feet wide. Wood and stone for bridge construction could be taken from lands adjoining the road. Where milldams and roads coincided to cross a stream, the law obligated owners of water-powered mills to construct their milldams twelve feet wide so that the top of the dam could be used as a road, and to build and maintain a bridge for public use.[25] Given the law's technical naïveté—road engineering and construction technology was rapidly advancing into a science in France and England by this time—roads remained the product of folk craft and artifice.[26] Travelers, in adapting to such conditions, often attempted to bypass the worst road sections on firmer or less rutted ground. In some places the bypass was directly beside the existing road, in others it might be several hundred yards away, following a parallel valley or ridge. The route way was therefore not a single road, but a braided skein of multiple tracks.

Although travel on the Maysville Road was difficult, it remained the region's overland lifeline to Ohio River navigation and to East Coast urban markets and goods suppliers. As the Bluegrass country developed at the hands of its rural farmers and urban entrepreneurs, each county through which the road passed sought to make its own local road connections to the thoroughfare, linking the backcountry to a transport network that would enhance residents' economic livelihoods and social connections to the wider world.

If the pioneer road can be thought of as a "built road," it was the product of folk road builders who often neglected the optimum terrain and later paid for their indiscretion with precipitous grades or impassable mires for a substantial portion of the year. Modern road construction and engineering did not arrive abruptly but accreted over decades. Eventually modern engineers could ignore the elevation and drainage idiosyncrasies of the topographic surface with seeming impunity and place roads along the most direct routes, regardless of hills, boggy flats, or potamic barriers.[27] An informal alliance of economic, political, and engineering interests began to form around concerns for "internal improvements" by the nineteenth century's second decade, initiating a gradual change in road construction philosophy and practice. How this process evolved and how folk road making was superseded by the formalities of law, engineering, and science is illustrated by Kentucky's embrace of the turnpike road.

8

Turnpike Road

In November 1796 Andrew Ellicott, a surveyor, landed at Limestone on his way down the Ohio River. His journal entry about the site is not flattering: "arrived at Limestone about ten o'clock in the forenoon. It is a miserable village; left it in about an hour."[1] Fourteen years later, in 1810, Fortescue Cuming traveled through Kentucky, and his published account recorded the rapid changes under way as the region made the transition from the inelegant pioneer frontier that Ellicott had encountered to a place where people were actively establishing the social and economic institutions and physical infrastructure that converted open land into a considered landscape of habitation. Upon arriving at the Ohio River landing at Limestone Creek, and even though Cuming found the town's sixty houses tightly constricted by its narrow site between the bluff and the river, he thought Maysville was the greatest shipping port on the Ohio below Pittsburgh and an important stop on the most direct overland road from Philadelphia to central Kentucky and Tennessee. Although through traffic was active, giving the place the appearance of liveliness, the town did not appear to be growing, and the boat-building businesses at the riverfront were moribund.[2] Finding no overland transportation available for hire, Cuming set out on foot for Lexington. Above the river, at the top of the bluff, he found the Outer Bluegrass countryside developed into large farms, and as he proceeded south along the road, he noted, "The country on every side appears to be better improved than I have observed it in any other part of America, and wonderfully abundant in grain, chiefly Indian corn."[3] Washington, unlike Maysville, was a thriving town of ninety-six houses, a stone courthouse, and two churches, and here Cuming was able to rent a horse for the remainder of the trip to Lexington.

Cuming found the road south to be in good condition. He was able to cross the North Fork of the Licking on a well-made wooden bridge, some 230 feet long. South of Mayslick, then a small post town with only about ten houses, he entered the Eden Shale Hills, which he found less developed and the road "very bad, the hills being extremely steep."[4] While he was still some three miles away from the Blue Licks, smoke from the seven salt furnaces there announced the approach to the Licking River's main channel. No bridge yet spanned the Licking, so Cuming had to ford the 240-foot channel, swimming his horse to the south bank. He obtained overnight accommodations near the licks at a roadside tavern that catered to people seeking relief from various illnesses by an efficacious intake of lick springwater—Cuming equated its taste and smell to those of "bilge water in a ship's hold."[5] Resuming his journey to Lexington the following day, he continued for several miles through the comparatively bleak Eden Shale landscape, the road passing along "a stony defile between barren hills."[6] The land improved near Millersburg, a village of about thirty houses. Though it was not thriving, the place held promise as a manufacturing town, Cuming believed, because of its position beside Hinkston Creek, a good millstream. A wooden bridge spanning the creek made for a much easier crossing than David Meade had experienced fourteen years earlier. Cuming completed the remainder of his ride into Lexington by way of a cross-country detour north of Paris. Off the main road, a countryside road network had not yet taken form, so Cuming found himself following a "labyrinth of cross paths" through fine, cultivated country that reminded him of Languedoc and Provence in France.[7]

Lexington and the surrounding farmland deeply impressed Cuming, and he spent the following days exploring the town, tabulating its commerce, and engaging the citizenry in conversation about the state of their businesses. The roads approaching the city were "very wide and fine, with grazing parks, meadows, and every spot in sight cultivated."[8] In town he counted 366 dwelling houses, mostly built of brick, besides barns, stables, and other business buildings. The small creek that bisected the town's center had been covered over to ease crossing. Main Street was eighty feet wide and well paved, and there were twelve-foot-wide sidewalks on each side. His informal census counted five churches, a new brick courthouse under construction, a library, and a highly regarded university. Cuming estimated Lexington's population at over 3,000, enslaved and free combined—the actual 1810 census count was 4,326. In the town market he was "astonished at the profusion and variety of most of the necessaries and many of the luxuries of life."[9] Farm products—beef, pork, lamb, cornmeal, butter—and garden produce were available in abundance and at good prices.

Fortescue Cuming's interest was piqued especially by the town's economic vitality. His account contains a detailed listing of artisans and manufacturers, including their level and value of production and the number of employees. A brief sample of what he found will illustrate the magnitude and diversity of production: three nail manufacturers producing sixty tons of nails annually—probably using iron produced in eastern Kentucky's charcoal-fired iron blast furnaces; three tanyards and five currying shops manufacturing $30,000 worth of leather each year—these yards supplied leather to seven saddler's shops employing thirty people whose labor was worth $25,000 to $30,000 annually; ten tailors and fifteen boot- and shoemakers employing sixty people; four ropewalks employing sixty and manufacturing three hundred tons of cordage from locally produced hemp; two tobacco manufacturers making snuff, chewing tobacco, and cigars from local tobaccos; and seven brickyards employing sixty people and producing 2.5 million bricks annually. Retail business and finance were represented by twenty-two retail stores selling over $300,000 worth of imported and foreign merchandise annually, an insurance company with banking functions capitalized at over $100,000, and a Bank of Kentucky branch office.[10]

The central Kentucky culture and economy that Fortescue Cuming described was enabled by land so rich that farmers soon produced commodities—tobacco, hemp, grains, and livestock—in excess of local market demand. Plenteous production elevated Lexington to the status of a central place for industry, wholesaling, and retailing, but it also drove down prices and invited speculation about the best manner to export farm surpluses. Whereas cattle and mules could be driven to markets outside the region at comparatively low cost, other farm products were bulky and of low value. When many products were shipped via Kentucky and Ohio river ports to New Orleans markets, high transportation costs often made them marginally profitable at best. Ginseng was the only local commodity of sufficient value that it could be exported east via New Orleans and reliably produce a profit.[11] Just so, the transportation costs on imported manufactured goods coming overland from Atlantic coast port cities were estimated at $65 per ton, for an aggregated average of $10,000 per day spent on transportation costs to bring imported goods to central Kentucky by riverboat and wagon. Transportation costs increased retail prices charged by Lexington shops by more than one-third and created a serious depletion of financial resources.[12] Such was the plight of businesses in a landlocked city, situated more than sixty miles from the nearest Ohio River port via roads that ranged from good to awful. The salient problem for Lexington merchants was not what they could sell but what they could haul and at what cost.

To counter this profound transportation disadvantage, as early as 1790 Lexington businesspeople organized a society for the encouragement of home manufacturers that produced sufficient investment monies to bring spinning and carding machines and looms to the city from Philadelphia.[13] This investment, as well as initiatives by other local entrepreneurs, such as Ed West, who invented a successful nail-cutting machine, increased manufacturing activity over fortyfold and impressed Fortescue Cuming some two decades later.[14]

Nevertheless, imported goods, especially from England, continued to pour into the city via Ohio River flatboats and Maysville Road freight wagons. Lexington area boosters—politicians, businesspeople, newspaper editors—petitioned the national congress for tariff protection of their local manufacturers. Henry Clay was by 1811 advocating a new "American System" that involved a planned national economy stressing tariff protection of home industries and internal improvements to enhance transportation through better roads and river navigation.[15] Some businesspeople thought that transport costs on imported goods could be checked if the Maysville Road could be improved. In 1811 the Kentucky legislature authorized a lottery to raise five thousand dollars to improve the road's northern segment from Maysville to Washington.[16] From the War of 1812 through about 1816, the Lexington area economy continued to boom. William Darby, in his 1818 guide for emigrants, commented approvingly about Lexington and environs: "No where in America has the almost instantaneous change, from an uncultivated waste to the elegancies of civilization, been so striking."[17]

But, with the first steamboat passage from Pittsburgh to New Orleans and back upstream to Pittsburgh in 1815, the economic power that Lexington had enjoyed began to shift to Ohio River port locations. Within a year steamboat construction was under way in Ohio River towns, and a Cincinnati company had started a steamship line to move cargo up and down the river at cost savings estimated at 50 percent over the established traditional combination of flatboat and overland road travel.[18] The net effect of rapidly increasing Ohio River steamboat traffic in conjunction with the financial panic of 1819 was a rapid decline of local manufacturing at inland centers. By 1820 Lexington and surrounding towns had nearly divested themselves of foundries and factories, and even the hemp and woolen mills that processed local raw materials failed.[19] The *Niles Register* reported that throughout Kentucky "nothing is seen but a boundless expanse of desolation. Wealth impoverished, enterprise checked, commerce at a stand, the currency depreciated."[20] Imploring congress to underwrite internal improvements secured no relief. Kentucky's legislature had supported improvements for the Wilderness Road in 1797 and approved the formation of a Maysville Road turnpike company in 1817 that would convert, through stock subscriptions and toll collections, the natural track into a stone-surfaced artificial road.[21] Yet road improvement advocates made little headway in obtaining financial support from either the state or federal government. Henry Clay, in a retirement speech made in Lexington in 1829, complained: "We want an efficient system of internal improvements adopted by the state. No Kentuckian who travelled in or out of it, could behold the wretched condition of our roads, without the deepest mortification." As an example Clay cited a recent trip that he and his family had made to Maysville from Lexington, the trip taking nearly four days "through the mud and the mire, a distance of only sixty-four miles, over one of the most frequented roads in the state."[22]

Lexington would continue to extend cultural influence across central Kentucky through institutions such as Transylvania University that were not sensitive to transportation issues. Educators, scientists, painters, architects, musicians, doctors, and their patrons moved to the city. Nevertheless, landlocked Lexington's inland position was suffocating other forms of economic development, and city boosters sought to counter the rapidly accelerating financial power of the Ohio River cities at Louisville and Cincinnati by advocating for better roads.[23]

Freight, mail, and passenger traffic continued to use the Maysville Road, however poor its condition. A stagecoach line established service between Lexington and Maysville in 1818, but service was intermittent. Not until a Pennsylvania native and Mason County resident, Joseph Desha, became Kentucky's governor in 1824 did the state seek to initiate systematic road and river navigation improvements. In his inaugural message to the legislature in 1826, Governor Desha strongly advocated for a turnpike road that would link Maysville to Louisville by way of Lexington and Frankfort.[24] The following year the Maysville and Lexington turnpike road company was incorporated again—the 1816 act of incorporation had expired by this time—with \$320,000 capital stock and the federal and state governments both authorized to subscribe \$100,000. The remaining stock was allocated for sale to local investors. Those who bought turnpike stock as an investment expected remuneration from dividends funded by tolls charged on road traffic.

In the 1820s and 1830s Kentucky's turnpike-building efforts focused geographically on the Bluegrass Region.[25] Creating a turnpike road represented a fundamental change in thinking about how roads could be used, how they should function relative to community and regional needs, and how roads could be made reliable and capable of enhancing vehicle speed and thereby reducing transportation costs. A turnpike was a constructed road, or what local people called an artificial road, and a radical departure from the natural beaten tracks that most roads had been until this time. Unlike the natural track, a constructed road required engineering technology, construction tools and materials, a willing and knowledgeable labor force, and, hence, substantial financial resources. Such a road had to be built and maintained as an extended linear unit, not in short, discrete sections. A road that crossed county boundaries and political jurisdictions had to maintain all its design and construction qualities over the course of its length; it could not be subject to changes in gradient or surfacing materials because funding or access priorities changed at a county boundary.

Building roads of resilient stone goes back to techniques developed by Roman engineers whose road network laced together Rome's European empire. In France Napoleon instituted technical training for road engineers that brought road-building principles to the level of a science and standardized road design in terms of appropriate alignment and grade, generous roadbed dimensions, thorough drainage, and high-quality surfacing materials.[26] In Great Britain the Scottish engineers Thomas Telford and John McAdam developed methods of building resilient, all-weather, broken-stone roadbeds. Telford's road required a foundation of large stones covered by a compacted layer of smaller, broken stones. In addition to providing support for the top layer of broken stone, the foundation stones provided passage for water drainage away from the road's surface. McAdam's method was simpler, as the road was built without a foundation course; his technique required less stone and was, therefore, cheaper and more straightforward to construct.[27] These were compelling qualities, given limited financial resources and an inexperienced, nonprofessional labor force, which was probably the reason that Kentucky road builders adopted McAdam's method in the 1820s. McAdam's principles were also widely adopted elsewhere, to the extent that broken-stone roads came to be known as macadam roads.

The chairman of the Maysville Turnpike Company's board of directors or commissioners, Valentine Peers, became a student of road-construction technology as part of his responsibilities to fund and direct the new road's construction. Peers manufactured salt at Lower Blue Licks in the early 1800s and thereafter lived in Paris and Maysville, operating cotton factories in both towns. The state legislature provided to the turnpike company little direction for road-construction planning or technical specifications other than the general guidance offered by the incorporating statutes.[28] In 1826 Peers sought advice from the directors of the Shelbyville and Louisville Turnpike Road Company, who were already engaged in planning and surveying their road.[29] He received from Basil Hobbs a detailed description of the procedures for clearing the right-of-way, leveling the roadbed, sizing broken stone, and estimating construction costs.

To build a proper macadam road and comply with state road-construction statutes, Hobbs recommended that a track for the road fifty feet wide be cleared of all trees, stumps, and other obstacles. A proper roadbed should be twenty-one feet wide and made as level as possible by cutting down hills and filling in depressions so that the final grade did not exceed three and one-half degrees. In cross section the roadbed was to be cut down below the surface five inches, tapering up from each side into a convex crown of three and one-half inches in the center. The raised or crowned roadbed, when covered in rock, would tend to shed water from the roadway. The dirt removed from the roadbed was placed beside the track to create a berm or curb nine inches high that would retain the stone covering. Road stone, obtained from roadside quarries where available, could be sized by heavy cast-iron sieves or "mortars," perforated with two-and-one-half-inch holes, which were mounted in wooden frames across the roadbed. Laborers, or turnpikers as they were called, were to place stones on the iron sieves and break the stone with three-pound hammers into sizes that would pass through the holes and fall onto the road surface below. As the stone accumulated to the required depth, laborers moved the sieves to the next section to be covered. Hobbs recommended turnpikers avoid wherever possible constructing water drainage culverts or "conduits" to direct water away from the road because of their expense and maintenance requirements—an idea that would prove ruinous for low-lying road sections where the waterlogged soil would not support the weight of heavy freight wagons. Hobbs estimated that construction costs would total $9 to $12 per rod, or $2,880 to $3,840 per mile.[30] At its completion in 1835, the sixty-seven-mile-long Maysville and Lexington Turnpike cost $426,400, including the price of thirteen tollhouses and six covered bridges, or an average of $6,364.18 per mile.[31] One-half the cost was borne by turnpike stock subscriptions of private individuals; the other half was funded by an appropriation from the state legislature for the purchase of turnpike stock.

Before construction could proceed, the turnpike company had to survey an appropriate route. By statute, the new road had be "the best and nearest route" from Maysville to Lexington, which implies that the surveyors be commissioned to survey the lands along which the road would pass and plat a direct yet low-gradient route.[32] James Darnaby and William Ellis Jr., Fayette County surveyors, completed the survey and submitted a map of their recommended route to the turnpike commissioners in August 1827. The map recorded the existing track and important settlements, rivers and streams, and roadside taverns and houses, as well as proposed alternative routes recommended by the surveyors.[33] The recommended route closely approximated the existing track in several places, such as the section from Millersburg north to Blue Licks. In other places the surveyors' recommended route departed from the original track, most notably between Lexington and Paris, where the old way followed Bryan Station Road and its extensions for nearly fourteen miles and passed several inns and farm homes established at the roadside. Here the recommended route lay a mile or so to the northwest but followed a nearly straight trajectory from Houston Creek south of Paris into Lexington. This new route was adopted. Local people referred to it as the "new cut," but its more formal designation was the Lexington to Paris Pike.

The first segment of the new "artificial" turnpike completed according to John McAdam's principles was the four-mile section from Maysville to Washington. Opened to traffic in November 1830, it was the first macadam road in the state and the first west of the Appalachians.[34] Toll fees, paid at tollhouses constructed at roadside every

During the toll-road era, Maysville-to-Lexington turnpike travelers paid tolls at thirteen tollgates spaced about five miles apart. Toll collectors lived in tollhouses at the gates. Collected tolls provided funds to repair the road, paid the tollgate keeper's salary, and perhaps yielded a dividend to turnpike company stockholders. In 1943 this tollhouse still stood beside the road in Nicholas County, near the Bourbon County line. This tollgate's location north of Millersburg would have complied with a state law that required gates be established no closer to a town than one mile. With the passing of the toll-road era, tollhouses were often converted to residences. (J. Winston Coleman Jr. Photographic Collection, Transylvania University Library)

five miles, were differentiated on the basis of the amount of wear or damage a vehicle or animal was thought to impart to the road, and enforced by legal statute. Light, wide-wheeled vehicles, for example, were favored with lower tolls, whereas owners of heavy, narrow-wheeled carriages and wagons paid higher rates. The state optimistically presumed that its investment in turnpike stock would be repaid by profits garnered from tolls; hence, the legislature passed a succession of laws regulating toll fees and setting penalties for vandalizing milestones, turnpike gates, and tollhouses.[35] People seeking to avoid paying tolls by detouring through farm fields to evade the tollhouses were, if caught and prosecuted, liable for a fifteen-dollar fine and court costs.[36] Shunning the pike, as it was termed, could be controlled if farmers built fences along their road frontage, thereby forcing road travelers to remain on the road.

Constructing a turnpike road was a large-scale undertaking that required hiring and organizing labor; hiring quarry masons to open quarries to supply stone for road pavement and bridge abutments, and providing tools, wagons, and explosives for excavation and quarrying; provisioning labor crews with food, water, and residential

Table 8.1. John McNamee Household, Fleming County, Kentucky, District 1, 1850

Name	*Age*	*Occupation*	*Birthplace*
John McNamee	26	Road maker	Ireland
Mary McNamee	20		Ireland
James McNamee	<1		Kentucky
Sarah McNamee	18		Ireland
William Bush	25	Laborer	Ireland
James Boyle	25	Laborer	Ireland
Andrew McNamee	20	Laborer	Ireland
Patrick Clane	20	Laborer	Ireland
Brian Roer	18	Laborer	Ireland
John Forty	20	Laborer	Ireland
Thomas Morley	20	Laborer	Ireland
John Maloy	32	Laborer	Ireland
John Flanigan	32	Laborer	Ireland
James Maloy	27	Laborer	Ireland
Michael Crow	18	Laborer	Ireland
Thomas Crow	26	Laborer	Ireland
James Laden	24	Laborer	Ireland
Michael Crain	32	Laborer	Ireland

Source: *U.S. Federal Census Manuscripts*, Fleming County, Ky., 1850.

accommodations; and solving logistical problems such as delivering timber to bridge construction sites. Counties bisected by the road participated in the road-building process by providing access to roadside land for stone quarries. Court-appointed commissioners in Bourbon County, for example, identified six quarry sites from which macadam road stone could be obtained. Spaced a mile or more apart and situated as close to the road as practicable, their remnants today are disguised by fill or vegetation cover—with one exception. The large quarry on Jacob Jacoby's land, at the famous Jacoby Curve south of Paris, was cut into a hillside on the road's southeast side and is still visible.[37]

Few construction projects, if any, of this magnitude had previously been attempted in Kentucky, so new, large-scale work methods had to be developed at the same time that engineering and financial problems had to be resolved. Turnpike companies hired road-building contractors locally. Many road laborers or turnpikers were Irish immigrants. John McNamee, for example, lived in Fleming County in 1850 and established a turnpike construction business. The Maysville Road traversed the western section of Fleming County from Blue Licks to Johnson Creek.

The McNamee household included John's wife, Mary, another woman, Sarah (possibly his sister), both also born in Ireland, and the McNamees' young son, James, who was born in Kentucky in 1849. John McNamee's occupation, as recorded by the census taker in 1850, was "road maker." Living in the same house were fourteen Ireland-born laborers, and one, Andrew McNamee, might have been a brother or other family member. This extended household probably represented John McNamee's road-construction crew.

Many other family-centered Irish turnpike contractors lived in the counties bisected by the Maysville Road, especially in Bourbon County, on the road's southern section, and in Mason County, at the road's northern terminus. They worked on the Maysville Turnpike, but they also built the neighborhood turnpikes or secondary roads that knitted a network of rural roads linking farms to other countryside neighborhoods, to the county seat, and eventually to a main or baseline road. Across Kentucky, if rural residents wished to be served by reliable all-weather, rock-surfaced roads, they had to build those roads themselves by forming turnpike companies, selling stock to local investors, and hiring turnpike construction companies to build the roads. Some 1,460 turnpike roads were built in Kentucky between 1810 and 1891. A few of them were state-sponsored baseline turnpikes that functioned as main thoroughfares that traversed the state—the Maysville Turnpike was one of these. But the large majority of these turnpikes were short neighborhood roads, often five miles or less in length.[38] In 1850 several turnpike contractors lived and worked in Mason County, and they were almost exclusively Irish.

As his young counterpart, John McNamee of Fleming County, had done, Michael Goest ran a turnpike-construction company out of his Mason County household. The couple's first son, John (or possibly Michael's younger brother), was born in Ireland in 1841, just a few years before the major emigrations of 1845–50 that were stimulated by accumulated economic and social maladies and exacerbated by the Great Famine. His son William was born in New York in 1849, which suggests that the

Table 8.2. Michael Goest Household, Mason County, Kentucky, District 2, 1850

Name	*Age*	*Occupation*	*Birthplace*
Michael Goest	31	Pike maker	Ireland
Catherine Goest	25		Ireland
John Goest	9		Ireland
William Goest	1		New York
Patrick Ryan	20	Pike maker	Ireland
Thomas Ryan	19	Pike maker	Ireland
Edward Burns	21	Pike maker	Ireland
Patrick Burns	19	Pike maker	Ireland
Thomas Coen	40	Pike maker	Ireland
John Finey	24	Pike maker	Ireland

Source: *U.S. Federal Census Manuscripts*, Mason County, Ky., 1850.

Table 8.3. William Lenihan Household, Bourbon County, Kentucky, 1870.

Name	*Age*	*Occupation*	*Birthplace*
William Lenihan	34	Turnpike contractor	Ireland
Kate Lenihan	27	Tollgate keeper	Ireland
Mary Lenihan	<1		Kentucky
Darby King	18	Pike laborer	Ireland

Source: *U.S. Federal Census Manuscripts*, Bourbon County, Ky., 1870.

family had successfully migrated and that Goest may have been working in one of that state's large road- or canal- construction projects then under way. The following year the census taker found Michael and Catherine Goest, their family, and six turnpike laborers living together in Mason County. Familial interdependence and social ties of affection and obligation to kith and kin were century-old traditions in Ireland and continued in the households that Irish labor contractors established in Kentucky. Few Irish contractors lived alone with their immediate families; most brought their laboring kinsmen into their homes as residents.[39] Once a turnpike was completed and the tollhouses erected, tollgate keepers, also primarily Irish, lived in the houses, collected tolls, and made minor repairs on the road.[40]

William Lenihan and his wife, Kate, for example, were Irish immigrants living in Bourbon County in 1870. They, together with their daughter, Mary, and a laborer, Darby King, lived in a turnpike tollhouse that Kate Lenihan operated while her husband worked on turnpike construction projects.

Though the Irish turnpiker era had passed by the turn of the twentieth century, and their roadside homes and tollhouses were by then a lost landscape, one can still find traces of the Irish presence along the road. Four miles south of the Ohio River, St. Patrick's Catholic Cemetery occupies a low hill just north of Washington, a few dozen yards from the Maysville Road. Many older gravestones bear Irish names and include the place of birth; for many that place was Ireland. The Mt. Olivet Catholic Cemetery in Paris, which adjoins the Paris Cemetery one block west of the Maysville Road, also contains the graves of many Irish immigrants.

All traffic on the surveyed and stone-paved Maysville Turnpike, especially stagecoaches and freight wagons, benefited substantially from its reduced grades, new bridges, and resilient surface. Coach lines that had struggled with poor conditions on the old road and delays caused by bad weather now found that their vehicles could average eight miles per hour on the newly rock-surfaced turnpike. The entire trip from Lexington to the Ohio River at Maysville now took less than one day.[41] From the mid-1830s to the early 1840s, as many as three stage lines served the Maysville-to-Lexington route, running in "opposition" or competition with one another along the road. The first stage line, called the Old Line, carried mail and passengers and featured both lightly loaded express stages and slower coaches that accepted heavy loads and accommodated passengers both inside and atop the vehicles. Stage lines commonly owned or held an interest in the taverns and inns along the road that company

A stagecoach office at Short and Mill streets in central Lexington, seen here in 1881, served stagecoach lines connecting the city to the surrounding county seats and more distant cities on the Ohio River, including Maysville. The stagecoach office also served as a social center for local residents who gathered news from distant places by talking with arriving passengers. The coach depicted here is a Concord, manufactured by the Abbot-Dowing Company's expansive coachworks in Concord, New Hampshire, at the north end of the industrial Merrimack River valley. Three benches inside provided space for nine passengers; nearly as many often rode atop the coach, beside the driver, or standing on the rear cargo boot. Concord coaches were known for their high quality and exceptional durability. This coach design was also used extensively by western stage lines such as Wells, Fargo & Company. (J. Winston Coleman Jr. Photographic Collection, Transylvania University Library)

coaches used as regular stops.[42] In 1837 a Pennsylvania stage company started the Good Intent Line, or General Opposition Line, advertising their business as "supplied with substantial Troy [New York] and Lancaster [Pennsylvania] Coaches, excellent teams, and careful sober drivers; all racing is expressly forbidden and baggage or parcels at the risk of owners thereof."[43] In 1839 a third stage line, the Peoples Line, was organized to serve the increasing demand by pike travelers.[44]

The sixty-seven-mile trip from Maysville to Lexington on the newly stone-surfaced turnpike included stops every ten miles to change horses; the fare was one or two dollars per passenger. The low fare charges, on the one hand, and stiff operational expenses, on the other, forced two lines out of business, which gave the surviving stage line a monopoly over the route. This line promptly increased its fares to five dollars per passenger and, to diminish the exertion required of the stage horses, reduced their speed to less than five miles per hour. An English traveler, James Silk Buckingham, generally a prideful critic of most aspects of the quotidian American life that he encountered, disembarked from the Ohio River at Maysville in the early 1840s and got aboard a Lexington-bound stagecoach with thirteen other passengers. He found the turnpike to be "one of the best in the Union, quite equal to the National Road from Wheeling to Columbus, and equal . . . to any road in England," but he railed at the exorbitant fare and the thirteen hours required to make the trip to Lexington under the avaricious regime of the single stage line.[45]

The new macadam turnpikes were not a panacea for the region's transportation problems. Though some believed that stone-surfaced roads generally benefited everyone who wished to use them, and that the new roads were even preferred to railroads in the Bluegrass agricultural countryside, other haulage concerns preoccupied area residents.[46] First, while the Maysville Turnpike connected an important Ohio River port town with the largest town in the Bluegrass Region, there were few country roads linking small hamlets and rural farmsteads with one another or with the turnpike. For the most part, people navigated the countryside not on established roads but along tracks that crossed farm fields and pastures, sure to arrive at their destinations only if they were local residents, familiar with the countryside, or if they had good directions and a well-drawn map.[47] Such was the experience of two English travelers, intent on inspecting the livestock at the James Letton farm near Millersburg. "To do this," they wrote, "we had six miles to thread out all alone, in a pretty blind way across the country. But a gentleman at the hotel where we stopped, drew a plain map of the route. . . . We pretty soon got into a large open park, then bearing to the left, and now taking to the right, and fording a wild crooked rivulet half a dozen times, opening and shutting as many different gates as we passed from enclosure to enclosure, we at last arrived at a snug farm-house," where they found a man to guide them the remaining two miles to their destination.[48]

High toll costs were a second issue weighing on effective road use. Though maintenance on central Kentucky's primary turnpike roads was generally adequate, most farm people could not afford the tolls. The cost of a two-horse farm wagon round-trip was about three cents per mile. For a farm family living five miles from town, a round-trip by wagon would have cost the equivalent of about $6.50 today. School attendance and social visits to neighbors and relatives were probably curtailed or otherwise influenced by such costs.[49] By the 1890s public concern for high toll costs resulted in a strong movement to abolish tolls and by 1900 most central Kentucky toll gates had been removed and the roads made free to travelers.[50]

Third, though the Maysville Turnpike Company adapted a version of the McAdam road-building technique, the road was nevertheless poorly built in some sections, and bridges were either badly constructed or placed on improperly engineered abutments that threatened collapse if undermined by high water. The road required constant maintenance. When repairs were not forthcoming, whether because of a shortage of toll revenues or a lack of materials or knowledge on the part of those assigned to the task, road quality suffered and travel slowed. These problems were not exclusive to the Maysville Turnpike but were endemic in most other road-improvement projects. At issue was a dearth of professionally trained engineers in Kentucky who could bring the engineering and science disciplines to road construction. The Kentucky legislature created the Board of Internal Improvement in 1835 to provide statewide oversight of road- and river-transportation-system development. The following year the board apprised the legislature that road construction should be directed by knowledgeable engineers. The board further observed that the transportation improvements contemplated by the state's political leadership were "well understood in other countries, [but] are, to most of us in this country, altogether new, and if carried into successful operation, will have to be done through the instrumentality of experienced and competent agents."[51]

To provide the state the required engineering expertise, the board looked toward those eastern states where large-scale transportation-improvement projects had already been completed. They hired Sylvester Welch from Pennsylvania as the state's chief engineer, a person of "great experience, and commanding reputation."[52] Welch had worked on New York's Erie Canal and in 1833 had served as chief engineer on the construction of the Allegheny Portage Railroad, which carried canal boats on the Pennsylvania Main Line Canal across the spine of the Appalachians in central Pennsylvania, a project widely regarded as a remarkable engineering achievement. The board also hired other engineers, including H. I. Eastin, who served as Welch's assistant and principal state road engineer.

Sylvester Welch quickly recognized the limitations of traditional road-construction methods in Kentucky, such as those recommended by Basil Hobbs, and in 1837 issued new, detailed specifications for constructing stone-surfaced turnpike roads. Building roads according to Welch's directives required extensive roadbed preparation, especially the carefully engineered placement of culverts and drains to remove water from under or alongside the road.[53] So effective were Welch's innovations that fifty-seven years after their publication they became the basis for the 1894 road law, often referred to as the Sims Road Law, the first major revision of the state's original 1789 road-building code.[54]

In the years subsequent to his appointment, Welch reported annually to the Board of Internal Improvement and offered his assessment of road conditions. By 1838 the Maysville Turnpike was in generally good condition, excepting those sections that were not drained by culverts and ditches where seeps and runoff water so softened the roadbed that heavy wagons cut through the stone covering. And, at the Licking River bridge, the abutment wing walls were so poorly built that they threatened to fall into the river unless reinforced with buttresses. The tolls collected during the year—October 1, 1837, to October 1, 1838—totaled $29,117.16, or $454.95 per mile, while repairs, pay for tollgate keepers, and other expenses totaled $325.96 per mile. The scanty toll returns were probably adequate to support nothing more than superficial maintenance. Road repair was further hampered by property owners whose land adjoined the road but who refused to allow the turnpike company to open stone quarries on their land or charged very high prices for stone. Welch also recognized that the ad hoc method of relying on tollgate keepers to make road repairs was woefully inadequate for keeping the road surface in acceptable condition. The solution he proposed required that the state adopt a process of appointing knowledgeable road superintendents who would regularly inspect the roads and sign formal contracts with reliable construction companies for needed repairs.[55]

Under Welch's leadership, and with enlightened and open-minded members on the Board of Internal Improvement, toll road management improved through the 1840s, although few state toll roads produced what was deemed by the state to be an acceptable return or profit on the state's investment in toll road stock. Initially, the Maysville Turnpike board was resistant or nonresponsive to admonitions by the Board of Internal Improvement to make annual reports of traffic, tolls collected, and road repair contracts. The turnpike directors did undertake repair of the Licking River bridge, but with low-grade materials and inexpert design. Apparently they chose to insure the bridge at an annual cost of forty-eight dollars rather than expend toll funds on qualified engineers and quality construction.[56]

A report made by the turnpike company's treasurer, William Huston, to the state auditor in 1845 illustrates how the company budgeted its toll collection funds. In the six-month period from June 1 to December 1 that year, the Maysville Road tollhouses collected $11,398. Expenditures included $67 for attorney fees, $151 for bridge insurance, $1,676 in salaries for gatekeepers, a superintendent, and treasurer, and $4,117 in road repairs. The directors declared the balance of $5,387 as a dividend on the 4,264 shares of turnpike company stock, half of which was held by the state, or a return per share of $1.27.[57]

Turnpike management proved problematic, especially in the view of the Board of Internal Improvement. The state funded its investment in turnpike shares from a sinking fund that included monies from a variety of sources, including state treasury surpluses, bonds, and, most important, dividends on stock shares that the state had purchased from the turnpike companies.[58] But when toll collections failed to provide sufficient capital to maintain the roads in good repair, and to meet state expectations for share dividends that could be used to recharge the sinking fund, the board reacted with harsh criticism for turnpike company directors. Turnpike shares initially cost one hundred dollars each. To reward investors, the Maysville Turnpike directors established a policy of allowing shareholders to use the road free of toll charges, a significant saving for regular turnpike travelers. Thus, for example, if someone made a round-trip from Lexington to Maysville with a four-horse wagon and paid the standard fifty-cent toll at each of the thirteen tollhouses, the cost of eight such trips would be the same as just one share of turnpike stock. The state board saw free road passage for stockholders as a transparent attempt to permit "a numerous host of useless directors or . . . stockholders . . . to use the road with wagons &c., free from toll. The consequence is, that an individual wishing so to use and ruin the road, purchases a share of stock for a trifle . . . without contributing a cent for its repairs."[59] The board's discontent deepened when querulous turnpike directors unilaterally reduced toll fees—in part a reaction to competition from the new Lexington and Ohio Railroad—while at the same time the state legislature was enacting laws mandating standard toll rates for all state turnpikes in the futile hope that toll dividends would one day be sufficient to repay state investments in turnpike construction.[60]

A further legacy of Sylvester Welch's foresight and engineering acuity was the completion of what he termed "lateral feeder" roads that would link outlying counties with the state's "great base line" cross-country turnpikes such as the Maysville

Road. By 1848 macadam feeder turnpikes, funded by local subscribers, linked Cynthiana to the road at Millersburg, and Georgetown and Winchester were connected at Paris. Carlisle and Mount Sterling established linkage to the Maysville Road west of Carlisle near Forest Retreat, the Nicholas County residence of Thomas Metcalfe. While governor from 1828 to 1832, Metcalfe was a stalwart advocate of state-supported transportation improvements, and when President Andrew Jackson vetoed legislation that would have provided federal funding for construction of the Maysville Road in 1830, Metcalfe vowed that the road would be built with state support. The lateral feeder pikes themselves were linked to smaller neighborhood turnpikes that provided farmers access to mill sites and their county seats, thereby increasing the value of road-adjacent property and opening the entire Bluegrass countryside to the ready movement of people, farm commodities, manufactured goods, and the mail.[61]

During the Civil War—1861 to 1865—Maysville Turnpike toll revenues declined precipitously, and road quality deteriorated because of deferred maintenance. After the war, railroads and interurban rail lines became progressively more competitive, and they increasingly siphoned business away from the turnpike. Toll collections failed to provide sufficient income to repair the pike, and people's disgruntlement at the prospect of paying tolls for access to a poor-quality road intensified. By the late 1880s the traveling public was in high dudgeon over regressive tolls and inferior roads. An anti–toll road movement garnered broad public support, and in 1892 and 1894 the Kentucky legislature passed bills that permitted cities and counties to acquire sections of toll roads within their jurisdictions through purchase of state-owned stock. The legislature followed, in 1896, with a new road law designed to provide free roads by permitting county courts to acquire all turnpikes within their jurisdiction by lease, gift, purchase, or contract.[62] By 1900 counties had acquired most of the state's turnpikes, often at bargain prices. That part of the Maysville Turnpike in Fayette County, for example, cost the county only $1,900 per mile to obtain.[63]

A state constitutional amendment in 1909 permitted the state to underwrite aid to counties for road projects. There followed in 1916 and 1921 federal legislation that provided aid to states for rural post or mail road construction and larger, interstate road systems, respectively. The Maysville Turnpike's toll road epoch ended some seventy years after it began, though the route would carry that name in vernacular place descriptions, on maps, and even on official road signs for decades thereafter.

9

State and Federal Highway

In 1912 the Kentucky legislature authorized the creation of the Department of Public Roads, which was initially responsible for advising the counties in road and bridge construction and maintenance. Although the department's formation marked a new era in the conceptualization of roads as developmental elements in state and regional transportation networks—rather than as matters of local travel convenience—and in the application of evolving engineering principles, legislators were reluctant to provide the financial resources required to adequately fund the hiring of departmental personnel. Road building now required technical expertise, a professional cadre of engineers, surveyors, draftsmen, and trained administrative staff. Nevertheless, state legislation provided a personnel budget of only $25,000, funded by a license tax on automobiles, and required that all hires be approved by the governor, which implied, of course, that Public Roads jobs were also patronage jobs.[1]

Though grossly underfunded, the highway engineers did begin to instill a new science-based discipline in the state's road construction enterprise. They standardized bridge specifications and circulated to county-level officials standards for macadam road construction that included blueprints of road cross sections and model forms for contracts, bonds, fiscal court proposals, and advertising construction jobs to road contractors. Bridge construction had previously been the purview of county officials; they delegated the task either to master carpenters, who erected wooden truss-covered bridges, or bridge-building firms such as Champion Bridge Company and King Bridge Company, both of Ohio, that erected bridges made from manufactured prefabricated iron components.[2] Department engineers decried the traditional practice of road maintenance performed by the old "militia" or corvée labor system, which compelled local residents to work a set number of days per year on the county's roads. The state highway engineer saw that system as "absolutely worthless and while some counties pretend to enforce the system there is usually more yarn spinning, tobacco chewing, and resting, done than work on roads."[3] The road surface of choice continued to be the venerable broken-stone macadam road, although engineers experimented with coverings of gravel and rock asphalt obtained from deposits in western Kentucky. New equipment began to replace the hand tools and wheelbarrows that were common in nineteenth-century road repair. Steam-powered rock crushers supplied macadam stone, and laborers used horse- or steam-powered plows, graders, scrapers, rollers, and water wagons to create level, low-gradient roadbeds.

Though trained nineteenth-century engineers such as Sylvester Welch had been keenly aware of the relationships between efficient road design and transportation costs, road economics became a priority for engineers in the new Department of Public Roads. Surveyors and road builders had long believed that the best road was the shortest distance between two points, yet this rule of thumb failed to recognize the costs associated with running the line of a road directly across rough topography, which resulted in steep road gradients on hills that reduced significantly a horse's tractive power. State engineers were able to demonstrate that by contouring road alignments to the topography, road gradient could be substantially reduced, thereby allowing both horse-drawn conveyances and motor vehicles to haul heavier loads, without significantly increasing road length. Moving freight on poor roads, be they inordinately steep or impassibly muddy, cost upwards of three times as much as moving freight on a high-quality road surface.

In making the case for better roads, Department of Public Roads engineers sought to remove road building from the purview of county-level political officials. They did this by broadening substantially the argument for quality roads, advocating for acceptance of proven engineering standards, hiring qualified road engineers in each county, and fostering the use of large-scale machinery. Engineers also argued that the modern state needed to concern itself with the complex linkages among long-term investment in transportation infrastructure, planning at a regional and statewide scale, and the beneficial economies that movement on quality roads produced. The department's advocacy for road improvement included a governor's proclamation declaring October 24 and 25, 1913, as "Good Road Days"; a state traveling exhibition of a model road; and a state fair pictorial exhibit of twenty-three different road-construction models as examples of good and bad roads.[4]

Until 1914 the Department of Public Roads acted in an advisory capacity to the counties, but new legislation in that year authorized the department to establish a road-building fund and allowed counties to obtain state aid for roads connecting county seats. This innovative legislation ended the long-standing tradition of funding roads by local residents or stock subscriptions and gave priority to road-network construction—county-to-county links—instead of building short road segments to serve county political favorites, wherever they might live in a county. Federal legislation in 1916 appropriated $85 million to the states for rural post-road construction, and a 1917 state act permitted counties to vote on a tax to provide funds for road and bridge construction. The state public roads commissioner identified five large-scale, cross-state road-construction projects to which federal aid would be applied. The Maysville Road was not among them, perhaps because the road was already in serviceable condition.[5] World War I curtailed most road building, but construction began on a limited number of road projects in 1919.[6]

Despite the state road commissioner's desire to construct long-distance roads, most road building before 1920 was limited to short segments extending from county seats into the surrounding countryside. Engineers completed several such projects on sections of the Maysville Road. In 1918 the four-mile section between Maysville and Washington was rebuilt with traditional water-bound macadam—that is, a broken-stone roadbed with rock screenings and stone dust washed into the small openings between stones—at a cost of about $21,000. Engineers cautioned, however, that this road surface would not withstand the heavy automobile traffic that was already using that road segment.[7] Other state-funded Maysville Road projects completed in Nicholas and Bourbon counties left only the road's south section in Fayette County and a north section from Blue Licks to Washington without a newly reconstructed bed and macadam surface.[8]

In 1920 Kentucky's road construction entered what we might term "the modern era." The state legislature enacted House Bill 60, which effected several major changes in road department administration and in how roads and highways were planned, engineered, funded, and built. The Department of Public Roads was reorganized into the Department of State Roads and Highways with a budget and authorization to hire qualified engineers. The old state aid system that initiated road construction at the county level was superseded. In part, the reorganization centralized control and enabled the state to take advantage of the new federal initiatives in funding post-road construction. The new department also embraced a planning function to set priorities, plan, and provide engineering oversight for the construction of a system or network of roads funded by state aid. To remove or reduce political influence in the choice of road alignments, prioritizing construction projects, and choice of road contractors, House Bill 60 authorized a bipartisan State Highway Commission of four members to be chosen from the professional business community—with equal representation from both political parties and different state regions. The commission also assisted the state highway engineer in matters of policy and decisions on the equitable distribution of road funds.[9] The state General Assembly also designated a system of primary state and federal highways in 1920. The Maysville Road was included as a state highway.

Kentucky drivers operated about 113,000 motor vehicles in 1920. Although these vehicles represented modern car- and truck-building technology, they had a corrosive effect on traditional macadam roads. Engineers estimated that the old mediocre roads, as they termed the macadam routes, would last only a few years under automobile traffic, or only a few days if traveled by heavily loaded trucks in wet weather. Engineers designated these roads as "light duty" and in need of replacement by "higher types" of surfacing, such as asphalt, as funding became available.[10] By 1923 the north half of the Maysville Road from near Carlisle to Maysville was either under construction or considered "poor but passable."[11] The availability of federal subsidies for road construction became an increasingly compelling rationale for regulating traditional practices in order to comply with federal engineering guidelines, as required for full participation in the aid program. County fiscal courts could no longer issue purchase contracts to bridge manufacturing companies whose practice was to supply narrow, lightly built, prefabricated bridges. Rather, new bridges had to comply with federal standards for width and load-bearing capacity before builders could install them on a road receiving federal aid.[12]

During the two decades preceding World War II, including the Great Depression, road building proceeded apace in central Kentucky. In 1925 the state completed construction on what were called the "great thoroughfares," including the north-south Boone Way from Covington to Cumberland Gap (later numbered U.S. 25) and the east-west Midland Trail from Louisville to Ashland (later U.S. 60).[13] Until federal legislation in 1926 created a uniform federal highway numbering system, roads retained their given names as their sole identification for construction and travelers' navigation.

That the Maysville Road should become part of U.S. 68 and be linked to other state roadways by a common route number was not simply a map exercise in linking roads into a basic north-south, east-west national grid. Rather, promoters in Kentucky and adjoining states urged the state's Highway Commission to acknowledge the state's potential tourist attractions and align their federally numbered roadways with those of adjoining states in order to provide maximum accessibility to interstate automobile traffic.[14] Anticipating that the number of tourist travelers would soon rival the numbers of commercial vehicles on the state's roads, if only potential tourists were properly courted, an editorial in the *Kentucky Road Builder* in 1925 offered the opinion that "even history becomes more interesting under the spell of motoring."[15] The Dixie Highway's director, J. Stacy Hill from Cincinnati, in an address to a highway engineers' convention in 1923 admonished Kentucky's political leadership to increase the rate of the state's highway construction programs to provide access to all its potential tourist attractions. "Cincinnati will spend large sums of money to bring traffic down to Kentucky where you have attractions we have not and I know of several very large advertising contracts which will be placed when your highways are in good condition. The success of any highway is in the co-operation of all its cities each with the other, the only idea being to create traffic."[16] Hill concluded his commentary on Kentucky's roads by urging the state to "drop every other line of road work and get all her North and South main highways completed at the earliest possible moment, so as to take her real place among the States of the country."[17]

Three years later, in 1926, Kentucky State Highway Engineer E. N. Todd proposed that a federal numbered highway link Maysville with western Kentucky by way of Blue Licks, Lexington, Shakertown, Harrodsburg, Perryville, Hodgenville, Cave City, Bowling Green, Hopkinsville, and Paducah "because of the many points of interest through which it passes." Todd recited the route's many potential tourist attractions—primarily natural features or historic sites—including the Indian battlefield at Blue Licks; Lexington as the home of Henry Clay and the first college west of the Allegheny Mountains; the Kentucky River and the Southern Railway's High Bridge over the river's palisades; Harrodsburg as the oldest town in the state; Bardstown as the site of "My Old Kentucky Home": and Mammoth Cave, which had been proposed as a national park.[18] The State Highway Commission began referring to the Maysville Road route as part of the state's "great Historic Trail."[19] The Maysville Road became part of U.S. 68, which linked Findlay, Ohio, to Paducah, Kentucky, in 1926, and two years later the highway department completed the installation of new U.S. 68 road signs along the Maysville Road. Maysville boosters seized on the federal highway designation to begin a publicity campaign promoting the city as a "solid, substantial city, founded more than a century ago, but a modern, commercial, industrial, tobacco, dairy, agricultural and tourist center." They even published a regional map drawn to place Maysville in the center of an Indiana, Ohio, and Kentucky highway network—including the Lincoln Highway (U.S. 30) and the National Road (U.S. 40)—and entitled the map "US 68, Historic Highway, the Short Route North to South through Maysville, the Pioneer Gateway."[20]

The traditional rationale for roadway construction that had been narrowly defined as enhancing local people's travel to their county seats, or serving local commercial interests by linking together a region's cities, had now been appropriated by larger commercial interests. But where Kentucky communities saw road-building progress, boosters in adjoining states saw Kentucky's road-building lethargy as an obstacle to their efforts to stimulate interstate travel and the economic benefits that they expected would accrue from increased road traffic. Confirming the volume of traffic flow on Kentucky's new roads was slippery guesswork until the state completed a traffic census in 1929. In October of that year, only days before the Black Tuesday stock market crash that triggered the Great Depression, state road engineers tabulated traffic counts for the state's major highways, including the Maysville Road. At three traffic enumeration points, Maysville, Millersburg, and Lexington, a Wednesday count revealed a total of 937, 951, and 2,455 vehicles passing the city limits of each place, respectively. A Sunday count at the same locations tabulated 1,466, 1,845, and 4,449 vehicles.[21] At both Millersburg and Lexington the Sunday road traffic was nearly double that of midweek. The "Sunday Driver" was on the road in substantial numbers, suggesting that the intoxicating "spell of motoring" was already affecting the driving public.

As a quality highway, the Maysville Road was now considered the equal of other major state thoroughfares, and engineers rated it as having "good surfacing," excepting the chronically difficult Fleming County section from Blue Licks at the Licking River crossing north to Johnson Creek at the Mason County line. This road segment lay in the rough Eden Shale topography, crosscut by two northwest flowing drainage basins, the Licking and Johnson Creek. A broad-backed, steep-sided ridge—also running southeast to northwest—lay athwart the route between the two streams. The old road traversed these barriers on steep grades and tight curves. Heavy erosion on the high-angle sections combined with damage from passing vehicles to degrade the roadbed into what state engineers rated as "poor surfacing."[22] Resurfacing this road section with bituminous macadam was under way in 1927, but the cost exceeded $23,000 per mile, a 30 percent premium over comparable Outer Bluegrass roads in Mason County, just to the north.[23] Road building on this northern Mason County section was not as problematic as on the Eden Shale country, in part because the stream and ridge pattern here trended northeast, toward Maysville and the Ohio River, which gave engineers long ridges or low-gradient valleys to follow.

The State Highway Department, supported by both state and federal highway construction funds, began a long-term program of realigning and rebuilding the Maysville Road in the late 1920s. Some road sections were in poor condition; others still followed closely an early alignment with steep slopes and flat, tight curves.

Nineteenth-century wooden covered bridges spanned creeks at some sites, though in 1928 the governor signed into law the Murphy Toll Bridge Act, which permitted the state to condemn or purchase privately owned toll bridges. The road's most substantial bridge construction project was the Simon Kenton Bridge, which spanned the Ohio River to link Maysville to Aberdeen, Ohio. Completed in 1931, the art deco two-lane cable-suspension bridge marked the end of 138 years of ferry service between Kentucky and the historic Zanes Trace route across southeast Ohio.[24] J. A. Roebling & Son's Company designed the new bridge using an advanced version of the cable-suspension technology invented by John Roebling and used in the cable-suspension bridge linking Cincinnati, Ohio, and Covington, Kentucky, in 1867. The Simon Kenton Bridge remained the Ohio River crossing point for U.S. 68 and the Maysville Road until 2000, when engineers completed a new cable-stayed suspension bridge about one mile west of Maysville.[25] When the new bridge opened, it became part of the new U.S. 68 bypass around Maysville, and the old Simon Kenton Bridge was designated as part of Business U.S. 68.

In 1932 engineers rebuilt the road section along Stoney Creek in Nicholas County just southwest of the Licking River crossing at Blue Licks. Five years later new construction realigned the old serpentine approach to the North Fork of the Licking River in Mason County. The original 1820s road had to accommodate a two-hundred-foot elevation change over this five-mile section. By 1937 a new alignment cut off the section's most abrupt curves and steep grades and left them orphaned alongside the new road. Approaching the North Fork from the south, the old road traversed a quarter-mile-wide floodplain before reaching the river, which it crossed via a wooden covered bridge. The river's meandering curve here scoured the channel's north bank into the base of a steep, 180-foot bluff. As the road emerged from the covered bridge, it made an abrupt ninety-degree right turn to follow the base of the bluff for several hundred feet before reaching Wells Creek valley. (Wells Creek is a North Fork tributary.) The old road then followed the creek valley north until it gained the upland above. Road engineers confronted several basic problems with this old road section—steep grades combined with switchback turns on both north and south approaches; abrupt right-angle turns at the bridge; a single-lane wooden bridge; and a low-lying floodplain susceptible to periodic flooding. Using extended cuts and fills, including a raised floodplain embankment and a new concrete bridge that carried the road directly up the Wells Creek valley, engineers modernized the old road by realignments that eliminated several curves while reducing its maximum grade.[26] Several farm buildings and other structures that had been built close to the old road had to be moved or torn down, including a gasoline filling station and several hundred feet of road-frontage rock fence. Though World War II disrupted the state's road-improvement program, construction began again in earnest in the mid-1940s. By the early 1970s the 1937 road segment was deemed outdated and was realigned once again. This most recent alteration relocated the entire roadway about one-third of a mile west, at the river crossing. The 1970s construction cut off extended sections of the 1937 road, leaving them either as closed cul-de-sacs or as bypassed road segments that detach from and reattach to the main road in orphaned loops of varying lengths. Engineers made

The original track of the Maysville Road is probably Burns Alley, the lower driveway immediately in front of this house on Mayslick's south side. The curving contemporary road to the left follows a raised embankment and may have been built in the 1930s.

further road modifications in the mid-1970s by rebuilding the entire road section from Mayslick to Maysville on a new alignment that included bypasses around Mayslick and Washington. Engineers completed a bypass around Paris by the late 1970s.

Along many road sections from Paris to Maysville, the 1820s road alignment is still visible to one side or the other of the current roadway. North of Millersburg, for example, south of the junction of U.S. 68 and State Route (SR) 36 to Carlisle, the old road is represented by a linear depression on the north side, some 250 feet from the highway, which was aligned to its present track in 1948. At the Carlisle Road (SR 36) junction, the old 1820s track made a long, sweeping curve to the east and north and now appears in a pasture to the right, or east. There it negotiates a steep bluff above Brushy Creek, dropping abruptly into the valley to cross and recross the current road while paralleling the creek to the northeast.[27] At Mayslick the 1820s road comes into the village from the south by way of Burns Alley, a narrow street immediately in front of a row of houses on the west side of the 1930s road alignment. From Burns Alley the old road crosses to the right side, where, as another alley, it fronts the fire station and emerges at the village center to cross Southworth Lane. From this crossing the old road follows the current access road north, crossing Lees Creek on a handsome dry-laid stone culvert before crossing the new U.S. 68 bypass, whereupon its name changes to Ross Road. As Ross Road the 1820s alignment forms a loop road paralleling Lees Creek, where it continues to provide access to those farms that fronted the old highway.

Post–World War I road construction methods sought to reduce grades, extend curve radii, and align road approaches to bridge crossings to improve safety while allowing higher vehicle speed and greater traffic flow. Meeting such demanding engineering requirements required large-scale steam- or motor-powered excavating equipment. Extensive volumes of earth and rock had to be cut from hill alignments and transported to depressions and valleys, where it became fill material for embankments that raised the roadbed above the flood zone. While extensive cut-and-fill work provided a new, low-gradient surface for road construction, it also created steep slopes on both cuts and fills, which produced a chronic roadside erosion problem that had to be addressed. Roadside ditches designed to drain water away from the road quickly filled with eroded silt and rock, compromising the ditch and introducing the threat that standing water could undermine the road. State engineers recommended planting the new road cuts in trees, shrubs, and grass, in part to beautify the new roadside but also to curtail the movement of silt and rock into the new ditches.[28] The Maysville Road's Fayette and Bourbon county sections received some $5,400 worth of roadside improvements and plantings in 1941, followed by the instillation of a new asphalt surface at a total cost of about $86,000.[29] Thus far we can summarize transportation morphogenesis by observing that as innovative technologies in transportation and construction came into common use, businesses advocated for their deployment, and governmental agencies saw to their adoption. Employing large earth-moving equipment to cut through hills and embank floodplain crossings to enhance passage of motorized vehicles illustrates a basic generalization of transportation geography—conformity to terrain declines with increasing economic importance of the route.[30]

Henry Ford's economical Model T automobile democratized highway travel by 1910 in the sense that middle-class folk could afford to own and drive cars for the first time, which gave them the luxury of discretionary mobility. The truck and bus soon supplemented the automobile as alternative transport modes for freight and passengers. When still dependent on horses for motive power, rural people had lived in comparative isolation, detached or remote from basic city amenities such as churches, schools, social clubs, shopping venues, and proximity to friends and relatives. Townspeople wishing to travel beyond the home community were dependent on train, interurban rail, or riverboats, which, of course, ran along narrow corridors according to predetermined schedules where these transport modes existed. The automobile offered access to any place that had a road at any time one wished to travel. It is difficult to overstate the magnitude of this revolution and the manifold and often unanticipated consequences that ubiquitous automobile access would have. The Kentucky Central Railroad (initially the Maysville & Lexington Railroad) track between Paris and Maysville opened about 1873. For some five decades the railroad ran in direct competition with road-borne stagecoach and freight-wagon lines in moving passengers and goods between Lexington and Maysville. World War I brought federal control of the nation's railroads and mandated increases in wages and freight rates. To improve movement of troops and materiel among factories, army camps, and ports, trucks and buses were pressed into service. After the war, competition from trucks and buses increased sharply, cutting into railroad profits. Initially, small trucks and buses focused on short-haul businesses that moved farm products to town and city markets and passengers from town to town. But by the mid-1920s trucks became larger, more powerful, and capable of moving cargo much longer distances. As states began to improve their roads through systematic construction programs, trucking became a large-scale business: from the mid-1920s to the late 1930s, livestock transported by trucks increased fivefold, whereas livestock transported by rail decreased by two-thirds. Rapidly increased automobile and bus use for personal travel dramatically cut passenger traffic on some railroads by nearly 70 percent during this same period.[31] The Louisville & Nashville Railroad purchased the Kentucky Central Railroad in 1891, including the line from Lexington to Maysville. Though city merchants and manufacturers along the route wanted access to the railroad, overall freight and passenger volumes remained limited, especially when compared with the flows between larger markets.[32]

People soon recognized that without quality all-weather roads, their newfound mobility was severely limited. As the Maysville Road story suggests, by the 1920s road reconstruction and new road building had become a state governmental priority. People traveled by automobile in rapidly increasing numbers—on business but also for recreation and leisure. Businesses serving the traveling public sprang up at the roadside to provide fuel, food, and lodging. Initially travelers purchased gas at livery stables, auto garages, and hardware and general stores that sold fuel hand-pumped from storage drums. Petroleum companies had invented the dedicated gas station by the early 1920s. The first-generation gas station is readily recognizable by its small, cubelike building, sometimes fashioned to resemble a small house, with an attached front portico over a concrete island on which the gas pumps stood. Franchise gas stations built by national gasoline companies in the form of an oblong box with large, plate-glass windows began to appear in the 1930s, a basic form that could be easily expanded by adding service bays and large overhead doors.

Entrepreneurs reinvented overnight accommodations for travelers—the roadside taverns of horse-drawn carriage and stagecoach days were closed or converted into residential houses. Auto-oriented travelers along the Maysville Road could stay in established central city hotels such as those in Lexington (the Lafayette and Phoenix hotels were among five central hotels in the city in the 1930s), Paris (the Windsor Hotel stood on Main Street), Millersburg, and Maysville (the New Central Hotel and White Manor Hotel). Public campgrounds established by municipalities and private camps provided by roadside landowners offered alternatives to travelers on a budget. Campgrounds became cabin camps, which in turn evolved into motels. City residents with large houses on a main thoroughfare might respond to travelers' demands for accommodation by converting part of their homes to tourist rooms—Maysville had three such establishments by 1950, for example.[33]

Local businesspeople established roadside restaurants in the 1920s and 1930s. Franchise chain eateries such as Howard Johnson's began to join them in the 1930s and 1940s. It is a considerable irony that however earnestly one seeks for evidence of this early automobile-oriented roadside along the modern Maysville Road corridor—be it relict gas station or motel buildings or recycled structures now occupied by other kinds of businesses—they are nearly absent. Yet there remain on the roadside, or its many cutoff loops, numerous buildings that served as stagecoach-oriented taverns. Roadside businesses intended to serve the automobile-riding public are prominent on other major federal highways, such as U.S. 40 (the National Road) in Ohio and Indiana, or U.S. 11, the Shenandoah Valley highway in Virginia. But along the Maysville Road, only a small number of early gas stations and motels still stand, and those are primarily in the terminal cities of Lexington and Maysville. Between these two end points few early auto-oriented roadside businesses remain. One of the last, a small 1930s motel in Fairview, was torn down in 2005.

10

From Turnpike to Parkway

From its inception, the most heavily traveled portion of the Maysville Road was the eighteen-mile section that connected Lexington and Paris—long known as the Paris Pike. Beginning at Main Street in central Lexington, the original track followed North Limestone Street to Bryan Station Road, which then angled northeast across open farmland, eventually arriving at the courthouse square in Paris. By the 1820s farms lined the route, and more than a dozen inns and taverns provided meals and overnight accommodations for carriage and stagecoach passengers and drovers. In 1827 James Darnaby and William Ellis Jr., the state-appointed surveyors, completed a general survey of the entire Maysville Road. Their map located the existing road and offered proposals for route alterations, the most substantive being a radical modification of the Lexington-to-Paris section. The surveyors suggested a new, nearly straight road from central Lexington to the fourteen-mile point south of Paris. The old track that traversed this section followed an irregular alignment on low land, paralleling creeks in some places, fording them in others—the track forded Houston Creek at least three times, for example.[1] Road builders completed the realignment proposed by Darnaby and Ellis by the mid-1830s; the road became part of the Maysville, Washington, Paris, and Lexington Turnpike, and tollhouses were installed at regular intervals. The new road flanked Houston Creek on the northwest and relegated the old track to the status of back road. Though local residents proposed modifications to the new road, largely to try to retain direct access to the road or make direct links between the old road and the new, the Darnaby and Ellis alignment remained the primary route for more than 170 years.[2]

Though the road's surface was periodically upgraded—in 1918 the Bourbon County section received a fresh, water-bound macadam surface, and the following year contractors applied hot asphalt oil to seal the surface—its historic turnpike configuration did not adapt well to motorized traffic as automobile ownership expanded in the 1920s.[3] Though engineers widened and realigned the road segment on Lexington's north side from North Limestone to North Broadway in the 1930s, the road's rural Fayette and Bourbon County sections retained its turnpike dimensions—the two narrow lanes, though asphalt-surfaced, were a mere twenty-two feet wide and had no shoulders or turning lanes. The Lexington-to-Paris interurban rail line was in

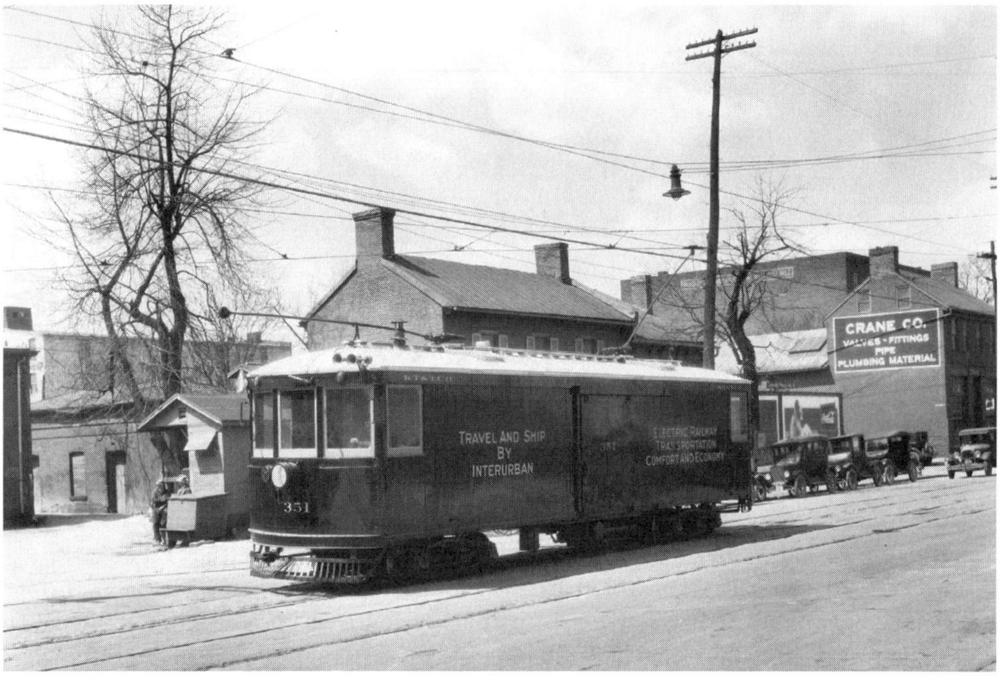

From 1901 to 1934 interurban railroad lines linked Lexington to the state capital and the surrounding county seats of Paris, Georgetown, Versailles, and Nicholasville. The Kentucky Traction and Terminal Company interurban system trackage was compatible with Lexington's streetcar tracks, and the rolling stock included both passenger and freight cars. An interurban freight car is shown here on West Main Street in Lexington circa 1926. In the era before widespread availability of the automobile and the truck, people living in surrounding counties could commute to Lexington for shopping and social events via the interurban. Lexington businesses shipped freight to farms and towns along the lines. The interurban track from Lexington to Paris lay immediately adjacent to Paris Pike. (J. Winston Coleman Jr. Photographic Collection, Transylvania University Library)

operation by 1912 and made its last run in 1934. The interurban ran abreast of the road on one side, and stone and wood-plank farm-frontage fences further encroached on the right-of-way, confining the entire roadbed to an aislelike passageway. More than two dozen farms fronted the road, and their slow-moving horse vans and hay wagons often traveled the road amid high-speed automobiles and heavily loaded tractor-trailers. The road's antique character and dimensions limited its capacity, while increasing traffic led to frequent accidents—from minor to horrific—and escalated concerns for travelers' safety among state transportation officials and road users.

Kentucky Transportation Cabinet engineers developed plans to rebuild the road and widen the Paris Pike to four lanes in the late 1960s, but protests and lawsuits by abutting landowners, public hearings and debates, and the development of revised construction plans and proposals protracted the reconstruction process. Farm owners and area citizens voiced concerns that the corridor's historic and aesthetic landscape qualities should be maintained, even enhanced, not obliterated by a four-lane highway insensitively built to the specifications of a functional but visually debased interstate highway. By 1993–94 a protracted process of landscape design, road engineering, and public review and discussion began, which yielded a master plan for a new parkway. Construction began in 1997 on the north section, near Paris, and the entire project was completed and opened to traffic in December 2003. The new road, though a divided four lanes with ten-foot grass shoulders, is visually two parallel two-lane roads, one northbound, the other south. Designers routed the parkway along the old turnpike corridor but varied the lane alignment and median width to avoid existing historic buildings, rock fences, formal stone farm entrances, and mature trees. In some sections the design aligned the road so that old, road-fronting rock fences would stand in the median. Local stonemasons trained in nineteenth-century Irish fence-building techniques by the Lexington-based Dry Stone Conservancy built several miles of new rock fence to replace fence removed or cut off by road construction. In recognition of the region's original savanna vegetation, the few remaining stands of ancient trees, especially on the Bourbon County road segment, were protected and supplemented by new plantings of native species. The completed parkway has received numerous accolades and awards for design, including recognition from the Federal Highway Administration, the American Association of State Highway and Transportation Officials, and the American Society of Landscape Architects.[4]

The Maysville Road segment from the north side of Paris to Ellisville is the only section that still retains its pre-1950s configuration. The remaining sections have been rebuilt to current engineering standards. As each segment is leveled and straightened, the traces and tracks established by Indians, buffalo, pioneers, and turnpikers, in turn, recede, eventually becoming lost landscapes.

Part III

The Maysville Road: A Landscape Biography

Is it not as well, or even better, to see a landscape than its picture?

—Daniel Drake,
Pioneer Life in Kentucky

11

The Road as a Corridor of Complexity

America's roads are enigmatic. Roads are linked together in local, regional, and national networks to the extent that they are essentially ubiquitous. Our modern day-to-day mobility is vested in roads that are so common that we tend to take them for granted until they are in need of repair or choked with traffic. We are inclined to regard the road simplistically, as though it were an accessory, a subsidiary feature lurking in the background. But historically, roads were often the foreground to travel—their routes and attributes such as gradient and condition were of primary concern to stagecoach line operators and carriage drivers. Whichever perspective obtains, background or foreground, roads and their attendant roadsides, which together constitute road landscapes, are very complex places and difficult to interpret.

Roads are the primary tangible links between the places where we conduct our lives—home and work, for example—a situation we may not recognize until our favorite route is closed for construction and we are forced to find an alternative road through unfamiliar territory. Road access permits straightforward observation of the towns and countryside through which they lead. More abstractly, roads affect our perceptions of places. We may, for example, associate dangerous, badly maintained roads with places that are politically and socially backward, whereas safe and superior roads may suggest that places are forward-thinking and economically robust. Road complexity is exacerbated through association with multiple legal jurisdictions—town or city, county, state, federal—each with somewhat different construction requirements and different rationales for maintenance. Some jurisdictions may promote the idea that roads serve as tools for economic development; others treat roads as subjects of political intrigue. Roads also provide the venue for linear marketplaces, roadside businesses that erect advertising signs to persuade travelers to stop for food, fuel, lodging, shopping, or other forms of financial or social transaction.

And consider how the traveler's relationship with the road, roadside, and fellow travelers changed through time. Eighteenth- and nineteenth-century travel via horseback or Concord coach (a stagecoach famed for its fine suspension) was a public experience that cast the traveler as a participant in local affairs. The traveling public shared coach seats and common tavern dining tables, they shared beds and sleeping rooms, they were engaged by local residents eager for news from beyond the horizon.[1] The enclosed automobile and truck provided private travel—people could now journey long distances as observers without directly engaging with anyone, provided they did not need to refuel or rent a room for the night. But even these social interchanges were conducted with a small cadre of trained company employees, rarely with "local people."

Road landscapes provide varied experiences for those who use the road or reside at roadside, and therefore roads are subject to multiple interpretations and understandings. Over-the-road truckers, highway patrol officers, firefighters, civil engineers, express delivery truck drivers, school bus passengers, farmers, commuters, and tourists experience roads and roadsides in somewhat different ways. Appreciating such widely disparate perspectives requires that we regard the roadway, in both its historic and contemporary guises, as a visual and experiential puzzle or palimpsest.[2] The road landscape has both material—and therefore subject to visual and tactile inspection—and behavioral dimensions that change through time. People who use roads are not automatons; their actions and experiences relate to their social, political, and economic milieus. It is difficult to identify or appreciate more than fragments of a road landscape's behavioral dimension, although we can enhance our understanding if we gain familiarity with how differing groups relate to the roads on which their mobility depends. What, for example, might an automobile traveler know about the tractor-trailers and truck drivers that cohabit the highway? The social world of the trucker and the car driver are radically different, and the points or places where their lives might intersect are limited. On the highway, encased in steel shells on wheels, the car driver and trucker are mutually anonymous. Should the car driver choose to learn something about the truck driver's world, however, he or she might patronize a truck stop. A trucker's life is strongly oriented toward the road rather than the home. A large truck stop provides diesel fuel, of course, but it also offers home-type accommodations, such as beds and large restrooms with showers. Banks of telephones permit drivers to contact their companies on secure land lines to provide shipping information and receive instructions on the location of their next loads. With some effort, the car driver can interact with other professional groups who frequent the road, be they construction crews, highway patrol officers, or postal service delivery people, and come to appreciate how their social milieus relate to their road experiences.

The modern road is a public space; therefore, understanding how roads work must include awareness of the vagaries of public support to underwrite construction costs, evolving construction techniques and technologies, the development of road-construction and road-use regulations by local, state, and federal authorities, and numerous other factors that control and direct road building and use. Understanding roads also requires that one consider the roadside landscape—the largely private space that lies immediately adjacent to the roadway and extends away to the visual horizon—which is shaped by the road and its traffic and, in turn, shapes the roadway.

Part III is biographical, a detailed narrative intended to assist the reader in interpreting the Maysville Road and its attendant roadside landscapes, historic and modern.

Part III is organized into three extended geographical sections: Lexington to Paris; Paris to the vicinity of Blue Licks; and Blue Licks to Maysville. Each section contains site commentary on present and historic routes, structures, and roadside landscapes that are keyed to mileage, beginning at Main Street in Lexington, and extending to the Ohio River's south bank at the foot of the Simon Kenton Bridge in Maysville. Where important bypassed road sections still exist we provide interpretations of them as well. To supplement the site commentaries, we provide short informational essays that will assist readers to interpret what can be seen, or, in some cases, describe lost landscapes that have been obliterated by subsequent construction or otherwise been rendered invisible. Although best read as a companion for inquisitive travelers, Part III is also a sequenced narrative that invites armchair reading by those interested in a geographical history of the road, its builders, its travelers, and its roadside residents.

12

Lexington

Mile 0.0 Lexington at Limestone and Main Street. On July 9, 1796, the general merchandise store operated by Abijah and John Wesley Hunt at the corner of Mill and Main streets, two blocks northwest of the Limestone and Main intersection, stood open for business. John Moylan operated another general store nearby. David Meade had arrived in central Kentucky two days earlier, having moved his family and belongings from Prince George County, Virginia, to his new Jessamine County farm home, La Chaumiere des Prairies, on July 7. This day Meade traveled the nine miles from his farm to Lexington in search of what we might consider rather exotic goods—given the time and place. At the Hunts' store he purchased one-half bushel of salt, probably the product of one of Kentucky's salt licks, one and one-half yards of cloth, three and one-half yards of black velvet, two skeins of silk, one and one-half yards of linen, and one plume. Though Meade's shopping list suggests that someone in his household had a special sewing project in mind, he could have chosen from a broad range of goods that the Hunts kept in stock, some of it supplied by local or regional sources, such as paper and hardware, butter, bacon, eggs, and whiskey. But the store also stocked items imported from distant foreign sources, some of which David Meade purchased, that had no doubt arrived in East Coast ports such as Philadelphia.[1] As account ledgers kept by John Moylan and the Hunts suggest, Lexington's residents and businesses had at their disposal by the 1790s commodities gleaned from sources around the world, assembled by coastal port merchants, and supplied by Ohio River boats and freight wagons negotiating the Maysville Road.

Lexington's original street plat was part of an application for town status made by early settlers and approved by the Virginia legislature in 1781. Two primary streets, Cross Street and Mulberry Street, ran northeast from the town common. Mulberry Street was renamed Limestone Street in 1887 because it connected directly with the Limestone or Maysville Road; Cross Street became Broadway. The intersection of Limestone and Main streets, where the Lexington end of the Maysville Road begins, became a key access node around which developed the city's commercial business area. Moreover, this intersection remained an important location in the city for more than a century and a half because it was the point where the region's major roads crossed. North Limestone was the Maysville Road. South Limestone extended southwest to

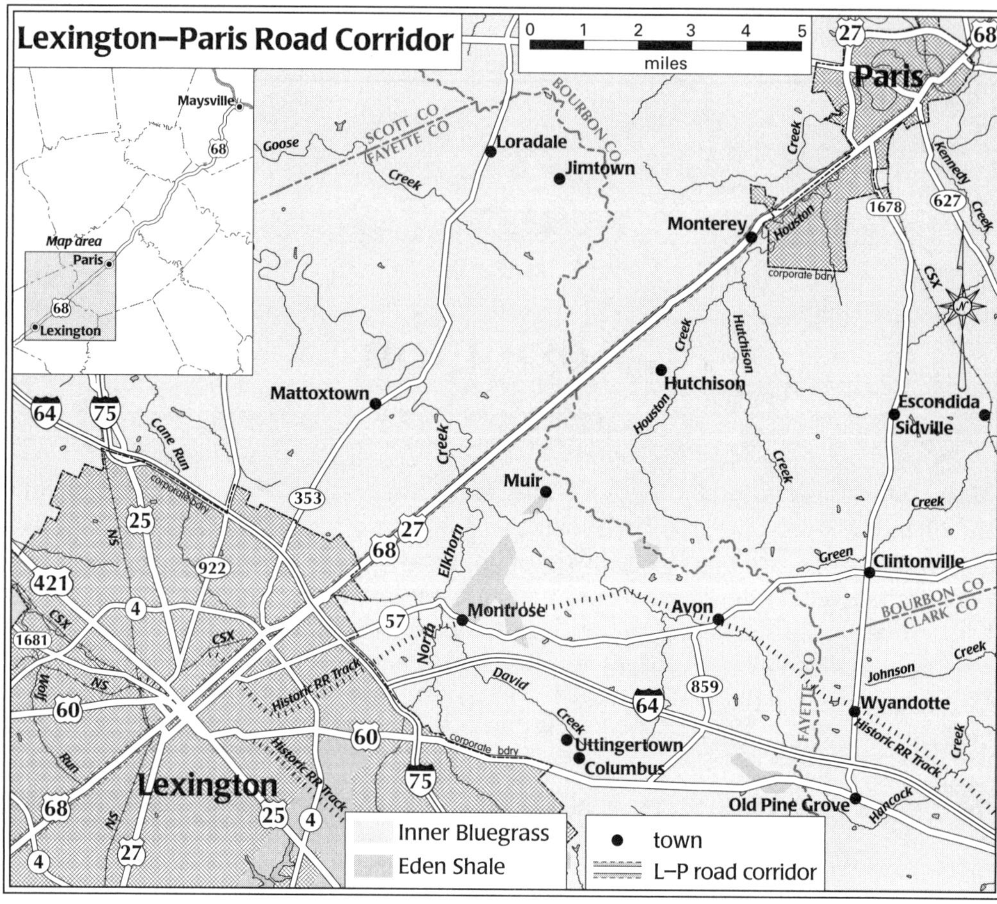

Nicholasville, the Jessamine County seat, and so became Nicholasville Road. The road to Richmond, the seat of Madison County to the south, became South Main Street. One branch of the Richmond road led south to Athens, and an additional road led to the Kentucky River near where the steep-gradient tributary Lower Howards Creek joins the trunk stream. The middle section of Lower Howards Creek would become one of Kentucky's first large-scale industrial sites, encompassing numerous mills and residences for mill operators and workers. On the Kentucky River's west side, not far upstream, stood Boonesborough, Daniel Boone's frontier fort. North Main Street connected to the state capital at Frankfort, to Versailles, the Woodford County seat to the west, and north to Georgetown. The road to Frankfort, in turn, ran west to Louisville. From Georgetown the road led north to Covington and Cincinnati. The intersection was therefore a major focus in the great road-and-river quadrilateral that linked Lexington to the Ohio River by way of Louisville, Covington, and Maysville.

In 1926 the city erected a Zero Milepost at the Union Railroad Station on Main Street. The venerable post, topped by a small statue of a caravan camel, marked the beginning point for measuring mileage from Lexington. Workers moved the marker

The Phoenix Hotel's classic architectural symmetry conveyed a sense of order and prosperity. Situated at the busy corner of Limestone and Main streets, the hotel was a hub of communication as stagecoaches arrived and departed, dropping off travelers and mail. Local residents stopped by to hear the latest news or read a newspaper, and various organizations and clubs held their meetings in the cozy confines of the gentlemen's parlor. The building depicted was built after the original log tavern burned in 1820. The proprietors promised "the best genuine red and white wines, Irish whiskey (10 years old), and other liquors of the best quality." The hotel was destroyed again by fire in 1879. (Courtesy of University of Kentucky Library Special Collections)

to the courthouse square when the railroad station was torn down in 1961. Today it stands here at the Main and Limestone corner, adjacent to Phoenix Park and across Limestone from its original location in front of the railroad station.

The dynamic nature of this downtown commercial center becomes evident in the evolution of land use at this intersection over the past century. Across Main Street to the northeast, in the place where Main Street commercial businesses once stood, is the 2004 Robert F. Stephens Justice Complex, containing the county's district and circuit courts. To the southeast, Phoenix Park, the Lexington Public Library, and an adjacent apartment building and parking ramp all occupy the corner lot where stood

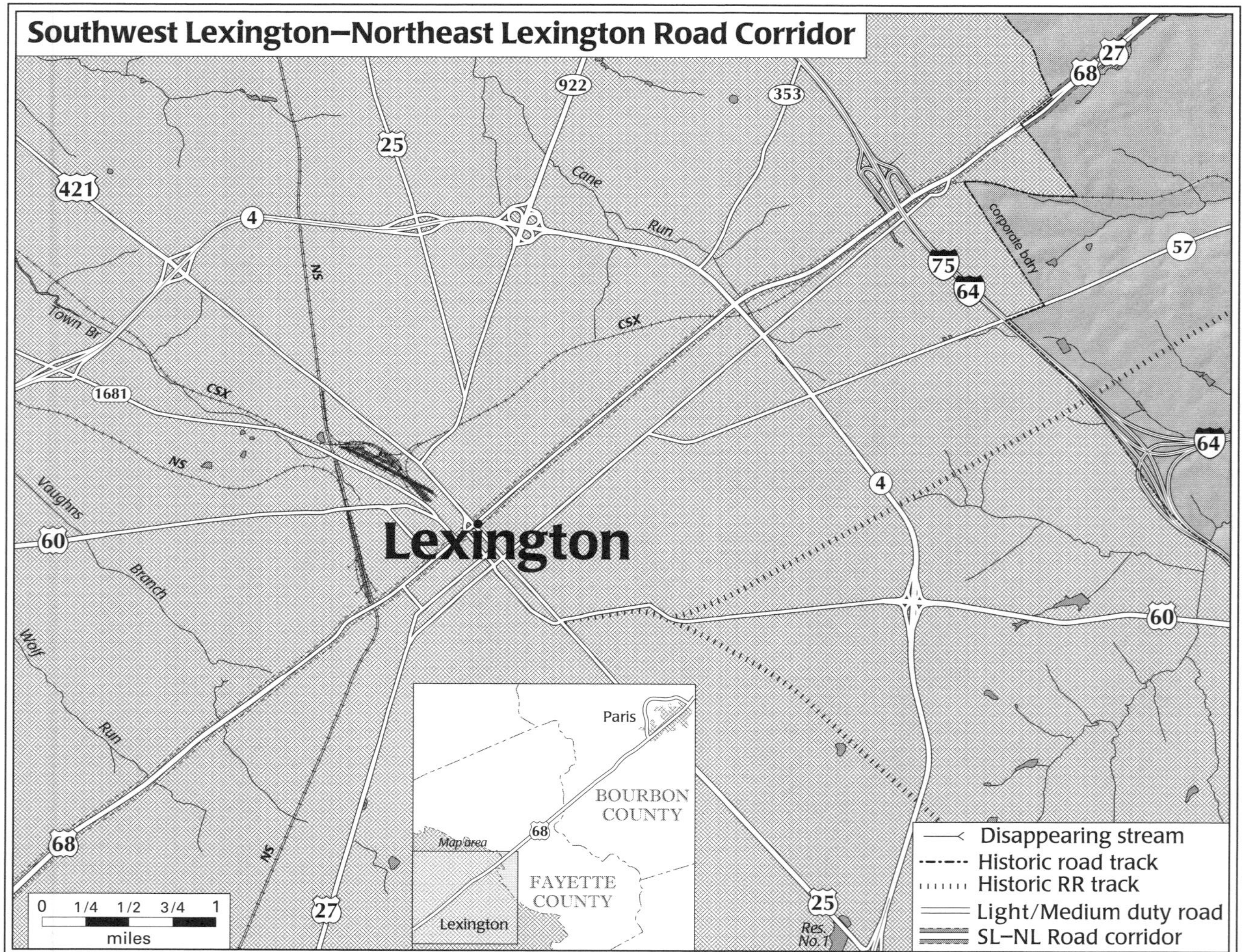
Southwest Lexington–Northeast Lexington Road Corridor
Lexington
922
353
25
421
4
Cane
Run
NS
CSX
Town Br
1681
Vaughns
60
Branch
Wolf
Run
68
27
75
64
57
corporate bdry
Paris
BOURBON COUNTY
FAYETTE COUNTY
Map area
Res. No. 1
0 1/4 1/2 3/4 1
miles
Disappearing stream
Historic road track
Historic RR track
Light/Medium duty road
SL–NL Road corridor

the Phoenix Hotel until it was demolished in 1982. This site anchored the south end of the first mail route west of the Appalachians and soon evolved into the most important crossroads location in the Greater Bluegrass Region. Hotels occupied the lot beginning in 1797, when John Postlethwait opened a tavern for travelers here. The first building burned in 1820, and its replacement was named the Phoenix. An 1879 fire destroyed the second building. The new replacement, also named the Phoenix, was a three-story brick building that had become the core of a modern eight-story hotel by 1910. One block to the southwest along South Limestone, Vine Street became the city's rail corridor.

By the 1880s the Chesapeake & Ohio Railroad maintained tracks and a passenger depot at the Phoenix Hotel's back door. Following the model of other modern central-city hotels at the time, the hotel's first floor included several retail shops, a billiards room, a barbershop, dining rooms, and a large room for traveling salesmen to set up their sample cases. A special railroad and hotel restaurant stood at the rear, adjacent to the depot. A large, block-deep livery stable stood next to the Phoenix along East Main Street, and beyond that to the southeast was a coal and lumberyard on a C & O railroad siding. Northwest of the Phoenix, across South Limestone, the three-story Florentine Hotel occupied the corner of Main and South Limestone. At street level, shops, offices, and a liquor store opened onto Main Street. In 2008 developers razed the block's remaining old buildings in preparation for construction of a new hotel and condominium complex. Opposite the Phoenix to the northeast, retail businesses and restaurants occupied several three-story buildings, including the Golden Horseshoe restaurant at 129 E. Main Street. In the post–World War II period, Duncan Hines noted, "This is a popular place in Lexington . . . specializing in seafood and prime ribs of beef."[2]

Proceeding north along North Limestone, the northwest or left side of the street was lined with two-story buildings that included dry goods shops, harness makers, a cobbler, and a plumber, as well as another hotel at the corner of North Limestone and Short Street. Across the street on the right, or northeast, side—now an expansive green space in front of the courthouses—the 1880s street front included barbershops, a restaurant, a billiards room, a harness shop, and a carriage manufacturer. Built atop this footprint, the new courthouse facades disguise labyrinthine interiors designed to hide hallways and sequester judicial chambers. Outside, the courthouses open onto an open plaza-type space graced with seasonal fountains. The potential of a predictable daytime clientele has encouraged investors to rehabilitate some of the old structures on the block's northwest side and convert the space into restaurants.

Limestone Street redevelopment here is a small segment of a much larger real estate renaissance under way in and adjacent to the old central business area as developers raze anachronistic buildings, convert the cleared lots into apartments and condominiums, and open new retail shops. The new residents include university students, young professionals, and jaded suburbanites who are seeking the convenience of low-maintenance loft living—no lawn to mow, leaves to rake, or snow to shovel. A large livery stable occupied the corner of Limestone and Short in the 1880s. A bulky structure, it extended back from Limestone to take up a large portion of the block. One

An eclectic collection of two- and three-story commercial buildings dating from the 1880s to the 1920s stand wall to wall in the first block of Limestone north of Main Street. The facades of the century-old structures have been altered; some were retrofit with recessed doorways and plate-glass windows, another has a decorative tiled pent roof jutting out above the second-story windows. In the central background the 1914 Fayette National Bank building looms fifteen stories above the courthouse square. McKim, Mead and White, the premier architectural design firm in the eastern United States at the time, designed the structure in the Beaux Arts style. Oddly, only the building's Main and Upper Street facades carry distinctive—and expensive—architectural details; the south and east sides seen from Limestone are plain brick-slab walls, which suggests that the building's owners either anticipated the construction of equal-sized buildings on adjacent lots or were turning their backs on the historic street corridor and presenting their formal facade to the other bank and office buildings that rimmed the courthouse square. After the onset of the Great Depression in 1929, the bank found itself in financial distress and closed in 1931. The space was subsequently occupied by another financial institution, an electrical utilities company, and other business tenants. Most recently the former bank lobby was a camera and photography-supply retail store. Many other southern cities exhibit business-area skylines with a single high-rise building—Wilmington and Charleston, for example—which indicates that the first two decades of the twentieth century were a time of general financial prosperity across the South. Yet few southern cities sustained this growth; the Depression and World War II halted much business construction, and their business areas were left with a single signature building.

block northwest along Short Street, the Fayette County Court House stood in the center of the public square that was part of the city's original survey plan.[3]

Fronting the plaza's fourth side at 101 Barr Street is the U.S. post office and courthouse building outfitted in art deco with Greek Revival flourishes. In the early 1900s the William Curran & Son Lumber Yard occupied this corner. The yard comprised a few small lumber sheds and large lumber piles in the open, exposed to the elements. A small carpenter's shop stood facing Barr Street where the post office sign now stands. Large Victorian houses on generous lots lined the rest of Barr Street as far east as Walnut (now Martin Luther King). Perhaps because it is a federal office building, the post office–courthouse is a rather reserved version of art deco style compared to privately owned structures built during the same 1920s–1930s period. On the second floor, the main courtroom is beautifully outfitted with a coffered ceiling and fine woodwork. Mounted against the back wall is a large oil painting by Ward Lockwood entitled *Daniel Boone's Arrival in Kentucky.* During the Depression a New Deal program authorized the U.S. Treasury Department's Section on Painting and Sculpture to commission hundreds of artists to prepare murals or paintings for the nation's post offices.[4] Lockwood was born in Atchison, Kansas, and studied art at the University of Kansas, the Pennsylvania Academy of the Fine Arts, and the Académie Ranson in Paris. His painting, completed in 1938, portrays Boone and five companions dressed in buckskin and broadcloth and carrying Pennsylvania long rifles as they emerge from dense woodland. The figures' coonskin caps are fallacious.

From Main Street north to just beyond Seventh Street, North Limestone passes through the center of Lexington's original 710-acre street and lot plat and the Mulberry Hill historic district. Pioneer surveyors platted the town following a long-established English habit, also used in many eastern seaboard towns, of laying out urban settlements in two sections—two or more rows of blocks dedicated to centrally located half-acre in-lots, and the remaining land surveyed into larger out-lots. Lexington's in-lot section centered on a common that paralleled Town Branch, the present route of Vine Street. The common was to be 165 feet, or ten poles, wide. Business and commercial properties occupied the in-lots that formed the city's core business area. From the common north along Main and Short Street the plat included twelve blocks in two rows. The plat designated one block in this group as the public square; it later became the courthouse square. The remaining eleven blocks were one-half-acre in-lots. South of the common, the third row of six blocks was also dedicated to in-lots. One row of out-lots extended southwest, beyond High Street to South Hill. A second row of seven out-lots followed the Town Branch valley to the southeast. The remaining hundred-plus out-lots extended northeast, paralleling the Maysville Road, across prime land beyond present-day Seventh Street. The five-acre out-lots provided small-scale farm and garden spaces; the out-lot plat was also a grid along which streets would run and a surveyed space into which residential neighborhoods expanded as Lexington grew. More generally, the out-lot plat also provided the grid orientation for the city street pattern as it extended from Main northeast to Seventh and Loudon.

Northeast from Main Street, North Limestone's frontage from Short Street to Church Street marked a transition to a mix of single-family homes and commercial businesses, including manufacturing firms. The federal post office building on the right stands on the site of an 1880s carriage factory and associated carpentry and harness shops, paint shops, and wood storage. A large wagon factory and related shops occupied the remainder of the block. The northwest, or left, side of the street included a jail on the corner of Short and Limestone; a leather shop, hay and feed store, and a

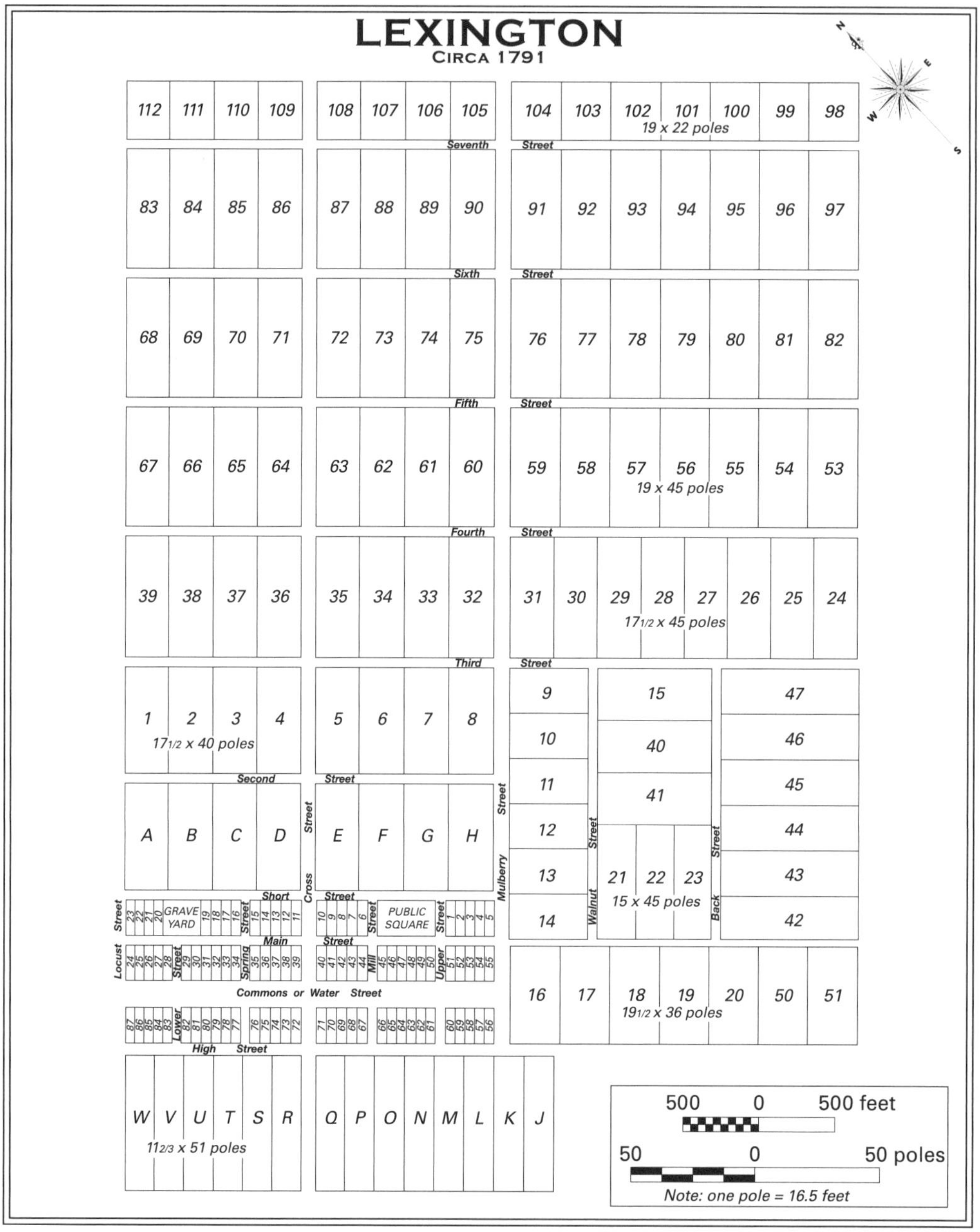

coal yard extended to the corner of Church Street. These businesses, some two blocks removed from the courthouse but lining the city's most important through street, are a reminder of the central role played by the horse in the nineteenth-century city. Narrow streets and business and residential lots made for a compact city. Most people moved about the city on foot. Dray work, on the other hand—moving lumber, brick, coal, industrial raw materials, food and feed, grain, and so on—required horse-drawn wagons. Stagecoach lines stabled their horses near their midtown stops, usually important taverns and hotels. Downtown business areas therefore included an amalgamation of horse-oriented space such as livery stables and feed stores, most often located with convenient access to primary thoroughfares. Lexington's horse transport–related businesses, including harness makers and carriage manufacturers, were concentrated along North Limestone in part because it was a primary cross-country road in the nineteenth century. Lexington's electric trolley system began service in 1890.[5] During the first three decades of the twentieth century, auto-oriented businesses such as gas stations, repair garages, auto sales lots, and motels clustered near the central business area, replacing shops that had supported horse transportation. Thereafter they were located beside the main highways at city gateway points.

From the post–Civil War period of the 1870s through the 1930s, few retail, financial, or specialized businesses stood along North Limestone. Instead, businesspeople created the city's commercial armature along Main Street and around the courthouse square, where telegraph and newspaper offices, banks, realty offices, attorneys' offices, large dry goods and department stores, and furniture stores were clustered. The lots closest to the courthouse square were especially coveted as potential commercial spaces.

Crossing Church Street to the northeast, Limestone in the 1880s passed a large lumberyard on the southeast corner, followed by single-family houses on both sides of the street. High-density ranks of two-story Federal-style houses fronted directly onto the sidewalk; they had no front or side yards. Behind the houses the blocks were largely open; the space was utilized for yards, gardens, storage sheds, and summer kitchens.

Mile 0.1 Pleasant Stone Street to Academy Alley. Beginning at this point and continuing north for the next half mile or more, North Limestone illustrates the distinctive character of an eighteenth- and early nineteenth-century pedestrian city. Before the nineteenth-century development of the horse-drawn omnibus, the horse-drawn trolley car, and the electric trolley car, individuals in most American cities had to walk anywhere they wished to go, be it to the workplace, stores, friends' or relatives' homes, church, or anywhere else. City dwellers were pedestrians unless they acquired sufficient wealth to own and maintain a horse and carriage. The pedestrian city had several distinctive characteristics, including a high-density central business area surrounded by residential neighborhoods differentiated according to wealth, class, and race or ethnicity. Direct access to the central business area was highly desirable because it reduced the time spent moving between home and places of business or employment. A city's wealthiest residents, therefore, tended to live as close to the central business area as possible, whereas the working class and poor lived on the city's periphery.[6] As rapid transit systems developed and the affordable personal automobile became available after about 1910, this pattern began to reverse: the wealthiest individuals moved out of the central city in favor of life at lower residential densities in distant suburbs. The city's low-income residents replaced them in the historic residential sections near the old central business area.

In the nineteenth-century pedestrian city, the central residential neighborhoods were prestigious, as were residential locations along the most important streets. People of wealth could assert their class position by building their homes, often designed by prominent architects and constructed of high-quality materials, along a major thoroughfare in or adjacent to the central business area. Such a location provided them with a prominent site where they could build a grand house and display their status through the visible and understandable language of the physical symbol. The calculated display of wealth through the size, design, and placement of one's home was not new to the American pedestrian city but emerged in fifteenth-century European cities.[7]

This section of North Limestone is also coincident with the out-lot section of the city's original plat that began at Short Street. From Main Street to Third, out-lots 9 through 14 present their short sides to the street. Beyond Third Street all out-lots are situated longitudinally with the street. Lexington's north-side out-lots share several common evolutionary characteristics. They are heterogeneous in period of development and construction and therefore in architectural scale and style. Early in the nineteenth century the lots were a mix of gardens and pastures, industry, and large estate properties. As the years and generations passed, residents and developers progressively subdivided the out-lots into smaller and smaller parcels. Because each subdividing stage occurred at a different time, houses built during each stage differ in style, scale, form, and placement, reflecting changing tastes and evolving building technologies. The balloon-frame house, probably invented in Chicago in the 1830s, began replacing the ancient post-and-beam, mortise-and-tenon construction. Slit nails mass-produced by the 1830s facilitated the new sawn-lumber construction technology. Mass-produced concrete block appeared in the late 1890s. Until then stonemasons had built house foundations out of mortared rubble stone.[8] Early Federal-, Italianate-, and Greek Revival–style town houses crowded the street, unencumbered by front or side yards. Estate houses occupied entire out-lots before later generations subdivided the properties and sold off sections for new residential development. Developers built post–Civil War clapboard cottages and shotgun houses along alleys or stub streets cut into the out-lots to provide accommodations for freed slaves. Massive brick, three-story Queen Anne houses appeared after the 1880s; Arts and Crafts bungalows and pyramidal-roofed cottages were the house forms of choice by the 1920s. Clients for the street's new houses, several designed by respected architects such as Cincinnatus Shryock and John McMurtry and constructed by the builder Garrett Wilgus, represented a cross section of Lexington's business and professional residents. The street's residents included artists, attorneys, coal dealers, doctors, grocers, hemp manufacturers, livery stable operators, merchants, millers, ministers, and saloon keepers.

Meanwhile, transportation technology was also evolving. Houses constructed after about 1910 sometimes included driveways and backyard garages for the mass-produced automobile. Earlier residence lots required some form of retrofit to accommodate the auto or the occupants would have to park on the street. The net effect in north Lexington was that most out-lots, especially those in proximity to the central business area, are not architecturally uniform but present an assortment of building styles, sizes, and orientations. Neighborhood diversity extends to differences in residents' class and race, which also changes and adjusts through time.

North Limestone still retains some of the city's most elegant homes built on out-lots between 1810 and the Civil War by several of the state's wealthiest individuals. Some original out-lot homes still function as residences; others have been converted to other uses such as schools and funeral homes. The first of these "grand avenue" homes is at 194 North Limestone. On the second half of the block, on the southeast, or right, side of the street, stood the Sayre Female Institute, which today is Sayre School, a private college preparatory school. In the 1840s Edward P. Johnson commissioned the architect Thomas Lewinski to build a large house here on out-lot 11. From the 1830s through the 1850s Edward Johnson operated the largest and most successful stagecoach company in central Kentucky. From offices in the Phoenix Hotel and Brennan's Hotel in central Lexington, Johnson's stage lines linked the city to the Ohio River: west to Louisville, north to Covington, and northeast to Maysville. An eastbound line ran to Owingsville, where one of the state's first iron furnaces operated. Other routes ran south and southwest to London and Nashville, with connections to Florence, Alabama.[9] A Lexington banker, David Sayre, founded his institute in 1854 and moved it to this site in 1855. He enlarged the house for institutional use by adding two additional floors to accommodate students, classrooms, and offices.[10]

Mile 0.3 In addition to serving as a through street for local and regional traffic, Limestone also became a trolley car route when the city's trolley car system opened in 1890. Considering that for most of its length through north Lexington the street was a modest fifty feet wide, and that on-street parking was permitted on both sides of the street, combined auto and trolley traffic produced substantial congestion.[11] Although city engineers recommended widening Limestone to accommodate more traffic, that project was never undertaken. Instead, the street was designated a one-way street north. Its companion, North Upper Street, which parallels Limestone one block to the left, or northwest, was converted to a one-way street for southbound traffic. By forgoing street widening, the city did not need to remove old buildings or yard space, so sections of this corridor remain today much as they were 120 years ago.

By the 1920s Limestone was still the most important arterial street in the city and the only outlet from the central business area to the northeast. Fayette County automobile registrations totaled about 4,500 in 1920 and had increased nearly fourfold to 16,000 by 1930.[12] North Broadway, the present-day route for U.S. 68–U.S. 27 and Paris Pike, went no farther north than Fairlawn Avenue, about nine-tenths of a mile north of Loudon Avenue, where it ended in a farm field.

On the south side of the Limestone and Third Street intersection stands the remnant of a 1950s Shell gasoline station. Since the station went out of business in the late 1970s, the structure has been converted to a variety of secondary uses. The parking lot serves the Atomic Café, a popular restaurant on the northwest side of the intersection that occupies a nineteenth-century commercial corner building. On the right, just beyond the Third Street intersection, at 312 North Limestone, a large white mansion in full nineteenth-century Greek Revival regalia served for many years as the White Hall Funeral Chapel—a common secondary adaptation for grand old houses. Built on out-lot 31 as a private residence for an Ireland-born manufacturer, James Weir, in 1832, the home was probably finished by a nephew, also named James Weir, in the

Evolution of Lexington's Out-Lot Blocks
1800 – 1990s
(Diagrammatic)

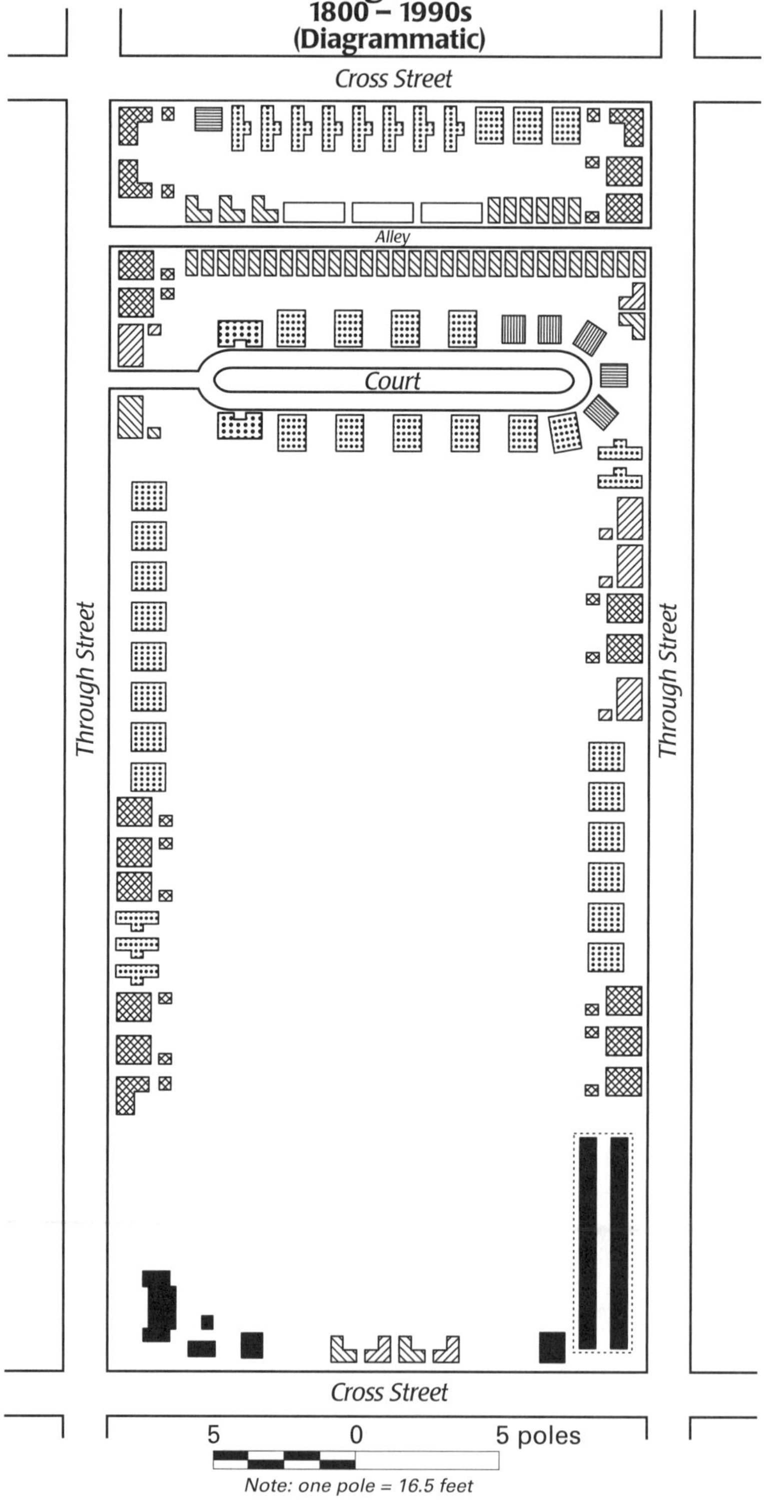

Evolution of Lexington's Out-Lot Blocks
1800 – 1990s
Legend

1800–1830

Entire block purchased for development by person of wealth. Large, architect-designed residence of brick or stone in period style (Federal, Georgian, ( ), with outbuildings, including slave quarters, kitchen, stable, smokehouse, icehouse. Part of lot used for kitchen garden, pasture for carriage horses, and industrial development with ropewalks (long, narrow buildings) or carriage manufacturing, etc. This house and some of the outbuildings may stand through the entire developmental sequence and be used as residences, funeral homes, schools, or other public structures.

1830–1860

Original out-lot owner, or heirs, subdivide the block into lots of varied size. Beginning to develop relatively high residential density, medium-size brick houses are constructed in a variety of period styles: Classical, Greek Revival, Gothic Revival, Italianate, etc. ( ). Large lots will later be subdivided and sold for house construction. Larger homes may include a carriage house at the back. Slave owners house their slaves in their homes or in quarters in the backyard. Most residents walk to work in the central business area. Some block faces fill in; others retain undeveloped lots. Industry continues to function or is removed and replaced by housing (indicates industrial buildings removed).

1860–1875

Post–Civil War demand for housing by freedmen addressed by developers who purchase undeveloped land interior to the block. Small, narrow lots laid out along an alley or stub street constructed across one end of the out-lot's and L- or T-plan clapboard cottages or shotgun houses ( ) constructed at high densities. Much of the out-lot's interior remains in gardens or undeveloped. A few larger brick homes ( ) built along street fronts although construction is probably slowed by the 1873 financial panic. The entire out-lot achieves its greatest overall class and racial diversity.

1875–1920

Large, multistory brick and stone Queen Anne, Gothic, Italianate, and Romanesque houses built on some remaining open or subdivided lots ( ). Developers obtain undeveloped land in the out-lot interior and construct a cul-de-sac court with large brick apartments ( ) and medium-size revival-style houses and bungalows ( ). A very steep social gradient established between residents of shotgun houses and the new apartments and revival-style houses. Some undeveloped block–face lots developed by contractors who build plan book bungalows. The trolley now provides transportation into the central business area and selected routes across the city. Some residents acquire automobiles and build driveways beside their houses and construct small garages in their backyards.

1920–1960

Little morphological change, as limited land remains available for development unless existing structures are removed; Tudor Revival is a favored style early in the period ( ). Some upper-income people move to the post–World War I or post–World War II suburbs; their large homes may be purchased by absentee landlords and subdivided into apartments for lower-income residents ( ). Black residents continue to occupy the L- and T-plan cottages and shotgun houses along the 1860s alley. Automobiles line the street, as off-street parking is not available for the residents of most small houses, and the trolley is replaced by the bus.

1960–1990s

Gentrification of some older homes constructed from the 1830s to the 1920s brings social diversity. Some post–Civil War housing in poor condition is removed and replaced by subsidized low-income houses and apartments ( ). Carriage houses and outbuildings associated with 1830s–1880s houses converted into residences.

Two different building forms stand at the Limestone and Third Street intersection. Two late eighteenth- or early nineteenth-century Federal-style houses on the left—one set back, the other fronting the sidewalk—feature roof gables that parallel the street. A newer building design, represented in the flat-roofed commercial building on the corner, became the favored street-fronting building form in American cities after the 1850s. This form allowed narrower street-frontage lots and had the advantage of directing rainwater off the back of the roof, away from the sidewalk and the building's sidewalls and foundation. Retrofit with large plate-glass windows and an awning, the structure's ground floor houses the Atomic Café.

early 1850s. The original plan was a two-story central block flanked by one-story wings on both sides. It is likely that the Weir house design was influenced by Transylvania University's Old Morrison building, two blocks to the northwest.[13] In 2007 the owners sold the funeral business and the building was reconfigured as an entertainment center for weddings and other special events.

Also at the Limestone and Third Street intersection but opposite White Hall is Transylvania University's John R. Hall Athletic Field. Transylvania, a small liberal arts college enrolling about 1,100 students, built the $2.5 million field in 1996 as a playing and practice space for women's softball, soccer, and intramural sports. The locker rooms and coach's office occupy an 1815 brick row house on Upper Street. A brick wall with wrought iron inserts screens the field from North Limestone traffic. The field is named for John R. Hall, who served during the 1980s and 1990s as chairman and CEO of Ashland, Inc., and was a member of Transylvania's Board of Curators.[14]

Transylvania's main campus stands just beyond Upper Street, one block to the left. The university's founding dates to 1780, when the Virginia Assembly chartered a school west of the Appalachians, or west of the woodland, hence the name Transylvania. Though originally established at Danville, an important early settlement on the Wilderness Road, the school subsequently moved to Lexington, where the first classes were held in 1789. A decade later Transylvania merged with a Presbyterian school, Kentucky Academy, to form Transylvania University. Under the vigorous and imaginative leadership of Horace Holley from 1818 to 1825, the liberal arts program expanded to include departments of law and medicine, which developed into outstanding programs with a national following. The medical and science faculty, for example, included Constantine Rafinesque and Daniel Drake while Henry Clay taught law. Since the 1960s Transylvania, through creative leadership and strong alumni support, significantly expanded its physical plant and financial endowment. The most distinctive building on campus is the Gideon Shryock–designed Old Morrison, a three-story Greek Revival structure facing Third Street. Completed in 1834, the building housed college administration offices throughout the nineteenth and twentieth centuries. Old Morrison underwent restoration in 1962 but was nearly destroyed by fire in 1969. Following reconstruction in 1971, the venerable structure reclaimed its role as campus administrative center.[15]

Mile 0.4 Salem to East Fifth Street. The evidence for the staged conversion of out-lots into period residential developments continues to accumulate along this section of North Limestone. Ideally, if nineteenth-century builders had access to

During the nineteenth century builders infilled Lexington's out-lots with a variety of housing forms as the owners of large estates subdivided their lots and sold off sections or individual lots. Some block faces were subsequently built up in large, brick, high-style houses, including Queen Anne, Italianate, Romanesque, and other revival forms. Other blocks, such as this one, filled in with working-class wood-frame, single-story L-plan or T-plan cottages or two-story houses that often included attenuated Queen Anne accoutrements such as projecting porches with spindled and bracketed balustrades and, as seen here, a vestigial turret with a conical roof.

large blocks of open land, as twentieth-century subdivision builders often did, they no doubt would have developed similar-sized residential lots sequentially and adopted the building style in vogue at the time. That process should have produced entire neighborhoods of similar houses—but that's not the case in north Lexington.

Mile 0.5 At the Fifth Street intersection, on the left, stands the John Brand home, Rose Hill House, built in 1812 on out-lot 60. Brand manufactured hemp in Scotland, and when the business failed in 1802 he migrated to America. In Lexington he established a hemp processing business with John Wesley Hunt and produced the first hemp bagging in the United States.[16] Ropewalks and other commercial structures, probably part of Brand's hemp-processing business, occupied the south part of his out-lot. The single-story Federal-style house includes a five-room central core building with three-room dependencies on each side. Eight fireplaces heated the structure in winter. A brick terrace opened to the backyard, across which stood a smokehouse and a two-storied structure that included a ground-floor kitchen and upstairs servants' quarters. A brick privy and stable stood to the left, or northwest, of the house, and an icehouse occupied an in-ground position on the southwest side. Slave cabins stood in the west yard. Though some of the outbuildings are gone, the house and its wrought-iron front gate remain little modified from the original construction. The house was partially restored in 1977–78. Several other houses of this same design were constructed in central Kentucky, including The Grange, built in 1818, four miles north of Paris on the Maysville Road.[17]

Mile 0.6 East Fifth and Limestone. Duncan Park, just beyond Fifth, occupies a dramatic rise on the right. This was out-lot 76 on the original Lexington plat. William Morton migrated from Baltimore to Lexington in the late 1780s and became a successful businessperson. His 1810 house still stands on its original site, well back from the street, so that today it occupies the middle of the park. The building's central structure is flanked by symmetrical dependencies; the whole is built of stucco-covered brick in a hybrid Georgian-Federal style with Palladian windows. Cassius M. Clay bought the house in 1838 and lived here until 1850. During this period Clay published Lexington's first abolitionist newspaper, the *True American*. Henry Duncan, a

Rose Hill House, circa 1815: front elevation. Drawing by Clay Lancaster. (Courtesy of the University Press of Kentucky)

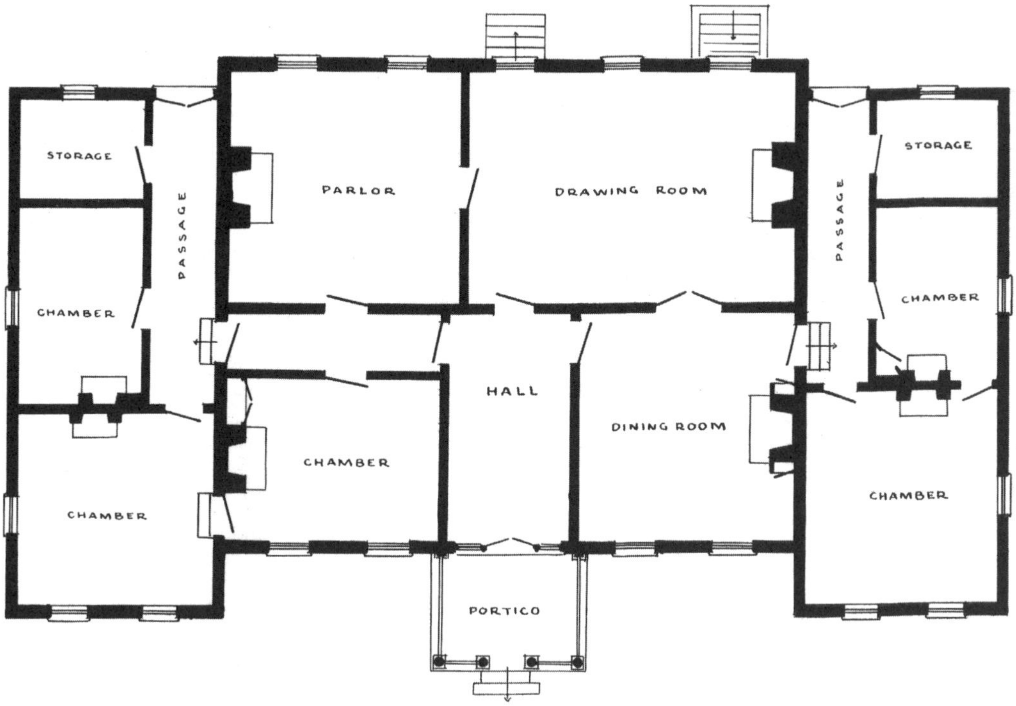

Rose Hill House: plan view. Drawing by Clay Lancaster. (Courtesy of the University Press of Kentucky)

Rose Hill House: perspective sketch, rear view. Drawing by Clay Lancaster. (Courtesy of the University Press of Kentucky)

two-term city mayor and cofounder of the *Lexington Daily Press* newspaper, bought the house sometime after 1850 and maintained the grounds in parklike condition. In 1912 the house and grounds became a city park. Following state-mandated segregation precepts, the city designated Duncan Park as a park for whites, and Douglass Park on the city's northwest side became a park for African Americans. Today Duncan Park and the original Morton house serve as a center for the Martin Luther King Neighborhood Association.[18]

From Main Street to Fifth, North Limestone climbs a distinct grade to crest just past Fifth, where the grade changes abruptly to follow a downhill slope all the way to Seventh Street. Fifth Street marks the divide between the Town Branch or Middle Fork and the Cane Run drainage systems. Town Branch runs northwest through the central business area at the lowest topographic point in central Lexington but is hidden in an underground conduit beneath Vine Street. Because the stream provided a necessary water supply for the early settlement here, in 1781 surveyors platted the Lexington street grid along this stream. The street grid was therefore oriented with the stream rather than the cardinal compass points, which has confused, from that time until the present, all those who find directional comfort in north-south, east-west street grids. Cane Run also flows northwest and joins North Elkhorn Creek at Great Crossing, west of Georgetown in Scott County. The Cane Run headwaters lie just beyond New Circle Road at *Mile 1.9* ahead.

Before the Civil War, the city's free African American residents lived in dispersed residential clusters, most of which were on the city's north side and in close proximity to factories, cemeteries, or vice districts. Most slaves lived in the same households as their owners, in residential enclaves, or in barracks provided by factories. After the war the city's African American population increased rapidly, from 3,080 in 1860 to 7,171 in 1870, as freed people from rural areas moved to the city seeking educational and employment opportunities and the protection of a federal army garrison and the Freedmen's Bureau.[19] Locating available building lots and erecting affordable housing had become a pressing problem by 1865. The city's major arterial streets, Main, Broadway, and Limestone, were already favored residential locations for the city's well-to-do, especially the higher sections, and streets such as North Limestone were referred to by real estate speculators as "grand drives."[20] The cheapest residential lots tended to be found on low-lying land afflicted by adjacent noise and nuisance land uses such as factories, slaughterhouses, and railroad tracks. Land developers created new residential clusters for African Americans in such areas, and the larger ones were often named for the developer. Several of these clusters became large neighborhoods on Lexington's north side, and two of them lie close to North Limestone. Taylortown was established in the open out-lots bordered by Limestone and Broadway between Fourth and Fifth in the 1860s and 1870s and expanded in 1877. The hemp manufacturer W. W. Bruce subdivided land adjacent to his north Lexington hemp factory in 1865 and sold lots to his employees, thereby creating Brucetown between Limestone and Broadway and north of Seventh Street.

African American residential clusters also grew up in street-front strip developments, often in areas where free blacks had lived before the war. In part to make land affordable, some landowners subdivided partially developed out-lots by running new streets or alleys through them. The out-lot fragments were then surveyed into small residential lots, often no more than twenty-eight feet wide by eighty to one hundred feet deep. Single-family frame dwellings had to be built to conform to the lot's shape and size, which often produced houses one room wide by three to five rooms deep, a configuration that yielded high population densities and a vernacular house form popularly known as the shotgun house.[21] If lots were as wide as thirty-five feet, other frame house forms could be built, including L- and T-plan cottages or single-story bungalows. Remnants of this residential development process can be seen along some sections of North Limestone as well as along connecting streets.

Four business structures cluster at East Sixth and Limestone, one on each corner, in the center of an otherwise residential neighborhood. During the trolley car's heyday retail businesses commonly congregated at street-corner trolley stops to capitalize on foot traffic going to and from the stop. A corner grocery store provided milk, bread, and other victuals for neighborhood residents who stepped off the trolley each

This Sixth Street commercial structure's recessed steps, transom windows, and large let-in doorway suggest that the previous occupants used the space for different purposes. Perhaps the building served as an auto-repair garage in an earlier incarnation. Given the dominance of cell phone technology, the pay phone on the left seems an anachronism.

afternoon on the way home from work. This corner included one of Lexington's venerable old neighborhood bakeries, Spalding's, which operated here until 2003, when the business closed. In 2006 Spalding's reopened in a new building on Winchester Road, near the intersection with Midland Avenue. The new bakery is a postmodern version of the historic structure on Limestone. Across the street from the original Spalding's, on the northwest corner, stands a liquor store in a building that served as a dwelling from the turn of the century until the 1930s. A wide door and transom windows cut into the building front left of the steps suggest conversion to commercial use as a garage sometime thereafter. Al's Bar stands on a third corner here, across Sixth from the liquor store. Al's is a longtime landmark business in the neighborhood, and its new owners refurbished the structure in 2007. The restaurant now serves organic foods produced by Kentucky farmers; local musicians present live music. Al's clientele includes a broad cross section of neighborhood residents, migrant workers, and university students. Residents of the north-side neighborhoods bisected by Limestone have voiced concerns about safety, security, and area redevelopment. Though a protracted process when undertaken by individual residents and entrepreneurs, change is occurring in this area. City planners view the upgrade of Al's Bar as one of the primary catalysts to redevelopment and an example of how a single individual or a small group can spur community confidence and investment. Property values here are comparatively cheap, and between Sixth Street and Loudon several urban pioneers have, during the past decade, remodeled houses and business buildings that are now occupied by artists, small retail shops, and restaurants.[22]

In 2008 the Lexington-Fayette Urban County Government and LexArts conceived of a community-based arts project that would sponsor the creation of wall murals at several sites across the city. The North Limestone Neighborhood Association commissioned a local artist, Michael Burrell, to create a mural for the south wall of Al's Bar that would celebrate the role that the bar and adjacent businesses played in fostering a vibrant music performance tradition in the neighborhood that included jazz, rock, blues, and bluegrass. The Lexington Outdoor Mural Project is one of three public art projects that one encounters along Limestone Street and the Maysville Road. At the road's northern terminus, Maysville has commissioned a number of flood-wall murals depicting that city's history. And, along the highway, farm owners are installing paintings of traditional Kentucky quilt designs on their barns as part of a statewide "quilt barn movement" that is coordinated by the Kentucky Arts Council, the U.S. Department of Agriculture, and the County Extension Service.

Mile 0.9 East Seventh Street was formerly known as Strodes' Road and led to Strodes' Station, near Winchester in Clark County.

Mile 1.1 An old brick barn on the left is now located in a Kentucky Utilities substation. Though today part of the CSX rail system, the railroad tracks crossing Limestone here were established by the Chesapeake & Ohio Railroad and were linked via a circumferential belt line to the Union Railroad Depot in the central business area at Main Street and Walnut Street (now North Martin Luther King Boulevard). The C & O belt line was connected to the main C & O rail yard and roundhouse near the present intersection of Walton and Midland, off Winchester

Road, and provided rail access to many of the city's east-side industrial and commercial sites.

Mile 1.3 Loudon Avenue. One of Lexington's trolley car lines, Route 3, ran along Limestone from downtown Lexington to Loudon. At this intersection the tracks turned right, or southeast, to Shropshire, where they turned right again, heading southwest toward Breckinridge and Chestnut to complete a loop back to Main Street. Loudon is wider here than the older Limestone Street, and one block south Loudon gains a raised, grass-covered median that demarcates the path followed by the trolley car tracks, which ran down the middle of the street. Given the highway and trolley line intersection here, the Limestone-Loudon crossing became an active suburban service area in the 1920s and 1930s: new brick commercial business buildings mixed with older business and residential structures dating to the 1880s. A 1930s gasoline station, an early version of the box-type station, still stands on the intersection's northwest corner, though it now functions as a used car lot, a very common secondary use for old gas stations. A business block occupying at least three lots stands on the opposite corner.

Commercial buildings from the 1920s line the east, or right, side of North Limestone from East Loudon Street to Wittland Lane. From Glenn Place to Burnett, Avon, and Arceme avenues, post–World War II infill residential housing dominates the street front.

13

The Original Limestone Trace—A Side Trip on Bryan Station Road

To follow the original Limestone Trace to its termination at Hutchison Road, turn right at the Loudon Avenue intersection and proceed for one block before turning left onto Bryan Avenue, which intersects Loudon on the left near the point where the raised median in Loudon Avenue begins. Bryan Avenue–Bryan Station Road is closely aligned with the old Limestone Trace, as its flexuous track suggests. The trace, in turn, is said to follow an old buffalo road that ran from Lexington to Paris and Millersburg.

At the Bryan and Loudon intersection (at 138 Loudon Avenue) stands a five-story redbrick warehouse building, one of the largest buildings in the city at the turn of the twentieth century. Because of the convergence of streets, old rail lines, and trolley car tracks here, the warehouse has an odd shape, and only a short wall section faces Loudon. Though many of the upper-story windows have been bricked in, the double freight doors, now painted dark red, are still in place on the upper floors. The structure's size and visibility probably prompted its owners to use its great walls as advertising boards for their business. Signs in the form of single words or short phrases encircle the facade in four bands that run between floors. The angled side facing old Bryan Avenue reads, from top to bottom, "Home of Blue Ribbon Twist," "Bluegrass Tobacco Works," "Coal, Hay, Corn, Oats," and "Lime, Sand, Cement." The top two signs advertising a tobacco product and the name of the business have been painted over, but the original wording remains legible. The narrow side facing Loudon reads, from top to bottom, "Coal," "Hay," "Corn," and "Oats." The long side of the building visible from Loudon and Limestone suggests that the building was also used as a general farm and hardware supply business subsequent to its use for tobacco warehousing and manufacturing. Here the signs read from top to bottom, "Coal, Hay, . . . Salt," "Charcoal, Coke, Firebrick, Fire Clay, Fire Backs, Sewer Pipe, Wall Coping," and "Roofing, Asphalt, Shingles, Galv'D Tanks, Sheetmetal, Building Materials." Such hand-painted wall signs were very common in American cities by 1900, especially on building walls that stood above surrounding structures or faced a vacant lot or side street.[1] Today such wall signs are rare.

Mile 0.1 The intersection of Bryan and Castlewood Avenue.

Mile 0.2 As Bryan Avenue bends to the left, Castlewood Park opens on the right. The old road crosses here the rural rim of the nineteenth-century city. Beyond the edge of Lexington's street and out-lot grid, large farm estates owned by the county's elite occupied much of the favored land across the Fayette County countryside. Smaller middling farms had in-filled between the larger properties by the eve of the Civil War. Large estate farms—many of them would later be termed gentleman farms in recognition that their owners saw farming as avocational and a venue for experimentation in progressive or scientific agriculture—could be found adjacent to large eastern cities such as Philadelphia, Baltimore, and Wilmington, Delaware, or in fecund areas of the South such as the great limestone basin around Nashville. Lexington and Fayette County, however, claimed the largest collection of estate farms. An architectural historian, Clay Lancaster, noted more than 170 such elite antebellum farm properties in Fayette County beyond the present-day New Circle Road.[2] Of course, large estate farms were not confined by the county boundary but extended across several adjoining counties. Expensive houses often punctuated the large rural estate properties, built by prominent architects according to the style and taste of the period.

The financial wherewithal to establish estate farms in the Inner Bluegrass countryside often resided in Lexington's business and professional families. During the last decade of the eighteenth century and for the first half of the nineteenth century, John Wesley Hunt operated a general merchandise store on Lexington's Main Street and was one of Lexington's most accomplished entrepreneurs. Hunt was born into a Trenton, New Jersey, merchant family in 1773. In 1795, with the assistance of Abijah Hunt, his cousin and a Cincinnati merchant, John Wesley Hunt became a participant in Lexington's emerging mercantile community. As pioneer merchants, the Hunts procured tools, hardware, foodstuffs, and dry goods on credit in Philadelphia. They commissioned wagoners to haul their goods 320 miles overland to Pittsburgh. There a forwarding agent put the cargo aboard flatboats for the four-hundred-mile trip down the Ohio River to Limestone, where it was transshipped by wagon over the Limestone Road sixty-seven miles to their Lexington store. Hunt's shipments completed the trip across the Appalachians from Philadelphia in about fifty-five days. Considering the high costs and risks associated with overland and downriver shipments, Hunt marked up the prices of his goods 75 to 100 percent.[3]

Cash was often difficult to obtain in pioneer Lexington, so John Hunt regularly accepted local produce as payment for his store goods. Abijah Hunt succeeded in obtaining a contract to supply the federal army troops at Cincinnati's Fort Washington, so John sent to him central Kentucky's bacon, butter, cheese, salt, tobacco, whiskey, and horses. In return, Abijah sent to John Cincinnati's products, including leather, shoes, and nails, and paid for the Kentucky products he purchased for the army with bills of exchange to be paid by the secretary of war. Such bills of exchange provided John Hunt with a negotiable equivalent of cash, thereby underwriting his credit with Philadelphia merchants. When the Kentucky River's flow was high enough to permit navigation, Abijah Hunt sent goods to Lexington via the river and Frankfort. Otherwise, in periods of low water, he made shipments by way of Limestone and the Limestone Road.[4]

By 1798 John Hunt bought locally produced tobacco and shipped it to New Orleans, where he could sell it for cash or bills of exchange. In 1800 the Hunts began exporting Kentucky slaves to Mississippi, a trade that continued to the eve of the Civil War.[5] The Hunts also speculated in land, buying and selling farmland and town lots in Lexington, Louisville, and Washington, Kentucky, and in St. Louis. John Hunt bought a five-hundred-acre farm in Fayette County where he raised cattle, hogs, mules, and horses. He imported blooded English racehorses and inaugurated the importation of trotting horses in the 1840s. Hunt was especially interested in importing high-quality stallions, which he stood at stud.[6]

In 1803 John Hunt established a hemp factory in Lexington to process raw hemp fiber purchased from local farmers. Using slave labor, he manufactured woven hemp material for shipment into the South, where plantation owners used it as cotton bale bagging. From 1809 to 1812, at the peak of his hemp manufacturing business, John Hunt owned more than seventy-five slaves, many of whom worked in his factory.[7]

The Ohio Valley economy settled into a financial depression in 1808 brought on largely by the inability of the valley's farmers to market their products anywhere other than by the tortuous journey south along the Ohio and Mississippi rivers to New Orleans, where commodity prices were soft at best and baneful at worst. England and France, at war with one another, confiscated American trade ship cargos on the Atlantic, cutting off export markets. In retaliation, the American Congress passed the Embargo Act in 1807 and Non-Intercourse Act in 1809; the intent of both acts was to curtail all foreign trade into American port cities, including foreign hemp and fiber products.[8] This action spurred the price of Kentucky hemp if a market other than New Orleans could be found. John Hunt had shipped hemp products throughout the South via the region's rivers, but in 1810 he began shipping his manufactured hemp rope and bagging northeast on the Limestone Road to Maysville and from there upriver by keelboat to Pittsburgh, its ultimate destination being Philadelphia.[9]

In 1813 John Hunt sold his hemp factory and most of his slaves. A year later, in 1814, he began work on a large town house in Lexington near the Transylvania University campus at Mill and Second streets, just two blocks west of Limestone. He named the Georgian house Hopemont. Today the structure is known as the Hunt-Morgan House and is maintained as a museum by the Blue Grass Trust for Historic Preservation. In 1816 John Hunt again shifted his investments, this time into banking, government stock, and insurance.[10] When he died in 1849, John Wesley Hunt's appraisers valued his estate at nearly $900,000. Given that appraisals typically undervalued real property, Hunt's actual net worth probably exceeded $1,000,000, and he may have been the first millionaire west of the Appalachians.[11] John Wesley Hunt established a family heritage of business and intellectual leadership that continued with his descendents. Among this group, his tenth child (of twelve), Francis Key Hunt, became a Lexington attorney, his grandson John Hunt Morgan served in the Confederate Army during the Civil War, and his great-grandson Thomas Hunt Morgan won the Nobel Prize in Physiology and Medicine in 1933.[12]

Also part of the Hunt family legacy is this historic farm property, a small remnant of which remains as Castlewood Park. When Francis Key Hunt married Julia Warfield,

The grand scale of Francis Key Hunt's remarkable Gothic Revival Loudoun House is roughly akin to that of the great country estate houses of England. From its position atop a low hill, the house still presents a capacious though regal facade to the small public park that surrounds it. Northward-expanding subdivisions have long isolated the house from the open farmland that once provided its pastoral context.

the daughter of Dr. and Mrs. Elisha Warfield Jr., in 1849, he received a fifty-six-acre tract of farmland here from the Warfields as a patrimony. Francis Hunt also received a handsome inheritance from his father's estate. Possessing both land and money, young Francis set about planning a grand home on the former Warfield property. The home that Hunt built, Loudoun House, faces southwest and stands on the south side of the present park space. To execute a plan in his preferred Gothic Revival style, Hunt retained the New York architect Alexander Jackson Davis, then regarded as the nation's preeminent designer of picturesque and Gothic Revival country houses. Davis built many of his commissions for New York millionaires along the Hudson River north of the city.[13] With plans in hand, Hunt next hired a Lexington builder, John McMurtry, to construct a Gothic Revival country villa. Completed in 1852 at a cost of $30,000, it was one of the most expensive buildings—never mind houses—in the state. The building's walls were of brick hollow-wall construction, perhaps the first building so constructed in Kentucky. The open space between the exterior and interior walls provided an insulating airway that reduced dampness inside the house. Workmen painted the exterior walls and covered them in a light dusting of sand to

Brick Cape Cod–style single-family houses built in the late 1940s and early 1950s stand in echelon on the former Warfield Farm near Loudoun House. The Warfields' 1830s house, The Meadows, was torn down in 1960 to make room for additional subdivisions of ranch-style houses.

simulate stone. Finish carpenters used walnut for the interior woodwork. The Hunts imported from New York enameled glass, plasterwork, marble mantels, and custom furniture. The building was called the grandest house in Lexington when completed and remained a showplace for decades thereafter. Francis Key Hunt lived in the house with his family until he died in 1879. His wife, Julia, sold Loudoun five years later and moved back to Mill Street, where she lived with her daughter Maria Hunt Dudley in a house next door to the John Wesley Hunt house. The grand old Gothic Revival Loudoun House is now the headquarters of the Lexington Art League.[14]

Across the street from Loudoun House and Castlewood Park, small T-plan and shotgun houses stand on land once part of Francis Key Hunt's farm. To the right, across the park, 1940s and 1950s Cape Cod–style houses occupy the land that was once part of Elisha Warfield's farm, the property where one of Kentucky's finest Thoroughbred stallions, Lexington (1850–75), was bred.

Mile 0.9 This northeast section of Lexington's circumferential New Circle Road was completed in the mid-1950s. The Bryan Station motel at the intersection was built shortly after the new bypass highway opened and today is rented as apartments by the week or month, a common conversion for old roadside motels that have lost their traditional traveling clientele to the modern franchise inns. Though planned as a limited-access bypass highway to relieve traffic congestion on Lexington's through streets, this section of New Circle Road was quickly converted to unlimited access as adjoining property owners built driveways directly to the highway instead of awaiting construction of a frontage road. The result, from the 1950s to the present, is one of the city's most congested roads, lined by road-oriented businesses and small shopping strips and constricted by traffic lights. This assemblage stands in wrenching contrast to New Circle Road's west section, which was completed in the late 1960s and maintained as a limited-access highway. Though some may find this kind of auto strip dreary to the point of repugnance, it remains an illuminating structural record of how such landscapes developed and what has become of them as new forms of roads and auto-oriented roadsides evolved. Of special significance here is the Burgers Shakes drive-in restaurant established to the right at 219 East Circle Road in 1957. The rare one-off restaurant specializes in economical hamburgers, milk shakes, and French fries. A cheeseburger, the most expensive item on the menu, cost twenty-four cents when the store opened. Customers ate in their cars until the early 1980s, when the owners enclosed the restaurant and installed booths for indoor eating.

Mile 1.2 The 1950s–1960s Rookwood Subdivision is on the right.

Mile 1.5 Intersection with Eastin Road.

Mile 2.0–2.1 Anniston Drive intersects on the right. The low area opposite the intersection may be the location of Wright's Pond, which was a wet lowland with a notorious reputation for miring wagons and coaches traveling along the original Limestone Trace. Constructing a bridge mitigated the hazard.

America's highway landscapes, be they two-hundred-year-old roads such as the Limestone Trace that recedes into the distance ahead, or Interstates 64 and 75, which pass almost anonymously beneath the overpass bridge, are intricately interlaced with intersecting technologies, politics, economics, law, and cultural traditions. Roads, old and new, enable movement, invite construction of commercial and residential structures at access points, and instigate a host of unintended consequences. In short, roads continually promote the creation of new geographies and modify old ones. As Bryan Station Road crosses Interstates 64 and 75 on the overpass, consider the historical and geographical presence of each road. Passengers in the 86,000 trucks and cars passing along the high-speed route below each day probably have no idea that they are crossing the path of the oldest highway west of the Appalachians, or that this road played a key role in the early development of the Inner Bluegrass country and its towns and cities. Just so, people riding in the 2,700 vehicles that drive Bryan Station Road daily may not reflect on the trucks on the interstates below, or their likely contents or destinations.[15]

Interstate 75 begins at Sault Ste. Marie in upper Michigan, near the Canadian border where the St. Marys River links Lake Superior to Lake Huron. From Michigan I-75 runs south through six states to Naples and Miami, Florida. Interstate 64 links Norfolk, Virginia, near the mouth of Chesapeake Bay, with St. Louis, Missouri, and the Mississippi River. Interstate 75, here routed in tandem with I-64, is one of the busiest truck routes in America. Since I-75 was completed in the late 1960s, it has become (together with the parallel route I-65 to the west) the transportation aorta for America's current industrial core—the automobile and truck manufacturing corridor that now stretches from southern Michigan into Tennessee and Alabama. Several major automobile manufacturing firms, many of them foreign owned, have established assembly factories along or close to I-75. The nearest auto factory to Lexington is the Toyota assembly plant at Georgetown, Kentucky, where nearly six thousand employees manufacture Camry and Avalon automobiles and Venza crossovers. More than sixty-five automobile parts manufacturing plants in Kentucky supply parts to Toyota and other assembly plants along I-75 and I-65, according to the "just-in-time" technique that requires delivery at the precise time that the parts are scheduled to be installed on the vehicle assembly line.[16] In this manner, delivery trucks become virtual warehouses, thereby eliminating a number of inventory issues, and the interstate highway becomes an extension of the factory's assembly line. Parts suppliers can minimize contingencies such as winter ice and snow storms by locating their plants as close to the factory as possible and along a federal highway or interstate to which highway maintenance crews assign a high priority.

The historic Manufacturing Belt, now maligned by some as the Rust Belt, once overlaid the Middle Atlantic states from Pennsylvania, New Jersey, and New York west through Ohio, Indiana, and Illinois, into southeastern Wisconsin. The region's heavy industries were predicated on blending Pennsylvania's anthracite and bituminous coals with Minnesota's iron ore and Michigan's limestone to produce the iron and steel that built much of the nation's transportation and commercial building infrastructure. The new manufacturing core is attracted not to physical resources and raw materials but to transportation access, nonunion labor pools, and state political and economic subsidies for industrial investment.

The U.S. Congress approved the North American Free Trade Agreement (NAFTA) in 1993. Since that time the nation's major north-south interstate highways have become trade corridors by hosting rapidly increasing truck traffic that links producers and consumers in Canada, the United States, and Mexico. The I-75 corridor carries NAFTA-related traffic, but the highway remains the route of choice for the nation's current auto and truck industrial corridor; 23 percent more trucks move on I-75 than on any other north-south interstate.[17]

The interstate corridor here is also closely associated with the Urban Services Boundary of the combined Lexington-Fayette Urban County Government. (The 2010 population of 295,803 includes residents of the city proper and the rural sections of Fayette County, not just those that live within the Urban Services Boundary.) Beyond the boundary, just ahead, the land is zoned agricultural and the sale of rural land for residential construction is restricted to forty-acre lots or larger. Farmland here can sell for $10,000 per acre and up; the forty-acre lot restriction is thus intended to deter leapfrog suburbanization. The dearth of urban services such as water and sewerage beyond the boundary and strict zoning controls offer further curbs on urban sprawl.

Mile 2.5 An old dry-laid rock fence lines the road on the left. The fence was probably built in the nineteenth century following design principles worked out in Ireland, Scotland, and England during the last millennium.

Mile 3.6 The road crosses the CSX Railroad tracks that are linked to Winchester and Paris.

Mile 3.9 A historical marker here identifies the site of Bryan's Station, an important Revolutionary War–era pioneer settlement that provided a safe haven for many settlers between 1779 and 1783. The station was initially settled by four Bryan brothers, William, Morgan, James, and Joseph, along with their compatriots, William Grant, Cave Johnson, and William Tomlinson. The Bryans were from North Carolina and were related to Daniel Boone by marriage. Boone married Rebecca Bryan, the daughter of Joseph Bryan, and William Bryan married Mary Boone, Daniel's sister.[18] The Bryan brothers accompanied Boone on his first attempt to settle in Kentucky in 1773, a venture that the party abandoned after an Indian attack killed several of their number, including Daniel Boone's eldest son, James. William Bryan, four of his brothers, and about twenty-five neighbors returned to Kentucky in 1775, arriving in Boonesborough in the fall. One of the group, Kasper Mansker, led an exploratory expedition west to the Green River country, the Barrens, and the Cumberland River. The Bryans returned to North Carolina to prepare for a spring excursion back to Kentucky. William became ill on the way and sent two of his slaves under the care of his brother in his place in July 1776. The party arrived at Boonesborough and then settled at a camp here on North Elkhorn Creek that became known as Bryan's Station. The settlers built half-faced camps—very crude huts that served as marginally adequate shelter—during this sojourn and they cleared sixty acres of land, planted corn, and built some fencing. Leaving two men to care for the corn, the others started back east to collect their families for the move to Kentucky. Upon their return, the Bryans found that the Indians had become so troublesome that it was too dangerous to attempt a settlement at that time, and they abandoned their plans for several years. Some of the Bryan men were part of a company that assembled in North Carolina and marched to Fort Boonesborough in 1777 to help in its defense. That year was so fraught with Indian troubles that it was known thereafter as the year of the "Bloody 7s."

News of Daniel Boone's capture by the Shawnee in 1778 thwarted yet another attempt by the Bryans to move to Kentucky permanently. After Boone's return from captivity and the successful defense of a siege against Boonesborough, the Bryans resolved to make the move to Kentucky because there seemed to be a lull in Indian raids against the fledgling settlements. In March 1779 William Bryan and his son Daniel, Samuel Bryan and his family of four, William Grant and his wife and a daughter, and some forty men met at Moccasin Gap, Virginia, and made the long trip to Boonesborough, arriving in late April. After a brief rest, they returned to the old camp on North Elkhorn Creek and commenced building a small fortified settlement and planting corn. Samuel Bryan, William Grant, Stephen Jones, and their families, along with fifteen other men, remained to watch over the new settlement while the remainder returned to North Carolina to gather their families for the final move west. Daniel Bryan, William's son, related that "we had to move on packhorse his family sadled 28 horses every morning including the packs."[19] Brothers Joseph, Morgan, and James Bryan also brought out their families, as did a number of their neighbors, making the move not only a family affair but one that included many members of one community.

This pattern of settlement by families related by blood, marriage, or friendship ties was the norm rather than the exception in the migration to Kentucky's frontier. Moving to an unfamiliar place, particularly during time of war, with people who shared a similar vision and commitment to mutual protection, cooperative work, and harmonious social interaction improved the chances for successful emigration. They arrived at Bryan's Station and began building log cabins that they arranged in a rectangular stockaded enclosure, the cabins forming part of the station walls. The fall of 1779 saw a large influx of settlers traveling through the southeastern Kentucky Wilderness, many of them moving along the Wilderness trail from Cumberland Gap to reach the Bluegrass, where they established many stations similar to Bryan's Station.

As additional families joined the Bryans, they enlarged their station significantly. The station site occupied a low rise overlooking North Elkhorn Creek valley, adjacent to two freshwater springs, one to the east and the other to the north. The cabins were crudely constructed—notched logs with the bark still attached, inward sloping shed roofs, chimneys set on low stone foundations and then built to height with clay and sticks; the open spaces between the cabins were filled with pickets. The Bryan's Station enclosure formed a long rectangle whose narrow ends had folding gates and blockhouses with projecting second stories at each corner. Single men or men unaccompanied by their families occupied the blockhouses, whereas families lived in the cabins. The stockade walls were log pickets split lengthwise and set into the ground to form a twelve-foot wall. The stockaded enclosure presented a formidable barrier to potential foes, but it was not completely impenetrable. Gaps between the pickets were filled with clay that sometimes fell out, leaving open spaces that Indians could successfully exploit.

The increasing flow of migrants into Kentucky did not go unnoticed by the Indians. During the spring of 1780 Indian attacks and raids increased, and the Bryan's Station families had lost most of their cattle by the following summer. Several smaller stations closed, and their occupants sought refuge in the larger stations and forts. Bryan's Station remained occupied during this perilous season, but on March 10, 1779, Indians killed William Bryan Jr. about six miles east of the station as he was coming in with a load of meat. The same day the Indians encamped about one mile from the station, killed two men and some cattle, and wounded another man. Bryan's Station men, with thirty reinforcements from the Lexington fort, set off to storm the Indian camp, only to find that their quarry had packed up and headed back north toward their Ohio River homes. The Indians stopped on the way at Martin's Station on Stoner Creek in present-day Bourbon County, Kentucky, and killed one man and all the cattle they could find. The Indians' superior numbers convinced the pursuing settlers to abandon their retaliatory expedition and return home. Several weeks later the Indians returned to Martin's and Ruddell's stations in the company of British and Canadian soldiers armed with cannons and seized control of both places. The blended Indian-British-Canadian force captured dozens of settlers whom they marched to Detroit, where most of them remained captives until the end of the Revolutionary War. This incident had a depressing effect on the Bluegrass settlements and was, until the end of the war, a serious deterrent to settlement beyond the triangular area anchored by Fort Boonesborough on the east, Lexington on the north, and Fort Harrod on the west.

The land courts held in 1779–80 to settle conflicting land claims acknowledged that another purchaser, Joseph Rogers, who had not yet moved to Kentucky, held superior title to the land on which Bryan's Station stood, thereby nullifying the Bryans' claim to the land. This ruling, together with the loss of William Bryan Jr. and other friends, so discouraged the Bryans that they returned to North Carolina in August 1780, although they continued to try to file other land claims in Kentucky. Some family members returned to Kentucky after the Revolutionary War ended but did not reoccupy the station. Their places were taken by other families who arrived the following autumn—John Ellis, who brought his family and slaves; Elijah, John, and Jeremiah Craig; Joseph Stucker and his relatives; John Martin, John Suggett, and the Henderson, Herndon, and Mitchell families, as well as others who arrived during the winter and into 1781.

Bryan's Station had grown to forty cabins by the summer of 1782, and settlers built several more cabins outside the enclosure. They also constructed outbuildings and other facilities such as tanning vats and a ropewalk. They cleared and fenced more land for cultivation, but wild rye and cane grew in extensive brakes and claimed the marshy North Elkhorn bottomland, while the creek banks remained sylvan. On the night of August 15, 1782, British Captain William Caldwell, his deputy Simon Girty, and a large force of Indians and Canadians reached Bryan's Station and surreptitiously made camp near the easterly spring, among the trees and corn where the Limestone Trace crossed North Elkhorn Creek. Guards at the station detected Caldwell's scouts, sent before daylight the following morning. A visiting Lexington resident, James McBride, killed one, and Elijah Craig assumed a leadership role in mounting a strong defense. Caught unprepared, the station's inhabitants had insufficient water stored within the station. The blended Indian-British force remained concealed and probably did not yet realize that the settlers had found them out. Given the need for water and gambling that the British forces were not yet ready to show themselves, the station's women went to the north-side spring to retrieve water, as was their daily morning custom. The gamble worked; the women brought enough water into the station to last for several days. Thomas Bell and Nicholas Tomlinson managed to depart from the station without detection and made their way to Lexington for reinforcements.

When the Indian-British force realized their presence was known, they pressed an attack. The two forces exchanged heavy gunfire; Caldwell's men set some of the station cabins afire. Reinforcements arrived at two o'clock that afternoon, but most were prevented from reaching the station safely and had to retreat. Simon Girty demanded surrender but was repulsed by Aaron Reynolds, who issued a defiant retort in which he compared Girty to a worthless dog. The siege lifted at sunset that evening, but before the Indian-British combatants departed, they employed the scorched-earth tactic of burning buildings, cutting down cornfields and gardens, and killing or stealing all the livestock outside the station enclosure. Although property damage and general destruction were heavy, casualties were minimal; only a few settlers were killed or wounded. Several days later settlers from the central Kentucky stations formed a retaliatory force and pursued the Indian-British force northeast along the Limestone Trace to the Lower Blue Licks. There the settlers were drawn into an ill-considered skirmish that turned into an ambush. Seventy-seven Kentucky men lost their lives in the most disastrous defeat Kentucky experienced during the Revolutionary War.

The Daughters of the American Revolution in 1896 erected a memorial wall inscribed with the settlers' names around the station's east-side spring commemorating the bravery and heroism demonstrated by the station inhabitants, male and female, during the siege. Although this was not the spring from which the station women gathered water before the battle began, the eastern spring was closer to Bryan Station Road and visitors' access did not require a trudge through the farm. Someone installed a stile in the fence bordering Bryan Station Road for visitors' convenience; current access to the property, however, must be sought from the landowner.

The winter of 1782–83 was the last in which Bryan's Station was garrisoned, and as the war with Great Britain drew to a close, the station's inhabitants began to disperse to their own land claims. By the spring of 1783 the station's population was quite low; the structure was used primarily as temporary shelter by incoming land claimants. Joseph Rogers and his family and slaves emigrated to Kentucky in 1784, evicted the settlers still living at the station, and occupied some of the cabins before building a one-story brick house in 1796. Some of the station's timbers were reused in the Rogers building and perhaps also in the slave quarters built behind the house. Over the next few decades, residents enlarged and modified the house twice, once in 1800, when the building acquired a two-story brick addition, and again in 1830. The house still stands and is occupied by descendants of Thomas C. Wood, who purchased the property in 1879.

North Elkhorn Creek—Entering Horse Farm Country

Mile 4.0 An old concrete bridge carries the road across North Elkhorn Creek here, and just beyond is the intersection with Briar Hill Road (formerly Hornback Mill Road). North Elkhorn Creek rises about six miles to the southeast at an elevation of about one thousand feet above sea level and flows northwest past Georgetown toward Frankfort. At the Forks of Elkhorn, east of Frankfort, the stream joins South Elkhorn Creek before the combined creeks flow into the Kentucky River north of Frankfort. North Elkhorn's drainage basin is about 276 square miles of prime Inner Bluegrass farmland. From its headwaters to its mouth, the stream's gradient is relatively low, and it is bedded atop stout limestones that resist downcutting. The creek's channel is broad and largely flat-bottomed; the water is often no more than five feet deep, and it flows in wide meandering loops incised thirty feet or more into the area bedrock. The creek did have sufficient flow, especially from late fall through spring, to provide waterpower to several mills erected along its banks in the nineteenth century. Several old milldams still span the creek, creating extended slack-water pools that local people favor for recreational canoeing and kayaking. The stream was recently ranked in the top ten of Kentucky's streams for flat-water boating. North Elkhorn Creek also supplies drinking water to Georgetown and Stamping Ground in Scott County.[20]

Mile 4.6 Johnston Road intersects Bryan Station Road here and provides a connection to Paris Pike; the road ahead leads into the Bluegrass horse farm country.

Mile 4.7 The C. V. Whitney farmhouse is on the left. (See *Mile 5.4–6.1* in chapter 15 for a description of the farm.) One of the distinctive features of the old Whitney farm is the Thoroughbred horse cemetery that is now part of the adjoining Gainesway Farm. The cemetery's burials include Broomstick, who was America's leading Thoroughbred broodmare sire in 1932–33, and Regret, winner of the 1915 Kentucky Derby. Only three fillies have won the Derby—Thoroughbred racing's most prestigious trial for three-year-old Thoroughbreds—Regret, Genuine Risk (1980), and Winning Colors (1988). Also buried here is Broomstick's grandson Equipoise, who was foaled in 1928 and went on to win twenty-nine races out of fifty-one starts. Equipoise was voted American Horse of the Year in 1932–33.

About one-half mile to the left, an abandoned Kentucky Central Railroad bed runs parallel to Bryan Station Road. The line opened in 1854 between Lexington and Paris and became part of the Louisville & Nashville Railroad in 1891. In the 1880s this line ran three passenger trains daily between Lexington and Paris and three freight trains per week. The line passed through or adjacent to several large horse farms, and the line often moved racehorses, Elmendorf Farm, to the north on Paris Pike, being one of its principal customers. Traffic on the line declined during the 1930s and 1940s as improved highways permitted an increase in automobile and truck traffic. The railroad abandoned this section in 1951 and removed the tracks by December of that year.[21]

Mile 5.9 Bryan Station Road crosses Lick Run here and an old buffalo trace that ran east of Lick Run, roughly parallel to the current road.

Mile 6.8 The intersection of Muir Station Road (CR 1973). A traditional country crossroads grocery store stood at the northwest quadrant of this intersection for several decades before it was closed and torn down after the millennial turn. In 2010 restaurateurs from Midway, Kentucky, opened Windy Corner Market and Restaurant on the site. The new facility was designed to echo the appearance of the country store and is constructed of recycled wood. Though the store was initially intended to serve the residents and employees on the surrounding farms, the clientele includes people from Lexington and the surrounding counties.

Mile 6.9 Low's Railroad Depot and Post Office was formerly located on the left. The abandoned railroad bed is visible along much of this section of Bryan Station Road.

Mile 7.2 The Fayette-Bourbon County boundary and the 0 mile marker.

Mile 8.4 A sunken lane on the left leads to the site of John Grant's Station (on a low rise about four hundred feet from the road), established in 1779 to house an overflow of people from Bryan's Station. Grant's Station was of sufficient size to house twenty to thirty families. In an April 24, 1780, letter to Colonel John Todd, Grant listed as inhabitants twenty-seven men whom he considered able soldiers and six others he could not "properly call effective." The station came under attack in June 1780, and the cabins were set on fire by Indians from Colonel William Byrd's war party, which also moved against Martin's and Ruddell's stations. The attack prompted residents to abandon Grant's Station and move back to Bryan's Station. John Grant returned in 1784, after the war, and built a log house here. He sold the station property to

George Berry in 1788. James Ingels Sr. bought the property in 1790 and established a farm and red-clay earthenware pottery here.[22] He built a stone house near Grant's log house. Archaeological excavations at the station site revealed charred remnants of log timbers lying where they collapsed when the station burned and thousands of shards of the pottery that the Ingels family produced here in the late eighteenth and early nineteenth centuries. Grant's log house was dismantled in the late nineteenth or early twentieth century and its timbers incorporated into an agricultural outbuilding that still stands across the road from the station.

Mile 8.5 Opposite John Grant's Station site and the site of the Ingels stone house stands James Ingels Jr.'s brick house, an excellent example of Federal-style architecture. The interior woodwork is of much higher quality and style than is common in rural examples of Federal-style architecture. The house stands amid an assortment of agricultural and domestic outbuildings that typify a nineteenth-century Kentucky Bluegrass farm.

Mile 8.6 Bryan Station Road intersects Houston-Antioch Road.

Mile 8.7 The fertile arc of Inner Bluegrass countryside that extends from Winchester on the east to Nicholasville on the west began to acquire an overlay of specialized horse and cattle farms by the mid-nineteenth century. Between the frontier period, when pioneers established small subsistence farms on their land claims, and the development of livestock farms, the region saw the growth of a diversified farming economy, built on slavery, and the creation of a landscape of fenced fields, multipurpose buildings, slave quarters, and substantial brick homes. The farm of Michael Huffman here is an example. The farmhouse, Wood Dale, stands on the left. The two-story brick hall-and-parlor front section was built in the early nineteenth century for Michael Huffman, a farmer who is listed in area tax records by 1805. The property on which the house stands was deeded formally to him in 1816, and he continued to purchase adjacent property in small amounts until he had amassed a farm of 155 acres. He owned no slaves in 1810 but had acquired an adult male and young adult female by 1830. Ten years later his slave holdings had increased to seven, including five males between ten and twenty years old and two females, one younger than ten and the other twenty-four to thirty-six years of age. Five household members were involved in farming. The family probably practiced diversified agriculture, producing livestock and grains. Certainly this strategy was in play in 1870, when the Huffmans raised horses, cattle, sheep, and swine and grew winter wheat, Indian corn, oats, buckwheat, and hay. Michael Huffman died in 1864, and his son Charles bought out his brothers' interest in the property so that he could continue farming. The Civil War and its aftermath caused considerable hardship among area farmers, and Charles Huffman was no exception. The loss of the family slaves compelled him to hire farm laborers at a cost of $600 in 1870. The value of agricultural goods raised in that year was only $750, leaving a very modest profit of $150, meaning that after emancipation Huffman's total labor costs increased to 80 percent of his gross farm income. The situation had improved little by 1880; farm product value climbed to $1,200, but wages amounted to $1,000 in that year, for a labor cost of 83 percent. A comparison of real and personal property values between 1860 and 1870 further illustrates the financial instability brought about by the war. In 1860 Michael and Charles Huffman, who lived and farmed together, had landholdings worth $8,800, while their personal property value, including their slaves, totaled $9,800. By 1870 Charles's land values had climbed to $14,400, but the value of his personal property had fallen to only $2,500. The depression of 1873 initiated a six-year period of economic stagnation nationally, and prospects for Bluegrass farmers did not improve until the 1880s.

Charles Huffman died in 1891, leaving his farm to his three daughters. His widowed daughter, Mary A. Edwards, received the house and some acreage. She was probably living with her father when he died. Her sisters, Lucy B. Beatty and Emma Huffman, received larger quantities of land to offset the bequest of the house to their sister Mary. Emma lived with Mary in the family home, and Lucy Beatty lived nearby in the Ingels house. The sisters extensively remodeled the house in the late nineteenth century by adding a frame wing set at a right angle to the brick front to form a T-plan residence. They also changed the front facade to a more stylish and contemporary Victorian. The property remained in the family until 1996, occupied by various family members until the early 1990s. The house is being restored by the current owner.

Mile 9.0 Bryan Station Road crosses a tributary of Houston Creek.

Mile 9.1 The Wilmot house is on the left. The Wilmot family members were early settlers in Bourbon County.

Mile 9.6 The road passes one of the elaborate entrances to Zanzibar Farm on the right, home to several exotic animal species. A massive mortared stone wall undulates between trees planted along the roadside frontage.

Mile 9.9 An earlier alignment of the Limestone Trace ran to the right of the current road and arrived at Shady Brook, a large Italianate dwelling built by Thomas Holliday in 1872 that is still occupied as a residence. William Moreland, a tavern keeper better known for his later inn on Paris Pike, had located his first tavern on this site; remnants of Moreland's tavern may be represented by a rear section that was incorporated in the construction of Holliday's house. Martin Hutchison built his home, Pleasant Retreat, nearby as well. Hutchison also built the first store and blacksmith shop at Hutchison Railroad Station when the rail line came through, and he served as postmaster (as did his widow). The house's driveway is part of the older Limestone Trace alignment; its current entrance is on Hutchison road.

Mile 10.1 Bryan Station Road now terminates at Hutchison Road, but the Limestone Trace once continued on across the country northeast until it reached the present location of Bradyleigh Farm, along the modern Paris Parkway where the McConnell Farmstead was located. The county court formally abandoned this road segment when the turnpike was built in the 1830s, although it continued in use by adjoining landowners and local traffic until the late nineteenth century.

Return to the Limestone-Maysville Road corridor in north Lexington.

14

The City-to-Country Transition

Mile 1.5 North of Loudon Avenue, from Devonia north to Carlisle Street and beyond, 1920s single-family residential housing predominates. The next intersecting street on the left beyond Devonia is Fairlawn Avenue. By the mid-1930s North Broadway Avenue, one long block to the left and the present route of U.S. 68, ended ignominiously in a farm field, and Fairlawn served as its connector with North Limestone (and Paris Pike–U.S. 68). In 1937 the Kentucky Highway Department developed plans to extend North Broadway 1.2 miles north as a bypass of North Limestone. Broadway was subsequently extended to connect with North Limestone beyond the Louisville & Nashville Railroad overpass.[1]

Mile 1.9 North Limestone intersects New Circle Road here. Beyond the intersection, the road's name changes to Old Paris Pike. In 1953 construction began on this eastside unlimited-access four-lane circumferential bypass, starting near Liberty Road to the south and extending north to North Broadway. The Parkette Drive-In restaurant near the Liberty Road intersection was built in 1951, preceding the new bypass, and other roadside businesses quickly appeared. At the North Broadway and New Circle Road intersection a box-style gas station still carries a sign on its front facade stating that the business has been in place "since 1954."

Across New Circle Road, the North Limestone–Old Paris Pike streetcar track moved from the road's center to the left, or northwest, side and became the Kentucky Traction and Terminal Railroad, with interurban service to Paris. Though the KT & TR tracks and right-of-way have vanished, one can still detect its presence in selected places where houses postdating the track are set farther back from the road on the left side than on the right.

Mile 2.2–2.3 The area from Northwood to Deepwood Drive includes a few remnants of Warrentown, a post–Civil War African American working-class neighborhood on the left and an early twentieth-century middle-class neighborhood on the right. Short segments of a pre–Civil War dry-laid stone turnpike fence are also visible on the right.

Mile 2.7 Just beyond Winston Avenue, on the right, is a beautiful architect-designed Arts and Crafts bungalow built in 1917 on a three-acre lot with a roadside cobblestone wall; a very small cobblestone waiting room for interurban passengers stands out front, next to the street. Perhaps the largest collection of cobblestone houses in the country was built during the 1830s to 1870s in the Genesee River country of New York near Rochester. The rounded cobbles used in those houses, most of them three to four inches in diameter, were of glacial origin, as the cobbles used on this house and fence appear to be. Since continental glaciation did not extend into central Kentucky, these cobbles were probably imported from some source north of the Ohio River.

Mile 3.0 A large "leg"-type freeway interchange just to the northwest, or left, gives access to a six-lane steel and concrete bridge that carries Interstates 64 and 75 over this section of Old Paris Pike. A leg-type freeway interchange resembles two horseshoes laid side by side and is employed if space limitations prohibit using the more common diamond or cloverleaf interchanges. The juxtaposition of North Broadway, a railroad track, and Old Paris Pike here required that highway engineers design a combined leg interchange and overpass to provide full access without disrupting any of the five routes that cross at this point. Because a leg interchange places highway off- and on-ramps side by side, this design has proven dangerous for travelers who are inattentive to the directional signs and attempt to enter the interstate via an exit ramp. About two miles to the south, I-64 splits from I-75 and heads east toward Virginia. Interstate 75 continues south toward Florida. In eastern Fayette County, I-64 carries about 37,600 vehicles per day. In southern Fayette County, more than 61,500 vehicles per day drive on I-75.[2]

This old section of the Maysville Road represents the 1920s transition from city to rural countryside. To provide services to city residents and to manage city growth, a new city charter in 1928 authorized the creation of a seven-member Fayette County Planning and Zoning Commission. The Board of Commissioners passed Lexington's first zoning ordinance in 1930 and adopted a comprehensive city plan the following year. In 1932 Lexington residents elected to adopt a city manager form of government. The city manager structure remained in place until 1974, when the city and county governments merged to become the Lexington-Fayette Urban County Government, one of the first such merged city-county governments in the nation.[3] The merged government included the innovative concept of an Urban Service Area, a key operational planning strategy designed to control urban sprawl and protect unique, high-value agricultural land, especially horse farms. Lexington-Fayette County, at 283 square miles, was divided into two zones, a 75.9-square-mile Urban Service Area and a 207.1-square-mile Rural Service Area. Beyond the Urban Service Area boundary, the merged government would not provide standard urban services such as sewer, water, and electric streetlights as a tactic to control leapfrogging suburban expansion or to divert it in desired directions. In 1980 the Urban Service Area boundary on Lexington's north and east sides was largely coterminous with Interstate 75, except for a small extension along North Broadway, Old Paris Pike, and U.S. 68 where developers had already established subdivisions. At the railroad overpass just ahead, a new subdivision on the right, served by Strawberry Fields Road, was in the Rural Service Area in 1988.

Mile 3.3 Old Paris Pike curves here and passes under the Louisville & Nashville Railroad to join North Broadway and U.S. 68. The Kentucky Traction and Terminal Company interurban line closely paralleled the road here and also ran beneath the L & N overpass. The Curb Bar stands at the junction of Old Paris Pike and U.S. 68. Bars and liquor stores commonly stand at gateway positions outside Kentucky's towns and cities that permit liquor sales in acknowledgment that people may have to travel a considerable distance to find the next legal alcohol sales outlet. Of Kentucky's 120 counties 75 are dry, and an additional 15 counties are dry but contain a wet town or city. Along the Maysville Road, Fleming and Robertson counties are dry; Bourbon, Nicholas, and Mason counties are wet.

To the left, at the Old Paris Pike and North Broadway–Paris Pike intersection, is an "interchange village" that offers food, fuel, and lodging to travelers. Immediately behind the Shell gas station on Haggard Lane is a motel and Transylvania University's ten-acre Marquard Field, a $1.7 million state-of-the-art baseball field that opened in 1999. Intended as a showcase for college baseball, the facility includes brick dugouts and a brick-and-wrought-iron border fence that matches the fence at Transylvania's John R. Hall Field at Third Street and Limestone. The infield dirt is, in part, red clay imported from Alabama. William Marquard was chairman and CEO of American Standard in the 1980s and the owner of Eaglestone Farm, a Thoroughbred and Angus breeding farm on the Maysville Road south of Carlisle.[4]

Mile 3.5 Just beyond the roadside gas stations and, on the left, Kingston Road, is the Joyland Park site. In 1923 Frank Brandt and two brothers, John W. and F. Keller Sauer, opened a twenty-five-acre amusement park here that they named Joyland Park. Attractions included a dance casino, a playground, a picnic area, the first

Joyland Park was a one-stop entertainment center for the entire family. Amusement park rides, picnic areas, and dancing to live music by headliners such as Harry James and Lionel Hampton provided entertainment for thirty-seven years before the park's closure in 1960. The park's location on the trolley-interurban rail line at the edge of the city was similar to that of amusement parks in many other American cities and had the effect of encouraging trolley ridership on weekends. (Courtesy of the University of Kentucky Library Special Collections)

public swimming pool in Fayette County, an eighteen-hole miniature golf course, and rides such as the wooden roller coaster called the Wildcat, and the Pretzel, which was billed as "that funny mysterious dark ride." Many famous big bands played at the dance casino during the 1930s and 1940s. Though the park had a five-thousand-car parking lot, visitors could also arrive via the interurban rail line or city bus. Thousands of visitors enjoyed the park's attractions for some three decades, but flagging attendance in the late 1950s caused its closure in 1960. Two disastrous fires in 1965 destroyed the casino and other buildings.[5]

Mile 3.9 The Lexington Country Club stands back from the road on the right along the recently rebuilt section of Paris Pike–U.S. 68, one of America's most extraordinary roadways. Dedicated by state transportation officials in 2003, this new parkway is twelve and one-half miles long and replaces the 1827 alignment of the old Paris Pike. After World War II, as automobile and truck traffic increased and slow-moving farm vehicles invited high-risk passing, the old highway became a dangerous place for travelers. The Kentucky Highway Department developed plans to widen the road in 1966. There followed a complicated thirty-seven-year vetting process that included engineering plans and proposals, protests and lawsuits by abutting landowners, public hearings and debates, and finally intensive consultation between engineers and landowners before and during road reconstruction. Engineers transformed what had been a narrow, shoulderless, two-lane asphalt track laid atop the old nineteenth-century turnpike into a four-lane parkway built to interstate highway specifications and carefully designed to preserve historic landscapes. The remarkably altered roadway cost more than $93 million, or about $4.5 million per mile, to build, nearly double the cost of any comparable road in the state. Horse farms line long sections of the route, their road frontage formally demarcated by plank or rock fences that required removal and reconstruction by expert masons. Since its completion, the road has won accolades from the Federal Highway Administration, the National Trust for Historic Preservation, and the Sierra Club as a premier example of context-sensitive design. Highway planners recognized that this roadway could not be separated from the natural and cultural landscapes through which it ran; rather, the road was a salient part of a larger historical and geographical unit.[6]

Mile 4.2 On the right, The Grange Lane leads to a 1990s gated exurban development of large single-family residences on ten-acre lots.

Northeast Lexington–Ferguson Road Junction Road Corridor

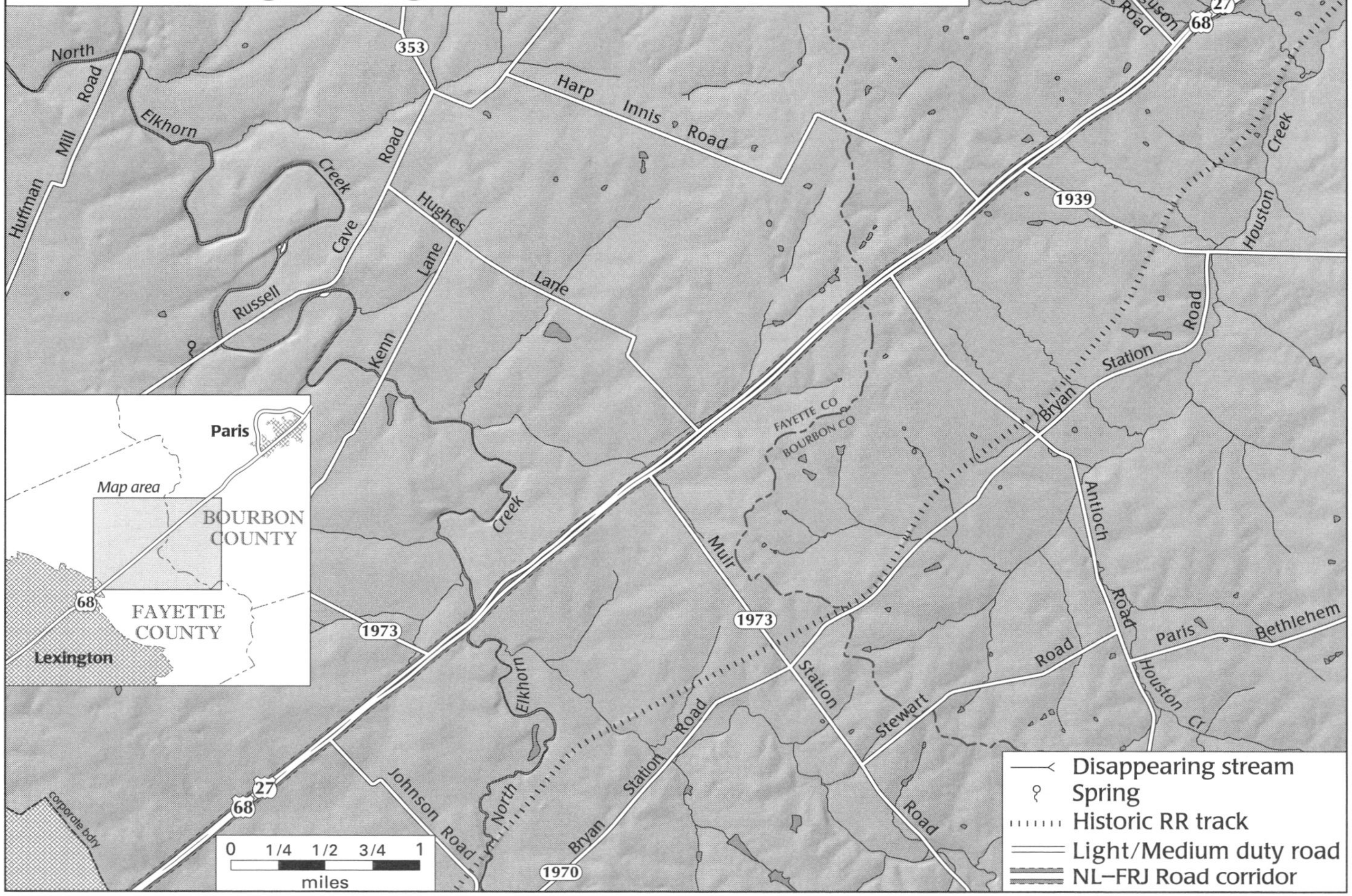

15

Gentleman Farms and the Inner Bluegrass Landscape

Mile 4.8 The roadside from this point to near Paris hosts a congregation of modern gentleman farms that produce horses, especially Thoroughbreds, and blooded cattle. This is one of the world's most extraordinary landscapes. A gentleman farm is often an avocation for the owner, rather than a vocation. The farm, furthermore, is often engaged in the production of amenity livestock such as racehorses, and much of the land is reserved for aesthetic bluegrass pastures enclosed by oak-planked fences. These are not, generally, traditional farms that produce grain and corn or swine and poultry for the commercial markets. Though rural landscapes are often beyond the awareness and understanding of those unfamiliar with specialized farming operations and management, the horse farm country here is, in addition to being an aesthetic showcase, a very complex node in an extraordinary national and international convergence of land and horse ownership; race and training tracks; support personnel, including trainers, equine veterinarians, exercise riders, and grooms; publishing and advertising; animals and money. One farm may represent a net value of more than $50 million, including the value of land, buildings, infrastructure such as roads and fences, and horses. Financing may originate in New York, property owners may reside in California, Ireland, Japan, South Africa, or Dubai, and the farm's horses might be bred in France, England, Ireland, or Kentucky.

On the left, a modern stone fence on Fairholme Farm introduces the gentleman farm district. In the 1960s through the 1980s, this property was Bwamazon Farm, one of the most successful Thoroughbred horse-breeding and racing farms of the period. At the Keeneland Race Course spring racing meet during the decade of the 1970s, for example, Bwamazon Farm, under its owner, Millard Waldheim, and his trainer, Anthony Basile, was the top stakes racehorse owner and breeder for seven of ten years. The farm entered several three-year-olds in the Kentucky Derby, including T V Commercial, their best showing, with a third-place finish in the 1968 Derby.

Mile 5.0–5.4 The Thoroughbred Center, on the right, was initially developed in the early 1970s as a Thoroughbred training facility by a California horseman, Rex Ellsworth, and the Lexington veterinarian A. G. Pessin at a cost of more than $5 million. The facility included prefabricated barns that could accommodate more than six hundred horses and a covered five-eighths-mile training track, which, at the time, was the only example of its type in the world. Today the Thoroughbred Center is owned by the Keeneland Association, the organization that operates Keeneland Race Course on Versailles Road on Lexington's west side. The center now has a second, seven-eighths-mile training track and a full complement of employees and trainers who exercise and train young Thoroughbreds for a fee. The 240-acre facility features a historic barn and other service buildings that include a 920-seat auditorium, which is available for conventions, conferences, theater productions, and other social events; a 2,400-square-foot lounge for banquets, wedding receptions, and company parties; and other meeting and conference room spaces. The center also manages a custom farm-maintenance program. The center's employees provide a broad range of farm services, including building entire horse farms—constructing roads and driveways, building and painting horse barns and wooden paddock and pasture fences, and clearing and mowing pastures.

Just beyond the Thoroughbred Center entrance is Johnston Road, on the right, which links Paris Pike to Bryan Station Road, about one mile to the northeast. On the left, across from the Johnston Road intersection, is Walmac International Farm. Ford Motor Company used a scene photographed here in a national automobile advertising campaign in 1991. Walmac Farm was part of James Ben Ali Haggin's Elmendorf property about 1900 (see *Mile 6.3,* below). In the post–World War II era the farm was owned by Robert Wallace McIlvain, a Pure Oil Company executive and Thoroughbred breeder who named the farm Walmac. The McIlvain family sold the farm in the 1980s to John T. L. Jones Jr. Jones had grown up in Texas and bred quarter horses and longhorn cattle at his Two Creek Ranch there before expanding his interests into Thoroughbreds about 1970.[1] The farm's primary business is Thoroughbred stallion syndication and management. Horses bred here have won major stakes races in the United States as well as England.[2] Well-known stallions that have stood at stud here include Nureyev, sire of 111 stakes race winners, Alleged, and Miswaki. In 2004 Jones sold Walmac to Walmac Stud Management LLC, a joint venture between his son John T. L. Jones III and Robert B. Trussell Jr. Trussell was director of sales and research at Gainesway Farm (see *Mile 6.2*) from 1979 to 1985 and the founder and CEO of Lexington-based Tempur-Pedic International, a mattress and pillow manufacturing company.[3]

Mile 5.4–6.1 The C. V. Whitney Farm (now part of the adjacent Gainesway Farm) begins at the corner of Paris Pike and Johnston Road. Because the main house, Maple Hill, faces Bryan Station Road roughly one mile to the east, this is in effect the farm's back boundary. The Whitney connection to this property began in 1914 when Harry Payne Whitney bought land from the James Ben Ali Haggin estate and moved his stable of horses here from a farm in New Jersey.[4] H. P. Whitney was the son of William C. Whitney of New York, whose considerable fortune was based on control of the New York City rail and trolley car systems.[5] The Whitney stable was one of the most successful in American Thoroughbred racing history. The 1915 Kentucky Derby winner, Regret, was bred by H. P. Whitney and was the first filly to win this major stakes race. Whitney won the Derby for a second time in 1927 with the colt Whiskery.

When Harry Payne Whitney died in 1930, his son, Cornelius Vanderbilt Whitney, inherited some $20 million and the Whitney farm. In addition to polo and Thoroughbred breeding and racing, C. V. Whitney's interests included a 1927 partnership that founded Pan American World Airways, production of Hollywood films—*Gone with the Wind* among them—large lumber holdings in New York's Adirondacks, and a mining operation in Manitoba. By 1933 the C. V. Whitney stable had completed a four-year run as the leading Thoroughbred racing operation in the country, during which sixty-two of his horses won 136 races and over $240,000 in prize money.[6]

The C. V. Whitney Farm home, Maple Hill, was an eighteenth-century farmhouse that Whitney and his wife, Marylou, refurbished and expanded. The property encompassed prime pastureland, a section of North Elkhorn Creek, a one-mile training track, numerous barns and outbuildings—including one of James Ben Ali Haggin's twelve-sided yearling barns—a horse cemetery, and eleven matching employee houses that lined Johnston Road, two of which still stand. In 1965 Whitney sold a five-hundred-acre parcel to his neighbor John Gaines. By 1975 Whitney had bred more than 150 stakes-winning horses, more than any other stable in the country. Whitney was a philanthropist, donating funds to Sayre School in Lexington for a new gymnasium and elementary building in the 1960s and 1970s. He died at Saratoga Springs, New York, in 1992 at age ninety-three, leaving to his wife an estate estimated at $100 million.[7] In 1997 the South African Graham Beck, owner of the adjoining Gainesway Farm, bought some 420 acres of the Whitney farm, leaving Marylou Whitney with about 145 acres. (See *Mile 6.2.*) In 2004 her horse Birdstone won the Belmont Stakes in New York, beating Smarty Jones, the national favorite. Smarty Jones had already won the Kentucky Derby and the Preakness Stakes that year; had he prevailed in the Belmont Stakes, he would have also won the Triple Crown, one of the most difficult challenges in sports.

Rock Fences

Along this section of Paris Pike vestiges of nineteenth- and early twentieth-century rock fences line one or both sides of the road. Masons began building dry-laid (without mortar) rock fences in central Kentucky as early as the 1790s, although the peak fence construction period was probably from the 1830s to the mid-1860s. Most mid-nineteenth-century rock fences were built by immigrant Irish stonemasons following Celtic masonry designs and traditions that are two or more millennia old. By about 1920 hundreds of miles of rock fence enclosed fields and farmsteads and lined roads across the Kentucky Bluegrass Region, but especially in the twelve counties that constitute the Inner Bluegrass subregion that centers on Lexington. Irish rock masons often worked under contract with area farmers and were generally paid three dollars or less per rod (sixteen and one-half feet) of finished fence. Construction included quarrying the building stones from limestone bedrock, hauling rocks to the building site, and erecting the fence.

Initially built to comply with Kentucky's trespass law, which required farmers to fence in their valued crop fields, the typical rock fence was twenty-four to thirty-two inches wide at the base, tapering to eighteen to twenty inches in width at the top horizontal course. In cross section the fence had a basic form: large foundation rocks laid below the frost line in a shallow trench; building rocks, which formed the body of the fence; through rocks, which were long enough to be laid entirely across or through the fence; a cap course across the top that, together with the through rocks, held the fence together. A top or copping course of rocks set vertically on edge and angled downhill added height and structural integrity.

Many different limestone formations underlie the Inner Bluegrass counties and can be readily quarried at the surface, especially on side hills and creek banks. Most Inner Bluegrass limestones are horizontally bedded—excepting those exposed at major faults—and each bed is only a few inches thick. Once the rocks are quarried and broken into manageable pieces, their flat sides made them nearly ideal building material. Masons readily laid the limestone in horizontal courses much as one would build a coursed brick wall.

To quarry building rock, masons first removed topsoil to expose a rock bed. They then drilled a line of boreholes an inch or so in diameter using hand-held iron drills. Wedges placed into the boreholes, when hit with a sledgehammer, broke the rock into manageable pieces. Alternatively, the boreholes might be filled with black powder that, when ignited, produced an explosion that lifted the rock without shattering it into fragments. If masons quarried stone in the winter they might fill their boreholes with water, which would freeze and expand and thus split the rock. Masons worked or "dressed" most rocks with a stone hammer only minimally before placing them into the fence. They carefully packed the open void in the center of the fence with small rocks, or spalls. The completed fence stood about five or five and one-half feet high and was held together by weight and friction. These non-mortared, dry-laid fences were superior to later structures that were often built with cement mortar. Rainwater ran off or through the dry-laid fence, providing no reservoir of moisture that could freeze and expand in cold weather.

On some large farms Irish masons were assisted by farm slaves who learned the Celtic tradition of the rock-fence craft. With emancipation after the Civil War, former slaves who had learned masonry skills often formed their own masonry companies and continued building fences and other dry-laid rock structures such as building foundations and chimneys.[8]

Macadam road-building and rock-fence construction occurred in tandem on some sections of the Maysville Road. The Bourbon County road section, for example was constructed by the Woods and Cain Company in the 1870s. Edmond P. Woods was an apprentice stonemason in County Limerick, Ireland, and moved to America in 1846 or 1847 and eventually made his way to Paris, Kentucky. His daughter married John H. Cain, also an Irish immigrant who migrated in 1877. Woods and Cain formed a construction partnership for road and fence building and won a contract to build the Bourbon County section of the Maysville Road. The company employed hundreds of men, some of them African Americans.[9]

From the Depression of the 1930s through the present day, many more old rock fences have been removed than new ones built. Fences come down when engineers widen roads, when farmers enlarge fields, or when tree seeds sprout along a fence line and eventually grow to a size sufficient to push the fence over. Though a full rock-fence census has never been undertaken, it is likely that fewer than 10 percent of the fences that once lined Bluegrass roads and field boundaries still stand. Each remaining yard of old rock fence is a prized historic reminder of the application of an ancient craft and of the masons who contributed their labor and knowledge to make a living for themselves and their families. This is why preserving the fences that lined the old Paris Pike was so important, and one of the reasons the design of the new highway has been so aesthetically and culturally successful.

The original Paris Pike rock fences represented a broad range of designs and building techniques. Some farms retained nineteenth-century Irish-built fences; others built new road frontage fences from the 1870s through the 1920s and 1930s using traditional dry-laid or "new" mortared-fence designs. In designing the new Paris Pike Parkway, landscape architects and engineers paid particular attention to preserving historic landscapes and viewsheds (environmental elements visible from a given point), including realigning highway lanes so that some old roadside rock fences would stand in the median, rather than be torn down. Fences that could not be saved were carefully removed and rebuilt. Local masons trained by Dry Stone Conservancy master masons built several miles of new rock fence on both sides of the new road, and in some cases even re-created mortared fences.

The new highway little resembles the straight, old, shoulderless road built atop the narrow nineteenth-century turnpike. The parkway's graceful, terrain-following alignment is flanked by old and new fences, historic buildings, and pastures punctuated by groves of ancient trees that together make up one of America's most beautiful roadways.[10]

Mile 6.2 Gainesway Farm, on the right, was owned by Graham Beck of South Africa and managed by his son, Antony. This is Kentucky's third Gainesway Farm. Clarence F. Gaines established the first Gainesway Farm on 350 acres south of Lexington on Tates Creek Pike in 1944. Gaines, originator of Gaines Dog Food, had been raising Standardbred horses (trotters and pacers) at his home in Sherburne, New York, but decided that "Kentucky offered better soil, climate, and atmosphere" for his horses.[11] For eight years Gainesway Farm was the nation's leading Standardbred market breeder.[12] In the late 1950s Gaines's son, John R. Gaines, moved to Kentucky and helped his father develop Gainesway into a new subdivision, and by the early 1960s he had established his own farm, the second Gainesway, on the historic Keene property adjacent to Keeneland Race Course on Versailles Road west of Lexington. John Gaines initially raised both Standardbred and Thoroughbred horses. Planning to expand his Thoroughbred operation, he bought thirty broodmares and five hundred acres of prime land along the Paris Pike section of the Maysville Road from C. V. Whitney in 1965. In partnership with John Hanes and John Olin, Gaines acquired the champion Thoroughbred colt Bold Bidder and retired the horse from racing to stand at stud at Gainesway. Bold Bidder sired Cannonade, winner of the 1974 Kentucky Derby. That same year Gaines moved his breeding and racing operation to the third Gainesway Farm at the Paris Pike location. Bold Bidder also sired Spectacular Bid, winner of the 1979 Kentucky Derby.

Gaines was an innovator in racing and strong advocate for higher education. In 1970 Kentucky's governor named him to a committee that planned the nation's first park devoted to horses, which today is the Kentucky Horse Park on Iron Works Pike at I-75. Gaines was elected to the Kentucky Horse Council in 1974, and in the early 1980s he developed the idea for a multirace, multimillion dollar racing series that became the Breeder's Cup. He donated $500,000 to endow the University of Kentucky Gaines Center for Undergraduate Studies in 1984.

On his farm Gaines developed a new concept in stallion-barn construction. His cluster of eight, four-stallion barns won an Honor Award from the American Institute of Architects in 1984 for excellence in design.[13] In 1989 Gaines sold Gainesway for $7.5 million to Renwick PLC, a British-based company owned by Graham J. Beck, a leading South African horse breeder who also had interests in winemaking, shipbuilding, and coal mining.[14] Later that year, Beck bought the 600-acre Greentree Farm, which adjoined Gainesway on the northeast, for $5.4 million. This, together with the 420-acre C. V. Whitney farm that he bought in 1997, gave Beck most of the farmland in the rectangle delimited by Paris Pike, Bryan Station Road, Muir Station Road, and Johnston Road, some 2,000 acres in all.[15]

BLUEGRASS PARKLAND

Mile 6.3 Two driveway entrances on the left provide access to Elmendorf Farm. For those traveling the Paris Pike–Maysville Road for the first time, it should now be clear, after the last two miles, that this is a remarkable landscape, a place that is radically different from any other rural countryside in America—indeed, the world. If the Inner Bluegrass has a heartland or an essence, this is it. The defining physical attributes of this area were outlined in Part II. Here one can begin to see how individuals, often people of great wealth, have added material artifacts to the topographic surface—houses, barns, fences, and the like—to create an archetypal landscape of horse and cattle farms. The Paris Pike transect represents a small segment of this landscape; nevertheless, one can sense the aesthetic qualities that reside in thousands of acres of bluegrass pastures and groves of venerable trees, punctuated by clusters of extraordinary farm buildings. Grazing livestock and farm mowers maintain the pastures and groves. In concert, the verdure of grass and trees form a regional-scale, English-style parkland—that is, a wooded pasture grazed by animals.[16] Whether farmers here have consciously followed the landscape design principles developed by classic English park designers such as "Capability" Brown and Humphry Repton or their own tastes, their judicious enhancement of the region's natural environment has transformed vast tracts of countryside into visually stunning parkland.

But this is not a simple landscape. Though agrarian, it is a very complicated place that reflects the efforts of many contributors applying different technologies, financed by monies produced by local and international businesses, and directed by ideas that span almost two centuries and several continents. Here one encounters two general types of farms. One is usually owner-occupied, is of moderate size, and is a working farm producing feeder cattle, corn and fodder crops, and, at least historically, burley tobacco. Houses, barns, and outbuildings may be historic and vernacular, but they are usually functional and scaled according to practical needs.

The second is the gentleman farm, which is often owned by someone whose considerable wealth springs from a source other than farming. Some owners are residents; others are absentees who may visit their farms only a few weeks of the year—during the Kentucky Derby in May, or for the horse sales at the Keeneland or Fasig-Tipton auctions. Farm owners may relegate day-to-day farming operations to a manager and staff. This kind of farm may be moderate in size or very large. It probably produces blooded horses—Thoroughbreds, Standardbreds, or Saddlebreds—and purebred cattle. Architects have designed the specialized farm buildings. Large homes, some historic, most constructed with expensive and exotic materials, display period architectural styles. Horse barns are models of carefully considered design—often paneled in hardwoods with brass fixtures. Fields and grounds are divided into pastures and paddocks dedicated to the exclusive use of stallions or mares or yearlings. This farm landscape is carefully considered and manipulated to be functional and efficient, and it is designed by landscape architects to exude aesthetic dignity. Maintenance is intensive. Serpentine driveways and fences measured in miles follow the land's contours, largely avoiding regimenting grids. Asphalt drives obviate muddy tires in foul weather. Asphalt-based black paint lends longevity to oak-planked fences. White paint turns the same fence into an exclamation of affluence when it encompasses a closely cropped emerald greensward. The four-plank black or white painted fence is nearly ubiquitous here and is synonymous with the image of gentleman farms. Such fences, while both functional and aesthetic, are more economical to build than modern rock fences. A wooden fence, constructed new with one coat of paint, costs about $26,000 per mile. Some farms have more than ten miles of fence. The symbolic representation captured by the combination of buildings, fences, and wooded pastures here is not far removed in suggested meaning from the grand houses built along North Limestone in Lexington in the early nineteenth century.

The Inner Bluegrass country has been the epitome of the gentleman farm landscape in America for nearly two centuries. It is clustered in a broad, multicounty arc to the west, north, and east of Lexington and includes important extensions toward Danville, Harrodsburg, Frankfort, and Cynthiana. Blooded racehorses came into Kentucky with eighteenth-century settlers from Virginia and Maryland. Henry Clay and his farm, Ashland, serve as exemplars of the process of gentleman farm genesis. Clay moved to Lexington from Virginia in 1797 to establish a law practice. He served as a U.S. senator and secretary of State. His farm on Lexington's south side along Richmond Road (later an extension of South Main Street) was his avid hobby, and he embraced the most progressive agronomic methods of the day to produce superior crops and livestock.[17] Clay was a pioneer in importing high-quality livestock—horses, cattle, and sheep—from Europe. A successful attorney and a revered public servant, Henry Clay embraced the science, economy, and aesthetic of his farm, and he enunciated what he saw as a clear difference between vocational yeoman farming and avocational gentleman farming. "There is a great difference," he said "between a farm employed in raising dead produce for market, and one which is applied, as mine is, to the rearing of all kinds of live stock. I have the Maltese ass, the Arabian horse, the merino and Saxe merino sheep, the English Hereford and Durham cattle, the goat, the mule, and the hog. The progress of these animals from their infancy to maturity, presents a constantly-varying subject of interest, and I never go out of my house, without meeting with some of them to engage agreeably my attention."[18] In 1831 Clay built at Ashland one of the first private racetracks in the state. He and many others who shared his interests and his means provided the impetus for horse breeding and racing in central Kentucky and the initial model for the gentleman farm landscape.[19] Succeeding generations have extended and elaborated the theme.

ELMENDORF

A singular example of how the concept and scale of the gentleman farm could be updated and articulated occurred here at Elmendorf Farm in the late nineteenth and early twentieth centuries. A local horseman, Daniel Swigert, developed Elmendorf into a "splendid estate" in the 1880s and sold it to C. J. Enright of Louisville in 1891. It was, the editor of the *Livestock Record* wrote,

> probably the most perfectly equipped breeding farm in Kentucky. It contains 545 acres of the richest and most superb bluegrass land. The stabling is first class and very expensive, including 150 loose boxes and stables for stallions, brood mares, yearlings, and livestock of all kind. The residence is one of the best and most desirable in the state. It has every modern convenience, gas, water works, etc. It is excellently watered by a beautiful running stream [North Elkhorn Creek] and has an abundance of lofty shade trees. Mr. Enright . . . will import a stallion from England and stock the farm thoroughly with the best brood mares obtainable. The price paid was $65,000.[20]

Enright sold Elmendorf by public auction in Westchester, New York, in 1897. The *Thoroughbred Record* described the farm: "Elmendorf is an ideal gentleman's country residence, with all the conveniences of a city house."[21] The farm's new owner was James Ben Ali Haggin; the price for the 545-acre property was one hundred dollars an acre.[22]

Haggin lived in California and New York, but his paternal grandfather had been a pioneer at Harrodsburg, Kentucky, in 1775. His father practiced law in Mercer County and married the daughter of a Turkish physician, Ibrahim Ben Ali. As a young man Haggin attended Centre College in Danville, Kentucky, and worked in his father's law office. By 1840 he had been admitted to the Kentucky bar and begun a legal practice in Shelbyville. With the discovery of gold in California in 1848, Haggin and his law partner, Lloyd Tevis, moved to Sacramento, where they opened a practice.[23]

Over the next five decades, not only was James Ben Ali Haggin a successful California attorney, but he also invested in Central Valley farmland, acquiring 400,000 acres on which he raised cattle, sheep, and Thoroughbred horses. He bought stock in silver, gold, and copper mines—Homestake in South Dakota's Black Hills and Anaconda at

James Ben Ali Haggin's New York architects completed the design and construction of his Green Hills mansion at Elmendorf Farm in 1902. Built in a subdued Beaux-Arts style, the structure nevertheless exudes classical Greek and Roman design elements. Joseph E. Widener razed the building in 1929, leaving only the front marble step ensemble of Corinthian columns and rampant lion statues to stand alone in a horse pasture. (Courtesy of the University of Kentucky Library Special Collections)

Butte, Montana, among them—and participated in numerous other business enterprises. He also bought Thoroughbreds from Kentucky farms, including Elmendorf, which he shipped to his California ranch for training. In 1886 his horse Ben Ali won the Kentucky Derby.

Upon acquiring Elmendorf Farm in 1897, Haggin began to move his interests from California to Kentucky and New York City. That same year, three years after the death of his first wife, Haggin married his twenty-eight-year-old niece, Margaret Pearl Voorhies of Versailles.[24] Though the C. J. Enright house on Elmendorf Farm was regarded as one of the best in the state, Haggin hired the New York architects H. I. Copeland, E. S. Hall, Latham Mollen, and J. L. Wells to design and build a $300,000 mansion that Margaret Haggin called Green Hills. Built of marble and limestone probably supplied by Charles McDonald of Covington, the home, which a Lexington newspaper dubbed the "Biltmore of Kentucky," stood embowered atop a low hill about one-half mile west of Paris Pike overlooking North Elkhorn Creek.[25] Haggin's architects moved the farm's entrance drive from Paris Pike southwest to Iron Works Pike, where a large gate and stone gatehouse formalized the entry.[26] A year after acquiring Elmendorf,

Haggin began to purchase adjoining properties that he integrated into one large farming unit, clearing away dozens of old tenant houses in the process. By 1900 he owned over 3,200 acres. His acquisitions continued, and by 1914 the property exceeded 8,000 acres. Haggin's Elmendorf extended from Bryan Station Road on the east to Russell Cave and Huffman Mill Pike on the west.[27] Though only a fraction of the size of his California farm, Elmendorf would have been equivalent in its dimensions to a large cattle ranch in west Texas or Wyoming. Considering that it encompassed more than twelve square miles, and given its placement on Kentucky's highly valued and incomparably fecund Inner Bluegrass land, Elmendorf's scale was Herculean.

In 1905 Haggin closed his Thoroughbred breeding and racing operation in California and moved some six hundred mares and stallions by train to Elmendorf.[28] He built a four-hundred-cow dairy on the east side of Paris Pike, where he filled a model stone barn with cows imported from the Isle of Jersey. His dairy marketed fresh Elmendorf milk and milk products in Lexington and Cincinnati.[29] So admired was Haggin's dairy that the Louisville & Nashville freight shipper's directory fervently exclaimed, "The dairy products from this farm are conceded to be the best that money, science and skill can produce—and there is not a more sanitary dairy farm in the world than the Elmendorf Farm."[30] Haggin, following the example of Henry Clay a century earlier, collected and bred some of the finest shorthorn beef cattle, sheep, and poultry in the country.[31] A private powerhouse electrified the farm; that building's shell still stands a few yards from Paris Pike, about a quarter mile northeast of Elkhorn Creek.[32] More than one thousand employees worked on the farm, many of them commuting from Lexington on the Kentucky Traction and Terminal Company's interurban railroad that ran beside Paris Pike. The stone waiting room building that served as a rail stop still stands along the Pike's southbound lanes in front of the farm. The Louisville & Nashville Railroad Company constructed a spur track into the farm from its Cincinnati line in 1904, giving the farm direct access to Paris Pike, the interurban rail, and the railroad. The rail spur allowed Haggin to board his private railroad car in New York and remain aboard until he arrived at Green Hills.[33]

Haggin's architects also designed many new farm buildings. Foundation and building stone came from a large quarry opened into North Elkhorn Creek's south bank. During Paris Pike's reconstruction in 2003, the entire quarry was filled in to accommodate the northbound lanes.[34] Haggin favored brick, stone, stucco, and tile or terracotta building materials. The Iron Works Pike gatehouse, the interurban line's waiting room, and some horse barns built from these materials still stand.[35] Haggin's architects also built experimental structures, including three twelve-sided barns.

Haggin died while at his summer home at Newport, Rhode Island, in September 1914. His great Elmendorf Farm was thereafter subdivided to become numerous new farms, each with its own character and equine heritage: Buckland, C. V. Whitney, Clovelly, Dixiana, Domino, Duntreath, Faraway, Gainesway, Greentree, Hagyard, Lann-Mark, Leatherwood, Man O' War, Mt. Brilliant, Normandy, Peckhamhurst, Spendthrift, Tree Haven, and Walmac.[36] A Philadelphia traction magnate, Joseph E. Widener, purchased the core Elmendorf farm and adjoining tracts totaling over 1,200 acres.[37] In the late 1920s Widener, preferring to live in another house on the farm, had

J. B. A. Haggin's Elmendorf Farm included property on both sides of the Paris Pike section of the Maysville Road. The Bluegrass Traction Company's interurban line paralleled the road on the left, and Haggin's architects designed a stone waiting room for placement at trackside. Many of Haggin's farm employees lived in Lexington and commuted to their jobs via the interurban. Haggin also commissioned the Louisville & Nashville Railroad to build a siding that connected the rail line on the farm's east side to the interurban tracks near the waiting room. The interurban tracks are gone, but the stone waiting room still stands beside the southbound lanes of the Paris Pike parkway. (Courtesy of the University of Kentucky Library Special Collections)

Haggin's Green Hills mansion torn down to avoid paying taxes on it, leaving only the marble entry steps, Greek Revival Corinthian columns, and lion statues that still stand in a pasture at the original building site. Widener hired the Philadelphia architect Horace Trumbauer to design and build new barns on the property. Many of these distinctive structures still stand on the adjoining Clovelly and Normandy farms. One of them, the 1928 training barn, included two rows of twenty-one stalls flanking a courtyard. The connecting stall rows were enclosed within an oval one-sixth-mile training track for use in inclement weather. Nearby, laborers built a full, one-mile training track with a starting chute.[38]

James Ben Ali Haggin's tenure in central Kentucky punctuated the Inner Bluegrass region's development as the nation's archetypal horse farm landscape. For more than a century before Haggin's assembly and transformation of the Elmendorf property began, people of financial means had established showplace farms and bred racehorses here. Many of them adapted to the Bluegrass environment farm design borrowed from English country estates. Buildings designed by Haggin's architects were either out of scale or so idiosyncratic in plan or appearance that they were copied by few other farms. The patrons who succeeded him, especially Joseph Widener and Horace Trumbauer, built structures that resonated with other farm owners, who soon copied them on their own properties. Trumbauer's wooden horse barns blended ideas from English country estate buildings such as Paladian, or arched windows, roofs punctuated by cupolas and dormers, and cross-braced Dutch doors. Haggin's preferred massive Victorian proportions gave way to a refined functionality in building form. New designs combined aesthetic proportions and shapes with a pragmatic appreciation for animal health and well-being by the control of natural light and airflow through the building. The new barns could be further augmented by contrasting paint color schemes that in turn became distinctive visual signatures for each farm.[39] Widener directed that his barns be painted white and dark green, a combination also adopted at neighboring Domino and Dixiana farms. Across Paris Pike to the east, C. V. Whitney adopted yellow and brown for his farm's barns and employee houses.

Maxwell Gluck bought Elmendorf Farm in 1952 and won national titles as the leading Thoroughbred farm owner in 1977 and 1981, and the leading Thoroughbred breeder in 1973, 1981, and 1982. Gluck was born in Texas in 1899 and moved to New York City when he was twenty. He founded the Darling Stores, a nationwide chain of 150 women's clothing stores. In 1957 President Dwight Eisenhower appointed Gluck ambassador to Ceylon, now Sri Lanka, a position that he held for a year before resigning. In 1983 Gluck contributed $3 million to the University of Kentucky to establish an equine research center.[40] Today that center stands on the university campus, along South Limestone.

After Gluck's death in 1984, Jack Kent Cooke bought the farm for $43 million. Cooke had investments in radio and television and was the majority owner of the Washington Redskins professional football team for twenty-three years. When Cooke died in 1997, his net worth was estimated at $825 million.[41] Elmendorf was subsequently sold, to a Louisville insurance executive, Dinwiddie Lampton Jr. Lampton had long-term interests in steeplechase, polo, and collecting antique horse-drawn carriages. He died in 2008.

Mile 6.4 North Elkhorn Creek. U.S. 68 now crosses this stream on two new bridges. At the point where the northbound lanes approach the creek, they occupy the old Elmendorf Farm quarry floor.

Mile 7.0 Paris Pike's northbound lanes track along the original turnpike, and nineteenth-century dry-laid stone fences line the roadside.

Mile 7.4 Greentree Farm is on the right. The rose-colored brick main house presents a large, two-story, Corinthian-columned portico to Paris Pike. Thomas Hughes built the house in the 1850s and named it Fairlawn.[42] Although now part of Gainesway Farm, Greentree was a key part of the James Ben Ali Haggin–Whitney farm for more than a century. In 1925 William Payne Whitney and his wife, Helen Hay Whitney, bought land here from the Haggin estate to establish a stud farm. Whitney's financial interests included oil, tobacco manufacturing, and banking. When he died in 1927, Helen Whitney and their two children, John Hay (Jock) Whitney and Joan Whitney Payson, continued the farm's Thoroughbred business.

Joan Payson was part owner of the New York Giants baseball team and later was cofounder and owner of the New York Mets. Her philanthropy earned her an honorary Doctor of Humane Letters degree from Hofstra College.[43] This branch of the Whitney family was nearly as successful in the Thoroughbred business as their first cousin, C. V. Whitney, whose farm was next door. Between 1931 and 1968, for example, Greentree Thoroughbreds won the Kentucky Derby twice (Twenty Grand, 1931, and Shut Out, 1942); the Preakness Stakes (Capot, 1949); and the Belmont Stakes four times (Twenty Grand, 1931, Shut Out, 1942, Capot, 1949, and Stage Door Johnny, 1968).[44] Joan Payson died in 1975, and her brother, Jock Whitney, died in 1982.

Muir Station Road intersects the Maysville Road on the right.

Mile 7.7 Just before the Hughes Lane intersection, the entrance to Normandy Farm opens onto the Paris Pike's southbound lanes on the left. This 260-acre property was part of James Ben Ali Haggin's Elmendorf and Joseph Widener's farm. The main house, a two-story, five-bay, brick structure, was built in 1804 by Abraham Bird. Called Kenney House, it faces Paris Pike at the end of a quarter-mile driveway.[45] E. Berry Ryan transferred his breeding, training, and racing operation here from a farm in Paoli, Pennsylvania, when he bought Normandy Farm from Widener's son Pete in 1950. Ryan's great-grandfather Thomas Fortune Ryan owned traction companies in New York and, together with George Widener, owned the Philadelphia trolley system.[46] The farm boarded about thirty broodmares, two-thirds of which belonged to the owners of top American and international stables, such as Paul Mellon's Rokeby Stables in Virginia. Ryan also raised registered Black Angus beef cattle.[47] He sold the farm in 1987.

The property still contains several Horace Trumbauer–designed barns, and it hosts two stunning horse-related artifacts from the early twentieth century, a horse cemetery and the Normandy Barn. Though picking the best Thoroughbred racehorse of the past century is a slippery and subjective matter, many would agree that Man O' War's record on the racetrack and the breeding barn place him at the top of the list. He was foaled at August Belmont's Nursery Stud on Georgetown Pike north of Lexington in 1917. During a comparatively short sixteen-month racing career that began in June 1919, Man O' War won twenty of twenty-one races while carrying weights of 130 pounds or more. His wins included the Preakness, Belmont, and Travers stakes races. As a stud he sired sixty-four stakes winners, including the 1937 Triple Crown winner, War Admiral. Here, at the Normandy Farm cemetery, Man O' War's sire, Fair Play, and dam, Mahubah, are buried side by side, in the shadow of a life-size bronze statue of Fair Play.

Joseph Widener commissioned the L-shaped Normandy Barn in 1927. The barn stands just northwest of the cemetery and was patterned after a barn that stood on a farm that Widener owned in Normandy, France, the Haras du Mesnil. Each section has six stalls, and a clock tower rises from the crux of the L. The slate roof, punctuated by gable-end jerkinheads, dormer windows, and cupolas, overhangs the stall doors in a forebay that provides shelter from the elements. The clockworks and other fixtures are said to have been removed from the original barn when France was being invaded by Germany in World War I. Metal ornaments grace the roof—birds, cats, and other creatures, which, according to rural French superstition, were supposed to frighten off evil spirits. The barn stands near the back of the farm about one-quarter mile behind the house; it is in good repair and remains one of the architectural gems of the Bluegrass gentleman farm landscape.[48]

Throughout this section of Paris Pike, the original stone farm entrances and some of the rock fences that once fronted the road now stand in the median between the north- and southbound lanes.

Mile 8.1 Hughes Lane is on the left. This road's first mile includes two ninety-degree turns that followed historic metes and bounds property boundaries. In some sections the road is deeply entrenched, which suggests its great age as an old farm service road. The land at the intersection of Hughes Lane and Paris Pike is currently open pasture and is part of Hagyard Farm. A turnpike tollhouse operated at this corner by 1861, or perhaps even earlier. R. P. Kenney, a retired farmer who owned several land parcels along the road, owned the land surrounding the tollhouse. By 1877 a small roadside community had developed here. O. O'Neal and J. Anderson lived in houses that triangulated with the tollhouse. The tollgate keeper may have been Z. T. Levi, and Jefferson Harp lived nearby. The principal landowners adjacent to the tollhouse were J. T. Hughes, who raised fine coach horses at his Elton Stock Farm, and the Harp family. Both the Hughes and Kenney farms had tracks for horse training and racing. W. M. Kenney, son of R. P. Kenney, owned land in the area and raised Alderney cattle, Southdown and Cotswold sheep, and trotting horses. The Alderney cow was a native of the English Channel islands, Guernsey, Jersey, and Alderney, and was favored by the English gentry for its rich milk and yellow cream. Bluegrass farmers, many of whom were Anglophiles at heart, had long imported blooded livestock from England, Scotland, and Ireland, and in the late nineteenth century Alderney cattle began to arrive in America.[49]

By the 1880s several African American families lived in the area and worked on the large farms nearby. The presence of black farm laborers here underscores the dominance of blacks in agricultural jobs across the region, and particularly in the developing Thoroughbred horse industry after the Civil War. As the century drew to a close, however, Jim Crow laws and racist attitudes combined to exclude blacks from such positions as jockey and horse trainer. By the 1870s large stock farms lined many of the region's major thoroughfares, such as Paris Pike, and census information chronicles the presence of the people who provided the labor that ensured ongoing farm operations. The farmhands and their families, many of whom were African American, often lived in houses provided by their employers, although some managed to purchase small land parcels on which to build a house.

The small community here followed this pattern. Sometime before 1880, a black family acquired five acres next to the tollhouse, and the land continued to pass from one family descendent to another across four generations. The community remained a small black enclave occupied by related families through the first quarter of the

Nineteenth-century Bluegrass country roads were often built and maintained by the people whose property abutted the routeway. Local turnpike companies built the longer roads; shorter ones such as Hughes Lane served a limited number of farms and were semiprivate. Hughes Lane linked sections of Elmendorf and adjoining farms to Paris Pike. The road's right-angle turns suggest that it has long followed property boundaries. The large cherry, hackberry, and locust trees growing out of its banks testify to the entrenched road's considerable age.

twentieth century. By 1960, when Charles and Katherine Hagyard bought the property for their horse farm, the houses were derelict and had been vacant for a number of years. Though this community maintained its roadside presence for a half century—1880 to about 1930—its landscape imprint was eventually engulfed and then obliterated by expanding neighboring farms, a process repeated all along this section of Paris Pike. Gone too is the human diversity, people of different races and classes, people who labored in fields, tended livestock, cooked and cleaned, and provided other necessary work that allowed the farms to become thriving businesses.

Mile 8.3 Clovelly Farm has two noncontiguous sections. The larger, 420-acre farm stands along Hughes Lane and was owned by Robin F. Scully of Beatrice, Nebraska. A 74-acre section on the right along Paris Pike became part of the farm in the 1960s. Scully's family was in the oil business, and his grandfather acquired land in the Midwest and Great Plains that was later developed by transcontinental railroad companies. Scully owned 250,000 acres in Nebraska at one time. Clovelly Farm, under his ownership, was a Thoroughbred, beef cattle, and tobacco farm.[50] The farm specialized in boarding foreign mares from Canada, Ireland, England, France, and Switzerland to be bred to Kentucky stallions. All foaling mares were kept at the Paris Pike property. Farmworkers trained yearlings at the Hughes Lane farm; their duties included workouts on Joseph Widener's old one-mile training track.[51]

In 2011 the Kentucky Equine Education Project estimated the state's horse population at about 320,000. Horses are now the state's top agricultural cash product, surpassing tobacco. Considering the 128,800 people employed in the horse industry as farm managers, trainers, veterinarians, farmworkers, racetrack workers, publishers, and so on, the total economic impact of the horse economy is an estimated $4 billion.[52]

For more than two centuries, horse breeding and racing have been Kentucky's signature industry. Farming on this scale, especially for Thoroughbred horses, can easily require substantially larger volumes of investment capital than can be produced by the farming process. This demand has been met by a sustaining flow of wealth into the Bluegrass Region from national and international sources, even during the Great Depression of the 1930s. Ensconced on farms across the Bluegrass countryside is the world's most coveted Thoroughbred gene pool, the primary reason that the area remains the world's most important focus of Thoroughbred breeding and training. The present horse farm landscape, as sampled along this Paris Pike transect, is directly linked to historical precedents, the product of two centuries of evolving horse production practices and marketing concerns that link the aesthetics of style and taste to the image of quality horses. The horse farm landscape is generally not a place of architectural flamboyance, although homes and barns can be outsize and expensive. Rather, structural design is largely understated and conscious of prototypes and landscape context. These qualities are widely admired and help account for this region's becoming the archetypal model nationally for gentleman horse farm landscapes.[53]

This region possesses unique environmental attributes found nowhere else in the nation, and its two-hundred-year relationship with quality livestock farming has produced an unparalleled linkage among business, farm residence, and landscape. Nevertheless, large sections of the region, especially areas close to rapidly growing urban places and interstate highway corridors, are under pressure from residential and commercial development. In June 2005 the World Monuments Fund named the Bluegrass cultural landscape to its 2006 watch list of the world's most endangered sites. The WMF is the only international organization devoted to onsite conservation of irreplaceable historic sites worldwide. The fund's citation identified the Inner Bluegrass Region as one of North America's most distinctive cultural and agricultural landscapes.

Although Thoroughbred horse farms dominate the landscape between Lexington and Paris, they are a relatively late development, dating from the late nineteenth to early twentieth centuries, when breeding and racing Thoroughbred horses became an industry in its own right and not just a pastime for wealthy gentlemen. The historical landscape along the Lexington-Maysville Turnpike before the modern horse-farm era looked very different from the current scene. Pre–Civil War maps record a turnpike corridor that included tollhouses, brick kilns, blacksmith shops, schools, small crossroads communities, saw- and gristmills, and modest farmhouses. Though different in their building types and functions, they accorded with each other in their preferred orientation to the road. Very few of these places remain intact and in most cases represent a lost landscape that exists only as archaeological sites.[54]

One example of the nineteenth-century roadside farms along this section belonged to John Armstrong, whose land is now occupied by Clovelly Farm. Archival research and field excavations conducted in advance of the site's destruction by the construction of the Paris Pike's new northeast-bound lanes revealed that John Armstrong, an Irishman, lived at the site from 1846 until 1875 with his second wife, Mary, their daughter, Sarah, and several slaves, servants, boarders, and relatives. Armstrong had immigrated to the United States sometime between 1821 and 1828 and lived in New York and Pennsylvania before coming to Kentucky. He bought forty-four acres from Preston Cummins, who was living in a house on the property at the time. Armstrong's house was probably a frame structure built before turnpike construction—its foundation was not aligned with the road. Armstrong farmed his land, but he had other business dealings that may have been equally important to his income. In 1850 four Irishmen—including one with his Irish wife—lived with the Armstrongs. Two of the men were "McAdamizers" and two were laborers—all four undoubtedly worked on the various local roads, surfacing them with broken stone according to the McAdam technology of the period. The Irish connections were significant; Irishmen frequently worked on road crews as masons, quarrymen, rock breakers, and other difficult occupations involved in road building. Armstrong received payment for providing room and board, and he may have had other connections to the turnpike business.

John Armstrong was a farmer even though he had only forty-four acres of farm property. His principal products were hogs, corn, and wheat. Although shorthorn cattle production was popular and profitable in nineteenth-century Kentucky, a shortage of land for pasture and hay production probably discouraged Armstrong from becoming heavily involved in raising cattle. Nor was he a large slave owner, although he generally had a few slaves, both house servants and farm laborers. The size of his farm and its modest yearly agricultural output places Armstrong in the category of a small-scale farmer, but he also owned a carriage—a relatively expensive conveyance that was subject to local taxes—railroad stock, and urban property in Paris, all clues to a more nuanced business life and a more affluent position than that of a small-scale farmer. His wife also contributed to the family income as a "tailoress" who made men's suits, overcoats, and other garments that required talents more specialized than simply sewing. Artifacts collected during site excavations here also indicate that the family was middle-class in social position—buying more expensive cuts of meat, particularly beef, from local butchers rather than relying solely on butchering meat animals raised on their farm; using decorated tablewares, which were more expensive than plain ones; and dressing stylishly. Living on the major improved road between two thriving towns was a distinct advantage for the Armstrongs, giving them ready access to commercial and mercantile markets, local news via the stagecoaches that daily passed by—and perhaps sometimes stopped to water their horses—and facilitating their involvement in investment opportunities that increased their prosperity.[55]

Mile 8.6 Now enlarged and converted into an office for a horse farm, the core of the building on the left, or north, side of the road here is a one-room brick schoolhouse. A school stood near this site as early as 1861 and may have originated as a private academy that was later absorbed into the public school system. The current building once housed school number 40 of the Common School District, which was established sometime before 1898 on land belonging to David Harp. After Harp's death, his daughter Ada inherited the half-acre tract on which the school stood and in August 1898 conveyed it to the school trustees, H. T. Muir, J. H. Gaines, and W. L. Spears.[56]

One-room schoolhouses became the norm in Kentucky after the legislature passed the first act to establish a public educational system in 1838. Schools were racially segregated until the mid-twentieth century, and many children did not attend school beyond the fifth grade. Yearly school terms were only three months long in the early years, and they were not extended to nine months until much later in the nineteenth century. School attendance was not compulsory by law until 1896, but even with the law in place attendance was difficult to enforce. A wood-burning stove provided heat in the winter; outdoor privies substituted for indoor plumbing all year round. School supplies were limited: chalk and blackboard, wall chart or map, and a dictionary. Students often provided their own textbooks. Nineteenth-century Kentucky elementary students studied "the three R's" (reading, 'riting, and 'rithmetic), geography, and American history. Secondary grades added spelling, grammar, composition, and health. One of the most popular book series used in Kentucky schools were the *McGuffey Eclectic Readers* compiled by William Holmes McGuffey, Presbyterian minister and University of Virginia professor. McGuffey produced his first reader in 1836 and over the next two decades developed a series of six readers and a spelling book. The series dominated the American textbook market until the 1920s and was very influential in the nation's primary and secondary education systems. McGuffey was a professor of moral philosophy, and his textbooks were strongly moralistic in tone and promoted traditional values such as honesty, truthfulness, promptness, goodness, and kindness. The term *eclectic* in the book's titles referred to McGuffey's practice of including a wide selection of readings by important authors in American and British literature, including poetry by Wordsworth, Byron, Milton, Poe, and Shakespeare, and prose by Macaulay, Thackeray, James Fennimore Cooper, Washington Irving, and Samuel Johnson. The books had a pronounced influence on American literary taste.[57]

Mile 8.9 Rosemont Farm is on the left.

Mile 9.1 Antioch Christian Church is on the right.

Mile 9.2 The Fayette County–Bourbon County boundary. Bourbon County was the fifth county formed in what became the state of Kentucky; the name was chosen in honor of the royal Bourbon family of France. The Virginia legislature approved the county's formation in 1785; boundary delimitation and formal enactment occurred the following year. The land constituting Bourbon County was excised from Fayette County, and it originally covered a large part of northern and eastern Kentucky. Over time thirty-eight counties were formed, in like manner, from Bourbon's original territory. Residents established the county seat at Hopewell in 1789 and changed the name to Paris the following year. Today Paris lies in the center of the county, at the confluence of Stoner and Houston creeks, tributaries of the Licking River, which flows northwest to join the Ohio at Covington and Newport. Other small towns or crossroads hamlets in the county include Millersburg, North Middletown, Ruddles Mills, Little Rock, Clintonville, and Centerville. Paris and Millersburg are both on the Maysville Road.[58]

Mile 9.4 The junction of Houston-Antioch Road and the Maysville Road was once the site of Morelandsville, a crossroads community. William Moreland was an innkeeper, farmer, and entrepreneur who moved to the newly built Lexington-Maysville Turnpike in 1834. His first location had been along the original Limestone Trace, now Bryan Station Road. Moreland was plying his trade on the old trace as early as 1822, and his business, labeled as an "inn," was a prominent landmark by 1827.[59] During the 1820s he and a partner, John Strickler, also pursued mercantile interests in Paris. Moreland's move to the new turnpike was an astute business decision. The location permitted him to profit from the increased traffic along the turnpike; he provided a place for stagecoach drivers to water their horses, for stage passengers to refresh themselves, and for neighbors to receive their mail.

Moreland's inn was a "commodious brick building . . . so constructed and so located that it can be used either as a private residence or as a public hotel." The two-story structure had an ell on the north side that contained a dining room and bar, and a large dance floor upstairs.[60] The building stood at the end of a long circular drive on the road's north side, across from the Houston-Antioch Road junction, in association with quarters for slaves, stables, an icehouse, and tailor, saddler, and blacksmith shops. A large storehouse "for the sale of all kinds of Merchandize, to good and solvent customers," completed the business and residential building cluster. The inn served people who were wealthy enough to travel by stagecoach rather than drovers or wagoners, who stopped for the night at much humbler facilities. Stagecoach passengers were likely to stop at a tavern long enough to refresh themselves rather than staying overnight, although Moreland could accommodate a few overnight guests. In 1850 Moreland and his wife, Margaret, lived here with two young Moreland relatives (perhaps grandchildren). The family also boarded a young farmer, W. H. Clay; two merchants, Thomas C. Wood and John Rankin; a tailor named William Hulett (who was presumably plying his trade in the tailor's shop at the site); and a carpenter named Jeptha Searce.[61] A visitor at the inn was probably attended by one of the black servants, perhaps King, Miner, or John, while Ann and Milly cooked meals in the kitchen. Moreland supplied oats and hay for the horses, coffee for the teetotalers, and whiskey for those wishing to sample the locally distilled spirit. Moreland's obituary referred to him as an innkeeper, indicating that the terms *inn* and *hotel* were considered interchangeable by the 1850s.

Known as the Ten Mile House, given its distance from Lexington, Moreland's inn was the site of a "distressing stage accident" on August 20, 1838. A stagecoach containing nine passengers and an extra driver was leaving the property when the driver applied the whip with too much force, causing the horses to set off down the long driveway to the turnpike at top speed. As the horses attempted the acute angle from the driveway to the road, the coach was "upset with great violence, dashing the top into a thousand pieces." The horses ran off with the forewheels, leaving the coach body behind. Everyone on board was injured, some seriously, though no one was killed. Less than one month later, a race between the stages of the "Old Line" and the "Opposition Line" resulted in the Opposition coach's upsetting when the two collided here at Moreland's inn. Such stagecoach accidents were common; most were the result of driver recklessness.[62]

Ever the entrepreneur, Moreland also farmed, loaned money, and served as justice of the peace. He was a member of the Odd Fellows Lodge in Paris, and, a few years after his death in 1852, another lodge was organized and built near his tavern and named for him. He was clearly well connected with the county's social elite. Garrett Davis and John Giltner, two prominent citizens—one a politician and the other an important builder-architect—witnessed the writing of his will. Moreland was also a Freemason and was given a Masonic funeral at his burial in the Paris cemetery.

Moreland's estate included the furnishings and accoutrements of his inn and home. His belongings included eleven beds, some of which were probably used by regular boarders. His other furnishings included a pianoforte that he left to his daughter Mary Ann; a brass clock, a sugar desk (a commodity of sufficient value to warrant its own secure storage container), and a high-post bedstead, all evidence of a genteel social standing and better-than-average affluence. Abundant bed linens, dining tables, decanters and bottles, various side tables, kitchen items such as kettles, pots, ovens, coffee boilers, sausage cutters, and other cupboard ware, a dozen chairs, numerous knives and forks, and four barrels of soap collectively suggest that Moreland was a prosperous innkeeper.

Whatever the appearance of comfort, Moreland's prosperity ran largely on credit, and his estate settlement, while sufficient to pay all his debts, was a drawn-out process that left his four grown children with less than four hundred dollars each as an inheritance. Though he had substantial assets in land, slaves, personal belongings, and credit accounts owed him by other people, he also carried substantial debt. William Moreland's life and passing provides an example of how a nineteenth-century entrepreneur might have conducted his business and the effect that his death had on the local community. His creditors were his neighbors and, no doubt, his friends. His numerous debts varied from paltry sums of a few dollars to substantial amounts, several hundred dollars, owed to various individuals. His largest debt was over $2,000, which he owed the Fayette Circuit Court for a court case he lost (this debt would be roughly equivalent in purchasing power to about $48,000 today). As late as 1850, just two years before his death, Moreland took out a mortgage on his property.[63]

The sale of his farm, slaves, personal property, livestock, and crops, and the collection of the numerous amounts owed him on credit accounts and promissory notes, paid William Moreland's debts. His personal property brought $9,664.31 at auction; collected credit accounts amounted to $1,431.51; 113 acres of land brought $1,035.00 when purchased by Thomas C. Wood, one of the merchants living in Moreland's inn.[64]

His executor also sold the slaves that were not bequeathed to his heirs. These individuals included twenty-year-old Ann, twenty-seven-year-old John, and forty-year-old Miner, as well as Milly, who was an elderly woman, and King, whose age was not given. Ann and John were appraised at $700 and $900, respectively, while the values of the other slaves were much lower. Collectively, they brought $2,000. Milly was accorded no value, and she was not listed among the sales of the other slaves. She probably died during the settlement of the estate, as one of the bills filed with the county clerk was for a $7.00 "coffin for negro" filed by John Giltner. The buyers of the other slaves were not specified in the estate settlement documents, but their dispersal is a grim reminder of the personal effect that the death of a slave owner had on his slaves, particularly if they were members of the same family. Some of Moreland's loans were deemed "worth nothing," meaning that his debtors could not pay them back. In those cases, the estate was forced to write them off as uncollectible. Once everything that could be sold was converted into cash, the settlement of the estate's debts began. The settlement listed eighty-seven bills or debts that required payment, ranging from medical services and the price of his coffin—both expected debts after a death—to taxes due, attorney's fees, various "fee bills," notes, and accounts. The final estate settlement was filed with the county court on June 1, 1857, five years after William Moreland died.

Though his children had probably received some of their inheritance before their father's death, Moreland's estate settlement typifies a nineteenth-century economy that ran on credit, promissory notes, and mortgages in lieu of cash, specie being scarce and subject to wide variances in value at that time. Despite his outward image of prosperity, William Moreland did not accumulate a substantial amount of unencumbered wealth to pass on to his heirs, although at least his estate was sufficient to pay off his debts. With his death, his inn seems to have closed. The Moreland post office was eventually moved to nearby Hutchison, a small community associated with a railroad station. Thomas Wood sold the property a few years later to a local doctor, and the building became a private residence. It was torn down in 1913.[65] Even the nearby Odd Fellows Lodge named for William Moreland passed out of memory. The collection of buildings that Moreland once comprised is now a lost landscape; its extent and functions, its personal relationships and lives lived here, can only be inferred from historic documents. The Lexington-Maysville Road corridor is replete with such lost landscapes, represented today only by relict buildings, hints of building foundations, road realignments, tree clusters, volunteer clumps of daffodils or other garden flowers, and additional oddments that, by themselves, seem alien or out of context with the present scene. And, because principal roads such as this one were, and continue to be, points of conjunction between a region's peoples and their social, economic, and political institutions, the roadside represents an especially rich collection of diverse landscapes, lost or extant. William Moreland's community is also a vivid reminder that nineteenth-century road corridors could be vital umbilicals that nourished dynamic rural social collectivities and that the countryside should not be viewed solely as the reserve of farmers.

The modern-day road passes through classic Bluegrass parkland, an aesthetic admixture of mature trees with a grass understory. James Hall, traveling through the area in 1838, described the area:

> The woodlands are all inclosed; the underwood, and the useless trees are removed, while the valuable timber trees are left, standing sufficiently wide apart to admit the rays of the sun, and the free circulation of the air, between them. The ground is then sown with grass and extensive tracts, which would otherwise have been mere wilderness, are thus converted into spacious lawns, studded with noble trees. These are so numerous, and of such extent, as to form a prominent feature in the scenery, and it is hardly possible to imagine anything more beautiful, than the alternations of woodland and meadow, with hemp and cornfields, and orchards, which the eye here meets in every direction.[66]

Though land clearing has removed many old trees in favor of open pastures or fields, some wooded parkland remains, now with a bluegrass ground cover. Mature, high-branched trees can be of substantial benefit to the farmer who wishes to maintain a productive pasture that will endure the summer heat. Bluegrass is a shallow-rooted rhizomic plant that often turns a dormant brown during the summer months, when rainfall is sparse and temperatures high. Shade cast by an open grove of trees helps lower soil temperatures and reduces evaporation and plant transpiration, thereby prolonging the period during which bluegrass is actively growing and palatable to grazing animals.

Mile 10.0 Intersection with Harp-Innis Road on the left.

Mile 10.3 The intersection of the present Hutchison Road with the Maysville Road is anchored by the Hopewell Presbyterian Church and a large white frame house that was originally built as an Odd Fellows lodge. By 1861 a blacksmith shop stood at this intersection, together with a few houses. The Hutchison name originated with Martin Hutchison, who developed a community of the same name to the southeast at the railroad crossing. An earlier name for Hutchison Road was the Hopewell-Bethlehem Pike, which connected the Lexington-Maysville Road to the Bethlehem-Paris Pike, now known simply as Bethlehem Road.

The congregation at Hopewell Presbyterian Church petitioned the Presbyterian synod in 1784 to sanction their church, and it was first represented in assemblies the following year. A log schoolhouse on or near the old Limestone Trace (now Bryan Station Road), not far from John Grant's Station, provided a venue for the first services. Later the congregation built a brick church near the junction of the Houston-Antioch Road and the old Limestone Trace and established a cemetery for their members. The church relocated to its present site to take advantage of the increased access provided by the construction of the turnpike along the "new cut" between Lexington and Paris. The brick church here was in use until it burned around 1900. The current building was erected in 1904, reusing brick salvaged from the old structure.[67]

Currently serving as a residence, the two-story, white frame house standing at the corner of Hutchison Road and the Maysville Road was first built as Moreland Lodge no. 124 for the Independent Order of Odd Fellows. Alonzo Halleck, a Paris silversmith, established this chapter in 1855, but the land for the lodge was not conveyed until 1860, when John Smith Kennedy sold a half-acre lot to the Odd Fellows. The deed indicated that the sale was "for the purpose of furnishing a lot for the Lodge Room," which suggests that the building was not constructed until after the land was transferred. The lodge was named in honor of William Moreland, who ran the inn on the turnpike across from the Houston-Antioch road junction.[68]

The Independent Order of the Odd Fellows traces its origins to mid-eighteenth-century England. The derivation of the name *Odd Fellows* is not clear. One explanation is that the formation of a society of common laboring men for social unity, fellowship, and mutual aid was so unusual in mid-eighteenth-century England that the members were considered peculiar or odd, hence the name. Another theory is that the early members were engaged in unusual or "odd" trades. The order was also known as the Three Link Fraternity, the links being Friendship, Love, and Truth. The earliest American chapter, Shakespeare Lodge no. 1, was established in New York City in 1806 by five Brothers of the English Order, and other chapters were instituted in the New York City area and Pennsylvania. The order as it is known today, however, formed in Baltimore in 1819 under the guidance of Thomas Wildey, who is considered the founder of Odd Fellowship in North America.

As American settlement moved westward, members established Odd Fellows chapters in new communities. A primary reason for the order's existence was to provide help for people in distress, that aid including monetary benefits to members unable to work, education of orphans, caring for the needs of widows, and payment for burial services. But membership included a strong social element as well as the opportunity to participate in conferring dramatic degrees; there was also a program of lessons intended to improve one's character. Members kept the degrees secret from outsiders, although the organization printed books outlining the lessons for member's use. The order adopted distinctive clothing, such as black sashes and white gloves, which members wore on special occasions. Various insignia, jewelry, and other accoutrements identified the order's activities and degrees. Membership entitled one to a funeral service after death, and some lodges established cemeteries for their members. The Odd Fellows were similar to the Freemasons, and many people were members of both orders. An auxiliary, the Daughters of Rebekah, offered women participation, since they were not allowed to join the men's lodges. The services provided by the Odd Fellows and other, similar organizations were models for legally mandated social programs that today benefit those in need. The location of a fraternal lodge here, in the open countryside, seems unusual by present-day standards, but it suggests that the Maysville Road had become a very important linear community that attracted homes, farmsteads, and businesses, attended to road travelers, and also served a densely developed rural area.

Mile 11.4–11.7 Jacoby curve was one of only two significant curves in the original turnpike road between Lexington and Paris; it became necessary when road crews building the turnpike between the two towns met and discovered that the road had to be rerouted around a high creek bank and a large quarry excavated by turnpike masons to provide rock for the road's macadam surface. The hillside quarry was never filled in, and it can still be seen on the right, as can a segment of the old turnpike road. An abandoned frame house, now isolated, stands near the quarry on the hillside above the creek. The interurban train ran along the left side of the old road here. The traffic along this section of Paris Pike today exceeds 15,000 vehicles per day.[69]

The Idle Hour Farm, with the Jacob and James S. Jacoby house, lies opposite the Jacoby curve and quarry. The two-story log dwelling, now extensively renovated, was built on the hall-parlor plan in 1791 by the sons of Francis Jacoby, an early Bourbon County settler. David Hager II, the current Idle Hour owner, is a commercial Thoroughbred breeder who specializes in breaking and training horses for racing. The farm trains thirty to fifty horses per year for clients in England, Japan, and the United States.[70]

Mile 12.4 Lockhart Spears started a Thoroughbred breeding operation at the 550-acre Stoneleigh Farm, on the right, in 1957. Spears bred horses primarily for sale to the yearling market, and over the years he produced seventeen stakes winners here. The family's core business was Spears Kiser Company, a grower, producer, and distributor of bluegrass seed with extensive farming operations in Kentucky and Canada. Spears died in 2003.[71] The architect Kenneth Franzheim designed Stoneleigh, the farm's stone house, early in the twentieth century. The house replaced an earlier, nineteenth-century Italianate–Second Empire house built by Dr. George McLeod Sr. An older Federal-style house still stands on the farm along a section of the Limestone Trace that was abandoned in the late nineteenth century.

Mile 12.6 The open stand of mature hardwood trees on the left is a classic example of a Bluegrass woodland pasture or parkland. A Lexington architect-builder, John McMurtry, constructed the nearly secluded house here in the 1850s for Christopher C. Rogers. Set back among the trees, the house is appropriately named Woodland Villa. McMurtry's design was Carpenter Gothic Revival, a popular style locally, as there are several other examples in central Kentucky dating from this period. The house's distinctive features include vertical board construction, double-stacked clustered chimney pairs, and bracketed porch posts. Behind the residence, a carriage house and smokehouse remain as the only extant representatives of a cluster of functionally specific outbuildings that once made up the farmstead. The Rogers family sold the farm in 1859 to E. G. Bedford, a slave owner who was a highly successful breeder of shorthorn cattle and Berkshire hogs. Bedford was a director of the Bourbon County Fair and Agricultural Association and prominent in the elite social circles of Bourbon County and central Kentucky. The Bedfords lived on the farm until the early twentieth century, when the Thompson family bought the property and added additional bedrooms and a sun porch to the house. The Thompsons raised Southdown sheep and later began a distributorship for compressed air and hydraulic equipment. The property recently sold and is now owned by a local doctor.

Before macadam road surfacing added resilience to rural road surfaces, old roads rapidly became entrenched by heavy wagon and carriage traffic. The fence line between Woodland Villa and the adjacent Bradyleigh Farm on the left follows such a trench that was once Greenwich Chapel Road.

Bradyleigh Farm on the left contains the McConnell farmstead site, which William

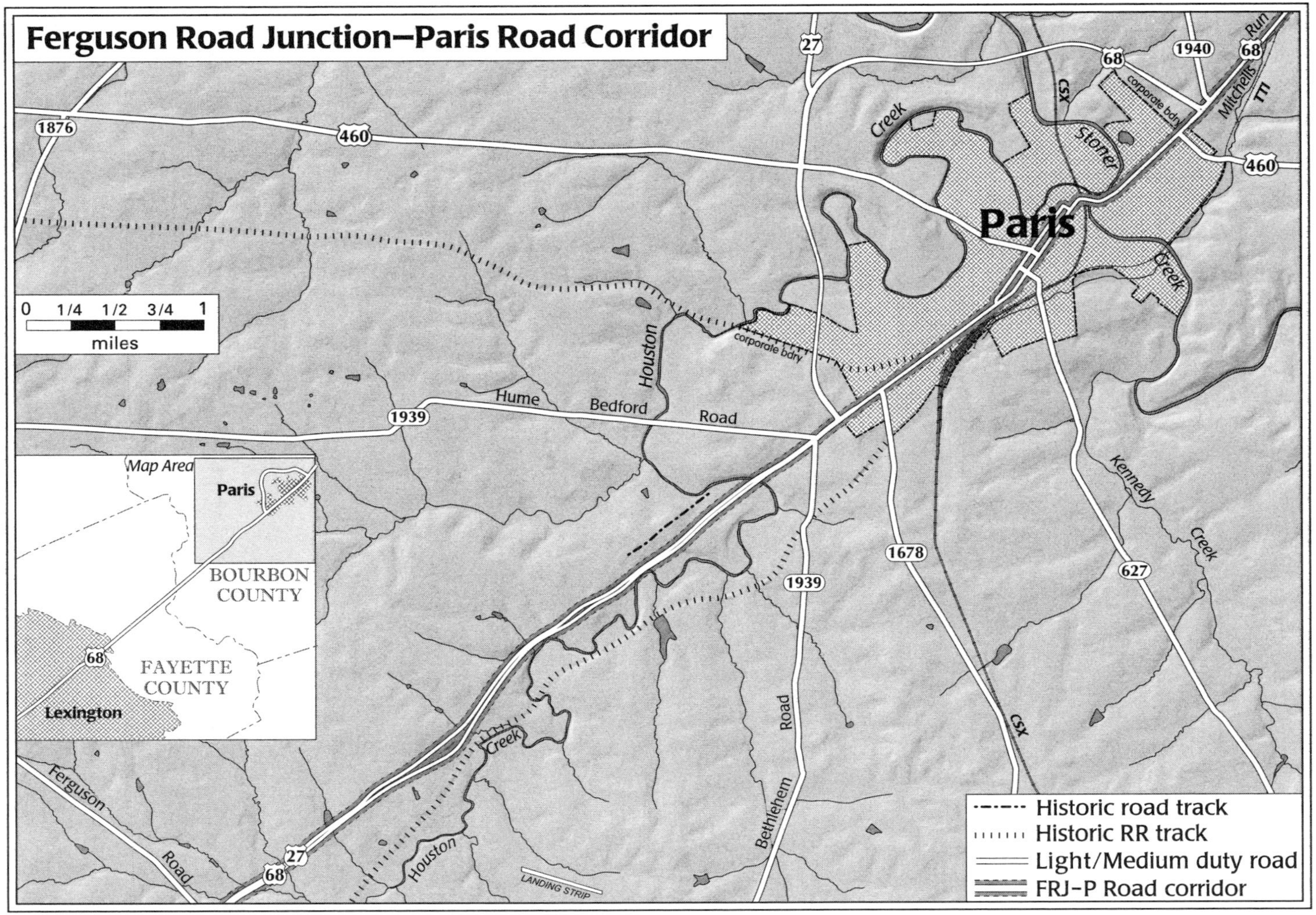

Ferguson Road Junction–Paris Road Corridor
0 1/4 1/2 3/4 1
miles
Paris
Stoner
Creek
Creek
Mitchells Run
TTI
CSX
CSX
corporate bdry
corporate bdry
Houston
Houston
Creek
Hume Bedford Road
Kennedy Creek
Bethlehem Road
Ferguson Road
LANDING STRIP
27
68
1940
460
1876
1939
1678
627
Map Area
BOURBON COUNTY
FAYETTE COUNTY
Lexington
Historic road track
Historic RR track
Light/Medium duty road
FRJ–P Road corridor

McConnell, a prominent farmer and slave owner of Irish descent, established around 1788. A stone house initially stood here, and the site was archaeologically excavated as part of the Paris Pike reconstruction.[72] The springhouse covering the perennial spring associated with the site is still visible at the base of the hill on which the house stood. William McConnell migrated to Kentucky from southeastern Pennsylvania about 1781, but he did not purchase his Bourbon County property until 1788. The original farm comprised one thousand acres of first-class land along the Limestone Trace about four miles from the center of Paris. McConnell built a stone house and established a prosperous livestock operation of middling size that was typical of a larger pattern developing across the Inner Bluegrass counties, western Kentucky's Pennyroyal country, and the Scioto Valley of Ohio's Virginia Military District. McConnell, a slaveholder, raised cattle, horses, sheep, and hogs, and his field crops were primarily hay and corn. His civic responsibilities included serving as road overseer, deputy surveyor, and a grand juror for the county, duties that placed him among the local middle-class gentry.

William McConnell represents a larger group of Bluegrass farmers who, by the 1830s, had transformed this fertile countryside into a major cattle-feeding economy. Farmers developed what they termed "the grazing system," which consolidated small properties into larger farms with extensive pasture. They planted cropland with a rotation of corn, rye, and clover and sowed their remaining woodlands with grass. By 1835 Bourbon County, in the heart of the prime Inner Bluegrass grazing lands, exported 10,000 head of fat cattle, 40,000 fat hogs, 3,000 horses and mules, whiskey valued at $70,000, bacon and lard worth $50,000, and various manufactured hemp products. Traditional crops such as wheat and tobacco were not produced in sufficient amounts to register as "exports."[73]

At his death in 1823, McConnell's estate provided his heirs with land, livestock, and other bequests. His daughter, Elizabeth, and her husband, John Ardery, took up residence at the family home. The Arderys continued farming the land Elizabeth had inherited and expanded their acreage through purchases from family and neighbors. Using enslaved labor, the Arderys continued raising livestock and grains. John Ardery had a financial interest in the Bourbon County fairgrounds and owned shares in the Covington & Lexington Railway Company and the Maysville and Lexington Turnpike Company.

After John's death in 1853, the Arderys' son, Lafayette, assumed farm ownership and management. Livestock feeding continued to be the farm's economic mainstay, but a rapid increase in the demand for mules during the Civil War was sufficient rationale for Lafayette Ardery to concentrate on raising mules for the Union Army—an ironic turn of purpose for a family farm steeped in the slaveholding economy. By the 1870s Lafayette and his family had left the family home and moved to another farm. The relocation may have been prompted by a fire that severely damaged the stone house. Whatever the reason for the move, by the late nineteenth century the old stone house would have been an architectural anachronism contrasting unfavorably with the new revival-style houses then being built across the county. The farm currently raises Thoroughbred horses.

Mile 13.0 The abandoned railroad bed of the Paris-to-Lexington portion of the old Kentucky Central Railroad is on the right.

Mile 13.5 Canefield Farm, on the right, underwent dramatic change after Paris Pike's nineteenth-century construction. The farm's original brick house, Locust Grove, fronted the old road, about one-half mile east from the present highway. That Federal-style house, with touches of Georgian architectural influence, still stands on the adjoining Monterey Farm, but the old road is extinct; only faint traces of it are visible in fence lines and at Houston Creek ford sites. About 1885, Matthew and Jane Kenney, the farm's residents, moved to the new house, a two-story structure called The Breezes, which faced the new Paris Pike. Jane Kenney is reputed to have said that she wanted no part of living off the highway.[74] After World War I the farm was sold to Julian Rogers, a Lexington livestock dealer. Rogers then sold the farm to a Saddlebred horse breeder, Douglas Davis, who modified The Breezes by adding the two-story columned portico that gives the house a distinctive facade that is still its hallmark. The 860-acre farm was subsequently sold to R. W. Ritter, owner of the Mohawk Carpet Company, who moved to Bourbon County from Amsterdam, New York, in the mid-1930s.[75] Ritter's son-in-law, James E. Clay, a commercial horse breeder, was in business here from the 1950s through 2006.[76]

Across the highway from Canefield Farm's Kenney House once stood the Monterey community, still memorialized in the name of the farm that now contains the site. Excavated as part of the Paris Pike reconstruction project, Monterey was first known as Houstonville in the early nineteenth century and was the location of the Houston post office and a blacksmith shop operated by William Hufford.[77] Although this might seem a rather remote place for a blacksmith to establish a business, such shops were common first-generation roadside businesses. Of course, blacksmiths flourished in towns and villages—tiny Flat Rock had one, and the milling center at Ruddles Mills north of Paris had two. But stagecoach lines, wagoners, carriage drivers, travelers on horseback, and local farmers patronized the roadside blacksmiths, who shod horses, welded broken iron wheel rims and double-tree chains, and made iron tools. The Houstonville shop was one of at least a dozen open-country blacksmith shops in rural Bourbon County in the early 1860s.[78] This hamlet was not renamed Monterey until after the Civil War. It grew up around tollgate house number 10, established here about 1835 by the Lexington and Maysville Turnpike Company. John Foote operated the tollgate and lived here with his family until about 1842, when the turnpike directors relocated the tollhouse closer to Paris. Willis Dorsey converted the old tollhouse building into a store where he sold dry goods, groceries, and boots and shoes. At least that was his legal business. County authorities charged him with running a "tippling house" in the 1850s. It seems that Dorsey not only sold liquor illegally, but also allowed slaves and free blacks to congregate on the property.

Monterey residents provided services to road travelers and adjacent farms. Though the settlement was never incorporated, it included a post office, wool-carding factory, school, church, and possibly a tavern. In addition to Foote and Dorsey, Monterey's early occupants were a diverse lot that included both black and white residents. Most were laborers, artisans, shopkeepers, or operated other small businesses. Samuel

Martin was a grocer. Thomas and Plunkett Armstrong established the wool-carding shop here about 1823. Jerome Crandall, a butcher, served in the Kentucky Mounted Rifles, a Confederate unit, during the Civil War. William and Harriet Moore, freed slaves, also lived in Monterey; William ran a blacksmith shop and built wagons. Franky Robison, a free black woman, bought a lot in 1834 and lived here with her husband, Henry Robison, until her death. Henry Robison and his next wife, Charlotte, lived in Monterey for many years until Charlotte, then widowed, sold the land in 1868. After the Civil War Monterey became a predominantly African American settlement, although whites owned some of the land parcels that they rented to tenants. The community persisted into the twentieth century and for a time supported an African Methodist Episcopal Church. Eventually the population declined and the property was enveloped into Monterey Farm, established by Edmund W. Brent in the 1930s.[79]

Mile 13.8 Shanty Springs flows under the current road to empty into Houston Creek on the right. A small frame house stood on a knoll overlooking the creek here by 1827. The provenance of the term "Shanty" is not known, but the term was commonly used in Bourbon County in the nineteenth century to refer to cheaply constructed temporary dwellings erected to accommodate the Irish turnpike laborers. The current house is probably a replacement of the 1820s building, but its architecture indicates that it was originally a single-story, four-room plan in which all the rooms were heated by individual flues built into a single central chimney. This dormitory-style floor plan may have been intended to accommodate single men working on the local turnpikes in the mid- to late nineteenth century and may be representative of an "Irish shanty."[80]

Mile 14.2 Fair View Stock Farm. The William Wheat house here was built in the Federal style with Federal-, Greek Revival–, Italianate-, and Colonial Revival–style woodwork that reflects modifications to the original structure.

Houston Creek was named for Joseph Huston, who explored the drainage in the 1770s, and the stream was known by this name by 1777. The change in spelling came about when another family named Houston claimed to have settled on the creek in 1780.

Mile 14.5 The James W. Wright house stands on a prominent hill above the west side of the road on Paris's south side. Andrew Wright was the son of an early settler, James Wright, who, at an early date, acquired thousands of acres of land in the Paris area. Although the house was thought to have been built by Andrew Wright, who inherited from his father the land on which it stands, it was built by James Wilson Wright, Andrew's nephew, in the 1840s. Built as a hall-and-parlor plan, the earliest house section is a timber frame laid on a limestone block foundation. A detached brick kitchen stood outside the back door, connected by a breezeway to the main house. The sawn lumber for the house was probably procured from James Wright's sawmill, located nearby on Houston Creek. In the 1850s the family expanded the house by adding a one-and-one-half-story chamber to the hall's west side, turning the building into a larger, central-hall plan. Nineteenth-century house expansion usually followed a change in household composition, such as an increase in family size or some other catalyst. James W. Wright was married to Harriet Thomas from 1846 to 1866, when she died. Together they reared three children here and the increase in house size

Situated on a prominent hill beside the road south of Paris, the James W. Wright house is an imposing building whose five-bayed front elevation belies its original one-room-deep design. Like vernacular housing across the state, the house's size and style were altered over time to better suit the owner's changing circumstances, whether greater prosperity or additions to the family.

probably was a response to the pragmatic need for more space. James W. Wright married Cynthia Jones in 1871 and sired three more children. Wright erected a one-and-one-half-story addition to the home's east wall and incorporated Italianate decorative details all around to produce an imposing, five-bay Victorian-era house that was only one room deep.

The Wright House illustrates a progression of modifications, stylistic updates, expansions, and reconfigurations that typifies many central Kentucky nineteenth-century houses. The alteration process was so common that it is rare to find an early house that has not been modified in some way to reflect changes in fashion, household composition, or wealth status. Houses that were not altered frequently were less likely to survive, since an important feature of their longevity was that they continued to function as the needs of their owners or occupants evolved over time. Concomitant with changing house styles, however, were shifting perceptions of what constituted an adequate house. The house's first occupant, James W. Wright, occupied the building from about 1846 until his death in 1898, during which time he made most of the architectural changes. The design decisions leading to each successive change in the house were undoubtedly consequent to the needs and desires of two families and two different wives. The original house's simple hall-and-parlor plan gave way to increasingly more imposing and ornamented additions. Not only did the final rendition provide practical interior spaces for the growing family, but the structure also became a visual metaphor that represented the Wright family's social prominence as a prosperous yet down-to-earth family whose pedigree reached back to the earliest years of county settlement. When highway engineers transformed Paris Pike into a parkway, the state purchased the Wright house and restored it. The structure now provides housing for women in the horse industry. Masons rebuilt the rock fence below the house yard to accommodate widening the highway at this point.

Mile 14.7 The Houston Oaks Golf Course entrance drive is on the right.

Mile 14.8 Lynnwood Farm is on the left, on the hill above Houston Creek. Also known as Forest Home, the house was originally constructed in the Gothic or Italianate style. It was altered at the turn of the twentieth century, and again in 1951 to resemble a "southern plantation" mansion. An old sunken roadbed, probably the 1830s turnpike, crosscuts the front pasture and driveway and continues toward Paris through the field on the left. Just beyond Lynnwood Farm the road enters Paris.

Mile 15.4 Houston Creek flows northeast from the drainage divide demarcated by the height of land at the Fayette County–Bourbon County boundary to join Stoner Creek just north of Paris. Houston's rock-bottomed channel drains much of southwest Bourbon County, and its low-gradient floodplain was long the preferred route from Lexington to Paris. The original Limestone Trace followed the creek as a northward extension of Bryan Station Road. Surveyors aligned the new 1830s Lexington-Maysville Turnpike parallel to the creek's north bank from here south to Monterey. Later the Lexington-to-Paris rail line also followed the creek valley.[81]

Houston Creek turns abruptly northwest here, cutting a broad, meandering loop across the traditional travel alignment, which necessitates a crossing. The current four-lane road crosses Houston Creek via a new double bridge. The old Limestone Trace approached the creek from the Paris, or north, side by dropping down into a short tributary valley that led directly to a shallow fording point at creek level, thereby avoiding the steeper bluffs that loomed on both sides. Once across on the south side, travelers followed the trace across a broad floodplain terrace—here about three hundred feet to the left, or northwest, of the present road—and then regained the upland via a low-angle point bar. The original historic track is still visible as the straight, deeply entrenched track that crosses the pasture to the left, crosscutting a farm driveway and continuing southwest on a trajectory parallel to the new road. In the late eighteenth century James Wright opened a mill upstream from the crossing, and his milldam probably stabilized the stream's flow during rainy periods, allowing travelers on the trace to cross with relative ease. When turnpike engineers considered the Houston Creek crossing in the 1830s, they deemed that routing the new road via the ford was not an acceptable option, and they built a covered bridge here east of the old road. In 1933, during the Depression, a concrete bridge replaced the old covered bridge.

Mile 15.5 An early Bourbon County settler, Captain James Wright, built a house sited on a prominent knoll overlooking Houston Creek and the Lexington-Maysville

Road. Wright, a Revolutionary War veteran and resident of Botetourt County in Virginia's Shenandoah Valley, migrated to Kentucky in 1785 and settled on one thousand acres of Houston Creek watershed land. His first log house still stands. By 1791 Wright had built a two-story brick house where he lived until his death. His son, James Wright Jr., inherited the property and added to the house a frame two-story section with Greek Revival interior woodwork sometime between 1825 and 1840. The two sections were visually united by an early twentieth-century two-story portico.[82] Both men established milling businesses nearby. The senior Wright built a log mill on Houston Creek that ground grain and produced sawn lumber. His son replaced the log mill with a three-story stone structure that no longer stands. The farm lane that runs behind the house may have been the original track to the mill site.

In the 1970s this property was part of an expansive Thoroughbred horse breeding and racing operation owned by Nelson Bunker Hunt, son of the Texas oil billionaire H. L. Hunt. Bunker Hunt's oil interests included a partnership with British Petroleum in Libya in the early 1960s. The Muammar Gaddafi government nationalized Hunt's Libyan oil holdings in 1973. Hunt's success in Thoroughbred racing earned him the Eclipse Award for Outstanding Breeder in 1976, 1985, and 1987. Together with his brother William Herbert Hunt, Bunker Hunt attempted to corner the world market for silver from 1973 to the early 1980s. Federal intervention led to a crash in silver prices in March 1980, and Bunker Hunt was forced into bankruptcy. The Bluegrass Farm property here was sold and the breeding stock dispersed. Today James Wright's land has been transformed yet again into the Houston Oaks Golf Course and a suburban residential community. The eighteen-hole, par-seventy-two course was designed by Jack Ridge, a golf course designer who has developed other courses in Kentucky, Georgia, and Alabama. Houston Oaks opened in 1996 as a semiprivate operation, and *Golf Digest* rates the links here as among the ten best courses in the state.[83]

Mile 15.6 A marker on the left designates U.S. 68 as a Blue Star Memorial Highway. During the final months of World War II, the New Jersey State Council of Garden Clubs decided to beautify a section of U.S. 22 near North Plainfield by planting several thousand dogwood trees as a memorial to the men and women from that state serving in the armed forces. The World War II service flag featured a blue star, and the star was often displayed in homes and businesses to denote a family member in the armed forces. After the war the program expanded to other states, including Kentucky. The designation Blue Star Memorial Highway honors all those who have served or are serving in the armed forces. Under the leadership of the National Council of Garden Clubs, the Blue Star Highway designation program broadened to link military service commemoration with highway beautification.[84]

Mile 15.8 Bethlehem Road on the right and Hume Bedford Road on the left intersect Paris Pike here. Bethlehem Road tracks south for several miles and is linked to Hutchison Pike and Iron Works Pike. A turnpike tollhouse once stood on the left side near this intersection. State road law required turnpike companies to erect tollhouses no closer to towns than one mile—though companies were permitted to place tollhouses at five-mile intervals in the open countryside. This location would have complied with that requirement and allowed toll collection from travelers on both the realigned Maysville Turnpike and the historic route that is now Bethlehem Road. Hume Bedford Road did not follow its present alignment in the 1860s but traced an irregular route well to the north as Fords Mill Road.[85] All that remains of Fords Mill Road today is a short spur that is linked to Cypress Street in Paris.

Mile 16.0 In 1973 highway engineers initiated construction plans to divert through traffic on U.S. 68 from downtown Paris to bypass the city on the west and north. The bypass begins here at a T-interchange and incorporates the local section of U.S. 27, which leads north to Cynthiana, the Harrison County seat. Traffic rejoins the old U.S. 68 alignment on Paris's northeast side. In principle, the bypass functions as intended. Traffic counts in 2009 suggest that about 17,000 vehicles reach this intersection from the south each day. The bypass carries some 12,300 vehicles north, and only 7,700 travel Paris's Main Street, many of them local vehicles. North of the bypass link with U.S. 68 only 10,300 vehicles traverse that road section daily.[86] On the other hand, the bypass has become an auxiliary Main Street by attracting new, auto-oriented businesses, including car dealerships, a strip shopping center, restaurants, and a Wal-Mart. In 2005, after two years of local debate, Wal-Mart announced plans to build a new store on farmland just to the left of the bypass–U.S. 68 intersection. By the fall of 2006 construction crews had cleared and leveled the site and completed construction on the new structure and its attendant access road and parking lots. The new store opened in January 2007, replacing an older store nearby. The new store, together with other businesses springing up on this leg of the bypass, promise lane-clogging traffic and calls for road widening. Additional turning lanes and a new stoplight at the store's main entrance are sure to follow.

16

Siting Paris

North, beyond Houston Creek, auto-oriented roadside businesses and subdivisions announce the entry into Paris; in 2010 the city was the third largest urban place on the road, with a population of 8,553 (a decline of 630 people from 2000).[1] The city's retail and commercial core, its oldest section, is two miles farther along the road. To interpret and understand transitional landscapes such as this one requires patience and considered observation. Imagine this transect two centuries ago, when the surrounding land stood open. The only landmarks here were isolated farm building clusters, the Limestone Trace's muddy track, and perhaps some smoke on the horizon ahead rising from the chimneys of a small cluster of buildings standing near Stoner Creek. Basic geographical decisions as to farm and town location were based on straightforward pragmatics. Farmsteads required a year-round freshwater supply, standing timber for fuel, fencing, and construction materials, and open expanses of fertile land. Central Kentucky's early settlers, therefore, often chose as their first priority first-generation farmhouse sites close to perennial springs. Prime town sites combined access to water, fuel and construction wood, overland roads, and streams that, if not navigable, had flow sufficient to power a grist- or sawmill.

When Virginia surveyors arrived in the Kentucky country in search of good land, the site that became Paris met their requirements. The meandering Houston and Stoner creeks, two major tributaries of the Licking River's South Fork, join here in a way that created a broad-shouldered peninsula flanked by streams on three sides, much as William Penn's site for Philadelphia was bounded east, west, and south by the Delaware and Schuylkill rivers. The Paris site featured a beneficial elevation of more than one hundred feet above creek level, which assured settlers that unless they defiantly erected structures directly on the floodplain, the menace of periodic floods could be largely avoided. The streams here offered modest navigability but had unambiguous potential for water-powered mill sites. And a minor alignment adjustment in the Limestone Trace allowed passage through the town via single crossings of Stoner Creek on the north and Houston Creek on the south, not the multiple crossings that a town site farther north would have necessitated.

If choosing a geographically propitious town site was more or less a straightforward process, the land patenting and surveying practices that permitted settlers to establish farms and towns was fraught with complicated legal entanglements. Colonel John Floyd, deputy surveyor for William Preston of Fincastle County, Virginia, completed the earliest land survey of two hundred acres here in 1776 on behalf of Walter Stewart. By virtue of his service in the British 44th Regiment of Foot during the French and Indian War, Stewart had earned a land claim right, which John Floyd surveyed for him here.[2] The land grant was delayed until 1780, and Walter Stewart never established residence in Bourbon County. Assignees of John May, John Craig, and Robert Johnston of Fayette County received an overlapping claim of 1,000 acres here in 1785. Craig and Johnston, in turn, assigned 500 acres to John Reed of Jefferson County, Kentucky, in 1787. Reed sold 250 acres to Lawrence Protzman of Hagerstown, Maryland, in 1789. Protzman moved to Bourbon County in 1788 and is credited with establishing the town of Paris.

Lawrence Protzman persuaded James Lanier of Cumberland, North Carolina, to join him in developing the town. The two men sent a petition signed by 117 Bourbon County citizens to the Virginia Assembly on September 2, 1789, requesting that a town be established around the courthouse that already stood on Protzman's land. The Assembly authorized the town, called Hopewell, in October 1789, designated Lawrence Protzman proprietor, and named nine citizens as trustees. On his behalf, Protzman's attorney, Thomas Jones, surveyed and marked town lots and conveyed and signed deeds in 1789.[3] Within a year the possibility of an overlap between the land claims of Walter Stewart and the land Protzman had purchased from John Reed came to the trustees' attention. Conflicts over land in Kentucky were so commonplace that it was a rare landowner who did not have to resort to the courts to establish legal title. Many people lost their land or suffered serious financial reversals, and Protzman was no exception. He was involved in several lawsuits, including one brought against him by his partner, James Lanier. Protzman's legal troubles alarmed the town trustees and citizens who already owned town lots. In October 1790 the town trustees petitioned the Virginia Assembly to condemn the disputed land and vest the title to the trustees to provide security to people who had already bought lots and convey lots that remained unsold. The trustees also requested that the town's name be changed to Paris.[4]

Lawrence Protzman had returned to Maryland by 1792, and by 1795 he was living in Rockingham County, Virginia, still trying to recoup his losses in Paris. He transferred his remaining interest in the town to his brother, John, in 1792, and except for a few transactions in 1795, probably abandoned his attempts to remain involved in Paris's development. By 1811 Protzman was living in Kanawha County, Virginia (now West Virginia), and that year he conducted his last land transactions in Kentucky by selling a few land tracts near Paris. Thereafter, the town trustees handled lot sales exclusively.

The early Paris plat ran from the present-day Twelfth Street north to the confluence of Houston and Stoner creeks. The entire grid of in-lots and most out-lots lay south of Houston Creek and west of Stoner Creek. The only town plat known to exist for Paris is dated January 1, 1799, and was drawn in response to an act of the Kentucky Assembly allowing "for the better regulation of the Town of Paris, and vesting the Trustees with Additional Powers." An explanatory note accompanying the map indicated that the plat was a reconstruction of the earlier survey. Some lots were assigned new numbers because their original numbers could not be ascertained. The Limestone Trace, which formed the town's Main Street, governed the town's orientation. The town's surveyor laid out a rectangular grid of in-lots that flanked three parallel streets running northeast-southwest. Pleasant Street paralleled Main on the east side, High Street on the west. Ten cross streets formed blocks of varying sizes, each most commonly containing four lots. The cross streets were named mostly for native trees, except for Mill Street (now Second Street), near the confluence of Houston and Stoner creeks, Church Street (now Fifth Street), and Main Cross Street (now Stoner Avenue). The plat included a large open square near Stoner Creek for the courthouse. Beyond the in-lots were larger out-lots of varying size and shapes. All the cross streets were later renamed; most of them are numbered today.[5]

Traveling through Paris north toward Maysville provides a vivid transition from twenty-first to nineteenth-century landscapes. New, road-oriented fast-food restaurants, big-box drugstores, and gas stations punctuate the twenty-first-century approach into Paris. Farther along the twentieth-century section are school buildings, a large 1970s supermarket, more gas stations, and earlier buildings that include 1920s bungalows and first-generation motels of the same vintage.

Mile 16.3 Clintonville Road (CR 1678), or East Nineteenth Street, leads almost directly south to Clintonville, an open country hamlet.

Mile 16.4 The James M. Brown house, on the left at 1831 Main St., built circa 1845, is a one-story brick Greek Revival structure with a central-passage plan. A subsequent owner was Robert T. Davis, son of Garrett Davis, a lawyer, politician, and state senator.

Mile 16.5 Following the series of 1990s lawsuits against the nation's tobacco manufacturers, the United States Department of Agriculture (USDA) restructured the federal price support and allotment system for burley tobacco. As the USDA phased out allotment regulations and price supports, tobacco production declined. Tobacco product manufacturers, in turn, changed the manner in which they purchased tobacco from farm producers. Tobacco companies discontinued their participation in the tobacco auction system, in place for nearly a century, and instituted tobacco sales by contract with individual farmers. Under the auction system, farmers took their cured tobacco to a central tobacco warehouse—usually in a county seat town at a location with railroad access—where buyers representing the tobacco companies bought at auction tobacco that they shipped to manufacturing plants for processing into cigarettes and other smoking products. Tobacco auctions declined rapidly after 2000, and traditional tobacco auction warehouses quickly became anachronistic. Owners converted some to alternative uses such as storage or antiques auction barns. Demolition crews eliminated others. Tobacco warehouse dimensions are impressive, especially in an urban setting. Though only twenty feet to the eaves, most warehouses enclosed floor space exceeding an acre (43,560 square feet). Removing just one warehouse within the city limits opened a football field–sized lot to redevelopment. Old tobacco warehouses here, ahead on the right, are now considered rare historic structures.

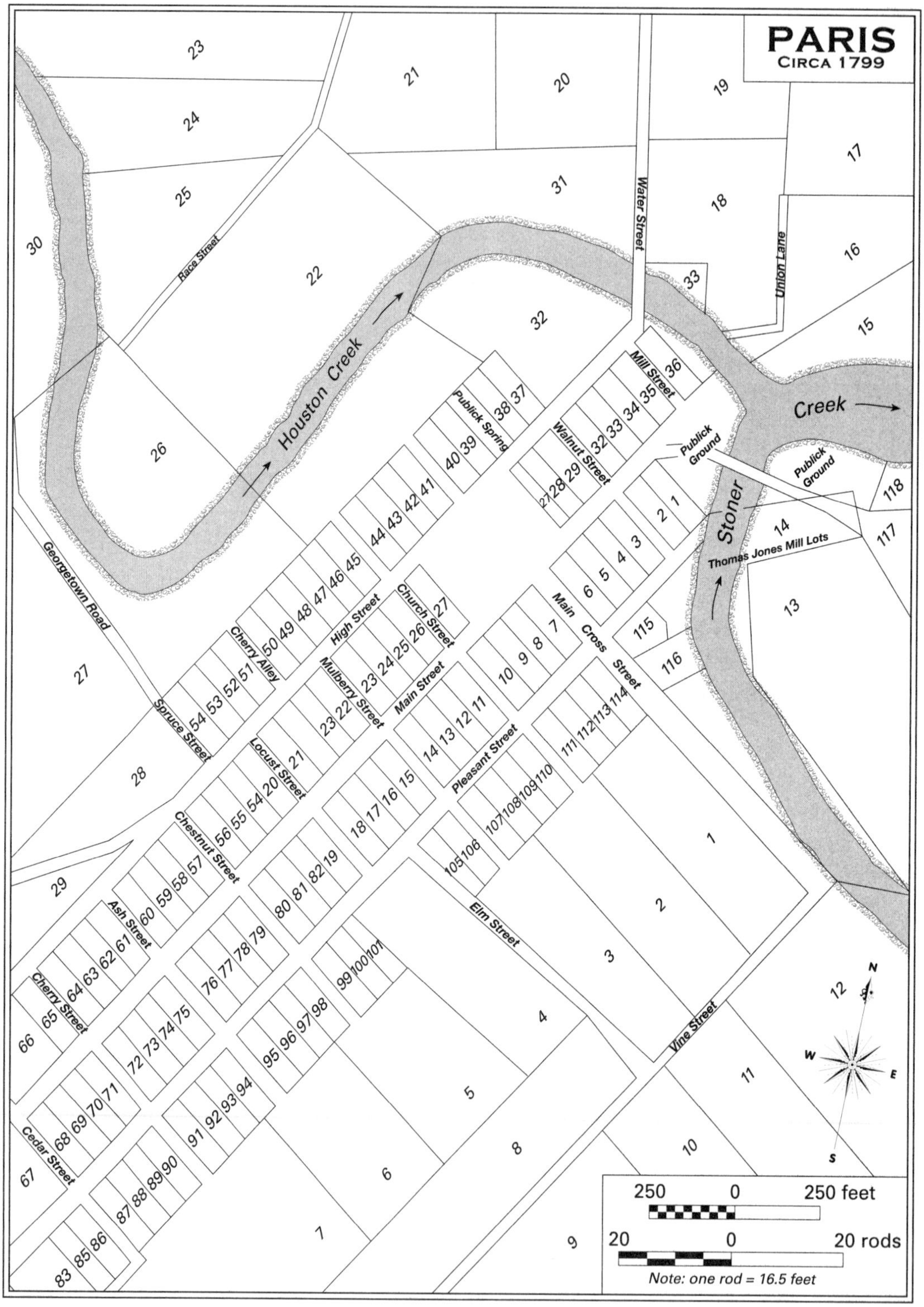

PARIS
CIRCA 1799
Houston Creek
Stoner
Creek
Race Street
Water Street
Union Lane
Mill Street
Walnut Street
Publick Spring
Publick Ground
Publick Ground
Thomas Jones Mill Lots
Georgetown Road
Cherry Alley
High Street
Church Street
Main Cross Street
Mulberry Street
Main Street
Spruce Street
Locust Street
Pleasant Street
Chestnut Street
Ash Street
Cherry Street
Elm Street
Vine Street
Cedar Street
N
W
E
S
250
0
250 feet
20
0
20 rods
Note: one rod = 16.5 feet

Mile 16.7 One of the first nineteenth-century structures one encounters is the Paris Cemetery Gatehouse, on the left, built in 1847 by John McMurtry, a prominent builder-architect. The striking Gothic Revival style is a design choice often associated with religious architecture of this period. Attached by cubiform blocks housing administrative offices, a three-bay arcade departs from the Gothic to embrace elements of the Tudor Revival style.[6]

On the right, across from the Paris Cemetery gate, a railroad-oriented industrial site now houses the Woodford Spears and Sons feed and grain business, established in the early twentieth century. The Spears family was also heavily invested in early flour milling, hemp processing, and bourbon whiskey production; they owned several facilities in Paris and the county.

Mile 16.8 A small, abandoned building identified on the relict sign as the Drover's Inn stands on the left. In 1877 a drovers' inn stood farther south, near the Paris Cemetery. Whatever the provenance of this building, the sign is a reminder that driving livestock along the Maysville Road was an important nineteenth-century business. Drovers commonly moved through the countryside from farm to farm consigning or purchasing livestock that they assembled into large herds and drove to eastern markets. On the road, darkness and animal fatigue obligated drovers to stop and put up their herds in large corrals or pens overnight. A large herd of beef cattle or hogs required water in substantial amounts and hay or other feed. Local farmers whose property fronted the road often provided the corral or fenced pasture and water for a set price per head of livestock.

Mile 17.1 Beyond the junction of Main and High streets, Main Street becomes one-way, northbound. The traffic flow transition also marks a transition to older houses and buildings. The original section of town in-lots begins at Twelfth Street. A sophisticated Richardsonian-style house introduces nineteenth-century Paris. Originally built as a private residence, St. Mary's parochial school now occupies the structure. The Roman Catholic Church of the Annunciation stands in the next block, an outstanding example of Gothic Revival ecclesiastical design. Parishioners began construction around 1858 and enlarged the building to its present dimensions and appearance about 1870.[7]

Traveling from Twelfth Street northeastward, the juxtaposition of structures originally built as residences and commercial storefronts signals the transition into Paris's downtown commercial core. The J. W. Muir building (1331 Main Street), built in 1913, retains its original cast-iron storefront. It was initially Muir's Insurance Agency's office. The Lusk Funeral Home at 1120 Main Street occupies an elegant Italianate-Gothic building. William M. Hinton, a prominent jeweler, built the house as his residence near the end of the Civil War. This structure's secondary use for funerary services is a reminder that American funeral directors often refer to their place of business as a "funeral home" and the location of choice for a "home" is a once-grand old house. The large interior rooms, often outfitted with churchlike pews, lend themselves to gatherings. The facade's architectural formality projects an appropriate sense of gravitas.

The Dr. John C. Grosjean house at 1102 Main Street dates from 1817. John

Metcalfe built the structure in the Federal style. Metcalfe was a well-known early builder and brother to Governor Thomas "Stonehammer" Metcalfe, a stonemason turned politician who owned Forest Retreat, a large farm on the turnpike north of Millersburg in Nicholas County. Dr. Grosjean, an early nineteenth-century physician, maintained a medical practice in partnership with John Metcalfe's son. In the eighteenth and nineteenth centuries, owners of well-built houses often remodeled them when the prevailing national architectural style changed. That occurred here when new owners remodeled the Grosjean house with Greek Revival–style elements shortly before the Civil War.

Mile 17.3 Main Street intersects Tenth Street, which is also named Winchester Road and State Road 627. The St. Charles Hotel, one of the city's oldest buildings, stands on the left at the corner of Winchester Road and Main Street. Sarah Stemmons and Samson D. Talbott lived in the structure, originally built in the early nineteenth century; later their son, J. D. Talbott, lived here in the 1870s. In the early 1890s Talbott sold the building to John M. Doyle, who converted it into the St. Charles Hotel. It now serves as office space and a day-care center.

About one-quarter mile east on SR 627 the old L & N Railroad depot still stands beside the railroad tracks. The rail line is now controlled by TTI Railroad Company. The company refurbished for their offices an old brick bluegrass seed stripping facility that stands opposite the depot.

Near the Ninth Street intersection stands another early nineteenth-century structure, the William W. Alexander house at 902 Main Street. Alexander, a prominent attorney, served as a state representative from 1848 to 1852. A later owner, Hugh D. Alexander, operated a saloon and restaurant here from the 1880s to 1908. The well-known portraitist William Edward West boarded here in the mid-nineteenth century.

Mile 17.5 Beyond Eighth Street, at 731 Main Street, the Edward Shinners Building houses a restaurant. The Richardsonian Romanesque–style structure is unusually tall and was described by *Ripley's Believe It or Not* as the world's tallest three-story building. The Shinners Building was constructed in the 1890s, when a grocery and general store occupied the first floor; until World War I space on the upper floors was rented to several fraternal organizations as lodge halls. The Robneel Building (800–806 Main Street) combines commercial shop fronts at street level and residential apartments on the two upper floors. Built in 1908, possibly by the architect Edwin Stamler, the structure currently houses the Odd Fellows Lodge 23.

The street-level facades of most buildings along Main Street have been radically transformed, although the second-story facades retain most of their original Victorian trim details. As originally constructed, the typical Main Street commercial building had two functioning sections. The ground- or street-level section was intended as retail sales or professional office space. The floors above often served as residential space for the business owner, rental apartments, office space, or storage. The street-level facade fronted a sidewalk and was usually constructed on either side of a central doorway. In modifying their storefronts, Paris Main Street property owners were part of a national trend that began in the 1880s and continued through the Depression to

The railroad closely paralleled the Maysville Road from Lexington to Millersburg. At Paris the historic railroad depot still stands a short distance southeast of Main Street. The TTI Railroad has refurbished an old bluegrass seed stripping facility along the tracks for use as company offices.

the eve of World War II. Storefront modification revived somewhat after the war as merchants sought to compete with new suburban shopping centers.

Initial storefront modification often began when store owners removed the first-floor store facade—or the entire storefront—and replaced it with a cheap cast-iron front made of prefabricated iron pilasters, cornices, window caps, and ornamental cresting. By adding sand to the paint used to cover the iron castings, a building could be made to appear as though it were constructed of cut stone, a much more expensive product.[8] A second wave of storefront modifications began during the Great Depression as a strategy to revive the national economy. In 1935 the federal government initiated a program of assistance for Main Street merchants through an amendment to the National Housing Act that guaranteed loans for commercial building modernization.[9] Merchants collaborated with storefront designers and materials manufacturers in remodeling projects. Architecture magazines began featuring illustrations of modernized street-front store facades created with new construction materials. Following ideas derived from the modern architecture movement, modified storefronts displayed smooth, clean, functional surfaces instead of "old-fashioned" Victorian details.

Many store owners, particularly retailers, modified their storefronts by removing the street-level front wall and replacing it with large glass windows set in aluminum or steel frames. Libbey-Owens-Ford Company, headquartered in Toledo, Ohio, advertised their new storefront redesign as the "Visual Front." Pittsburgh Plate Glass created a storefront design termed the "Open Vision" front.[10] To increase window display space and promote window shopping, store owners often set the front door back into the store space and surrounded it with angled glass windows—a structural modification that was already under way by the 1920s. Several types of setbacks were used, including extra-deep corridors that extended into the store space as much as ten feet. A popular facade modification included opaque colored Vitrolite structural glass panels in the bulkhead space below the windows or across the facade above the display windows. Vitrolite was a Libbey-Owens-Ford product. Its competitor Pittsburgh Plate Glass manufactured Carrara structural plate glass for the same applications. Black and white were among the most popular glass panel colors. Other new facade materials included porcelain enamel (widely used on gas stations, early hamburger franchise restaurants such as White Castle, and signs), glass block (Greyhound bus terminals), glazed brick (many different types of retail stores and theaters), stainless steel (diners, window frames), and polished stone and terra-cotta (Woolworths, among others). Manufacturers promoted these materials as symbols of progress and rejuvenation.

The Paris central business area extends from Seventh to Second streets and still retains many historic buildings—some modified with cast-iron or inset-glass fronts, some with near-original facades. Beige and maroon glass panels frame the show windows at 722 Main Street. Rabon's Furniture Store at 723 Main Street dates from the 1890s and has an inset cast-iron front across the first floor facade. The Daniel Roche Grocery Store building at 718 Main Street, built in 1888, is a high Victorian-Gothic commercial building of exceptional quality. Fit into a narrow lot, the new building housed a grocery store previously established here in 1879 by Daniel Roche. The Roche family continued using the structure as a grocery into the twentieth century.

Early in the twentieth century, Louis and Nathan Oberdorfer built the Drug Store Building at 708–714 Main Street, which features a handsome neoclassical facade. Louis Oberdorfer operated the pharmacy and his brother, Nathan, maintained medical and surgical offices here.

The two-story brick building at 704–706 Main Street began as a livery stable operated by A. J. Hook from 1865 to 1888. It continued as a livery stable and was later converted into an automobile garage by subsequent owners. In 1936 Charles P. Cook converted the building to a grocery store by refacing the facade with textured brick and adding a parapet, a process intended to make the building conform to other commercial structures along the street. Cook's Grocery was for many years renowned for its gourmet food (including truffles) and country ham. Across the street at 703, a two-story 1880s brick building includes a rare hand-painted advertising sign on its upper south wall that reads: "Fees, the Home of the Good Things to Eat."

Main Street's 600 block contains several commercial buildings, including the Schwartz Building at 619, built in the late nineteenth century as a saloon. It later was a dry goods store and in the 1950s became a clothing store operated by L. Wollstein,

This early gasoline station's cottagelike appearance stands in stark contrast to its original purpose. Though house-form gas stations were intended to mollify the perceived encroachment of industrial buildings into residential neighborhoods, those built in Tudor Revival style may have also evoked romanticized images of old inns or stagecoach stops. The customer so affected must have been brought abruptly back to reality, however, by the acrid gas fumes produced as the station attendant filled the auto's tank.

whose name can be seen in tile on the vestibule floor. Another saloon, operated by Thomas F. Brannon at 602 Main Street, dates from 1888 and first operated as a toy and millinery shop. The Bourbon Home Telephone Company had its offices here in the early twentieth century. This block also includes cast-iron-front buildings. At 615 a tiny building houses Jerome's Barbershop. The diminutive structure is pinched between two much larger buildings and may occupy a former alleyway. Jerome's is one of five barber shops or hair-styling salons that are clustered together at the north end of the 600 block. Such related business agglomerations were very common in larger cities and can still be found in small and medium-sized cities where banks and attorney's offices are often clustered near a courthouse or city hall.

A charming brick-textured building, first built as a Pure Oil gas station in 1926, anchors the corner of Fifth and Main streets. Remodeled as a clothing store in 1976, the old station then served as a florist's shop for a time, but in 2011 the structure was empty and for sale. In the 1920s, as the Pure Oil and other franchise oil companies

Paris's central business area cannot be properly appreciated from the window of an automobile. The narrow Main Street, flanked by tall commercial buildings with elaborate storefronts, reflects an era when shoppers walked from store to store, shopping, visiting, and enjoying the treat of eating out at local restaurants. (Courtesy of the University of Kentucky Library Special Collections)

attempted to domesticate their new gasoline dispensing stations and make them less conspicuous when inserted into residential neighborhoods or commercial strips, they chose standard designs intended to resemble houses. This 1926 station's picturesque gables, bay windows, chimneys, and steep Tudor Revival rooflines exemplify the strategy. The Hinton Block, built for John T. Hinton in 1891, stands opposite the Pure Oil Gas Station and is the largest nineteenth-century building in downtown Paris. The building's grand scale represents a dramatic departure from the more conventional single-lot-sized buildings in the adjoining blocks.

Built in 1881, the George S. Varden Drug Store building at 509 Main Street still exhibits a period pressed-metal facade with classical details. George Varden operated his pharmacy here for over seven decades, from its opening in 1881 to 1952. The store continued to operate as a pharmacy under other owners who continued Varden's traditional services such as home delivery and credit accounts. A gift and gourmet sandwich shop called Varden's until recently occupied the old business space.

The Odd Fellows Hall at 500–502 Main Street is one of Paris's most important historic buildings. Although it has been somewhat modified, its Greek Revival urban style is typical of this popular mid-nineteenth-century architectural fashion. The Odd Fellows shared their building with the Paris Opera House until a newer opera building was built down the street.

Mile 17.7 Main Street's 400 block includes more examples of modified store facades, such as 433, where an identification plate on the cast-iron front contains the manufacturer's name, Stewart Iron Works, Cincinnati. This block might aptly be called the "Bank Block" because it is dominated by the Deposit Bank Building site constructed in 1884 at 400–402 Main Street. The Deposit Bank, organized in 1851, was one of Paris's first financial institutions. John T. Hinton constructed four similar buildings here, and the Deposit Bank first occupied the corner building, while other businesses filled the remaining three. The Kentucky Bank now occupies the entire grouping. On the north, or courthouse, side of the old Deposit Bank building masons installed a carved stone "Green Man" face above the first-floor level near a side door. The Green Man image is usually depicted as a face covered or surrounded in leaves, branches, or even fruits such as grapes. The Green Man's origin has not been established but probably extends back to pagan Europe and perhaps to the Indian subcontinent. Thousands of Green Man images appear in stone buildings across Europe, where they grace gothic cathedrals, castles, and other large stone structures. The images are often carved into keystones atop arched doorways and in roof gables and pillars. In European folklore the Green Man was also known as Green George, Green Jack, or Jack-in-the-Green. One might imagine that the modern commercial image of the Jolly Green Giant bears a strong resemblance to the foliage-wrapped Green Man of yore.

The Bourbon Agricultural Bank Building, constructed in 1899, stands diagonally across the street from the Deposit Bank Building. It is now occupied by Kentucky Bank (which occupies several building on both sides of Main Street). Recently restored to its original appearance, the facade combines Italianate and Flemish elements in its corner turrets, buff-colored "Roman" brick, and extravagant stonework trim and a Flemish gable. During the 1880s and the early 1890s Main Street from Eighth Street north to the courthouse square was an active construction zone, a reminder that large, expensive commercial buildings were usually built in flush economic times, not periods of recession or depression. From 1879 to 1886 the national economy was recovering from the depression of 1873–79. By 1886 the economy had regained a comfortable level of prosperity that continued until the early 1890s.

Just past the bank buildings, Main Street opens into a square that commands the highest land in town and is sufficiently expansive, at about three and six-tenths acres,

The Paris city plat allocated the highest elevation in the city to the grand Bourbon County Courthouse; the building and its square serve as a perpetual reminder of the town's role as the center of county governance.

to accommodate the courthouse and streets while retaining a comparatively spacious open area in the midst of otherwise high-density lots and buildings. A. C. Nash, an architect from Cincinnati, designed and constructed the resplendently grand stone-and-brick Renaissance Revival–style courthouse, the fourth for Paris, in 1902–5.[11] During the nineteenth and early twentieth centuries, people crowded the large square on Court Day, a weekly or monthly meeting of the county court that drew vendors, merchants, shoppers, and others who had business with the court. For rural families, Court Day was a chance to travel to town, shop, visit friends, and catch up on the local news. Inside the courthouse, county court officials reviewed petitions for new roads, issued permits to construct mills and milldams, appointed commissioners for various court responsibilities, and carried out many other local government duties.

People thronged to Paris every month for Court Day to attend court, conduct business, shop in retail stores, buy and sell livestock, listen to political oratory, and catch up on the latest gossip. But changing priorities turned the event from a business asset into a public nuisance; complaints about congestion and animal waste on the streets led to the demise of Court Day in the early twentieth century. (Courtesy of the Hopewell Museum, Paris, Kentucky)

17

Side Trip

High Street from the Bourbon County Courthouse South to the Juncture of High and Main Streets

Beginning at the Bourbon County Courthouse, one may circle back on U.S. 68 by way of southbound High Street. High parallels Main Street and is now a one-way street that is connected to Lexington in the southwest.

Mile 0.0 St. Peter's Episcopal Church stands near the head of High Street across from the back door of the courthouse. It was built about 1833, and the parishioners subsequently enlarged and modified the church in the early 1870s. City officials erected the Paris City Fire Station nearby in 1874–75. Atop the town's topographic high point and directly across High Street from the courthouse stands Duncan Tavern, a stone structure built in 1788 and now operated as a house museum by the Daughters of the American Revolution. In 1806 Duncan Tavern, though near the center of Paris, was not a single building but a small grouping of structures that sustained its function as a hostelry and stopover for those traveling via horseback or carriage. The tavern's supporting buildings included "a good kitchen with a well of water nearby, a garden spot, a good smokehouse, dairy, outhouses and a large stable with a granary adjoining it."[1]

Opposite Duncan Tavern is the Deposit Bank of Paris/Memorial Building, built around 1859. The bank offices were located in the building's corner section. Attached living quarters provided housing for the bank's cashier or president. In 1922 city officials designated the building a commemorative for Bourbon County casualties of World War I and renamed it the Memorial Building.

Mile 0.1 At Fourth Street the Eads Tavern stands on the right. The clapboarded log structure served as Paris's first post office in 1795 and may have served as an office for Robert Trimble, a distinguished Kentucky jurist. Joseph Walker, publisher of the *Western Citizen* newspaper (still in operation), also lived here in the 1870s. Paris city offices occupy the old county hospital, which has been replaced by a new hospital building on the city's north side.

Mile 0.2 The Paris–Bourbon County Public Library stands at Seventh Street, a handsome building designed by the architect Edwin Stamler in 1904 and partially funded by the Carnegie Foundation.

Mile 0.3 The Paris Lodge, the second Freemason lodge established in Kentucky, is now housed in a modest brick building whose frontage belies its overall size. The Central Baptist and First Christian Churches stand in tandem. The First Christian Church, built in 1902, is nearly as prominent in size as the courthouse. Its striking octagonal shapes, arched openings, steep rooflines, and complicated spatial arrangement make it one of Paris's most impressive ecclesiastical buildings.

Mile 0.5 The St. Paul United Methodist Church at 1117 High Street is a transitional Greek Revival– and Italianate-style church built in 1876. It continues to serve as an important church for the African American community.

Return to the courthouse to rejoin U.S. 68 north.

18

Nineteenth-Century Paris

Since Bourbon County's inception, Paris has served as its political center. As county seat, the settlement was predisposed to become the county's largest town, an advantage that was unremittingly reinforced by its strategic location on the Maysville Road, a kind of transportation subsidy that greatly enhanced its political and economic position. Many county primary and secondary roads were improved with macadam surfacing from the 1830s through the 1860s, which allowed farm and small-town residents easier access to Paris markets and merchants, further advancing an expanding prosperity. Travelers availed themselves of the amenities offered by Paris hotels, and local merchants stocked their stores with a wide variety of merchandise obtained from Philadelphia and other eastern cities during annual or semiannual buying trips. Thomas K. Marsh, a local silversmith, fabricated his own distinctive silver pieces and sold jewelry and watches made by Philadelphia artisans. By the 1830s the *Western Citizen* newspaper carried a bounty of advertisements for imported goods—Franklin and cook stoves, bathtubs, pumps, safes; Shakertown brooms, baskets, and tubs; and, prominently, patent pharmaceuticals that promised to cure any and every ailment. Achy bones? Try Jew David's Ointment Plaster. Going bald? Indian Renovating Hair Oil was the solution. Gray's Invaluable Ointment took its claims further, promising to cure "swellings, tumors, ulcers, sores . . . , wounds, bruises . . . , corns, et cetera."[1]

A national depression reached Paris and Bourbon County in 1839, fostering rising prices and labor costs and causing numerous bankruptcies. Nevertheless, the county's agricultural economy continued to expand. Court Day in Paris, held on Mondays for much of the nineteenth century, brought hundreds of people to town to shop and to buy and sell livestock, particularly mules, cattle, sheep, and horses. Wealthy farmers sent purchasing agents to Europe in search of blooded livestock to improve their herds. Farmers exhibited their best stock at the Bourbon County Agricultural Fair, held yearly at the fairgrounds on Paris's north side. Here one so inclined could encounter shorthorn cattle, Spanish jacks, Cotswold and Southdown sheep, and Berkshire hogs—livestock whose ancestors had been driven from East Coast ports into Kentucky by way of the Limestone Road or some other overland trail.

Financial recovery and growing prosperity in the 1840s encouraged the improvement of local country roads. Residents held public meetings in Paris and other Bourbon County communities in support of macadamizing existing principal roads.[2] In 1848 the Kentucky General Assembly granted charters for turnpikes to be established from Paris to several surrounding towns—Cynthiana, Clintonville, and Winchester. By the 1850s seemingly all roads led to Paris, and local farmers capitalized on the improved transport network to send their livestock and crops to Paris markets and mills.

Paris also became a hub on the railroad lines that developed between Lexington and Maysville, and Lexington and Covington, although not without some opposition. Paris residents generally supported the railroad because they expected that rail access would bring an economic boost to the town's economy. Others were less sanguine, given the railroad's speculative financing and uncertain profitability. Paris residents engaged in an impassioned debate, from 1850 to 1852, but ultimately support outweighed opposition. The Bourbon County Court began raising funds to support railroad construction by offering $150,000 worth of stock in 1857, an offer contingent on a majority vote favoring the measure in the July election. The measure passed, 886 to 484. Shares sold at fifty dollars each. To further underwrite the cost of construction, the court approved a property tax of three cents per hundred dollars assessed value. The court raised the tax to eight cents in 1852 to cover shortfalls, and it approved an additional two cents for a sinking fund in 1853.

With financial matters addressed, decision making turned to finalizing the railroad's route. The Maysville line would run from Paris to Millersburg and Carlisle. This route raised concerns that the line would run too close to the Maysville Turnpike, which would allow the railroad to siphon toll-paying traffic away from the venerable road. Collateral propinquity proved impossible to avoid, however, in part because the road followed low-gradient creek valleys and because the road also marked the shortest and most direct route, qualities railroad surveyors found very compelling. The railroad tracks closely paralleled the road between Paris and Millersburg. Surveyors even overlapped the railroad tracks and the turnpike at Paris and Millersburg. Despite concerns that railroad and road proximity would work against turnpike shareholders, travel along the road was not adversely affected in the short term, except for the stage line that once carried mail and passengers from Lexington to Paris and points north. When the track from Paris to Maysville was finally completed in the early 1870s, however, the railroad established stations at regular intervals between Carlisle and Maysville and the effect on village growth along the Maysville Road's northern section was not benign.

The railroad proved to be a boon to Paris, supporting its position as a livestock trade center. Rail-oriented tobacco warehouses and other shipping facilities also attracted important commercial customers from the county's fecund farms. The area's rapid economic growth during the 1840s and 1850s began to slow in the winter of 1856–57. Seeking an explanation, the local newspaper editor blamed "excessive imports, debts, internal improvements, land speculation, easy credit, and the banks in general for the ensuing depression."[3] The railroads suffered financial difficulties as well, and for a few years the economy was stagnant. The general depression lifted by 1859, and the local economy quickly recovered. Main Street commercial establishments in Paris once more enjoyed profitable patronage.

When the Civil War began in 1861, the influence on Bourbon County's economic recovery was almost immediate. By October local politicians were urging loyalty to the Union, a position that prevailed despite considerable Confederate allegiance manifested in southern sympathy meetings, contraband runs, and enlistment of local men in the Confederate unit known as the Orphan's Brigade. As the county seat and largest town, Paris was able to capitalize further on its position astride both the Maysville Turnpike and the railroad to become a focus for Union troop movements and bivouacs. The 35th Ohio Regiment established a camp at the Bourbon Fairgrounds in late 1862, remaining on duty for several weeks. Local aid societies organized to bake pies and cakes, prepare food baskets and toiletries, and provide blankets and other necessities for the soldiers. A Home Guard was organized to protect the county from marauders and bushwhackers. The first serious conflict in Paris came on July 18, 1862, when Confederate Brigadier General John Hunt Morgan commanded the Union post to surrender unconditionally, to which Captain P. E. Pugsley defiantly replied, "If you want Paris, you must fight for it." Morgan invaded Paris that afternoon and seized the newspaper office, but the Home Guard and local citizens repelled his advance. This initial skirmish involved only a fraction of Morgan's troops, however, and his main force returned and destroyed several railroad bridges, cut telegraph lines, and occupied Paris for a short period, stealing horses, guns, and clothing. After a brief encounter with Union troops from Lexington, Morgan and his men fled town with their booty, having done minimal damage.

A more inconvenient occupation of Paris took place from mid-September to late October 1862, forcing closure of the newspaper, mail disruption, and suspension of normal railroad schedules. The Confederates also introduced their worthless Confederate currency by forcing merchants to accept it for purchases—in essence, another form of theft from the local people. Confederates burned several buildings, jailed uncooperative citizens, and commandeered without compensation livestock, food, and arms. Seven weeks passed before Union forces prevailed and drove the Confederates from town.

Despite considerable sympathy for the southern cause by some Bourbon County citizens, majority support went to the Union, even among slaveholders. The August 1863 election sent two prominent Unionist slaveholders, Brutus J. Clay and Garrett Davis, to Washington to serve in Congress. Clay and Davis were both Whigs and conservative on constitutional matters. As the war pressed on, they became increasingly disillusioned with Lincoln's prosecution of the conflict, particularly his decision to enlist African American men, mostly slaves, into the Union Army. Despite much opposition, black enlistments began in March 1864, and Bourbon County eventually contributed more than 350 soldiers to the "sable arm of the Union," one of the state's highest county enlistments. In the war's waning months, guerrilla raids kept Paris and the surrounding countryside off-balance even though the battlefront was miles distant. Paris residents did improve security by installing a public lighting system comprising coal oil lamps in front of public buildings and hotels. The Union Army assigned black soldiers to guard duty in Paris, a measure that increased protection but sometimes led to misunderstandings and confrontations between the soldiers and white civilians who resented their presence.

On April 14, 1865, the *Western Citizen* announced the war's end, to the great relief of its readers. The following issue reported President Lincoln's assassination. Paris and Bourbon County, like the nation, now looked to the future with trepidation, wondering what kind of postwar society would ensue.[4]

19

Paris toward Blue Licks

Mile 0.0 From the Bourbon County Courthouse Square, the road leads northeast toward Maysville. The Elks/Masonic Lodge/Bourbon Hotel building, built circa 1901–5, stands on the left at the corner of Main and Bank Row. The four-story structure is of brick construction with stone trim in a Romanesque-inspired style. The Elks Lodge, B.P.O.E. no. 373, erected the building and used the upper two floors as club rooms. The Freemasons rented part of the building for several years and then bought it in 1926. The Bourbon Hotel moved here in the 1940s from a former Main Street location. Along Main Street between Third and Second streets, several nineteenth-century commercial buildings front the road northeastward from the courthouse square.

In the nineteenth century's first decade, the town building pattern in Paris still exhibited the traditional habit of assembling dissimilar land uses and structures—business, industry, and residential—together in awkward ways. Yet the settlement also exhibited features of the newly emerging mercantile town in which superior transport links fostered the growth in local and regional commodity manufacturing, a proliferation of artisans' workshops—tailors, cobblers, bakers, and blacksmiths, among many others—and specialized retail activity.[1] In the block from Third to Second streets, for example, the businesses on the right side included a saddlery, a drugstore, two dry goods stores, and Hughes Tavern; the Indian Queen Tavern stood at the corner of Second and Main. Across the street stood two malodorous tanneries, a mere half block from the courthouse, nuisance industries that were usually banished to the periphery in larger settlements. Beyond Second Street, a saloon, bakery, cabinet shop, residence, blacksmith shop, and hat shop fronted the street on the left.[2]

Mile 0.1 The railroad bridge here crosses U.S. 68. The highway bridge replaced a covered wood-frame bridge named the Cottontown Bridge for the cotton spinning mills that operated at creekside during the nineteenth century. Early nineteenth-century industries such as grist- and sawmills depended on waterpower and were perforce located at those points along a stream's course where falls or rapids provided power potential to turn a mill wheel. Lacking sufficient natural falls along a stream, millers could dam a stream at a point near a road access point, such as this one, and build an extended millrace to bring water from a point well upstream, or use

In the first North Main Street block north of the Paris courthouse square, commercial buildings dating from the 1870s to 1890s undergo stabilization and refurbishing. The facades' formal cornices and window hoods disguise the complex land uses that coexisted here in the nineteenth century—taverns, blacksmith shops, and a bakery, residence, and tannery.

The Paris Milling Company was the latest and most modern of the mills that occupied this site from 1800. Traditional water-powered wheels turned millstones for eighty years, producing thousands of barrels of wheat flour and cornmeal. The arrival of roller-mill technology ushered milling into the modern era, which foreshadowed the end of small-scale traditional custom mills. Paris Milling Company marketed the "Purity," "Crystal," "Bourbon Belle" (for fancy baking), and "Success" brands, all made from Kentucky winter wheat, as well as cornmeal ground from locally grown corn. (Courtesy of the University of Kentucky Library Special Collections)

a different mill-wheel configuration to provide power. When stationary steam engines became available in the trans-Appalachian west, they were readily applied to small industrial operations such as cotton mills.

Mile 0.2 After we pass beneath the railroad viaduct, the small stone structure on the left is the old Paris Gas Works building. The Paris Gas Company was organized in 1866 and erected this building, complete with low, arched windows, in the late 1860s. Now painted white, the structure houses a veterinary clinic. Crossing Stoner Creek on the highway bridge, we come to the Paris Milling Company on the right, which operated a flour mill here. The mill buildings still stand and the milldam still spans Stoner Creek. Farmers' Tobacco Warehouse no. 3 stands adjacent to the mill buildings.

Mile 0.3–0.5 Just as the southern gateway into Paris featured a row of burley tobacco auction warehouses, the north entry also hosted a "tobacco row." Some tobacco warehouses still stand on the left along this section of Main Street, including Farmers' Tobacco Warehouses nos. 1 and 2. The oldest warehouse here was a two-story brick building with a street-side windlass apparatus attached to the front cornice, which workers used to lift tobacco from wagons parked in the street to the second-floor access door. A demolition crew razed the venerable structure in 2006 along with a more conventional single-story warehouse nearby. The remaining warehouses are either empty or used for storage.

Mile 0.6 Legion Drive on the left leads to several small businesses and the forty-four-acre Legion Park. One of the state's tuberculosis hospitals once stood beyond the park, in the grove of tall trees on the hillcrest to the northwest. Closed in 1979, the once-grand hospital's vacant shell stood forgotten amid overgrown plantings for years, and the structure was finally demolished in 2012. The Bedford limestone entrance surround bore incised double-barred crosses that represented tuberculosis hospitals nationwide—the logo of the long-standing Christmas Seals fund-raising effort and the American Lung Association. Though substantially constructed of brick, the building contained asbestos, which would have to be removed before the structure could be rehabilitated for secondary uses. In the nineteenth and early twentieth centuries, tuberculosis was the leading cause of death in America. In 1946, motivated by the continued threat of tuberculosis, the U.S. Congress passed Public Law 725, a grant-in-aid program popularly known as the Hill-Burton Act, which designated $75 million in annual matching funds to assist states in constructing general, mental, chronic disease, and tuberculosis hospitals. A subsequent program amendment in 1949 increased the annual appropriation to $150 million.[3] To ensure that those states where the need was most acute built new hospitals first, the government established a guideline for the minimum number of hospital beds per state in 1949 at 2.5 beds per average annual death from tuberculosis. Kentucky ranked with the bottom seven states nationally, being some 2,000 beds short of the federal recommendation. The state moved quickly to integrate plans for new hospital construction, including both general and tuberculosis hospitals.[4] The Paris hospital, under construction in the late 1940s and opened in 1950, was one of several tuberculosis hospitals built across the state, including facilities in Louisville and Madisonville. The Paris hospital was large and clearly intended to serve a multicounty area. It was positioned in relative isolation from the town's residential quarter and atop the highest hill in the area to promote fresh airflow through the building when the windows were opened. The west entrance section was three stories, the main section four stories tall. In 1944 researchers developed the antibiotic streptomycin for treatment of tuberculosis, which, together with other antituberculosis drugs developed in the 1950s and 1960s, helped reduce the scourge substantially and eventually rendered tuberculosis hospitals obsolete.

Mile 0.8 The road intersects North Middletown Road (U.S. 460) on the right at the modern Shell Oil station. Most franchise gas stations no longer feature service bays with hydraulic car lifts to facilitate oil changes and grease jobs. As automobile manufacturers increased vehicle computer applications in the 1980s and 1990s, general auto repair became increasingly intractable and required expensive specialized equipment, a strong motivation for mechanics operating small, multipurpose gas stations to convert their grease rack space to more profitable use. The most popular gas station transformation has been to convert the service bays into a convenience store that sells milk, soft drinks, and snacks at higher profits than the operator could realize selling oil by the quart or antifreeze by the gallon.

Across the road on the left is the Bourbon Community Hospital. Recent renovations created space for a new operating room and radiology department. The fifty-eight-bed facility includes a physician staff in family practice, internal medicine, and a variety of other specialties such as orthopedics and cardiology. The hospital is owned by LifePoint Hospitals Inc., which, through its subsidiaries, owns, operates, and leases fifty-three general acute-care hospitals in small communities in nineteen states. LifePoint is headquartered in Brentwood, Tennessee, a suburb of Nashville. Like the old tuberculosis hospital just to the north, this site near the junction of U.S. 68 and the U.S. 68 Bypass enjoys high accessibility for Paris residents as well as those in the rural area that extends to the north and east.

Mile 1.0 At the intersection of the 1970s' U.S. 68 Bypass and the Maysville Road the old highway tightens, funnel-like, into two narrow lanes sans shoulders. From this point to Forest Retreat, west of Carlisle, the highway resembles a 1930s road. In some sections mature trees lean ominously toward the road; in other sections shallow ditches break abruptly downward from the asphalt lane in readiness to swallow a swerving car wheel, which could initiated a catastrophic rollover. Some 8,200 vehicles pass along this road section each day, many of them driven by people commuting to jobs in Lexington, as early morning and late afternoon traffic columns will attest.[5] In 2004 engineers at the Kentucky Transportation Cabinet prepared plans to widen U.S. 68 from this point north to southeastern Nicholas County, and construction began in February 2012. The present road will be widened into a four-lane highway with 6-foot inside shoulders and 12-foot outside shoulders, the opposing lanes divided by a 40-foot median. When completed, the 24-foot road will flare to a 124-foot divided highway, not including right-of-way. Vestiges of earlier roadbeds that lie close to the present alignment will probably disappear.[6]

Mile 1.1 Ruddles Mills Road intersects on the left. About five miles north of Paris, at the intersection of Stoner and Hinkston creeks, a nineteenth-century milling center developed; dams and millraces supplied water to turn mill wheels for at least two gristmills, which, together with the related businesses that grew up at the site, became known as the village of Ruddles Mills. The milling site became the focus of numerous nineteenth-century road- and turnpike-construction projects.[7]

The L & N Railroad track on the right parallels the highway from Paris to Millersburg. The line is now operated by the TTI Railroad, a short line with offices near the depot in Paris and the motto "Rail to River" service. TTI is a major coal-hauling route offering rail-to-river barge-loading facilities on the Ohio River east of Maysville.

Mile 1.8 Jackstown Road connects to the Maysville Road on the right, and just beyond it is the Bourbon Drive-In movie theater. Jackstown Road was formerly known as Duggins Mill Road—a reminder that before federal and state road numbering systems were put into practice in the 1920s, most roads were named for their

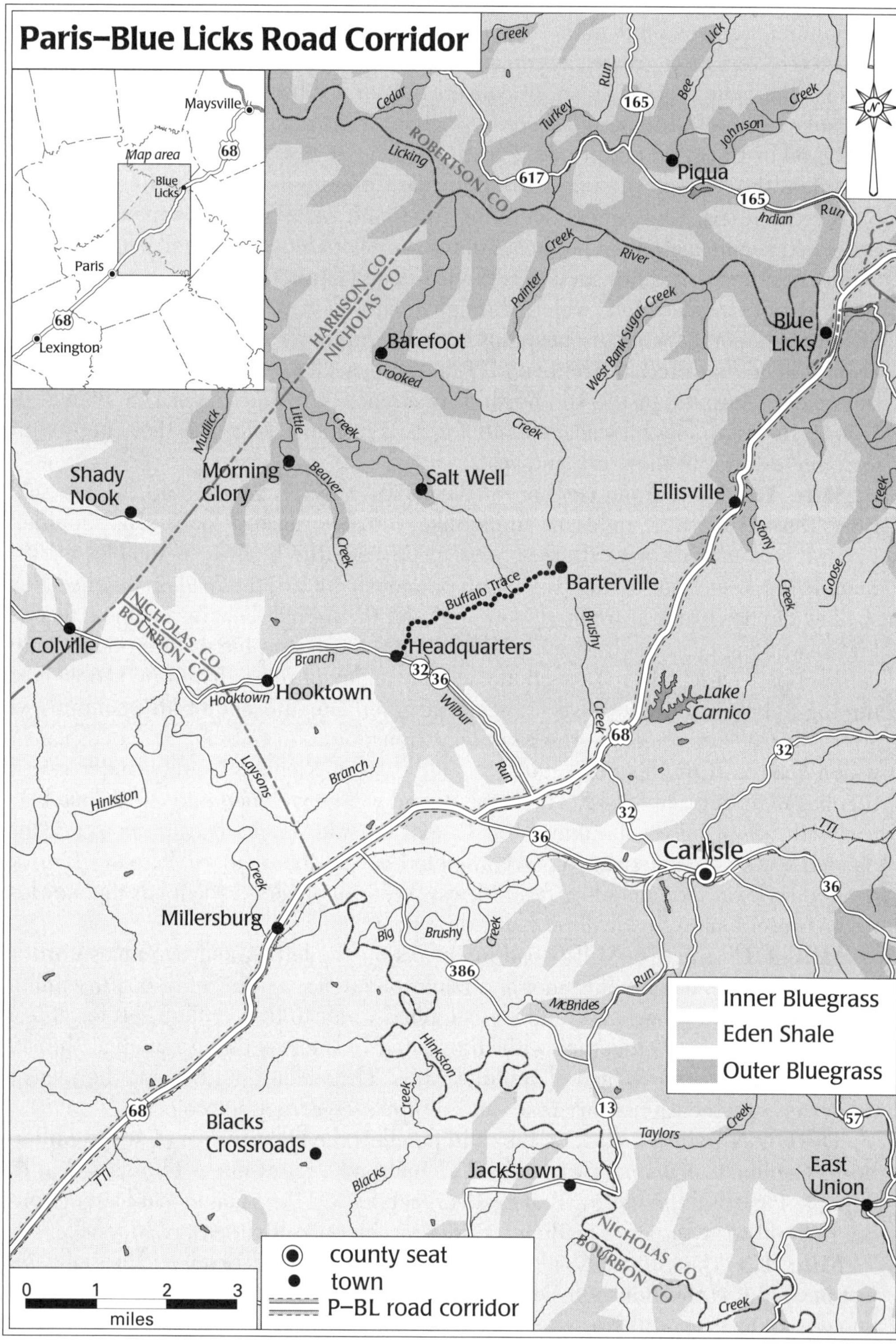
Paris–Blue Licks Road Corridor
Maysville
Map area
Blue Licks
Paris
Lexington
68
Piqua
Blue Licks
Barefoot
Shady Nook
Morning Glory
Salt Well
Ellisville
Barterville
Buffalo Trace
Colville
Headquarters
Hooktown
Lake Carnico
Carlisle
Millersburg
Blacks Crossroads
Jackstown
East Union
ROBERTSON CO
HARRISON CO
NICHOLAS CO
BOURBON CO
Licking River
Inner Bluegrass
Eden Shale
Outer Bluegrass
county seat
town
P–BL road corridor
0 1 2 3
miles

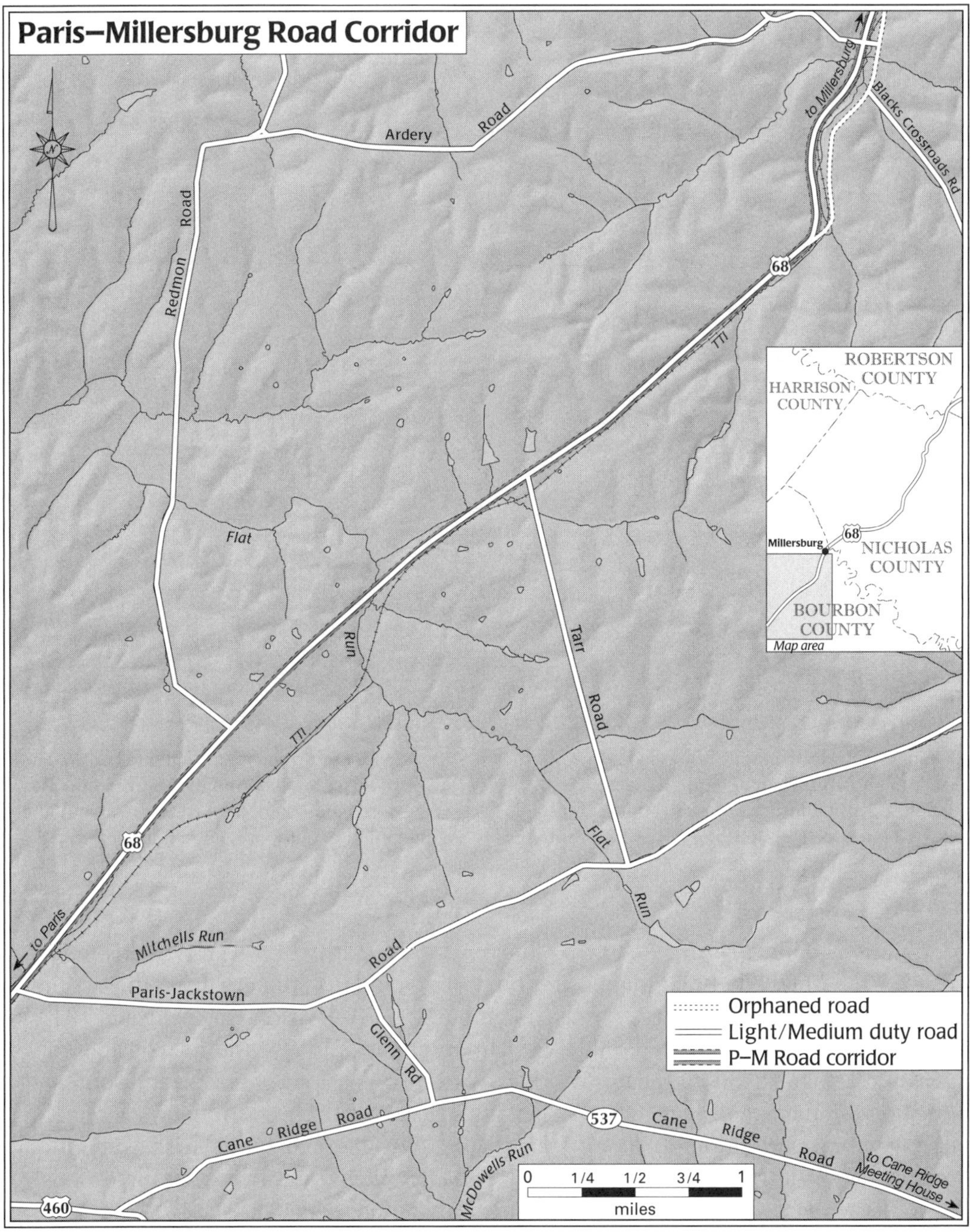

Paris–Millersburg Road Corridor
Ardery Road
Redmon Road
to Millersburg
Blacks Crossroads Rd
68
TTI
ROBERTSON COUNTY
HARRISON COUNTY
Millersburg
NICHOLAS COUNTY
BOURBON COUNTY
Map area
Flat Run
Tarr Road
Flat Run
to Paris
Mitchells Run
Paris-Jackstown Road
Glenn Rd
Orphaned road
Light/Medium duty road
P–M Road corridor
Cane Ridge Road
537
Cane Ridge Road
to Cane Ridge Meeting House
McDowells Run
0 1/4 1/2 3/4 1
miles
460

Though radically different from modern movie theaters with their comfortable seats, climate control, and state-of-the-art screening equipment, drive-in theaters were standard weekend-night entertainment for families and an inexpensive dating option for the local teenage population before the widespread availability of television. The Bourbon Drive-In is one of a very small number of outdoor theaters that still function during the summer months.

destinations. Duggins Mill Road also illustrates that many early county roads linked Paris or the Maysville Road to mill sites on Stoner and Hinkston creeks or their tributaries. The drive-in theater is a rare remnant of the pre-television era of the late 1940s and 1950s, when families could take a carful of children to a movie for considerably less money than an indoor theater would cost—one dollar for a carload was a common price on Sunday nights. The drive-in restaurant also contributed to the development of a novel form of automobility by encouraging customers to eat in their cars out of plastic baskets—fried chicken in a basket was a favorite—thereby saving the expense of constructing a formal restaurant that provided indoor service.

North of this intersection the road makes a transition onto younger bedrock—the Millersburg limestone—which has a higher shale component than the limestones to the south. This shale is soft and easily erodible, and as the proportion of shale content increases—up to 40 percent of the Millersburg vertical profile in some sections—the surface reflects the shale's presence in hillier topography.

Mile 2.0 The Paris/Bourbon County Stockyards are on the right. Beef cattle production in Bourbon County has a long tradition dating to the 1840s or before, and Bourbon and surrounding counties continue as major beef cattle producers. For the past decade the value of cattle sold by Kentucky's farmers each year has exceeded $500 million; the state's aggregate beef production ranks in the top ten nationally. Kentucky consistently produces more beef cattle than any other state east of the Mississippi River.[8]

The historic Mt. Gilead Meetinghouse site is adjacent to the stockyards. Though the meetinghouse was removed from the site years ago, its location is now commemorated by a stone monument that stands alone on a parklike lot beside the highway. A grove behind the meetinghouse lot shades a small cemetery containing graves of the Current and Isgrig families, both multigenerational families in the county. Eli Current operated an inn that once stood on or near the adjacent stockyards property. The inn was a favorite stop for stagecoaches and travelers.

Mile 3.3 The junction with Redmon Road is on the left. This road was formerly known as Steele's Road (circa 1818) and Mesles Road (circa 1827), and was an important early roadway that connected the Mt. Gilead Meetinghouse and Maysville Road to the surrounding neighborhood. The road had several forks and alternative routes that ran north to Ruddles Mills and a ford across Stoner Creek. In the winter old sunken or entrenched road tracks can be seen in farmers' pastures adjacent to Redmon Road.

Mile 4.0 In the open woodland back from the highway on the right stands an early nineteenth-century house known as The Grange (also called Oakland and Brentwood). Edward Stone, a local builder and slave trader, built the house around 1810–20. An excellent example of Federal-style architecture, the house closely resembles the Rose Hill House at Limestone and Fifth streets in Lexington. The Grange features a five-bay, central-hallway plan and large Palladian windows. Edward Stone and his brother were killed in 1826 on a boat trip to New Orleans while they were transporting slaves for sale in the southern market.

Mile 4.5 The Thomas Champ house, also known as Sulphur Spring, stands on the left. This house strongly resembles Rose Hill House and The Grange in style and probably was also built by Edward Stone, who owned it originally. It is likely that it was built around 1825 for a member of the Champ family.

Mile 5.2 Tarr Road intersects with the Maysville Road on the right.

Mile 5.6 Stream dissection is increasing, and pronounced hills appear on either side of the road. Hillcroft Farm, on the right, is owned by Misdee Wrigley, a great-granddaughter of William Wrigley Jr., who founded the Wrigley Chewing Gum Company in Chicago in 1891. During the late nineteenth century's Gilded Age, many of Chicago's successful industrialists and businesspeople built luxury summer homes in Lake Geneva, Wisconsin, some forty miles northwest of the city. In the 1920s William Wrigley acquired an established estate there, which became the original Hillcroft and included the famous Green Gables mansion and barns for the family's Arabian horses. The modern Kentucky version of Hillcroft is 850 acres of rolling Inner Bluegrass countryside dedicated to breeding American Saddlebreds and the rare Hackney horse for riding and harness-carriage driving competitions.

As the breed's name implies, the Saddlebred is an American-bred riding horse whose lineage can be traced to the Galloway and Hobby horses brought from England by British colonists in the 1600s. From this stock Rhode Island horse breeders developed the Narragansett Pacer; crossing it with the first Thoroughbred stallions imported from the Middle East, they produced the distinctive American horse by 1776. Settlers from the colonial states brought American horses into Kentucky, where they became the seed stock for Kentucky's horse-breeding industry. It is said that the Kentuckians who fought in the War of 1812 were mounted on American horses. Through continued selective breeding with Thoroughbred, Standardbred, and Morgan breeds, the American horse was further refined to become the American Saddlebred and was sometimes known as the Kentucky Saddler. The breed's foundation stallion, Denmark, was foaled in Boyle County, Kentucky, in 1839.[9] During the Civil War both Union and Confederate officers and cavalry troops rode Saddlebreds, including Ulysses S. Grant (Cincinnati), William Tecumseh Sherman (Lexington), Stonewall Jackson (Little Sorrell), and Robert E. Lee (Traveller). Today the American Saddlebred Association registers over a quarter million Saddlebreds and sanctions and organizes riding competitions. The Saddlebred is usually shown as a three-gaited or five-gaited horse, but it also participates in dressage, show jumping, cross-country jumping, driving, and cutting exhibitions. The Hackney is a distinctive high-stepping trotter developed in Norfolk, England, in the late 1700s whose specialized use as a carriage horse developed in parallel with the improvement of English roads in the mid-1800s. In 1878 Alexander J. Cassatt imported the first Hackney to Chesterbrook Farm, a palatial estate that he established along the Main Line in Berwyn, just west of Philadelphia. Cassatt was instrumental in founding the American Hackney Horse Society in 1891; today the society is headquartered at the Kentucky Horse Park north of Lexington. Cassatt worked as a civil engineer and administrator for the Pennsylvania Railroad and became president of the company in 1899.

The main entrance to Hillcroft Farm from the Maysville Road involves traversing a rather awkward trench cut by railroad engineers to reduce the grade through this hilly section. An arched bridge with stone abutments carries a gated driveway across the track and into the farm proper. Atop the hill opposite the entry gate stands a modern multifunctional barn that houses farm offices, tack and storage rooms, a farrier shop, show harness room, horse stalls, and a large, attached show arena. Misdee Wrigley's horses have garnered many major awards. Raffles was the 2001 Dutch National Champion, and Callaway's Independence Day won the 2003 Reserve World Championship for five-gaited geldings.[10]

Mile 6.8 The old U.S. 68 roadbed leaves the current highway here and runs parallel on the right. In 1956 the Commonwealth Department of Highways prepared plans to bypass the old road from here to Hinkston Creek on Millersburg's west side. Engineers aligned the new highway to the left of the old route, following the floodplain of a small creek that joins the Hinkston just ahead. While the new road made a more direct connection with Main Street in Millersburg, it also eliminated two at-grade railroad crossings with the Louisville & Nashville tracks, one here, the other ahead near the bridges that carried the road and the railroad across Hinkston Creek.

Not only were at-grade crossings dangerous, but long trains often caused major road traffic delays.[11] By 2007 highway traffic south of Millersburg averaged about 7,700 vehicles per day, or about 500 fewer vehicles per day than the number on U.S. 68 on the north side of Paris.[12]

The Kentucky Transportation Cabinet's plan to rebuild U.S. 68 includes a bypass around Millersburg's northwest side, or left of the present right-of-way. Each successive adjustment of the Maysville Road here has moved the roadway farther to the left. By routing the new bypass road northwest, highway engineers can avoid constructing two expensive railroad crossings that would have entered the calculus had they chosen a southeast bypass route.[13]

Mile 7.8 State Road 1893 intersects on the left. This old road arcs northwest and west to connect Millersburg with Ruddles Mills.

Mile 7.9 Old U.S. 68 rejoins the present-day road.

20

Millersburg

Mile 8.0 U.S. 68 crosses Hinkston Creek entering Millersburg from the southwest. In 1950 the highway followed the old track that crossed the river upstream of the dam spillway and stands left, or west, of the Louisville & Nashville Railroad bridge. Upon crossing the creek, the road followed an S-curve that connected to the old turnpike route, later renamed Main Street.[1]

Millersburg is in Bourbon County, just south of the Bourbon County–Nicholas County boundary. The town was established on land owned by Major John Miller. A native of Pennsylvania, Miller emigrated to Kentucky in 1775 with his brothers, Robert and William, William Steele, William McClelland, and others seeking suitable land for farming. After completing their surveys and planting corn crops under the duress of continual Indian harassment, the party returned to Pennsylvania to prepare their families for permanent emigration. The group made their return trip by flatboat down the Ohio River, which was, given the ongoing Indian threat, a dangerous gauntlet for emigrants. The trip proved fatal for Robert Miller, who was killed by Indians shooting at the party from the river's north bank. The tragedy compelled the Miller party to bypass landing at Limestone (Maysville), choosing instead to continue downriver to the Beargrass settlements (later Louisville), where they stayed until the conclusion of the Revolutionary War. When the Millers returned to the Millersburg area, the Indian threat had not been completely extinguished. The surviving brothers and their fellow settlers erected defensible log buildings to house and protect their families as they began developing their land claims into prosperous farms.

John Miller built the first mill for grinding grain and sawing logs on the east bank of Hinkston Creek at the Limestone Trace crossing. The mill was operating before Bourbon County was legally organized. Farmers often paid an in-kind milling fee of 10 percent of the flour or meal that mill operators ground for them. In this way millers accumulated substantial flour and meal stocks that they could sell locally; provided farm production was sufficient, they could ship their surplus downriver to New Orleans for sale there. After Bourbon County and its court were established, William Miller petitioned the court in 1788 for permission to erect a water-powered gristmill on the Hinkston "where the waggon road [Limestone Trace] leading from Bourbon Courthouse [Paris] to the Blue Licks crossed the creek," opposite his brother's mill.[2]

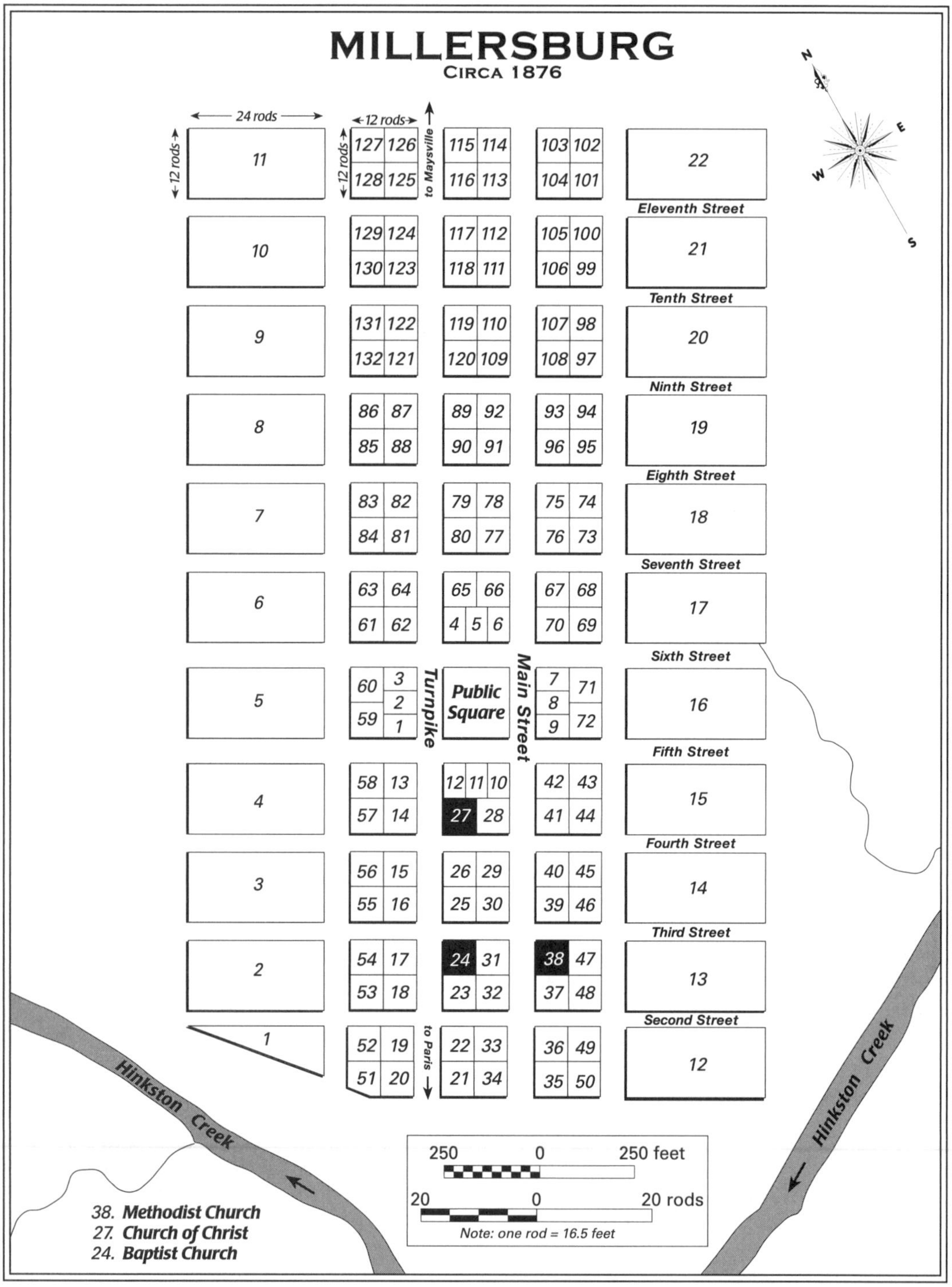
MILLERSBURG
CIRCA 1876
N
E
W
S
24 rods
12 rods
12 rods
12 rods
to Maysville
to Paris
Eleventh Street
Tenth Street
Ninth Street
Eighth Street
Seventh Street
Sixth Street
Fifth Street
Fourth Street
Third Street
Second Street
Turnpike
Main Street
Public Square
Hinkston Creek
Hinkston Creek
250
0
250 feet
20
0
20 rods
Note: one rod = 16.5 feet
38. Methodist Church
27. Church of Christ
24. Baptist Church

William Allison attached fulling equipment to this mill and in 1797 advertised his fulling business at this location. Because fulling mills typically processed wool cloth by pounding it in a slurry of potash soap and fuller's earth to remove lanolin and thicken and felt the fabric, area farmers were doubtless producing sheep in numbers sufficient to warrant mill construction before the turn of the nineteenth century. Needham Parry passed through the settlement in 1794 and found the Hinkston Creek banks bustling with millworks. "There is," he noted, "a dam & on one side of it there is a grist mill & saw & on the other side, right opposite, there is a grist & fulling mill: all of which are supplied out of the same head, one dam answering the whole."[3] Mills operated here throughout the nineteenth century under various owners.

The Kentucky General Assembly authorized the establishment of Millersburg on December 19, 1796. The town was not laid out until 1798, following an order by the Bourbon County Circuit Court. The town site of choice was similar to Paris's: astride the Limestone Trace and at the point where the road traversed an important regional perennial stream. Millersburg's original plat was lost but was redrawn by Alfred N. Gilbert in 1857. The town plan aligned with the Limestone Trace, which gave North Main Street a bearing of north 30 degrees east. North Main Street later became part of the Lexington-Maysville Turnpike. Main Street had three flanking streets, West Back Street on the westerly side and South Main and East Back streets on the east. The cross streets carried numbers, Second through Eleventh. An extension of Eleventh Street leading to the town cemetery was later surveyed and named Cemetery Street. The town plan comprised a total of 132 in-lots and twenty-two out-lots. The plat allowed for a public square bordered by North Main, Fifth, East Back, and Sixth streets. Between 1891 and 1897 Millersburg's major street names were changed. North Main became Main Street, South Main Street was renamed Vimont Street, and West Back and East Back became Trigg and Miller streets, respectively. The new names commemorated notable families who had been part of Millersburg's development since its earliest settlement.

Millersburg's town plat is generally similar to the Paris plan and has close relatives in south-central Pennsylvania. In detail, however, the Millersburg and Paris plats are substantially different. The Millersburg plat is based on square blocks, the Paris grid on rectangular blocks. The square block, usually divided into four square lots, is the basic city land division unit in many ancient Roman cities, a plan that in turn was based on Mediterranean traditions of agricultural land organization. A west and central European tradition of allocating land in long, narrow 120-acre "hides" of equal width to individual farmers was translated into urban rectangular blocks in hundreds of towns and cities where a guiding developmental principle was to allocate land, albeit for mercantile and residential use.[4] On the American frontier the square-block town found applications from the East Coast to the West, but the rectangular-block plat found wider favor among real estate developers. The rectangular block lent itself to repetitive subdivision into long, narrow, uniform lots while limiting the amount of space given over to streets. And fewer streets translated into fewer intersections, which rapidly became points of congestion in the era before traffic management was codified through regulation and signage.[5]

John Miller, Millersburg's founder and namesake, was from the Sherman Valley in Perry County, Pennsylvania. The seat of Cumberland County, Carlisle, lay in the legendary Great Valley just to the south across Blue Mountain on Forbes Road, which linked southeastern Pennsylvania and Pittsburgh. Carlisle is based on a linear, square-block plat similar to that of Millersburg. The nearby towns Newville and Mount Holly Springs, among several other towns in adjacent counties, have linear plats at their historic cores. The linear town plan was substantially different from the grid plan adopted by Lexington and was a clever adaptation to a roadside location. As employed in Millersburg and Paris, the linear plan included parallel backstreets on each side of the through road. The plan allowed the maximum number of lots facing the road, and road frontage was the most desirable location for both business and residence. The twin backstreets—in Millersburg these streets were originally named Back Street—provided room for residential expansion, yet these lots were only one block removed from the road.[6]

Initially, because John Miller donated one hundred acres of land for the town, he sold town lots as a proprietor. Eventually, however, the town's trustees controlled lot sales, although town governance was immature and record keeping was casual. Deeds filed with the county clerk record that lots were sold, traded, or transferred from one person to another quite informally for the first few years. A notable example is a deed filed in 1807.[7] The trustees transferred ownership of in-lot 16 to Alexander McClintock, documenting the previous transfer history within the text of the deed. William Kinnit and Jonathon Jonstone bought the lot from John Miller, then transferred it to Themson Ware, who subsequently transferred the lot to Michael Witch; there were later transfers to William Holliday, Robert Dudley, William Porter, and William McClintock before the final transfer to Alexander McClintock. Only at this point did Alexander McClintock seek a legal deed for the lot, which suggests that most early lot transfers were speculative investments, often very short term, as people sought to profit from frontier land fever. Millersburg and other frontier settlements along the Limestone Trace should therefore not be conceived of as stable, steadily growing settlements, which might be inferred from plat maps and abstracted histories. Rather, for at least two decades after their founding, these incipient urban places, in part because of their superior accessibility, were rife with speculation that bred economic and demographic instability.

In addition to its early focus on milling, Millersburg developed into a viable nineteenth-century trading and road-traffic service center. Nevertheless, the town's population increased only moderately between 1810 and 1840. In 1810 Millersburg tallied thirty-five households with 238 residents, 49 (20.6 percent) of whom were slaves. No free blacks lived in town at this date. A decade later Millersburg's total population had increased to 385, of whom 72 were slaves and 13 were free blacks. By 1830, sixty-three households accounted for 450 individuals, including 111 slaves (24.7 percent of the population) and 11 free blacks. The town had lost population by 1840, 427 individuals in fifty-six households, but slaves had increased in number to 133, or 31.1 percent.[8] During the last half of the nineteenth century Millersburg's population doubled, the most rapid growth occurring after the close of the Civil War. The increase is attributable in large part to emancipated blacks' leaving nearby farms and moving into town, and to the student body at Kentucky Wesleyan College, which accounted for nearly a quarter of the white population in 1870.[9] Most of the employed blacks in Millersburg in 1870 were female domestic servants (64 of 102). The only other gainfully employed black women worked in child care, and only 11 women were housewives without other employment. Among employed black males, farmhands were most numerous (19 of 38), followed by 11 domestic servants, 3 laborers, and a blacksmith, a wagoner, a hostler, a shoemaker, and a barber.

Whites worked at a variety of occupations, largely typical urban jobs for the period. Among the professional class were professors of ancient languages and mathematics who taught at the Millersburg Female College and Kentucky Wesleyan College, and several physicians and ministers. Dry goods merchants, druggists, and grocers and their clerks represented the retail establishments. Two hotel proprietors provided room and board for passing travelers. Town security was the responsibility of a single constable.

Several carpenters, a cabinetmaker, a stonemason, and a few painters represented the building trades in Millersburg. The presence of tradespeople in a town is a reliable indicator that the settlement is demographically stable and has potential to grow. Skilled tradespeople were mobile; they could often find work in multiple locations and had no need to tie themselves to a place with limited prospects. Two livestock traders took advantage of Millersburg's location on the road to serve the drovers whose stock drives regularly passed through, and wagon makers, saddlers, and blacksmiths served the road's more conventional horse-drawn travelers. Millersburg became a post town, requiring the services of a postmaster and assistant. Other services included a woman milliner and several tailors, a tinner, two butchers, a whiskey dealer, and an undertaker.[10]

A cholera outbreak in 1873 caused seventy-six deaths in Millersburg; the town's black and Irish citizens were especially vulnerable. Local doctors blamed stagnant, polluted water and poor hygiene practices and attributed some recoveries to the judicious consumption of calomel and charcoal, a treatment that no doubt did more harm than good, since calomel contains toxic quantities of mercury.[11]

Despite cholera's tragic toll, the town's population continued to increase, reaching 858 citizens by 1880.[12] Though many traditional commercial establishments and services continued in operation, some notable changes were under way in post–Civil War Millersburg. African Americans represented just over half the town's population; most blacks still worked as farm laborers, in domestic service, or in child care. Before 1870 the black residential pattern included family-based households scattered throughout town, and individual black workers living within white households. By 1880 the black population had become largely segregated in a residential enclave called Judyville on the town's east side. The development of residential segregation may have started as early as the 1873 cholera outbreak, which sickened mostly black citizens who lived in a "negro settlement along the course of a branch running on the eastern border of the town and parallel with the railroad."[13] Racially segregated neighborhoods became commonplace in Kentucky's towns and cities in the score of years following the Civil

War. In the countryside new black settlements took the form of small hamlets, but in towns blacks occupied neighborhoods or subdivisions usually named after the white landowner who subdivided land to provide residential lots that blacks could rent or purchase.[14]

Millersburg in the 1880s is profiled in period business gazetteers and censuses. The Kentucky Central Railroad tracks skirted the northeast edge of town and gave employment to a brakeman, three travel agents, a porter, and a civil engineer. Another rail agent doubled as the operator of a recent technological innovation in communication, the telegraph. The railroad did not eclipse the need for traditional wheeled conveyances. Millersburg had three wagon makers, two carriage makers, a carriage trimmer, and five carriage painters. A construction boom stimulated the building trades; the results can still be seen in the town's collection of Victorian-era architecture. Millersburg remained an important center for higher education with the continued operation of the Millersburg Female College and Kentucky Wesleyan College. The Millersburg Deposit Bank handled financial transactions, and a lawyer was on hand for legal issues. Local production of clothing and footwear also increased as women entered the workforce in greater numbers as milliners, dressmakers, seamstresses, and mantua makers as well as the usually male occupations of shoemaker and tailor. Retail establishments remained much the same: groceries, general stores, dry goods, butchers, bakers, and coal and lumber yards. The Millersburg Coal and Lumber Company was one of the railroad's largest customers; the building still stands, now in faded red paint, along Vimont Street, one block east of Main Street, where it would have been closer to the railroad track, an important convenience in the transfer of bulky deliveries.[15] The company's vehicular in-street weight scale is still in position in front of the building.

Approaching the turn of the twentieth century, Millersburg continued to gain population but remained a small town with a maximum of 950 inhabitants. In 1896 the *Kentucky State Gazetteer and Business Directory* advertised many businesses typical of a small urban community of the time. Along with an assortment of grocery, dry goods, and drug stores, local citizens could avail themselves of medical and dental professionals, the building trades, dressmakers and milliners, barbers, confectioners, blacksmiths, livestock dealers, an elocutionist, and other service providers. The new Opera House provided entertainment, as did two bands—the Millersburg Cornet Band and the Colored Cornet Band. The Millersburg Military Institute, then known as the Millersburg Training School, was one of four schools, including the female college and two public schools. (Kentucky Wesleyan had moved to Winchester in 1890.) The local flour mill was still in business and the increasing importance of tobacco as a cash crop prompted several growers to include their names in the gazetteer even though they did not live in town.

Millersburg's quintessential small-town milieu and diverse matrix of class, race, and occupation persisted into the early twentieth century, and for decades thereafter the town quietly served its surrounding hinterland as a central place for retail goods and professional services. As the century wore on, businesses decreased in number and variety, and the town gradually lost the historic range of social classes and ethnic diversity. In 2010 Millersburg's population was 792, approximately the same size as it had been 120 years earlier. African Americans constituted 2.7 percent of that number, while 3.7 percent were Hispanic.[16] The Pruitt Funeral Home is one of few surviving businesses from the early twentieth century. Most recently, the town lost its last bank, and its elementary school and Millersburg Military Institute closed. The W. R. Stamler Manufacturing Company, which makes mining machinery, was one of the town's major employers, but the company moved to Lexington. Millersburg today serves mainly as a commuter-residential community with only a few basic businesses and churches.

Mile 8.1 Old Main Street enters from the right. The turnpike entered town on the west end and crossed Hinkston Creek via a covered bridge just above the milldam. The pike then split to follow the course of North Main Street (present Main Street). The present-day U.S. 68 leads directly into town on a post-1950s bypass and becomes Main Street, crossing Hinkston Creek and its nearly thousand-foot-wide alluvial floodplain via a modern steel and concrete bridge. The road's original trajectory into town is still visible as a section of roadway called Old Millersburg Road. The milldam is also still visible upstream from the modern bridge.

Mile 8.3 Millersburg's Main Street is an eclectic mix of structures of the late eighteenth- to early nineteenth-century, later antebellum, and late nineteenth- to early twentieth-century periods whose architecture chronicles the town's growth. As the road curves right to engage the town's street grid, a row of stone and brick houses fronts the road on the left; these are superb examples of early town houses and commercial buildings with exceptional masonry and beautiful millwork, inside and out. James McKee, an early Millersburg merchant, was responsible for building a stone house and shop, a stone bank, and a brick town house. McKee built his stone house and shop about 1791. The stonemasonry was probably done by McKee or Thomas Metcalfe, two important early builders and stonemasons. The adjoining stone building in the middle of the row was built as the Bank of Hinkston about 1809. The brick town house on the corner dates before 1830.[17] The buildings were later purchased by Louis Vimont, another prominent merchant, who emigrated to the United States from France and moved to Millersburg about 1795. In addition to his mercantile interests, Vimont also served as postmaster and road contractor, and he was involved in the macadamization of sections of the turnpike in the 1830s.[18] Being a block removed from the high-traffic Main Street, Vimont Street attracted a variety of businesses, small churches, and residences.

The house at 206 Main Street is an unusual conversion and reuse of the former First Baptist Church, built around 1825 on a nave plan, with separate entrances for women and men. The church was converted to a dwelling around 1886 with the addition of side gables and a one-story filigreed Victorian porch. Former First Baptist Church members organized the First Christian Church at the corner of Fourth Street and Main in 1831. They completed the nave-plan brick church in 1842. There followed two substantive remodelings; after the Civil War the congregation converted the entire structure to Gothic Revival style, and in 1926 they further modified the church with Tudor-style elements in the brick addition on the front.

In 1900 the U.S. Patent Office issued a patent for a machine to manufacture hollow concrete blocks. The machine, available from Sears, Roebuck and Company and many other retailers, produced standard-size blocks with a face side that resembled rusticated stone. Between 1905 and 1930 builders erected thousands of commercial and residential buildings using rock-faced concrete-block, among them this two-story version that stands one block south of the Millersburg town square. The building has served as an implement dealership and general mechanic's shop. It is surrounded by a collection of venerable fifty-year-old International Harvester Farmall tractors, including a Model H that was introduced in 1940 and sold for less than $1,000 if equipped with rubber tires—if equipped with steel wheels, the tractor was some $200 cheaper. The H was rated as a two-plow tractor, ideal for use on small farms with light soils.

Mile 8.4 On the right, an 1882 iron fence encloses Millersburg's town square, a central feature in the 1780s town plan. Residents built a Republican or Union church on the square in the early nineteenth century; the structure served as a common meetinghouse until the various religious denominations built their own churches. The church was later torn down, and the public square thereafter has been maintained as open green space for community activities and events.

The main Millersburg business area between Third and Seventh streets contains numerous late nineteenth- and early twentieth-century commercial buildings that are visible evidence of the town's prosperous past. By the close of the Civil War in 1865, the Millersburg commercial area included furniture dealers, druggists, dealers in dry goods, groceries, hardware and other commodities, milliners, saddle and harness makers, shoemakers, physicians, and millers, totaling twenty-eight separate businesses. By

Like many small towns, Millersburg supported small banking institutions throughout the nineteenth and during most of the twentieth centuries. Bank investment in local businesses fueled a small town's prosperity. Here, at the Exchange Bank on Main Street, a patron could get a loan on a handshake because the loan officer knew which community members were reliable risks and which were not. As banking firms consolidated and large concerns bought out the small ones, branch banks closed for reasons of cost efficiency, and small-town banking became much less common.

the 1890s the street's commercial buildings had begun to acquire decorative cast-iron fronts; many survive as exemplars of late nineteenth-century building technology and style. These buildings, constructed or rebuilt when the town's population peaked at 950, represent Millersburg's commercial apogee.

The block from Fourth Street to Fifth includes the Millersburg Opera House at the middle of the block, flanked by a narrow commercial building constructed in 1898 and the Miller Block building, where John Miller's grandson ran a grocery. The Miller Block's second floor served as a lodge hall for various fraternal organizations, including the Freemasons. The Odd Fellows met in the building on the corner of Fourth and Main Street. A unique example of early log construction, the two-story, weatherboarded log house at 407 Main Street stands close to the street and has only two upstairs windows (typical of late eighteenth- and early nineteenth-century log dwellings). The diminutive single-story frame house at 413 Main Street is a rare survivor of a house form and scale that was common in the early nineteenth century. In contrast, the larger, two-story homes nearby were built later, after architectural tastes shifted to more elaborate styles, greater square footage, and ornate embellishments. From Fifth Street to Sixth, bank buildings dominated the block, illustrating that even in relatively small urban places, functions such as banking tended to cluster or "localize" to mutual advantage. Various late nineteenth-century hotels also used some of the commercial buildings.

Mile 8.5 Millersburg's Presbyterians formally organized in 1818 and worshiped initially in the common meetinghouse that stood on the public square. In 1870 they built the First Presbyterian Church on the left in the popular Gothic Revival ecclesiastical style.

Mile 8.6 Beyond the business district, nineteenth-century houses line Main Street in an eclectic mix of architectural styles—Gothic Revival, Greek Revival, Roman Classical, Queen Anne, and Italianate. The 1950s' Millersburg Motel on the right is a classic small-town motel. A small parking lot that opens directly to the highway fronts the L-shaped building. In the late 1950s or the 1960s the owner sacrificed part of the parking lot and added a small swimming pool beside the highway, a strategy followed by many independent motels during this period, when new franchise motels festooned the American roadside, many featuring such amenities as swimming pools. Small independent motel owners had to consider adding similar features or lose customers. The motel was one of the few local places offering visitor accommodations during the Millersburg Military Institute graduation celebrations, family reunions, and other special events. In the 1990s, as the traveling public sought accommodations in larger towns, the motel's owners converted the business to apartments rented to local residents who paid by the week or month, an operational strategy adopted by the owners of thousands of old roadside motels nationwide. The motel swimming pool has been filled to the top with crushed limestone chips, a strategy intended no doubt to avoid accidents and lawsuits.

Mile 8.8 Standing back from the road on the right among grand old trees is the campus of the eighteen-acre Millersburg Military Institute, established here in 1893. The institute was housed initially in William Nunn's 1852 Greek Revival residence. Nunn was heavily involved in educational projects in Millersburg, including the Millersburg Male and Female Institute, which became Kentucky Wesleyan College in 1858 (later moved to Winchester and then Owensboro, Kentucky). Colonel C. M. Best established the Millersburg Training School, first housed in the old Kentucky Wesleyan College building across the street (now replaced by Millersburg Elementary School). Colonel Best purchased the college grounds and buildings in 1898. He converted the structures into a military boarding school and named it Millersburg Military Institute. The campus included the Nunn house, which operated as the administration building and president's home; Moffett Hall, built in 1921; a brick-veneered gymnasium built in 1916; Rankin Hall, built as a classroom and dormitory; and a chapel. In 1947 the institute added a new building, the construction of which required eight massive wooden timbers whose considerable length obliged the contractor to ship them on the railroad—each timber occupying two flatcars.[19] Although the school operated for 113 years, it was plagued by financial difficulties and closed in August 2006.[20] In 2008 the U.S. Army Cadet Corps of Dayton, Pennsylvania (not

The Millersburg Cemetery, situated beside the highway on the northern outskirts of town, contains the remains of Millersburg's founder, John Miller, as well as other early families. Supplanted by the public cemetery established in the center of town, this early cemetery's antiquated tombstones, standing in the gloom cast by old trees, would seem almost gothic were it not for the modern-day traffic on the Maysville Road.

affiliated with the U.S. Army) bought the site with plans to establish their National Cadet Training Center here.

Mile 9.0 CR 1879, or the Cynthiana Road, intersects here with U.S. 68.

Mile 9.1 Maplewood House, on the left, is believed to have been built circa 1850 for John Clark Miller, grandson of Millersburg's founder, John Miller. The Greek Revival house also includes Italianate and Gothic details.

Mile 9.4 Located at the Bourbon County–Nicholas County line, the Millersburg Cemetery is the town's oldest cemetery and the final resting place of many of Millersburg's early prominent citizens. A turnpike tollhouse once stood next to the cemetery.

Mile 10.1 SR 386 intersects U.S. 68 on the right. As U.S. 68 tracks northeast toward Carlisle, it crosses a gradual topographic transition—the surface becomes rougher, the valleys deeper, and the slopes steeper—as the road leaves the Inner Bluegrass and enters the Eden Shale Hills. By taking a short side trip here on SR 386,

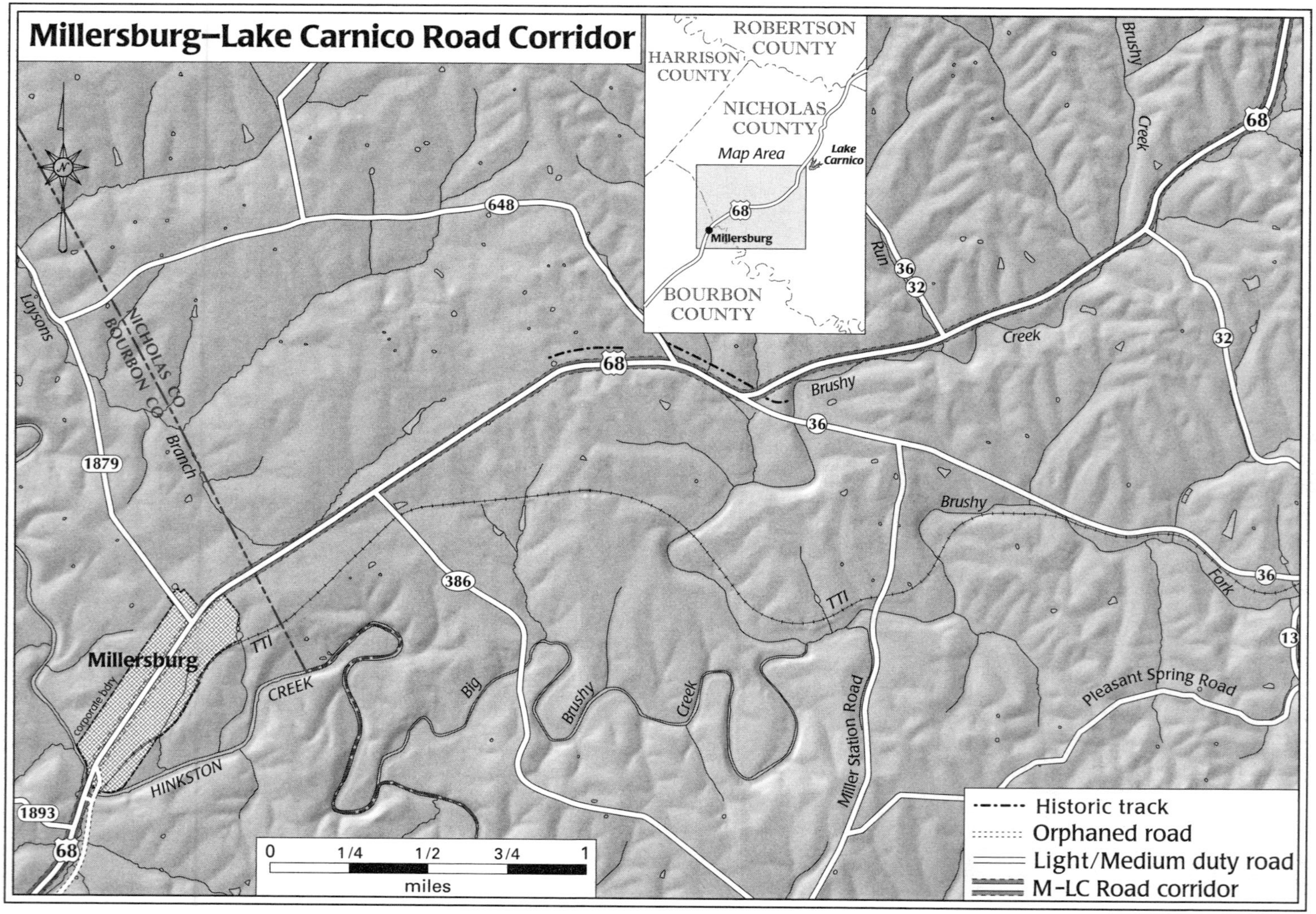
Millersburg–Lake Carnico Road Corridor
ROBERTSON COUNTY
HARRISON COUNTY
NICHOLAS COUNTY
BOURBON COUNTY
Map Area
Lake Carnico
Millersburg
68
648
1879
1893
386
36
32
13
NICHOLAS CO
BOURBON CO
Laysons
Branch
Brushy Creek
Run
Brushy Fork
TTI
Big Brushy Creek
HINKSTON CREEK
corporate bdry
Miller Station Road
Pleasant Spring Road
Historic track
Orphaned road
Light/Medium duty road
M-LC Road corridor
0
1/4
1/2
3/4
1
miles

one can encounter the Eden Shale country more directly. During any season of the year this is visually interesting country. SR 386 is paralleled by some historic road sections, now cut off by new alignments but still clearly visible beside the present road. One orphaned road section has nineteenth-century rock fences running along one or both sides.

Mile 11.2 The old turnpike road alignment is visible here to the left of the present highway.

Mile 11.3 The farm site on the left includes a house that stood here in 1827. It probably corresponds to the Johnston house that fronted the old pike at the three-mile mark north from Millersburg. In 1948 State Highway Department engineers straightened this road section to the Carlisle cutoff about three-quarters of a mile ahead. The effect was dramatic. From this point to the junction with SR 648 ahead, three different road alignments follow the old road corridor. The pre-1948 road ran to the right, crossed to the left, then recrossed to the right at the rock quarry ahead. Meanwhile, a still older road track can be seen in the field to the left, paralleling the current highway; it is probably a first-generation organic roadbed and may also be an

As viewed from SR 648, the sunken track of the old Maysville Road crosses a pasture to pass by the front of the farmhouse in the grove of trees at Eaglestone Farm. The old road's shallow trench is roughly fifty feet wide and can be traced across sidehills paralleling the present road for nearly a mile.

old buffalo trace. This early road is entrenched—it does not follow a built-up roadbed—which suggests that it predates formal road engineering and construction and was a simple cross-country track or way. It followed the side hill above the eastward flowing intermittent stream toward Brushy Creek at the SR 36 intersection.

The traffic count average on this road segment in 2008 was about 7,000 vehicles per day. The Kentucky Transportation Cabinet plans to begin rebuilding this section into a four-lane highway from Millersburg to CR 1455.[21]

Mile 11.7 At the intersection with SR 648 the first-generation buffalo road–organic trail is clearly visible crossing the pasture to the left. By driving a short distance north on SR 648, one can intersect this old track, represented here by a shallow trench some thirty feet wide. Upon crossing SR 648, the track climbs the hill and passes close to the front of the Eaglestone Farm house. In 1948 nineteenth-century dry-laid rock fences lined both sides of SR 648, then called Stone Road. The fences extended east and north along U.S. 68 well past the Carlisle cutoff. Most roadside rock fences were removed in 1948 when engineers realigned and widened the highway. Construction plans called for the removal of 1,158 yards of rock fence along the next two thousand feet of roadway.[22] As highway designers learned when rock fences along the Paris Pike section of U.S. 68 were rebuilt or built anew to accommodate the new road alignment, replacement of professionally built dry-laid rock fence can cost up to $300 per linear yard. At that rate, the 1948 realignment of this short section of demolished rock fence would cost about $347,000 at present-day replacement prices.

Mile 11.8 Eaglestone Farm's formal entrance is on the left. The old road track ran directly in front of the present house. During the 1980s and 1990s, Eaglestone Farm was owned by the William Marquard family. Marquard was chairman and CEO of American Standard, a multinational manufacturing company, before retiring in the 1980s. The farm bred and raced Thoroughbred horses and raised purebred Angus cattle.[23]

21

The Eden Shale Hills

Mile 12.1 At the junction of U.S. 68 and the SR 36 connector to Carlisle, the old Maysville Road turned nearly 90 degrees to the left, or northeast, to follow the Brushy Creek valley. The creek flows south toward Hinkston Creek, the trunk stream in this section, so the road was heading up gradient into the heart of the Eden Shale Hills. A small tributary of Brushy Creek runs through this intersection, necessitating two bridges or culverts, one under U.S. 68 and the other under SR 36. Before 1948 the road continued about two hundred feet beyond this intersection and then turned northeast. The old track is still visible crossing the hill to the right and descending a steep grade to the Brushy Creek floodplain before reconnecting with the present alignment. Rock fences lined both sides of this old road segment until the late 1940s.

Mile 12.4 The modern U.S. 68 follows the historic road's track very closely through this section, clinging to the low side hill above Brushy Creek's floodplain. The road crosses several small tributaries, such as Wilbur Run, necessitating culverts at each crossing. SR 32 and 36 follow Wilbur Run upstream to the village of Headquarters, three miles to the west. Positioned parallel to U.S. 68, an old road called Buffalo Trace Road runs from near Headquarters northeast to Barterville. Vandals have stolen the official road signs, but some property owners include the Buffalo Trace address on their roadside mailboxes.

Mile 12.6 Old Carlisle Road heads off to the right just beyond the Rock Haven Auction House. The road is just discernible as an entrenched depression heading up the creek bank to higher ground.

Mile 13.1 SR 32 to Carlisle intersects the Maysville Road here. Ready Money Jack, a colorful character during the early historic settlement era, once lived in the vicinity. John Hedges said Ready Money Jack was from Pennsylvania's Monongahela country, where Indian encounters were common, and thus he was not afraid of Indian attack. Jack operated "a kind of tavern" at this location. Joseph Luckey claimed Ready Money Jack was a freed slave. Luckey explained his nickname as "must have the ready money," implying that he preferred monetary transactions to those involving barter, trade, or credit. Holladay's Inn stood in this area in 1827.[1]

Traffic along this section of U.S. 68 averaged about 4,200 vehicles per day in 2008, or only 59 percent of the 7,100 vehicles per day carried by the highway segment only four miles to the south near the Nicholas County–Bourbon County boundary. The Nicholas County seat, Carlisle, lies just three and one-half miles east of the SR 36–U.S. 68 intersection. Traffic on SR 36 to Carlisle is typically about 3,900 vehicles per day, or nearly equal to the traffic load on U.S. 68, which suggests that the local two-way, seat-to-seat traffic from Carlisle to Paris and Lexington is nearly as great as the long-distance flow from Paris to Maysville.[2]

Mile 13.6 The road follows Brushy Creek upstream here, passing a rare nineteenth-century stone barn on the right. The surrounding hills are capped with Kope formation rocks, which in vertical profile are roughly 80 percent soft shales interbedded with limestone.[3] The shale readily dissolves when exposed to precipitation—easily seen in road cuts—and it slumps and slides with alacrity, soon filling the roadside ditches with mud that highway crews must periodically load onto trucks and haul away. One enters the heart of the Eden Shale Hills here, and much of the land from here to near Mayslick is steeply sloped; there is only a thin veneer of soil that if farmed is best left in grass pasture, as one sees here on all sides.

Mile 13.7 The state historic marker number 1230 here suggests that a restored log cabin reputed to be Daniel Boone's last home in Kentucky stands on the hillside to the right. Boone and his family lived in the vicinity until they moved to Missouri, then in the Louisiana Territory, in 1799. The log building originally stood near the road next to a small stream that periodically flooded. To preserve the structure, Dr. Eslie Asbury, the owner of Forest Retreat, ahead on the left, moved it to its current location.

Mile 13.9 Dry-laid rock fences once lined the road's left side near the intersection of U.S. 68 and SR 1244 and extended several hundred feet along the county road to the north. A small stone gable-roofed stable stands just beyond the intersection, also on the left. Roughly two miles to the left or northwest, along SR 1244 at Johnson Road, the Eden Shale countryside provides the natural backdrop for Artcroft, conceived in the late 1990s as a retreat for artists and writers. Artcroft's rationale is based loosely on that of the McDowell Colony in Peterborough, New Hampshire. The retreat's core is a four-hundred-acre cattle and goat farm. An 1840s Greek Revival farmhouse provides living space for artists-in-residence. A 1910 tobacco barn has been converted to artists' work space, and a new two-story studio building provides additional work and living space. Fellowships and work exchange programs support the artists who come to work here.[4]

Mile 14.1 Peyton's Tavern, now a private residence, stands beside the road on the right. The tavern is one of the few nineteenth-century roadside taverns remaining along this section of the Maysville Road. The building's form includes a large two-story great room on the left, or north, end, flanked by an extended ell to the right, which contained individual single-story rooms for travelers. Each room had an entry door on the front and a rear door that opened onto the backyard, which gave guests access to an outdoor privy that stood near Brushy Creek. In 1948 a small log cabin also stood in the backyard. An outside stair leads to rooms on the second floor. When the building was rebuilt as a private home, the front outside doors were sealed and inside connecting doorways were opened to link all the rooms to the great room, which is now a kitchen and living room.

Across the highway to the left is the entrance to Forest Retreat, the former home of Thomas Metcalfe. The handsome stone house stands at the top of a hill about a quarter mile back from the road. Metcalfe was a prominent nineteenth-century Kentucky politician who served in the Kentucky General Assembly and the U.S. Senate and was governor of Kentucky from 1828 to 1833. Born in Fauquier County, Virginia, in 1780, Metcalfe came to Kentucky with his family in 1785, initially settling in Fayette County. Thereafter he relocated to Nicholas County. Metcalfe was one of sixteen children, and, owing to his father's modest financial means, at age sixteen he apprenticed to an older brother to learn stonemasonry. Metcalfe excelled at his craft and worked on the second courthouse in Paris, the McKee house and shop in Millersburg, and many other area buildings.

In 1812 Metcalfe was elected to the Kentucky General Assembly from Nicholas County and served for several years. Because of his occupation as a stonemason, he became known as "Old Stonehammer," a nickname he embraced with pride. He raised a company of volunteers in 1813 and served with distinction under Colonel William E. Boswell at the Battle of Fort Meigs during the War of 1812. His military service caught the attention of General William H. Harrison. Metcalfe helped Harrison campaign in his successful bid for the presidency; his assistance included making a nomination speech at the nominating convention.

Thomas Metcalfe continued his political career in the U.S. Congress as a representative in 1818. He supported protective tariffs and internal improvements, and he advocated for easier sale of public land. In 1827, for example, Metcalfe proposed construction of a mail road to begin in Zanesville, Ohio, and run southwest through Maysville and Lexington to Nashville, Tennessee, and Florence, Alabama, en route to New Orleans. He also convinced the secretary of war to order a survey of the road section that was to begin at Maysville in May of that year.[5]

Metcalfe resigned his representative's seat in 1828 to run for Kentucky governor as a National Republican, an election he won by a narrow margin against William T. Barry, the Democratic candidate. Metcalfe's single term as governor was quite progressive; he believed that internal improvements were necessary for the economic development of the state and strongly endorsed and encouraged such projects as the Portland Canal at the Falls of the Ohio, the Lexington & Ohio Railroad, the Green River Navigation Company, and the Shelbyville-Louisville Road. After President Andrew Jackson vetoed federal aid for the Lexington-Maysville Turnpike, Metcalfe provided state funds so the project could move forward.

Metcalfe supported the American Colonization Society and was in favor of the emigration of slaves and free blacks to Liberia. After his governorship, he continued to hold public office, serving again in the Kentucky legislature, and filled the unexpired term of John J. Crittenden in the U.S. Senate.

Metcalfe served as president of Kentucky's Board of Internal Improvement in the 1840s and was a strong advocate for construction and maintenance of high-quality roads, including the Maysville Turnpike. His position as board president set him at odds with the Maysville Turnpike directors over road management, toll collections, and other issues. Through purchase of turnpike company stock, the state invested in

Thomas Metcalfe's country estate, Forest Retreat, stands on the low hill beside the Maysville Road in Nicholas County. Born in Virginia's Piedmont region in 1780, Metcalfe was in his twenties when he moved to Kentucky and Nicholas County. His skills as a stonemason earned him the nickname "Old Stonehammer." Metcalfe served on the state Board of Internal Improvement and was a strong advocate for improving roads. He served a term as governor from 1828 until 1832. The dry-laid rock fence bordering the farm's frontage on U.S. 68 was probably built in the nineteenth century. The small, square hole in the fence near the corner is a passage for small animals and is termed a cripple, lunky, smoot, or thawl hole in Scotland and northern England. Just out of the frame to the left stands a dry-laid stone barn; across the road to the right is Peyton's Tavern, one of the few remaining nineteenth-century taverns remaining at the roadside.

the construction of more than twenty major roads across the state and by 1840 had acquired more than $2 million in turnpike shares. Toll collections were intended, by statute, to pay dividends to stockholders, including the state, thereby gradually repaying the state's investment. In 1839, however, the tolls collected on all turnpike stock totaled $9,471, or less than one-half of one percent of the capital invested. And tolls from the previous six years added up to only $29,100. At fault, in the opinion of the Internal Improvement Board, were the turnpike company directors, who spent too little time and effort properly managing turnpike business.[6] Furthermore, the Internal Improvement Board believed that turnpike directors capriciously managed the pike to suit their own interests rather than those of the stockholders, and the Maysville directors were perhaps the worst of the lot. Turnpike companies, it seemed, appointed too many directors whose entitlements included using the road toll-free. Even stockholders so benefited. And, in defiance of state law, the directors unilaterally reduced toll fares. All this greatly perplexed Metcalfe, who called a convention of state turnpike directors at the state capitol in Frankfort in April 1847 for the purpose of forcing them to adopt a uniform toll rate for all toll roads—rates that had already been set by the General Assembly. Some toll road companies complied. The Maysville Turnpike Company did not.[7]

Failing health caused Metcalfe to decline a federal appointment as secretary of war, and he retired to his Forest Retreat farm in 1849 to live out his remaining years. Metcalfe had purchased the farm in 1816. Throughout his political career, he entertained many dignitaries at Forest Retreat, including Henry Clay, Andrew Jackson, and William Henry Harrison. The farm property included a separate building used as a tavern, the stone stable that still stands at the corner of U.S. 68 and SR 1244, and other outbuildings. Cholera took Thomas Metcalfe's life in 1855 at the age of seventy-five. He is buried in the family cemetery near his home, along with his wife, Nancy Mason Metcalfe, who died in 1852.

Mile 14.1–14.4 On the left, a considerable run of nineteenth-century dry-laid rock fence still stands, demarcating the Forest Retreat property from the road right-of-way.

Mile 14.2 The intersection of SR 32, an old turnpike linking Carlisle, the Nicolas County seat, to the Maysville Road, is on the right. In 1948 a country store and gas station with two pumps stood here on the right at the SR 32–U.S. 68 intersection.

Mile 14.4 When this road segment was rebuilt in 1948, the alignment remained essentially the same; a few small curves were eliminated, but the road was widened, resurfaced, and reconfigured to accommodate wider shoulders using materials excavated from nearby road cuts.

Brushy Creek, a south-flowing tributary of Hinkston Creek, has cut a low-gradient valley into the south rim of the Eden Shale country. The Maysville Road has long followed this natural route. This view from SR 1455, or Lake Road, is southward from the Lake Carnico dam. The golf course fairway in the foreground gives way to valley-bottom tobacco fields and hillside pastures in the middle distance.

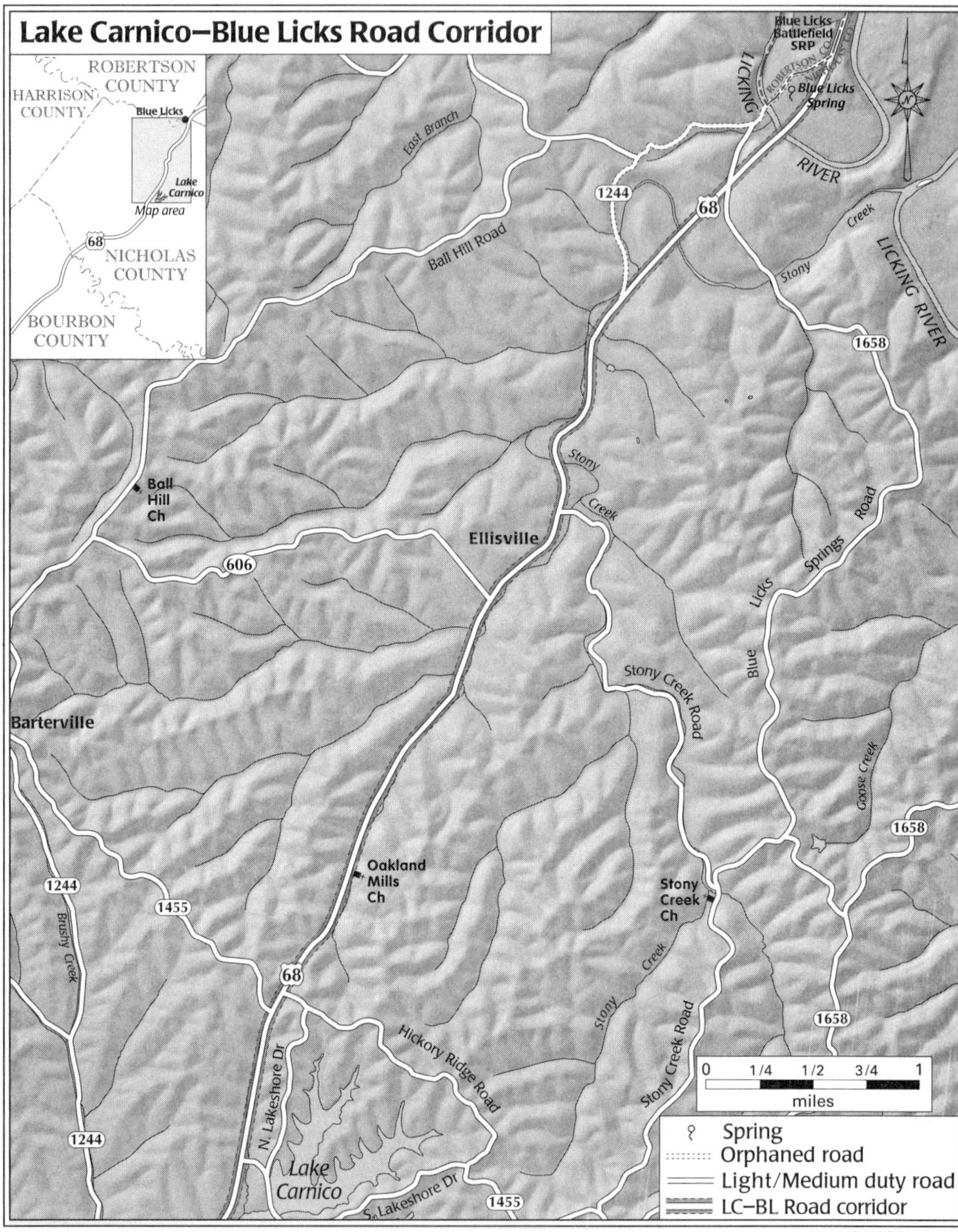

Mile 15.3 County Road 1455, another link between Carlisle and U.S. 68, intersects here on the right. The 500-acre Lake Carnico Development District on the right dates from 1994 and includes a nine-hole, par-thirty-six golf course, and a 114-acre lake; both front on U.S. 68. The 4-H youth development program at the University of Kentucky maintains four 4-H camps across the state. The North Central Camp is

"Over Here!" The plaint articulated in red paint on a shed wall summarizes the effect that a new highway bypass has on traditional roadside businesses. Selling secondhand goods, whether at antiques stores, flea markets, or rummage shops, is one of the most common business activities to reoccupy road-front stores in small towns and roadside settlements bypassed by new highway alignments. When the 1990s bypass around Ellisville was completed, an antiques dealer erected signs facing the new highway and set up a display of old horse-drawn moldboard plows in an attempt to entice potential customers back to the old road.

part of the Lake Carnico site and serves thirty-four counties. The camp's 350-acre site includes heated cabins, bathhouses, a dining hall, and other facilities sufficient to accommodate more than three hundred campers.

Mile 16.0 The road to the hamlet of Barterville, SR 1455, intersects U.S. 68 here on the left.

Mile 16.2 On the right, Hickory Ridge Road intersects U.S. 68.

Mile 16.6 The old road alignment parallels the modern U.S. 68 on the right.

Mile 16.9–17.6 The old road parallels U.S. 68 on the left as the highway approaches Ellisville, a string village (that is, strung out along a road instead of being set on a grid or other, more complex street configuration) aligned along the old highway ahead.

Mile 18.3 The junction with SR 606, also called Sugg Road, is on the left. About 2.3 miles west on SR 606 is Ball Hill Road, which follows the same general alignment as Buffalo Trace Road and may be a remnant of that early track. The present Ball Hill Road leads directly to the Lower Blue Licks, which is about three miles ahead on U.S. 68. Ellisville is an unincorporated collection of roadside homes lining the old highway. An old clapboard general store, now an antiques shop, stands on the right; some of the original store shelving is still in place. A Stony Creek tributary flows parallel to the road, and the new 1990s bypass runs to the right, or east, of the creek. Recognizing that potential customers are now bypassing them, some Ellisville entrepreneurs have erected hand-painted signs on their buildings or along the bypass to remind travelers that they can still find antiques along the old highway.

Mile 18.6 The old road closely parallels U.S. 68 on the right here, and a twentieth-century schoolhouse still stands along the old alignment.

Mile 18.8 Stony Road intersects U.S. 68 on the right.

Mile 18.9 Ellis Tavern stands on the left here, at the base of a steep hill and fronting on a fragment of the old turnpike. James Ellis built this stone house in which he operated a tavern along the original Limestone Trace in 1807. The building replaced a log station that he had built before 1782—the eighteenth-century forest that covered these hills included black oak, white oak, hickory, and beech trees. In 1804 Nicholas County officials established the county seat here, which necessitated construction of a log courthouse, jail, and stray pen (a pound for wandering livestock), and the place was named Ellisville. In 1814 the seat moved east to Carlisle. Ellisville remained a small roadside community throughout the nineteenth century and into the twentieth century, its importance highlighted by the presence of a post office from 1879 to 1906, a flour mill, a school, blacksmith, cobbler, wagon and cooper shops, and several stores. Part of the small community was called Shake Rag by some of its citizens who disliked the name Ellisville.[8]

The creek valley is comparatively wide here, and, given its general position in the Eden Shale Hills, Ellisville may have been a favored site for the development of small bottomland farms that provided water and fodder for drovers moving herds of livestock along the road, and for coach horses during the stagecoach era.

Mile 19.0 Stony Creek, flowing north toward the Licking River, crosses the road here from right to left. Three bridge sites, two of them extant, stand side by side, marking three different bridge-building technologies. The oldest crossing is the farthest west, or left. This approach and crossing is now represented by an old road fragment and stone bridge abutments that probably supported a wooden covered bridge. The old roadbed on the creek's south side has grown up in trees. The old bridge was superseded by an early 1930s approach and concrete bridge that parallels the original alignment here and crosses Stony Creek.[9] In 1967 transportation engineers drew up plans to bypass the 1930s road with an alignment that crosses the creek on a steel and concrete bridge of modern design.[10] The 1930s road is now an orphaned cutoff loop used primarily by local farm residents. The multiple bridges and old road cutoff loops represent increasingly sophisticated engineering solutions and the application of evolving road-construction technologies. When large, steam-powered tractors and shovels replaced hand picks, grub hoes, and wheelbarrows, engineers could assertively cut roadbeds through rugged land rather than timorously routing them along

Offering concrete tchotchkes to suit every taste, this new roadside business in Ellisville capitalizes on the popularity of treating residential yards and gardens as yet another canvas for the home decorator. One might choose from elegant fountains and classical figures, whimsical gnomes, and ethnically inspired donkeys and sombrero-topped youngsters; whatever one's preference, an ambitious gardener-decorator can convert a yard or garden into another room of the house with themed decorative statuary.

the gentlest gradients that the difficult topography permitted. Highway construction contractors using power earth-moving equipment and explosives could create roadbeds by crosscutting deep trenches into hill spurs and utilizing the excavated rock and overburden as embankment fill across interstitial valleys to a depth sufficient to create nearly level road surfaces. Engineers designed the new highway to eliminate tight curves, decrease gradients, increase sight-line distances, and increase load-carrying capacity. Where the new alignment approximated the original roadway the resulting superimposition of the straight new road onto the old serpentine curves created a pattern of interlaced loops that isolated islandlike land parcels between two or more roads.

Mile 19.2–19.4 The winding 1930s road follows the hilly topography, continuing on the left side of the modern alignment along this section. A new roadside business on the left offers concrete yard gear for sale behind a chain-link fence befitting a secret military instillation. The level sales lot is covered in stone chips to eliminate mud splash on the merchandise, which includes every manner of urn, planter, and statue. Interspersed, frozen in gray concrete, is a small army of gnomes, fauns, gargoyles, and Greek goddesses awaiting their new assignments to guard patios or add mass-produced "classic" dignity to bowered and bluegrassed backyards.

Mile 19.9 SR 1244 intersects the 1960s alignment of U.S. 68 here.

Mile 20.6 On the right, the Ishmael Chapel Church Road intersects U.S. 68.

22

Blue Licks

Mile 21.0 The old turnpike road, the Blue Licks cutoff, ran to the left here on its southern approach to the Licking River crossing. To follow the old route, turn left and cross Stony Creek on the concrete bridge. At the junction with SR 1244 stands a small frame building at the corner; a Freemason emblem is attached to the front facade. The upper story now serves as Blue Licks Lodge no. 495. The stone foundation and an unusual water-control structure behind the building suggest that it was once a hillside mill, although it is not clear how water would have reached the building. The structure's facade intimates that the original building was modified into a store. About a mile and one-half from U.S. 68, an iron bridge—now closed—carried the old road across the Licking River. On the river's north side, the embanked roadbed crosses the Licking's broad floodplain. A few houses and a large two-story commercial building, now used for storage, is all that remains of the old Blue Licks settlement here. The current U.S. 68 crosses the Licking River on a modern bridge to the east, or right, of the saline springs.

In the 1790s Isaac Drake of Mayslick traveled here to the salt-boiling operation to barter for salt. Though the area later attracted visitors seeking cures for their physical ailments by drinking and bathing in the mineralized springwater, the water's saline content was relatively low for efficient salt recovery. Drake bartered for salt with corn or hay, because the surrounding area produced neither. By bringing as much meadowgrass hay as two horses could pull, he could obtain one bushel of salt in trade.[1]

The mineral-rich water attracted large numbers of herbivorous animals and their predators (including humans) from the Pleistocene era to historic times. In addition to creating a trail network that focused at the lick, large numbers of bison, deer, elk, and other animals trampled and uprooted vegetation for a considerable distance around the lick in search of salt deposits. Animal grazing and rooting may have discouraged tree growth and encouraged the formation of glades or tree-fringed open areas colonized by grasses and other herbaceous plants. One plant that apparently adapted to such unusual environmental conditions was Short's goldenrod (*Solidago shortii*). This rare goldenrod species was initially discovered by Charles W. Short on Rock Island at the Falls of the Ohio at Louisville in 1840. After engineers built the lock and dam there in the 1920s, the species was thought extinct. In the 1930s the ecologist E. Lucy Braun found the species growing on barren, overgrazed hillside pastures around Lower Blue Licks, and plant ecologists have documented several Short's goldenrod populations that survive in the area, especially along the old buffalo trace and along both the old and new sections of U.S. 68.[2] The Blue Licks Battlefield State Resort Park sponsors a Short's Goldenrod Festival each September, when the goldenrod blooms.

Many Pleistocene animals became trapped in the mire surrounding the lick; excavations of their fossilized bones began at Lower Blue Licks as early as 1784, when entrepreneurs erected saltworks here. Subsequent saltworks proprietors continued to find fossilized bones as they attempted to improve the salt springs by digging them deeper and enlarging them. The proprietors of the summer hotel at the Licks in 1897 hired a local resident, Thomas W. Hunter, to dig a series of trenches near the salt springs in the hopes of determining why the water volume was declining. Hunter assembled the bones that he found in an extensive collection that was eventually installed at the Blue Licks State Park museum.[3]

Prehistoric and historic peoples alike boiled down Blue Licks water to extract the salt, a necessary mineral nutrient for good health and a fundamental requirement for food preservation. The spring's strategic location and value is pointed up by several incidents, including a visit by Daniel Boone and a party of settlers who came here in 1778 to boil water to obtain salt for the settlers living at Fort Boonesborough in present-day Madison County, Kentucky. Boone's work crew produced several hundred bushels of salt during weeks of difficult work in miserable winter weather. In early February, while Boone was hunting with his son-in-law Flanders Callaway and Thomas Brooks, they encountered a large party of Shawnee who were on their way to attack Fort Boonesborough. Boone convinced his men to surrender to ward off the pending attack on Fort Boonesborough. The Shawnee took the captive salt crew to their Scioto River settlement at what would later become Chillicothe, Ohio. Boone escaped in June and returned to Fort Boonesborough to warn residents of another planned attack.[4]

In 1784 David Tanner began a saltworks here that consisted of four kettles that he rented out to people who wished to make their own salt. He enclosed the mineral spring and the kettles with a log palisade, "closely chinked and daubed and carried up about ten feet high and twenty feet or more square but left with an open top and having a strong door."[5] Tanner's dwelling, also strongly picketed, was on the hill about one hundred yards south of the spring and kettles. A guard of a dozen or more men kept constant vigil over the site, watching for Indians, who also frequented the area. Tanner even instructed his guards to use a password to identify friendly visitors, as Ben Guthrie discovered when he and his companions sought refuge and were initially refused entry because they did not know the countersign that Tanner required to distinguish friend from foe.[6]

Under the best of circumstances, boiling Blue Licks water to obtain salt was a laborious undertaking. Those who established the industry had to assemble three basic resources: brine water of sufficient salinity to make the operation economically viable, ample hardwood to maintain large fires for extended periods, and iron that could be cast into boiling kettles. Lower Blue Licks water proffered comparatively weak brine.

To obtain one bushel of salt required boiling down roughly one thousand gallons of springwater. By comparison, the brine waters in the Ohio Valley's major salines, such as the Scioto Salt Works in Ohio and Ohio Salt Lick east of Maysville, contained salt in much higher concentrations. At the Ohio Salt Lick, for example, three hundred gallons of water would produce one bushel of salt.[7] Firewood was readily obtained in the Eden Shale Hills, although the extensive barrens around the Blue Lick created by buffalo and other animals prompted wood cutters to travel well beyond the immediate area to obtain wood sufficient to keep the burners in operation. Eastern Kentucky frontier iron-blast furnaces near Russell in Greenup County, and the Slate Creek furnace near Owingsville in Bath County, provided the forty-inch iron kettles that the Blue Licks salt boilers required. The early iron furnaces were called "salts" because much of their initial production was cast into kettles for the salt industry.[8]

By Ohio Valley standards, the Lower Blue Licks salt-boiling operation was a low-profit operation that maintained production during the early years by supplying local markets. As road and river transportation improved, however, salt produced in greater volume and at much lower cost at other salines made the Lower Blue Licks an improvident operation, and salt making declined. The site, nevertheless, attracted hunters and salt makers during the pioneer era and was a place coveted by Indians and white settlers alike. A battle fought at the Lick in 1782 between the American settlers and a consortium of British regulars, Queen's Rangers, and Indians from the Wyandot, Ottawa, Ojibwa, and Potawatomi tribes resulted in a disastrous defeat for the settlers. What began as a retaliatory chase after an Indian contingent that had attacked Bryan's Station and other settlements in the Lexington area ended with a fierce engagement at Blue Licks. Sixty-four settlers were killed, including Daniel Boone's son Israel and nephew Thomas, as were many prominent officers, such as John Todd, Stephen Trigg, Silas Harlan, and John Gordon, as well as numerous privates. The ambuscade became known as the Battle of Blue Licks.[9]

The Licks' economic potential attracted early surveyors who sought legal title to the real estate surrounding the springs. Richard Johnson was the first; he received in 1774 a military warrant of 2,000 acres issued by Lord John Murray Dunmore, royal governor of Virginia. Francis Scott received a military warrant for 50 acres, which was subsequently assigned to Turner Hunt Hudson, then to Philip Love, and finally to John Floyd over a period of a few months in 1774. Floyd assigned the 50 acres to James Parberry in 1778, who also claimed an adjoining 450 acres here in 1780. About 1787 Parberry assigned half of the 450-acre tract to James Buchanan, who also wished to establish a ferry across the Licking River, and the other half to James French. Thereafter, French's half was assigned successively to Littleberry Bedford, Henry Clay Sr., Henry Clay Jr., and finally George M. Bedinger in 1791. The conflict between the Parberry and Johnson claims was apparently resolved in Parberry's favor, and Johnson never gained title to any Blue Licks land despite his early warrant.[10]

As the dangers of the Kentucky frontier receded, Lower Blue Licks attracted more economic development. Major George Michael Bedinger, an early entrepreneur, built gristmills on both sides of the Licking and eventually added a tobacco warehouse, sawmill, general store, and blacksmith shop. James Buchanan's widow and heirs conveyed their property interest to William Bartlett in 1816. Bartlett laid out lots for a town to be called Bartlettsburgh and held a public sale in March 1816. The plat for Bartlettsburgh was filed in the Nicholas County clerk's office in 1817, but Bartlett's death in 1820 quashed plans for town development.[11]

Developers built several resort hotels at Lower Blue Licks during the nineteenth century, and visitors traveled the Maysville Turnpike to the site, where they could "take the waters." The medical wisdom of the day heralded the benefits of bathing in and drinking the mineral waters. Though the promise of Lower Blue Licks springwater was probably barmecidal (that is, imaginary) as a curative medium, people of all classes traveled long distances over bad roads to imbibe. Francis Cuming visited the Blue Licks in 1808 and stayed at a tavern hosted by Mrs. Williams and her sister, Miss Howard, both agreeable women whom Cuming found to be "better bred, and better informed than most of the tavern ladies we had seen since we left Pittsburgh." Cuming encountered other visitors who were there to drink the mineral waters, "which are esteemed as efficacious in some disorders." He described the water's smell and taste as "exactly like the bilge water in a ship's hold." The nauseous water was sometimes cathartic and sometimes emetic in its effect, but it did not cause "griping or sickness of the stomach."[12] By 1827 four innkeepers, Bedinger, Boolingal, Moor, and Throckmorton, were operating establishments at Lower Blue Licks. The Good Intent stagecoach line began operation in 1825, and the route included the Blue Licks inns. The completion of the Lexington-Maysville Turnpike further enhanced Lower Blue Licks' attraction as an important tourist destination. To improve access to the resort, Lewis Wernwag built a covered bridge across the Licking River at Blue Licks, and a post office was established.[13]

In 1842 Thomas and Louis P. Holliday leased land belonging to the Bedinger family and built a large, three-story resort hotel boasting three hundred rooms, an expansive dining room, a ballroom, and three elegant parlors. The facade featured deep galleries to accommodate lounging visitors. Known as the Arlington Hotel, it hosted hundreds of visitors until 1862, when it burned to the ground. The Bedinger heirs built a smaller hotel nearby in 1870. They named it the LaRue House after its proprietor, John LaRue. About 1877 a well-known Paris innkeeper, Captain Daniel Turney, built a new hotel on the Arlington Hotel site, which became known as Turney's Arlington House. By the 1880s the site had become a popular spa, and area newspapers extolled the Lower Blue Licks as the "Saratoga of the South."[14]

Lower Blue Licks was also home to the Western Military Institute for a brief period when the school moved from Georgetown in January 1850. The institute catered to the sons of wealthy southern planters and emphasized engineering, mathematics, and military science. The school buildings accommodated three hundred cadets, but allegations of inadequate housing arose toward the end of 1850, and school administrators resolved the issue by moving the school to Drennon Springs in Henry County, where it reopened in 1851.[15]

Though many visitors came to Lower Blue Licks to sample the water personally, entrepreneurs formed several companies to bottle the water for retail sales elsewhere. Pierce and Stanton of Maysville and the Blue Licks Water Company of Covington

Blue Licks offered many entertainment and accommodation options to visitors during the nineteenth century, when "taking the waters" constituted a fashionable vacation, made more desirable by the prevailing belief in the medicinal benefits of the mineral water that flowed from the springs. Four innkeepers plied their trade here by 1827, and the springs remained a popular destination until they ceased to flow in the late nineteenth century. (Courtesy of the Kentucky Historical Society, Frank Dunn Collection)

marketed the water in their communities from the 1850s to 1870. The Lower Blue Licks Spring Company formed in 1889 to exploit the springs. That same year Turney's Arlington House burned, and E. T. Calvert of Louisville purchased both the springs and the hotel site in 1892. The tourist industry continued to thrive for several more years, but the springs began to fail in 1896 and efforts to revive them were unsuccessful. By 1904 the springs had ceased to flow entirely and financial ruin loomed. Tourists stopped coming, and the remaining hotel went out of business.

A radical realignment of U.S. 68 bypassed the historic Lower Blue Licks settlement in the 1960s. The old road intersects U.S. 68 on the left and crosses the Licking River on an aged iron-truss bridge downstream from the modern crossing. One of the historic saline springs was sited about 650 feet north of the river and about 120 feet west of the present road. The cycle of development, growth, and demise of the Lower Blue Licks settlement created one of the most extensive lost landscapes that developed along the Maysville Road. Few material artifacts remain to suggest the magnitude or sequence of spring-oriented development that occurred here; even the Eden Shale woodland has recovered, and black oak, hickory, hackberry, and juniper trees now inhabit the surrounding hills.

Mile 21.4 The old road reenters the 1960s highway from the left. Based on the most elementary road-building technology, the old road was extremely sensitive to

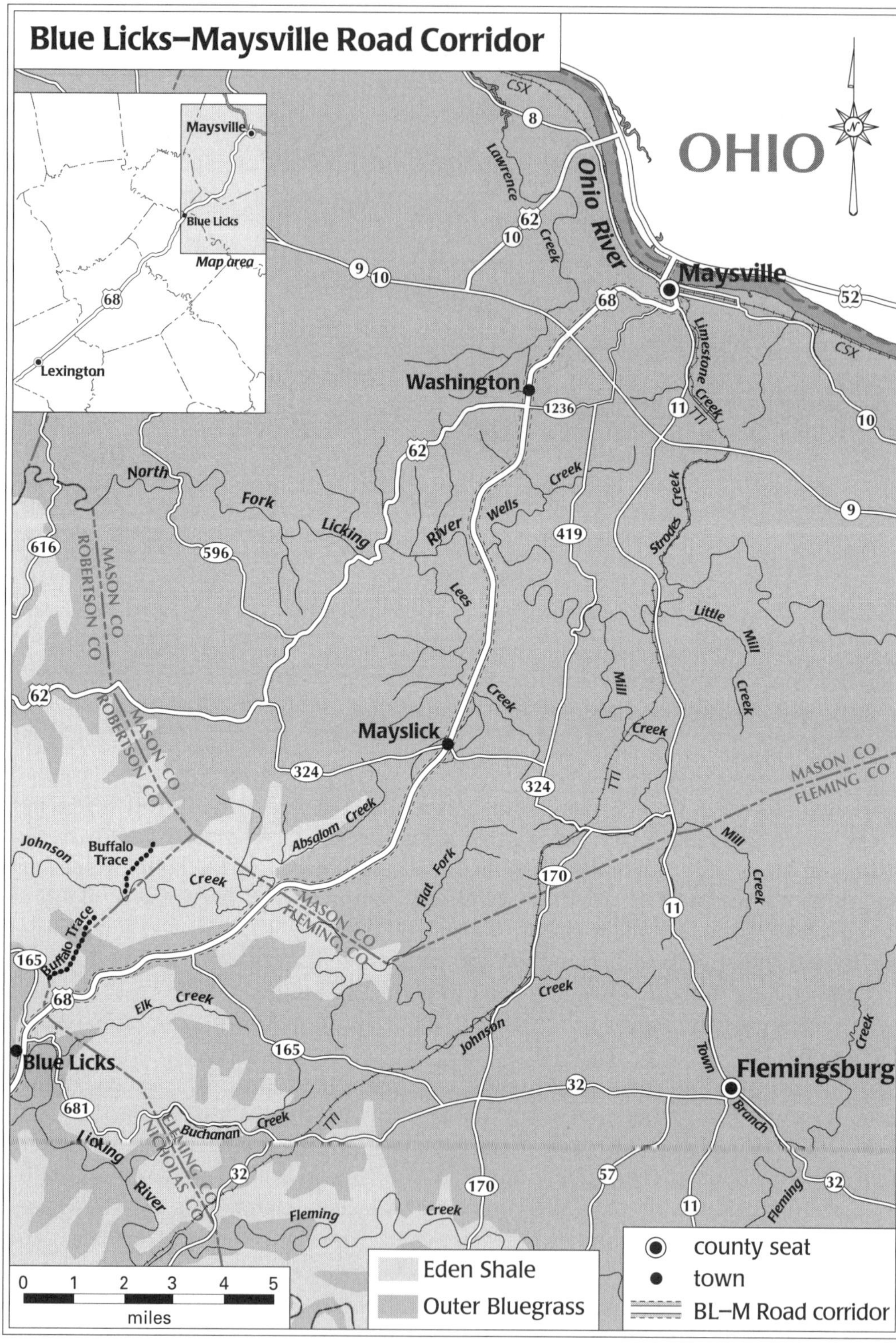

Blue Licks–Maysville Road Corridor
OHIO
Ohio River
Maysville
Washington
Mayslick
Blue Licks
Flemingsburg
Lexington
Map area
MASON CO
ROBERTSON CO
FLEMING CO
NICHOLAS CO
North Fork Licking River
Licking River
Lawrence Creek
Limestone Creek
Strodes Creek
Wells Creek
Lees Creek
Little Mill Creek
Mill Creek
Absalom Creek
Flat Fork
Johnson Creek
Elk Creek
Buchanan Creek
Fleming Creek
Town Branch
Buffalo Trace
CSX
TTI
Eden Shale
Outer Bluegrass
county seat
town
BL–M Road corridor
miles

topographic form and amplitude. As it did in many other places in the fractally complex Eden Shale countryside, the original track skirted hills and followed creek valleys wherever possible to reduce grades.

Mile 21.5 Stream patterns, county boundaries, and altered road alignments interweave here to yield a complicated geography of splintered political jurisdictions. The Licking River follows a wide S-shaped double loop from the mouth of Stony Creek, just over the hillside spur to the right, to the mouth of Indian Creek, which joins the Licking downstream to the left. The "as-the-crow-flies" distance between these two stream junctions is two and one-half miles. Following the Licking's meandering channel requires five miles to link the same points. Robertson County's boundary with Nicholas County formerly followed the Licking River channel upstream until it reached the old highway alignment, whereupon it followed the road's centerline past the Blue Licks Battlefield State Park, skirting the north end of the Licking's loop to intersect the Fleming County boundary just to the north. The north and south county boundary sections retain their road centerline position. Just north of the Blue Licks settlement site, at the intersection with the 1960s bypass, a tiny sliver of Nicholas County now stands on the west side of the realigned road. Two hundred feet farther north, the new highway replaced an old curved road section, thereby isolating a narrow slice of Robertson County on the east side of the present highway near the entrance to Blue Licks Battlefield State Resort Park.

23

Commemoration, Heritage, and a Battlefield Park

Mile 21.7 The entrance to Blue Licks Battlefield State Resort Park is on the left. The Kentucky General Assembly established Lower Blue Licks State Park on March 27, 1926, to commemorate the settlers who fought and died in the Battle of Blue Licks in 1782. The Blue Licks Battlefield Commission acquired land here that included the battlefield and presented a deed to the Kentucky State Park Commission on January 25, 1927. Officials formally dedicated the park the following August. After making a dedicatory speech, former governor William J. Fields unveiled a new cenotaph modeled after the Revolutionary War monument erected at Yorktown, Virginia, by the Colonial National Monument Association.[1] Over the next few years the state built a museum here to house the Hunter bone collection and to interpret the area's history. The site included a custodian's house, an internal road system, and picnic areas. Additional excavations below the main spring in 1946 by Victor Dodge and Willard Jillson of the Kentucky Geological Survey recovered more Pleistocene-era bones, including a mastodon tusk with a full tip that became part of the museum's exhibit. The present road alignment here dates from the late 1960s. In 1991 the park's roads were upgraded, and in 1999 the Kentucky Department of Parks built a new lodge here with thirty-two rooms for overnight guests, in addition to conference and dining rooms. The lodge is named for Marvin Lewis "Pete" Worthington, who served as a representative in the state legislature from 1978 to 2000. Worthington was known to his legislative peers as "the Gentleman from Ewing." The L & N Railroad station town of Ewing is about seven miles due east from the park.

It is illuminating to pause here to contemplate the original rationale and purpose for creating a state park at this site. At least six different historic events or geographic sites or situations might have been commemorated here: the salt lick as an environmental feature, with its attendant prehistoric bone deposits; the eighteenth-century salt extraction industry; the 1782 Battle of Blue Licks; the venue for one of Daniel Boone's better-known frontier experiences; the early Maysville Road, with its important river crossing, concentration of taverns, and flow of commerce into and out of the region; or the nineteenth-century spas that earned this site the sobriquet "the

Saratoga of the South." Of these, the state chose to commemorate the battle and the battlefield site and its linkage to Daniel Boone.

Americans have long chosen to commemorate wars or battlefields as important elements of their past in part because such places can be made to represent lessons about heroic responses to tyrannical threats to freedom or the triumph of justice over injustice.[2] As citizens of a country with just over two centuries of national history, Americans have struggled to develop a sense of collective memory, and they have cast some of their efforts in the direction of developing a sense of heritage. Though difficult to define, heritage might be viewed as "people's history," though we need to recognize how selective and subjective individuals, communities, and nations can be about selecting fragments of their history they value enough to commemorate as heritage.[3]

Only after the 1850s did Americans began to embrace large-scale commemoration projects as heritage markers. The Mount Vernon Ladies' Association, formed in 1856 and the oldest historic preservation organization in America, and the Ladies' Hermitage Association, patterned after the Mount Vernon group and founded in 1889, incubated the sense of common heritage through preservation of presidents' homes. Nationally, until the 1890s women's groups such as these were the primary champions of linking heritage to memory, and memory to monumental commemoration, be it as a preserved home, commissioned war monument, or tributary park space.[4]

The rationale for creating the Blue Licks Park was probably to acknowledge the battle as the last military engagement of the Revolutionary War, to celebrate the Kentucky participants as heroes, and to cast the battle as a formative event in Kentucky's frontier history, even though it was a calamitous defeat born of clever deception by the blended British and Indian force and ill-considered bravado on the part of the Kentucky contingent. Land acquisition for a commemorative park at Blue Licks began in 1926. Samuel Wilson, a Lexington judge, served as a spokesperson for groups concerned about patriotic causes and historical events who wished to erect a memorial monument in time for Daniel Boone's two hundredth birthday anniversary, variously reported but commonly acknowledged as 1734. The governor approved the creation of a Daniel Boone Bicentennial Commission in 1934 to commemorate Boone's birth. Through the efforts of Kentucky's U.S. Senator Alben Barkley and Representative Virgil Chapman, the Congress authorized acquisition of four Kentucky sites closely associated with Daniel Boone's frontier exploits: Boonesborough (Madison County), Boone's Station (Boonville in Owsley County), Bryan's Station (Fayette County), and the Blue Licks Battlefield (Nicholas and Robertson counties). The four sites were to be turned into formal shrines curated by the National Park Service and linked by a federal highway. The Bicentennial Commission's efforts to purchase the four sites for historical development were thwarted largely by a dearth of funding and recalcitrant landowners who were unwilling to sell. The site-linking highway was never built. Any demonstrable concern for material exemplars of heritage, be it individual and local or regional and corporate, was still subservient to other priorities. The commission did obtain some 250 acres at Blue Licks in 1943, but negotiations for the Boonesborough property plodded into the 1960s. In 1963 the state, operating in place of the venerable

Bicentennial Commission, purchased seventy-five acres of the Boonesborough site, and the state dedicated Fort Boonesborough State Park two years later.[5]

Since the mid-nineteenth century, then, Americans and Kentuckians alike have become obsessed with seeking out and enthroning their heritage. Today heritage not only is a matter of museum commemorative policy, but has also been embraced by revenue-strapped communities as a tactic to attract tourist dollars, a trend that has spawned the phrase "heritage tourism." But heritage should not be misconceived as history. As the geographer David Lowenthal reminds us, heritage consoles us with tradition, it links us with ancestors, certifies identity, and roots us in time-honored ways. But as the "people's history," heritage is highly selective of historic events, and this selectivity can undermine historical truth with twisted myth; it can breed bellicose discord.[6] At Blue Licks Battlefield, a commemorative granite obelisk and pioneer graveyard became key symbolic site elements, and the place became another of many "Indian Wars" heritage sites across the nation. The park thus supports the heroic image of frontier folk such as Daniel Boone. Missing from the park is any illumination of those events that were central elements in the tragic destruction of American Indian cultures.[7]

Mile 21.8 Park expansion in the late 1990s included this walkway over U.S. 68.

24

Blue Licks toward Maysville

Mile 22.1 The back road into Blue Licks Battlefield State Resort Park intersects on the left. The old Maysville Turnpike alignment, now renamed Redbud Road, departs from the modern road here and for about a mile and one-quarter loops east and north before rejoining U.S. 68. Most of the abandoned segments form short loops that now function as farm and residence driveways. About one-half mile ahead on Redbud Road, one may gain a spectacular view of the Licking River valley to the south, or right. A Kentucky Historical Society roadside marker here identifies the home and grave site of George M. Bedinger; born in Pennsylvania in 1756, he served as an officer in the Revolutionary War and at the siege of Yorktown in 1781. Bedinger helped defend Boonesborough in 1779, and he returned to Kentucky in 1784 as a surveyor. He was the first surveyor to operate in the Lower Blue Licks area. He served as a Kentucky legislator from 1792 to 1794 and as a member of the U.S. Congress from 1803 to 1807. At the top of the hill a nineteenth-century farmstead fronts the old road. One of the few extant Maysville Turnpike iron mile markers stands in the front yard, near the road.

In the crux of the angle between U.S. 68 and Redbud Road is an expansive, nearly level area that seems out of place among the surrounding hills. This is a remnant of the ancient Licking River floodplain that lies more than one hundred feet above the existing river channel. The ancestral river deposited silt and gravel comprising chert, limestone, and quartz pebbles as channel deposits here. As the river eroded its channel downward, these deposits were left behind as extensive flats. Another area of old channel deposits lies along Redbud Road beyond the Bedinger historical marker, and expansive areas can be found near the Licking River up- and downstream from here.[1]

Mile 22.5 In 1928 State Highway Department engineers developed plans to rebuild this section of the old Maysville Road from the north boundary of Blue Licks State Park to the junction with SR 165 here on the left as part of a larger project to upgrade the road that linked Mt. Olivet, the Robertson County seat, to U.S. 68.[2] The 1920s alignment very closely followed the old turnpike road in this section.

Mile 22.8 The 1960s highway alignment intersects the Fleming County–Robertson County boundary at this point. The boundary follows an old buffalo trace in a broad loop about a mile and three-quarters to the west and north before transitioning into a straight survey line.[3]

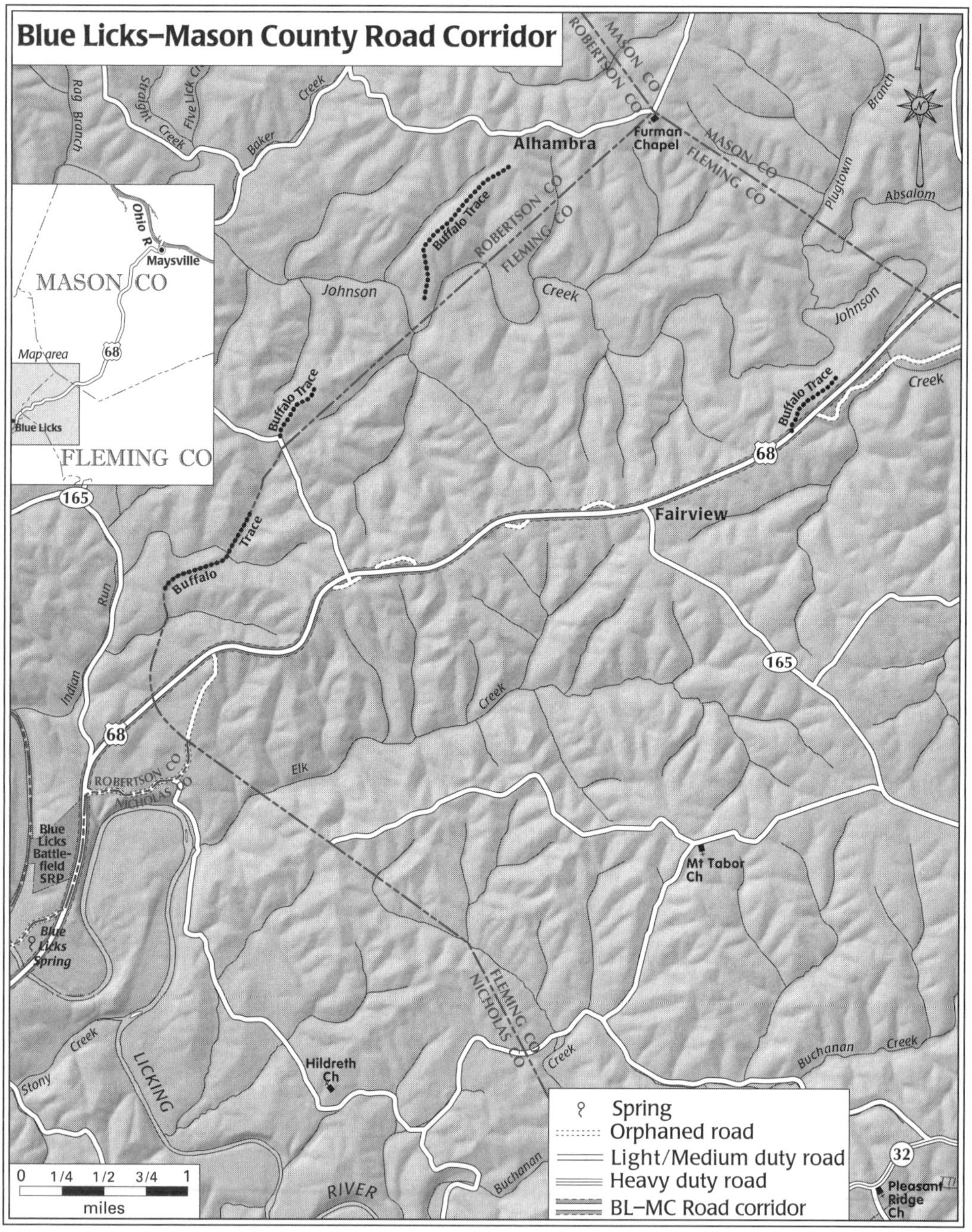
Blue Licks–Mason County Road Corridor
MASON CO
ROBERTSON CO
FLEMING CO
NICHOLAS CO
Alhambra
Furman Chapel
Fairview
Mt Tabor Ch
Hildreth Ch
Pleasant Ridge Ch
Blue Licks Battlefield SRP
Blue Licks Spring
Buffalo Trace
Johnson Creek
Elk Creek
Indian Run
Rag Branch
Straight Creek
Five Lick Cr
Baker Creek
Plugtown Branch
Absalom
Stony Creek
Buchanan Creek
LICKING RIVER
68
165
32
Ohio R
Maysville
Map area
Blue Licks
Spring
Orphaned road
Light/Medium duty road
Heavy duty road
BL–MC Road corridor
0 1/4 1/2 3/4 1
miles

Mile 23.3 Redbud Road intersects again with the 1960s highway. Increased road-building funds from state gasoline taxes and large-scale earth-moving equipment available to road builders in the 1950s and 1960s allowed engineers to combine hill cuts with valley fills to construct a straighter, low-gradient roadway that superseded the old turnpike's winding route through the Eden Shale Hills. The process orphaned seven 1920s road segments as cutoffs between Redbud Road and Fairview; the bypassed road loops are now identified primarily by the names of trees.

Mile 24.2–24.3 The Willow Road cutoff leads off to the right.

Mile 24.5–24.7 The Evergreen Road cutoff is on the left.

Mile 25.3–25.4 To follow the Pisgah Cemetery Road cutoff, bear to the right past the hillside cemetery.

Mile 25.7 The Dogwood Road cutoff is on the left.

25

Fairview and Ewing

Mile 26.1 The intersection of U.S. 68 and SR 165 marks the drainage divide between the Licking River to the south and Johnson Creek to the north and the center of the small roadside community of Fairview (also known as Oakwood). In the 1950s Bill's Snack Shop and Gas Station replaced a wood-frame grocery store that stood at the corner. The concrete-block building has since entertained sellers of used home furnishings and used cars. Crossroads country stores are common across the greater Bluegrass, and although such stores do not provide the breadth of goods sold at a grocery store on a town's main street, they often function as rural community centers. In addition to purveying selected canned and fresh foodstuffs, the country store is often a neighborhood gathering place at noon and early evening.

Other than the recycled gas station, only scattered houses, farmsteads, and the Mt. Pisgah Baptist Church demarcate the contemporary Fairview site. U.S. 68 follows a ridge crest here for more than a mile; to the east, SR 165 also follows a ridge crest, the routeway of choice in crossing the Eden Shale's abrupt topography. Ridge roads attract farmsteads and rural nonfarm houses as though the road were magnetic and the buildings were ferric because the Eden Shale valleys are narrow and flood-prone and acceptable building sites are limited. Most slopes are too steep to invite house or barn construction. Farm buildings accordingly adhere to SR 165 at a density sufficient to compel the highway department to mark the twisting road with yellow diamond-shaped signs that designate the ridgetop a "Congested Area."

Four miles east, the Maysville & Lexington–Kentucky Central–Louisville & Nashville–TTI Railroad parallels U.S. 68 as the rail route and highway converge north toward Maysville. Nineteenth-century engineers built the railroad north from Carlisle and south from Maysville. The track ran parallel to the Maysville Road, but two miles or more to the east. After the first through rail line here opened in 1873, the railroad established freight and passenger depots at important road crossings; the depots served local farms and attracted businesses and residential housing. The rail depots, from south to north, were Myers (also known as Myer Station), Pleasant Valley, Cowan, Ewing, Nepton, Flemingsburg Junction (also known as Johnsons Junction), Helena, Marshall's Station (Lewisburg), Clark's Station, and Dimmitt's Station.[1] Most stations attracted a cluster of houses and perhaps a store, post office, and livestock

Fairview and Ewing, ca. 1950s
Fleming County, Ky.

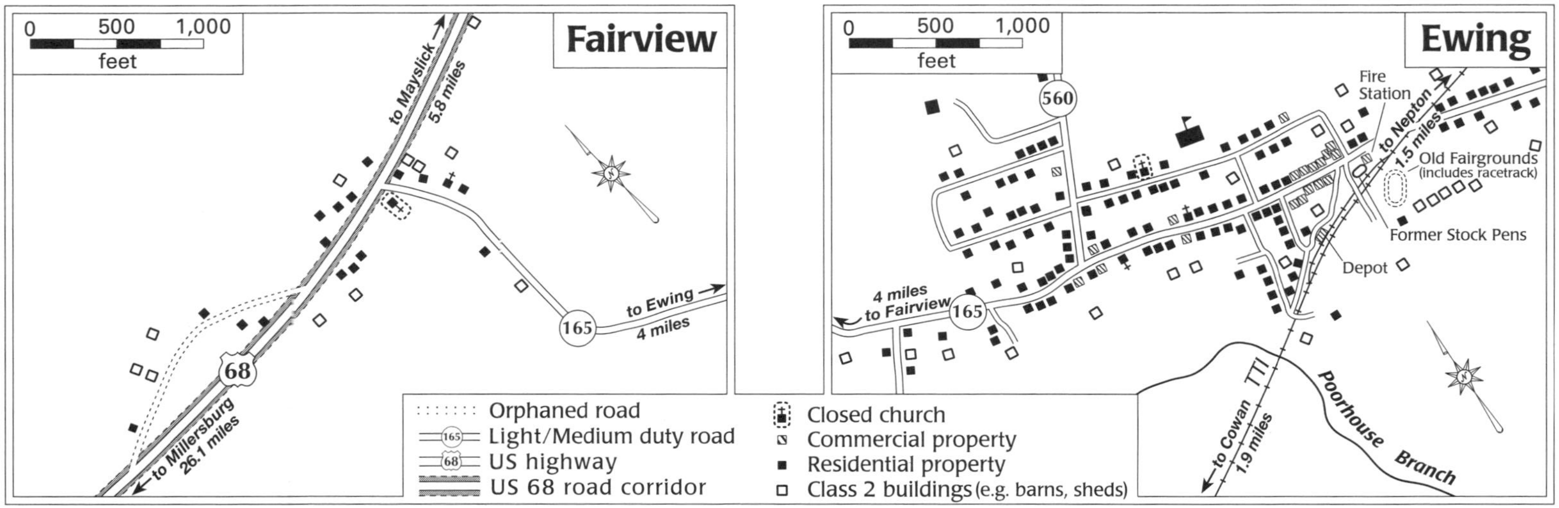

From Millersburg to Maysville the railroad departed the road corridor and ran a parallel track some four miles to the east. The Louisville & Nashville railroad established depots at primary road crossings along the route, and small rail-oriented towns grew up around them. Although the Ewing depot has not served passengers for decades, the town's residents have refurbished the building. The county fairgrounds once occupied the hillside where a farmhouse and silo now stand.

pens beside the tracks. Some developed into small villages with churches, retail stores, and a school.

The Ewing station opened in 1871 with H. M. Ewing as the first agent, and the town grew up at a point where the road to Fairview intersected the tracks.[2] Though four miles east of Fairview and the Maysville Road, Ewing is several times larger, its population at six hundred. In addition to the train depot, the nineteenth- and twentieth-century Ewing business area is remarkably intact and includes several buildings that still function as businesses or are empty and awaiting reuse. A two-story brick bank remains in business, but the frame-and-clapboard Powell Hotel is closed.[3] Other businesses included grocery stores (converted to other uses), a barbershop (closed), a farm hardware store and lumberyard (closed), and a machinery dealer and repair garage. Several other business buildings once housed doctors, a dentist, an attorney, a veterinarian, and the *Ewing Inquirer* newspaper. Service structures include the Ewing Christian and Baptist churches and a new fire station. The blacksmith shop and

Model-T Ford repair shop are gone, as is the grocery store that sold gasoline.[4] A modern gas station–convenience store now dispenses fuel and snacks. Fleming County consolidated the rural schools in its western section in 1924. The small school at Fairview closed and students traveled to Ewing via school bus or horse-drawn school wagon to attend both elementary and high school. The large, two-story elementary school on Euclid Avenue dates from 1926, when the new Ewing Consolidated High School opened. Vacant lots scattered throughout the town suggest that many structures are missing. Some houses have burned down and not been replaced. The furniture store, millinery shop, and funeral home are gone. A grocery store and dairy have closed. Across the railroad tracks, the fairgrounds, with its floral hall and one-half mile trotting track, have been absorbed by the adjoining farm. The depot, though refurbished and in excellent condition, no longer retains its former functions. And the daily sequence of six passenger trains, two mail trains, and assorted freights that polished the tracks in the 1930s have been replaced by one TTI train per day hauling coal to Maysville and irregular freight service.

Given Fairview's seemingly enviable position on the Maysville Turnpike and the road's status as an important twentieth-century federal highway, it is counterintuitive that Ewing, located on a small state road four miles away, would possess a much larger

SR 165, which links Ewing to the Maysville Road, functions as Ewing's Main Street. The Powell Hotel featured a full-width porch for guests to relax on at the roadside. The brick building on the highway's south side houses the town's bank.

complement of urban services and a substantially larger population. Fairview is more than eighteen miles north of Millersburg and seven miles south of Mayslick. If merchants had established retail businesses in Fairview instead of Ewing, their potential consumer base would have been considerable. The reason that Ewing was able to outstrip Fairview as a business and residential center relates to the comparative logistical advantage of nineteenth- and twentieth-century railroad access and the role that the railroad played in supporting Ewing's acquisition of centrality: that is, the ability of a place—a village, town, or city—to produce goods and services in excess of what its residents can consume.[5]

Fairview stands at the intersection of a state and federal highway and is thereby a transport network node or has a nodal character. An intersection or nodal location might be a convenient place for local residents to establish a store or tavern. But such locations might provide basic services primarily to roadway travelers; the location

Across Main Street from the Baptist church, a farm machinery yard offers used Belarus tractors for sale. Manufactured in the Republic of Belarus in the former Soviet Union by the Minsk Tractor Works, one of the largest tractor manufacturers in the world, the Belarus tractor has been sold in the United States since the 1970s. Belarus tractors provide basic utility at much lower prices than American-built brands such as John Deere and International Harvester. The model 825 has seventy-five horsepower and would be an attractive choice for Eden Shale farmers, whose small-scale operations require a considered budget.

offers no assurance that the place will also produce the surplus of goods and services that attract businesspeople whose trade and exchange activities create centrality. There were probably at least three reasons that places such as Fairview and Ewing exhibited strongly contrasting historic growth. First, during Kentucky's nineteenth-century turnpike era (1830s to 1890s), road quality was marginal, toll fees were high, and the time schedule of movement on a high-friction road was malleable at best—all of which conspired to make road travel a high-cost proposition. By comparison, the logistical costs of moving freight and passengers by low-friction rail were modest. The railroad, moreover, offered shippers and receivers the luxury of a predictable, reliable schedule and thus offered the better option for farmers to ship bulky or nondurable commodities—tobacco and hemp, cattle and hogs, milk and cream—to market, for local merchants to receive manufactured goods, and for local people to ride passenger trains to Maysville, Lexington, or beyond.[6] Express shipments of perishable foods and drugs could be made in a single day if punctually delivered to a shipping station.[7] Ewing did not have a bakery, but each Saturday in the 1920s and 1930s, Traxel's Bakery in Maysville shipped six dozen loaves of fresh-baked bread, among the most perishable of foodstuffs, to the Ewing depot. From the depot John Hildreth used his Model-T pickup truck to deliver the bread to his grocery store, where it usually sold out within the hour. Ice shipments also arrived on the Saturday freight. A Mr. Williams hauled the ice from the depot to his icehouse on Maple Street, where he offered it for sale to local customers. He used the surplus to cool his basement creamery.[8] Neighborhood residents found the opportunity to "shun the pike" by patronizing the modern railroad too compelling to disregard.

Farther south, where the railroad ran beside the turnpike, local farmers and the wholesale and retail businesses in the towns where the road and rail conjoined could easily patronize either or both transport modes. Both road and railroad directly served Paris and Millersburg, giving those places exceptional locational advantage. Businesspeople there could realize profits that would generate increases in employment and payrolls that accrued to the same place. North of Millersburg, where the rail swings away from the highway to serve Carlisle, any locational advantage gained by a roadside or rail-side location was apportioned between competing sites such as Fairview and Ewing, and the rail-oriented places were favored over the old toll-road sites.

As burley tobacco production moved south from its nineteenth-century Ohio Valley cradle, farmers in Fleming and Nicholas counties could use the railroad to deliver their crops to Maysville auction warehouses before trucks and high-quality road surfaces made traditional roadway market trips an acceptable alternative. Reciprocally, Maysville plow manufacturers could ship their implements south along the railroad to machinery dealers in rail-side villages such as Ewing.[9] As the surrounding farming economy developed in the late nineteenth century, additional production and consumption functions might have emerged that would find the rail-side locations superior to those at the roadside. The railroad delivered bulk fuel oil to local retailers, as well as lumber, brick, and other construction materials to local building-supply businesses. Farmers shipped livestock via rail to markets in Maysville, Lexington, and Cincinnati, and they sent grain to distant mills.

Compared to Fairview, Ewing's growth may also relate to its position astride one of the radial roads leading toward Flemingsburg, the county seat. Modern-day traffic along U.S. 68 near Fairview, for example, is about 2,700 vehicles per day, whereas some 3,400 vehicles per day travel SR 32, which links Ewing to the county seat at Flemingsburg.[10] Ewing's topographic context is also superior to that at Fairview. Ewing's site is near the boundary of the Eden Shale Hills and the Outer Bluegrass, whereas Fairview was ensconced well within the Eden Shale country. Eden Shale farms were generally smaller and rural population densities lower than in the Outer Bluegrass counties; the people of the Fairview hinterland probably had less buying power than those who patronized Ewing's merchants.[11]

Fairview, though on a federal trunk highway, was unable to compete successfully with Ewing—though highway travelers patronize gas stations and restaurants, they do not, as a matter of course, seek out hardware stores and lumberyards. And although the railroad still provides service along the TransKentucky Transportation line (TTI), Ewing's inertia is strong enough to retain businesses and residents and sustain its size advantage over Fairview.

26

Fairview toward Mason County

Mile 0.0 Fairview marks the point where the Maysville Road traverses the center of Fleming County's western "panhandle," which stretches from Blue Licks Battlefield State Resort Park to the south to the vicinity of Johnson Creek to the north. In 1947 the road at Fairview was bituminous packed macadam, a road surface of sufficient quality to be rated as "paved road" by the State Highway Department.[1] The use of bituminous or asphaltic materials in road paving marks a transition in highway construction from basic broken-rock macadam-type road surfacing commonly used in the nineteenth century to the modern hard-surface asphalt or concrete road. Natural bitumen materials were first used in street construction in Paris, France, in 1854 but proved too expensive to have wider practical application. America's first sheet-asphalt street was laid in front of the Newark, New Jersey, city hall in 1870, yet the material, especially in sheet or pavement form, remained expensive and had limited application outside central cities.[2]

As asphalt became more readily available, road builders used it in combination with sand and stone to produce several different road surfaces. Rock asphalt is limestone or sandstone that contains a small amount of naturally occurring asphalt. When broken or crushed, the stone can be laid into an "asphalt road." Asphalt mastic used asphalt refined from bituminous rocks, which was melted and mixed with sand to make pavements. Asphaltic concrete was a mixture of broken stone bound together with asphaltic cement, a product that included a solvent to increase its plasticity and adhesiveness.[3] It is likely that the 1947 road surface here was a transitional surface, a broken-stone macadam base covered with a thin layer of finely crushed-stone binder material that, in turn, was covered by an asphalt sheet.

Just to the north, across the county boundary in Mason County, the 1947 road surface changed to water-bound macadam that had been surface-treated with a thin layer of asphalt, one of the most common road forms in the eastern United States during the early automobile era. Though the term *macadam* conjures images of the hand-broken stone roads built by turnpike contractors in the mid-nineteenth century, this road was probably made of machine-broken or machine-crushed stone laid on a carefully leveled and ditched surface to form a stout base. Large, steam-powered rollers compacted the stone into a crowned profile that sloped from the road's centerline

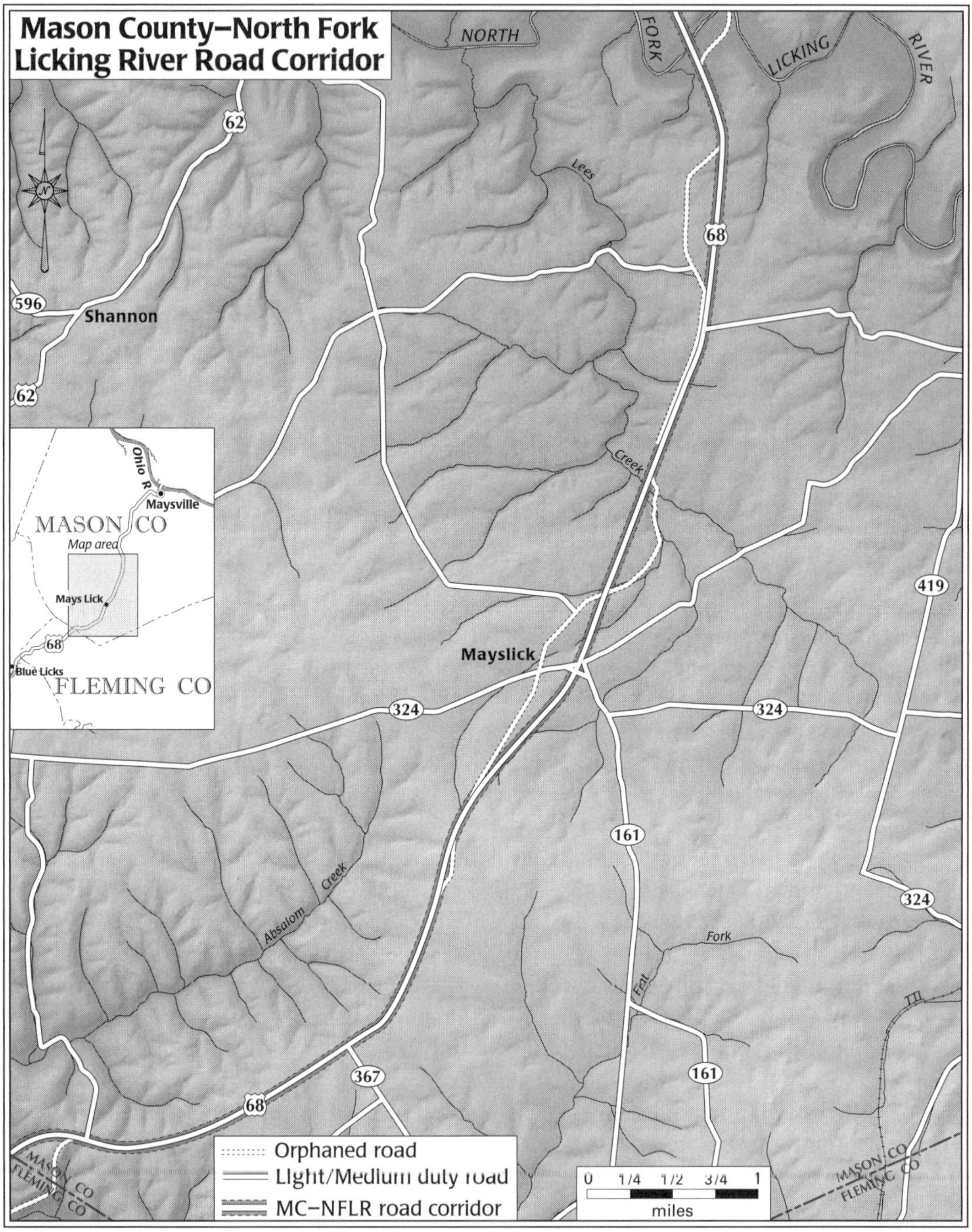
Mason County–North Fork Licking River Road Corridor
NORTH
FORK
LICKING
RIVER
Lees
Creek
62
68
596
Shannon
Ohio R.
Maysville
MASON CO
Map area
Mays Lick
68
Blue Licks
FLEMING CO
419
Mayslick
324
324
161
324
Absalom Creek
Fork
Frat
367
161
68
TTI
MASON CO
FLEMING CO
MASON CO
FLEMING CO
Orphaned road
Light/Medium duty road
MC–NFLR road corridor
0 1/4 1/2 3/4 1
miles

to the ditches on either side to assure rainwater drainage from the surface. The road surface was finished with a binder of stone screenings that varied in size from dust to three-quarter-inch diameter. The screenings were spread on the packed broken-stone surface and rolled in with the steamroller. A common street sprinkler then watered the road surface, washing the fine stone dust and chips into any remaining voids between the larger stones. When dried, the finished road surface became a nearly solid pavement, largely impervious to water, and performing somewhat like concrete. A thin slurry of asphalt atop the stone surface would reduce dust and help hold the screenings in place against traffic and heavy rain.[4] The water-bound macadam road, while relatively economical to build and maintain, could not withstand modern truck traffic and was eventually superseded by heavy asphalt and reinforced-concrete pavement construction.

When the term *gravel* was used in Kentucky road construction, it usually referred to broken stone, limestone primarily. North of the Ohio River and across the glaciated Midwest and New England, gravel refers to a mixture of small stones, largely of metamorphic origins, from pea-size or smaller to half-dollar-size or slightly larger. The continental glacial advances across the northern states during the Pleistocene era—the Wisconsin (10,000 B.C.E.) and Illinoian (140,000 B.C.E.) are the two most recent—terminated as far south as the Ohio River. As vast ice lobes moved across Canada and the northern states, the weight and motion of the ice crushed and abraded metamorphic bedrock. The product was sand and rounded stones from pebble-size to boulders, much of which became incorporated in the ice and was carried long distances as the ice moved south. Vast quantities of glacial meltwater washed the sand and gravel into concentrated deposits—some dozens of miles across, others in lenses only a few feet in diameter. For a century or more, road engineers in the northern states have used sand and gravel from natural glacial deposits for road construction and surfacing. Kentucky is largely south of the glacial boundary or terminus, so rock used in road construction had to be quarried from ancient sedimentary limestones, broken and crushed into small sizes appropriate for construction, and hauled to the construction site for application. While the term "gravel" is sometimes used to describe the smaller limestone pieces, it is not usually gravel of glacial origins, but the product of expensive quarrying and crushing operations.

Mile 1.6 Greenhouse Road, an old Maysville Road cutoff, intersects on the right. A toll house stood near here in 1877.

Mile 2.0 As the present-day highway approaches the Johnson Creek crossing, the old road runs parallel on the right, crossing Johnson Creek on a low, narrow 1930s concrete bridge. As the old highway climbs out of the valley, it wraps around a small farmstead in a tight U-turn before rejoining the new highway alignment ahead. The combination of a short radius curve, hill, and bridge crossing probably made this one of the most dangerous sections of the old highway, especially in rain or snow conditions.

Mile 2.1 U.S. 68 crosses from Fleming County into Mason County. From 1923 to 1929 the Mason County section of U.S. 68 was resurfaced with crushed limestone, although the alignment remained the same as the old roadway.

Mile 2.4 The Greenhouse Road cutoff reconnects to U.S. 68.

27

The Outer Bluegrass

Mile 3.4 The large, shallow-angle sinkhole on the left signifies that the road has regained the Outer Bluegrass limestone country. Sinkholes such as this one drain vertically into an unseen underground drainage system that probably includes cracks and crevices enlarged by solution, and perhaps an underground cave. This sinkhole has served as a local landmark for more than a century.

Mile 3.7 Intersection with Nepton Road.

Burley Tobacco

Mile 5.2 The old road alignment is to the right here. A Maysville Turnpike tollhouse may have stood near this point in the nineteenth century. A burley tobacco–curing barn stands near the entrance of the old road. Burley tobacco, one of the primary constituents used in blending tobaccos for cigarette manufacture, has been grown in central Kentucky since the 1860s.

The first tobaccos grown in Kentucky were not the modern burley type but varieties imported from Cuba into Virginia by John Rolfe in the early 1600s.[1] Virginians migrating to eighteenth-century Kentucky brought tobacco seed with them and began growing the crop for their own use. As Kentucky's settlement density increased and river navigation improved, farmers packed surplus tobacco into wooden barrels or hogsheads for shipment downstream on the Ohio River to New Orleans, where it was sent on to East Coast and European markets. Tobacco became so highly valued that it was in some places used in place of currency.

Before shipping, tobacco had to be processed by air or fire curing. To ensure that farmers sold and exported only high-quality tobacco, Virginia passed a law in 1783 requiring that tobacco be inspected before going to market. Erection of tobacco-inspection warehouses promptly followed. Given the difficulty of moving bulky tobacco hogsheads over bad or nonexistent roads, the preferred transport routes were navigable rivers, so Kentucky's tobacco-inspection warehouses were built along the largest streams. Maysville became the site of one of the first warehouses, built in 1787. A warehouse in Paris was completed in 1790, along Stoner Creek.[2] Although Bluegrass soils produced abundant tobacco yields, much of the region's best farmland lay

Farmers harvest burley tobacco in August and September and hang the green plant stalks in large wooden barns to cure. Small roof ventilators and narrow side doors manage airflow through the building during dry fall weather to promote curing. The building in the right foreground is a tool and stripping shed, where workers remove cured tobacco leaves from the stalk for grading and baling in preparation for marketing.

well away from navigable streams such as the Licking and Kentucky rivers, so production either remained in the northern counties near the Ohio or migrated west, where farmers had direct access to the Green, Cumberland, and Tennessee rivers.

Farmers developed improved tobacco strains, such as Red Burley and Little Burley, which, although gummy and leathery, could command high prices in the New Orleans market.[3] But a new strain, White Burley, found in a seedling bed in Brown County, Ohio, in 1864, radically altered Kentucky tobacco production patterns. White Burley cured to a bright yellow or tawny ocher color and quickly became the manufacturers' tobacco of choice. As the demand for plug chewing and light smoking products such as cigarettes increased after the Civil War, White Burley production increased as well. And, because road conditions improved and new rail lines connected most Bluegrass county seat towns to the national railroad grid, by 1900 tobacco production was no longer tied to navigable rivers but relocated according to the distribution of productive soils and marketing outlets. Thereafter, tobacco production spread rapidly south into the central Bluegrass, and whereas Maysville had been an important sales and shipping center—Mason County farmers produced more than 1 million pounds in 1850, while Fayette County production that year was zero—Lexington became the state's new center for tobacco auction sales by about 1910 and soon boasted of being the largest burley tobacco auction market in the world.

The burley production calendar follows a regular annual round and yields a distinctive farming landscape of seedbeds, fields, and specialized curing barns. In January a farmer selects the field, tests the soil, and orders fertilizer. Tobacco is a voracious consumer of minerals, especially phosphorus and potassium. A farmer may also purchase hybrid tobacco seed at this time. Because burley seed is very small, only a small amount, if measured by volume, is required to plant enough seedlings for an acre or more of tobacco. F. W. Rickard Seeds of Winchester, Kentucky, is one of the largest hybrid tobacco seed producers in the nation.

Because tobacco seedlings are vulnerable to a variety of diseases, the seed is first planted in a small, sterilized bed. In February, weather permitting, the farmer tills the tobacco seedbed to prepare it. The seedbed is treated for weeds and disease in March and covered in plastic to prevent contamination by wind-borne weed seeds and disease spores. Seedbeds are usually planted in March and immediately covered with a cotton muslin cloth to further protect the bed and provide a shaded, humid environment for seedling development. Under favorable conditions, a one-hundred-square-yard seedbed will produce between ten and twenty thousand seedling plants. In April the farmer dusts and sprays the seedbed with insecticides and fungicides and weeds the bed while keeping it well watered. By May the main tobacco field is prepared for transplanting. The seedbed is heavily watered and the seedlings, now six to eight inches tall, are pulled and wrapped in bundles for transport to the field. Transplanting usually takes place from May 25 to June 10, though the weather may contract or expand that window. Using a single- or two-row transplanting machine, the farmer sets the seedlings in rows thirty-eight to forty-two inches apart, the plants in each row spaced at eighteen- to twenty-inch intervals.

In June the farmer replaces those field plants that did not survive the initial transplantation; spraying the field for disease and insect pests continues. Vigorous tobacco plants will set a seed head, but to ensure that all the plant's energy is diverted into producing leaves, the farmer will "top" the plants, or break off each plant's seed head when the plants are four to six feet tall, in July or early August. After topping, most tobacco varieties will develop suckers, or new lateral shoots, that must also be removed at frequent intervals to ensure proper leaf development.

Plant harvesting begins in late August or early September. Laborers cut the individual plants, now five to six feet tall, and impale stalks on a four-foot hardwood tobacco stick, five to six plants per stick. Workers load the tobacco sticks onto a flatbed wagon and haul them to a curing barn. Inside the barn, workers hang each stick on an internal framework of cross rails—from top to bottom—to begin the curing process. Burley tobacco is air cured. Tall, narrow doors in the barn side walls—sometimes painted a contrasting color—permit airflow through the building to speed plant dehydration. The doors are generally closed in cool, damp weather and opened in warm,

When farmers terminate tobacco production, their curing barns might be used for other purposes—storing hay bales or farm machinery, for example. Or the barns may be torn down to make room for other structures. Only the internal framing of this burley tobacco barn remains after the roof and exterior wall planks have been removed.

dry conditions. Curing time varies from four to eight weeks. After the tobacco field is cleared, it is usually planted in a grass or grain cover crop to reduce soil erosion.

In October workers take down the tobacco sticks from the barn and strip the cured leaves from the plant stalk for sorting into federally approved grades according to color, texture, size, and other qualities. Leaves of similar quality are then baled together and stored for a few days before being loaded onto a truck or wagon for transport. From the 1920s through the late 1990s most Kentucky burley tobacco was sold at auction warehouses strategically located in prime production areas. Along the Maysville Road, Lexington was the region's anchor auction market—it had dozens of warehouses concentrated along railroad tracks on the southwest, west, and north sides of the city. Paris also hosted tobacco auctions, and Maysville, for a time, was the second-largest tobacco auction center in the state. So important was tobacco marketing to Maysville that the city's adopted nickname was "the Golden Buckle on the Burley Belt."[4] Tobacco auction warehouses are vast structures with acres of floor space to provide temporary storage for thousands of pounds of cured tobacco under one roof.

Skylights provide auction floor illumination. Auctioned tobacco moves into the manufacturing process. which has historically required transport to Louisville or North Carolina, depending on which company bought the crop.

Because of health-related lawsuits against the major tobacco manufacturing companies and rapidly increasing production and importation of foreign tobaccos, the auction sales system has given way to a contract system whereby growers produce a crop at an agreed-on price for a specific company. The old auction warehouses are no longer needed. Some have been converted to other uses; some have been torn down to make space for urban redevelopment. Many farmers are forgoing tobacco for other crops. The landscape signature of such a decision is a farmstead tobacco barn converted to machinery storage or other uses or simply abandoned to the elements.

Mile 5.7 The old highway forks off of the present U.S. 68 alignment near a large, white, two-story frame house on the left, which stands very close to the road.

28

Mayslick—"The Asparagus Bed of Mason County"

One enters Mayslick (also spelled May's Lick) from the south on Pike Street (as in Turnpike Street), at the point where the new road begins a sweeping curve to the right, bypassing the village on the east. The ruins of a brick house stand in the field to the left, or west, at the turn, marking what may have been the old turnpike track. Ahead, Pike Street passes the town cemetery on the right, followed by a Baptist church on the left and a Christian church a block or so farther along. Burns Alley begins about six-tenths of a mile from the bypass junction, and it closely parallels the present road on the left, extending to Franklin Alley. Now fronted by several small frame-and-clapboard houses, Burns Alley is said to be part of the original Limestone Trace. Just ahead, the old trace alignment crosses Pike Street to the right, where it becomes Wilson Avenue. The town's new fire station is on the right. A short distance ahead at Nicholas Street, Wilson emerges into the historic town common, or "Public Avenue" as some termed it, a polygonal acre-sized space created by the acute-angle intersection of the original trace, the turnpike or Pike Street, and the crossing road to Sardis, now Sherman Street, to the west and Nicholas Street to the east. Victorian brick buildings—the Bank of Maysville (1902), the Presbyterian church (1877), and the Odd Fellows Lodge (1847–1904)—enclose the common on the south and east sides. The old trace continues north across Nicholas Street to become Salt Lick Lane, a narrow street that descends into the creek valley. The lane passes the historic salt spring now enclosed by a small brick municipal building before turning right at the creek to become a long driveway that provides access to a church and historic school on the town's east side. Pike Street, also extending north from the common, crosses Lees Creek on a spectacular dry-laid stone culvert, visible only from Salt Lick Lane, before climbing out of the creek valley and heading north toward Washington and Maysville. The town's earliest settlers established homes and taverns along this section of the pike. The unusual road configuration gave Mayslick a double crossroads for a time, both commanded by the medial common, which became the focus for local businesses, including dry goods stores and blacksmith shops.

Mayslick's site enjoyed several advantages that made it a compelling place to

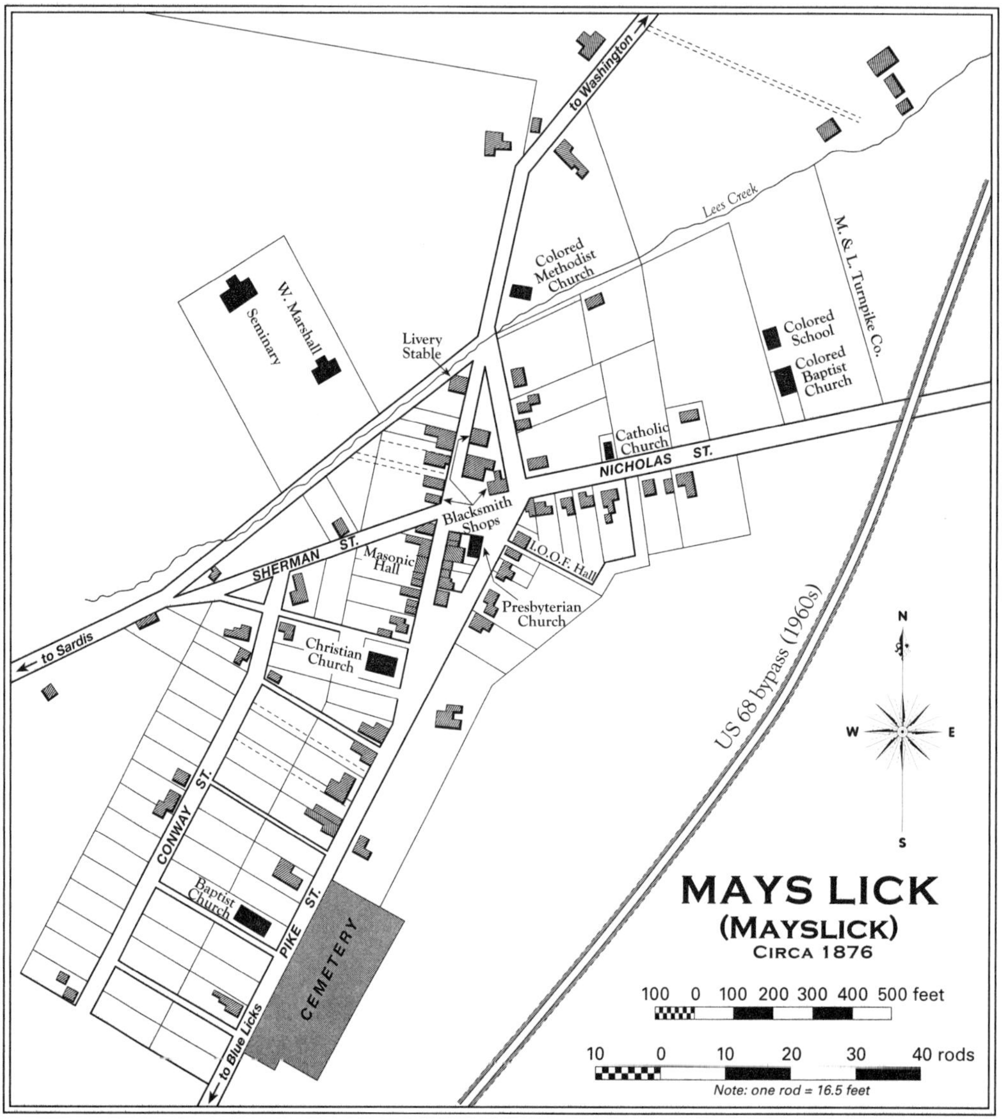

establish a settlement in the 1780s. A buffalo trace to Blue Licks and the wagon track to Lexington passed a saline spring here. When evaluated by southward-moving migrants, this was the first place south of the Ohio River where frontier folk could obtain salt, albeit in the form of weak brine water initially, a resource that ranked second only to potable water, given its critical role in enabling settlement to move inland.[1] The surrounding area offered fertile uplands in expansive acreages that had excellent farming potential, contrasting starkly with the troubling, steep-sloped shale lands that lay just to the south. And finally, a group of settlers from New Jersey found

Nineteenth-century roadside hall-and-parlor brick row houses on Pike Street in Mayslick suggest that the town was attracting residents who were interested in real estate development. Some Mayslick commercial buildings stand empty, although most residential structures function as homes or retail shops.

a 1,400-acre land parcel here that the owner offered for sale and warranted to have a clear title, a salutary advantage on the Kentucky frontier, where land ownership disputes were legion.

Pioneer settlers in Kentucky are usually given perpetual pride of place in county histories, and the first claimants to land around Mayslick are little different. The Isaac Drake, David Morris, and John Shotwell families, all from Plainfield, New Jersey, arrived to settle here in the late 1780s. Cornelius and Abraham Drake, Isaac's brothers, subsequently joined the settlement.[2] Isaac Drake's son, Daniel, grew up along the Great Road, as local people termed the early track linking Maysville and Lexington. Daniel later observed that living in Mayslick and spending time in his uncle Abraham's store and tavern, which fronted the road, allowed him to observe "aspects of things and people, which I should not have seen had we lived off the Road, and the sight of which was no doubt intellectually beneficial. Many of the travelers were wealthy; and as the Road did not well admit of carriages, they journeyed on horseback. Thus I often saw ladies and gentlemen riding side by side, and remember I thought the latter must be the happiest persons on earth."[3] As a young man, Daniel Drake studied medicine in Cincinnati and at the University of Pennsylvania. He became a highly regarded nineteenth-century physician and naturalist, teaching at Transylvania University in Lexington and at the University of Cincinnati and working largely in the Ohio Valley until his death in 1852.[4] Drake was a keen observer of people and the physical environment and in his later life wrote letters to his children that served as memoirs of his early years. The initial Mayslick settlers were, according to Drake, a "colony of East Jersey people, amounting in the aggregate to 52 souls."[5] These settlers apparently migrated as a group or chain; the first to arrive may have sent a positive assessment of the Mayslick area back to friends and relatives in New Jersey who then moved west, effectively transplanting their families and communities to the trans-Appalachian country. Drake's assessment of the other immigrants who joined the early Mayslick settlement was not as charitable as it was of the estimable folk from New Jersey:

> The immigrants from other states were almost entirely Virginians and Marylanders. All were country people by birth and residence—all were illiterate, but in various degrees—& all were poor, or in moderate circumstances—a majority or, at least a moiety, however, were small freeholders. As to religious and moral refinement & a knowledge and use of the domestic arts of civilized life, the Jersey emigrants, as a body, were superior. Next came the Virginians, and last and lowest, the Marylanders. The Jersey people were generally without slaves, partly from principle, and partly from the want of means. Most of the settlers from Virginia and Maryland brought slaves with them, though the number in each family was small—often only one.[6]

By the 1790s, though with scarcely enough buildings to be termed a "village," the settlement was an emporium for a tract of country—much of it still covered in deciduous forest—six to eight miles in diameter and occupied by several hundred families.[7] Though Mayslick was not the county seat, it did serve as a seat of justice. Each Saturday two or three justices of the peace came to the settlement to hold court, at which local litigants presented their cases and complaints. Farm people also scheduled their shopping visits to the Drake store, the blacksmith, or other businesses for Saturday, and the day's activities expanded to include horse trading and racing, cockfights, wrestling matches, and heavy drinking. (Drake strongly advocated temperance.)[8]

Just north of the town common, in the valley along Lees Creek, early settlers used the brackish springwater and well water to produce salt. François André Michaux, son of the French botanist André Michaux, visited Mayslick in August 1802. He found the salt-production technique in use similar to that used in France to produce lye. Workers drew water from wells that they poured into twenty-five-gallon metal pots. They placed ten or twelve pots in a row over a four-foot-deep pit. Burning wood billets in the pit boiled the water, which produced small quantities of salt. The process was labor-intensive, consumed a great deal of wood, and yielded very expensive salt.[9]

Mayslick's population has not been systematically reported by the federal census, but from 1890 to 1930 the residential count fluctuated between about 360 and 260. The town's small collection of businesses and general stores—including two blacksmith shops—served three different constituencies: townspeople, families from the surrounding farms, and road travelers. The town's six church congregations circa the 1870s probably served members from across the southern part of the county, rather than only town residents.

Mason County has long been productive farm country. Eighteenth- and nineteenth-century farmers produced cattle, horses, and mules, as well as corn and wheat, and fodder crops as livestock feed. Mason was one of six northern Kentucky counties that produced tobacco in the late 1700s—Maysville, recall, established a tobacco inspection station in 1787. Today the county has some 726 farms, averaging 176 acres—small by modern standards. More than 80 percent of the county land, some 128,000 acres, is in farms, and of that amount, about 46,000 acres is harvested cropland. The market value of agricultural products sold per farm averages about $31,000 per annum, and after subtracting operational expenses, the average net cash income per farm annually is $5,900, which suggests that many farm families supplement their income by working at jobs off the farm. Beef and dairy cattle are the primary livestock produced, corn (for grain and silage), hay, soybeans, wheat, and tobacco the main crops. County farmers grew tobacco on 2,280 acres in 2007—from which they produced over 4.8 million pounds of burley tobacco—compared to only 60 acres of vegetables harvested.[10] Though Mayslick is proud of its designation as the Asparagus Patch of Mason County, one is very hard pressed to find asparagus grown in commercial amounts anywhere in the county. Rather, the nickname is credited to S. M. Roff, a cashier in the Farmers Bank of Mayslick in the early 1900s. Because asparagus is reputed to grow only in the most fertile soils, Roff's phrase was suggestive of the area's high fertility and productive farms rather than the plant's abundance.[11] The county's best soils do indeed lie along a broad ridge that extends from Washington south past Mayslick, the same ridge followed by the Maysville Road. These are primarily brown Lowell soils, derived from weathered limestone and siltstone, and the fuscous Shelbyville soils that formed in a mantle of wind-borne loess (very fine silt) and weathered materials from underlying limestones.[12] Townspeople celebrate their "patch" tradition with an asparagus festival each May.

Mayslick's churches remain active centers of community life. Historically, six congregations maintained churches here—Baptist, Colored Baptist, Christian, Presbyterian, Catholic, and Colored Methodist. The first settlers were Baptists, according to Daniel Drake, and had belonged to the same church in Scotch Plains, New Jersey, before they moved west.[13] The settlement's first church was established in 1789 as the Church of Jesus Christ. After meeting for several years in a local barn, the congregation constructed its first church building in 1804 near the Great Road, on property that now includes the Mayslick Cemetery. By 1830 the congregation had split, and one of its offshoots became the Baptist church whose most recent building is the 1870 brick edifice that now stands across the road from the mother church site.[14] These early Baptists believed in baptism by immersion—sprinkling was deemed unscriptural—yet there was insufficient water in the immediate area to conduct proper baptisms. This necessitated long horseback processions traversing a narrow road through the woods north to Lees Creek or south to Johnson Creek, where the congregation would assemble on the creek bank to witness midstream baptisms.[15]

Modern land-development pressure on town lots is relatively low in Mayslick; vacant lots lie open, and old buildings such as the old St. Rose of Lima Church stand vacant.

The St. Rose of Lima Catholic Church stands along Nicholas Street just east of the town common. Established here in 1867, St. Rose is a descendent of an 1847 mission church served by a priest from Maysville. Mason County's Catholic population arrived somewhat later than the pioneering settlers from New Jersey, Maryland, and Virginia; they were largely German and Irish immigrants. The old white clapboard chapel stands adjacent to the modern brick edifice. The church was named for Saint Rose, born in Lima, Peru, in 1586, whose life of perpetual penance and exceptional self-mortification earned her canonization by Pope Clement X in 1671, the first person born in the Americas to be so designated.[16]

From its inception in 1789 to 1868, African Americans—many of them enslaved—worshiped at the Baptist church. In August 1868 black congregation members split off and formed their own church, the Mayslick Second Baptist Church, at the east edge of town on Nicholas Street (now State Road 324). When highway engineers constructed the Mayslick bypass, they redirected Nicholas Street farther south. The white clapboard Second Baptist Church stands near the inflection point of the new road; the abandoned Nicholas Street stub has become a parking lot for truck trailers.

An early African American school building, built after the Civil War, in 1868, still

The bypassed section of old SR 324 now functions as a parking lot for truck trailers. Awkward shed additions front and rear disguised one of the few Rosenwald schools still standing in Kentucky. The four-square school building has a pyramidal sheet-metal roof and tall windows along the east side, which now faces the U.S. 68 bypass. Since this photograph was taken in 2006, the shed additions have been removed and the structure has undergone restoration. The gable-roofed Second Baptist Church stands behind the school.

stands at the rear of the Second Baptist Church lot on Nicholas Street. Though overgrown by volunteer vegetation and in derelict condition, the old building represents a watershed in the education of African American children in Mason County. Standing across an alley from the Second Baptist Church, and fronting on the old Nicholas Street alignment, a square brick building was until recently encased within a seemingly random collection of additions and lean-to sheds. The building functioned as an auction barn and mini-storage. The sheds have been removed to reveal one of the county's most important buildings—the Mayslick Negro School, which opened in July 1921. This school for African American students is one of two in Mason County—the other was in Washington—built with financial support from the Rosenwald Fund.

Born in Springfield, Illinois, to a family of clothiers, Julius Rosenwald established a clothing business in Chicago in 1884; he then became a manager at Sears & Roebuck in 1897, and the Sears company president in 1909. Long interested in philanthropy and improving educational opportunities for poor and disenfranchised people, Rosenwald developed a professional partnership with Booker T. Washington, founder of Tuskegee Institute, and became an institute trustee in 1912.[17] Washington, in collaboration with executives of the Standard Oil Company, devised a program whereby rural schools for African American students could be financed by local funds and built by local people, a portion of the building material costs being underwritten by the company. Julius Rosenwald, through a fund named for him, provided incentive monies to carry the program forward after 1912. A community could qualify for Rosenwald funds if it could meet a number of requirements, including the ability to raise money locally to obtain land and building materials and in-kind labor contributions to erect the structure. The building design had to be approved by the Tuskegee Institute and the state's department of education. Furthermore, the school year had to be extended from five to seven months with a concomitant salary increase for the teacher—a grant of thirty dollars was deemed sufficient to pay a teacher to teach two additional months of school each year.[18] Julius Rosenwald died in 1932. As a legacy, his fund helped construct over five thousand schools, industrial instruction shops, and teachers' homes in fifteen southern states.

In Kentucky the Rosenwald Fund provided financial support for 158 schools built between 1917 and 1932. The selection of school designs available ranged from one-teacher to twelve-teacher plans. Each design included tall windows to admit sunlight and provide ventilation; a directional orientation to reduce glare was recommended. Schools for three or more teachers included an auditorium and a stage, a space that could serve as a gym in bad weather or as a place for performances and special lectures. So configured, the school could serve as a community center in addition to providing educational space.

The Mayslick Rosenwald school is a four-teacher plan—with an auditorium—and cost $17,650. The local African American population contributed $10,800, the general public $5,650, and the Rosenwald Fund $1,200.[19] Once disguised by wooden additions, the brick structure is largely intact, its front door topped by a date stone that declares the building's heritage. The building's hip roof and large windows closely resemble those of a Tuskegee school plan.[20] The buildings' eastside elevation provides a clear measure of size—the east wall is about fifty-four feet long. Eight tall, six-over-one, double-hung sash windows illuminate the first-floor space; the basement workspace below has six windows.

In 1891 a revised Kentucky constitution legalized a state segregated school system, and in 1904 the legislature passed the Day Law, which made illegal teaching black and white children in the same classroom. The U.S. Supreme Court found legal strictures such as the Day Law unconstitutional in 1948, and in 1954 the Court in the case *Brown v. Board of Education of Topeka* found segregated school systems to be illegal. Mayslick's African American Rosenwald school remained in operation until 1960.

From the central crossroads in Mayslick the road toward Washington and Maysville ran north across the Lees Creek headwaters, past the site of the town's nineteenth-century livery stable, and up the hill past the Drake family home—on the left and now marked by state historical marker number 1628. The commemorative plaque summarizes Daniel Drake's professional life as the Ohio Valley's most prominent nineteenth-century physician. About a mile north of the central town common, the Palmer Funeral Home on the left occupies a historic building. Just ahead, Latham Pike intersects the Maysville Road. During the nineteenth century's turnpike period, a tollhouse stood

Daniel Drake's family residence was a large central-hallway clapboard house that still stands beside the old Maysville Road on Mayslick's north side.

on the right, or north, side of Latham Pike approximately a mile from its intersection with the Maysville Road, one of four tollhouses positioned on the main roads that led to Mayslick. The other three tollhouse sites were along the Maysville Road (U.S. 68) about two miles south, along the road southwest to Sardis (SR 324), and along the old Nicholas Road (SR 324) about one mile east.

The education theme exemplified by the small school building behind the Second Baptist Church and the Rosenwald school on Nicholas Street materializes again on Mayslick's north side, but in a different context. As the road approaches the intersection with the Mayslick bypass, Kentucky's first consolidated school building stands on the hill to the right. At the turn of the twentieth century the state had some 2.1 million residents, about 80 percent of whom lived on farms and in small towns. The state's educational system was still centered on public and private academies and rural one-room schools. Most students in 1900, especially those living in rural areas, did not progress beyond the eighth grade. Those families with the financial wherewithal might send their children to a town school for ninth through twelfth grades, boarding them in private homes for the school year.

When completed in 1910, the hilltop Mayslick school was one of the largest buildings in town and the pride of the county as the state's first consolidated school.

In 1908 the state legislature passed the Sullivan School Law, which included a number of provisions intended to organize education at the county level, including systematically dividing the state's 120 counties into school districts based on student density. Its primary objective, however, was to invigorate educational standards by mandating construction of a high school with free tuition for rural children in each county.[21] William E. Pyles, a prominent landowner whose large farm lay adjacent to the Maysville Road at the North Fork of the Licking River north of Mayslick, argued strongly that the Mason County consolidated school should be located in Mayslick, not Maysville. Pyles and Mayslick community residents formed the Mayslick Improvement Company, which sold stock and raised funds to build a $32,000 school building that opened in 1910. Consolidating seven rural school districts into one necessitated transporting children from remote farms to Mayslick each school day. Using funds provided by a self-imposed school transportation tax, the consolidated school purchased a fleet of mule-drawn wagons—similar to the omnibuses used in cities before the advent of the streetcar—and established pickup routes through the county. By the third year of operation, the school had seven teachers and operated eleven student pickup wagons.

The benefits of school consolidation were manifold. Not only did the students' parochial world of small, one-room schools broaden significantly, but school attendance exceeded 90 percent—compared with a state average of about 58 percent—and most students completing eighth grade went on to high school. School Principal R. F. Gaithey believed that the consolidated school was a major boon to the "tenant class" students, as he termed them, who now enjoyed the same educational opportunities as the students who came from wealthy landholder families. Although it was unanticipated, the Mayslick consolidated school also had the effect of increasing farmland values as farmers sought to gain access to the school for their children by buying land in the district.[22] When a new Mason County high school opened in Maysville in 1960, Mayslick lost its secondary education classes to the new school, although it retained its elementary classes until 1979. In 1981 the school property was sold; the buyers remodeled the structure into fifteen apartments. The building stands as a reminder that Mayslick was the first community in the state to create a consolidated school that provided transportation to students at public expense.[23]

Mile 7.3 As the old Maysville Road exits Mayslick to the north, it intersects the bypass. A Shell gas station stands on the hill to the right, conveniently accessible from the old road and the bypass. In 1955 the state authorized construction of a bypass that would carry U.S. 68 around Mayslick's east side. J. J. Pollittee, the chief engineer, announced the project, which included funding for a bypass at Washington. The project provided for 6.4 miles of roadway from Mayslick to Washington, forty-four to fifty-six feet wide, including ten-foot shoulders and a twenty-four-foot driving lane, at an estimated cost of $150,000 per mile. Mayslick residents voiced concerns that the new bypass would draw traffic away from the town's businesses, although it is likely that most town businesses catered to local customers rather than people passing along the road.[24]

As the old road alignment crosses the U.S. 68 bypass here, its name changes to Ross Drive; it rejoins the new road one mile ahead. The old route descended an easy hillside grade into Lees Creek valley. Daniel Drake's uncle Abraham Drake built two water-powered mills on Lees Creek just north of Mayslick in the 1790s. As a nine-year-old, young Daniel was entrusted to take corn and wheat to the mills to be ground. For the return trip, he packed the meal or flour on his horse and followed the mill path through the trees back to Mayslick, a route that very probably approximated the present road.[25]

Mile 7.5 On U.S. 68 north of the Ross Drive intersection, the Mayslick Mill stands on the right, beside the new road alignment. Eighteenth- and nineteenth-century water-powered mills stood beside creeks that could be dammed to provide sufficient fall to turn a waterwheel. Late nineteenth- and early twentieth-century mills were typically built along railroad tracks, which allowed economical export of large volumes of locally produced surplus grain. The Mayslick Mill is road- and truck-oriented and an indicator that the surrounding farms are active livestock producers. The mill's sign declares that "Bulk Feed & Fertilizer/Country Ham" are its primary products, but the mill's actual function is more diversified. Area farmers can purchase livestock feed at the mill, some of it custom-ground from local grains. Also for sale are selected livestock management items such as fence gates, water tanks, salt blocks, round hay-bale feeding frames, and assorted hardware.

A historic marker here commemorates Confederate General John Hunt Morgan's last Civil War raid in June 1864. Born in 1825 in Huntsville, the heart of north Alabama's fertile Tennessee River Valley, Morgan moved with his family to Lexington,

Holstein heifers in a pasture on Mayslick's north side seek shade on a warm summer day. The Mayslick Mill stands along U.S. 68 in the distance. This mill has two "legs," or vertical elevators, that employ gravity to deliver grains and other feed components through angled downspouts to storage bins.

Kentucky, in 1831. He served in the Mexican War (1846–48) and joined the Confederate forces in 1861, early in the Civil War. Morgan operated primarily in the Virginia, Tennessee, and Kentucky theaters, and his preference for detached guerrilla cavalry tactics often caused Union forces to divert from established battle lines, thereby winning for Morgan renown and promotion. In June 1863 Morgan initiated his last raid into Kentucky. His skirmishers briefly occupied Mt. Sterling—where his troops robbed the bank of some $60,000—Lexington, and Cynthiana, where a Union Army counterattack drove Morgan and his men from the state. Confederate sympathizers much admired Morgan's exploits. The Kentucky Historical Society has erected seventy-two historic roadside markers across the state that commemorate Morgan's Civil War routes and battle sites. Fourteen markers, many with the same text as this one, mark the route and incidents of his last raid.[26]

Mile 8.1 On the left, running parallel to U.S. 68, is a cutoff section of the 1930s Maysville Road track, which becomes SR 2514.

Mile 8.9 U.S. 68 intersects Clift Pike, which runs east, or to the right.

Mile 9.2 SR 2544 continues to parallel the new highway on the left, intersecting the Old Sardis Pike on the left.

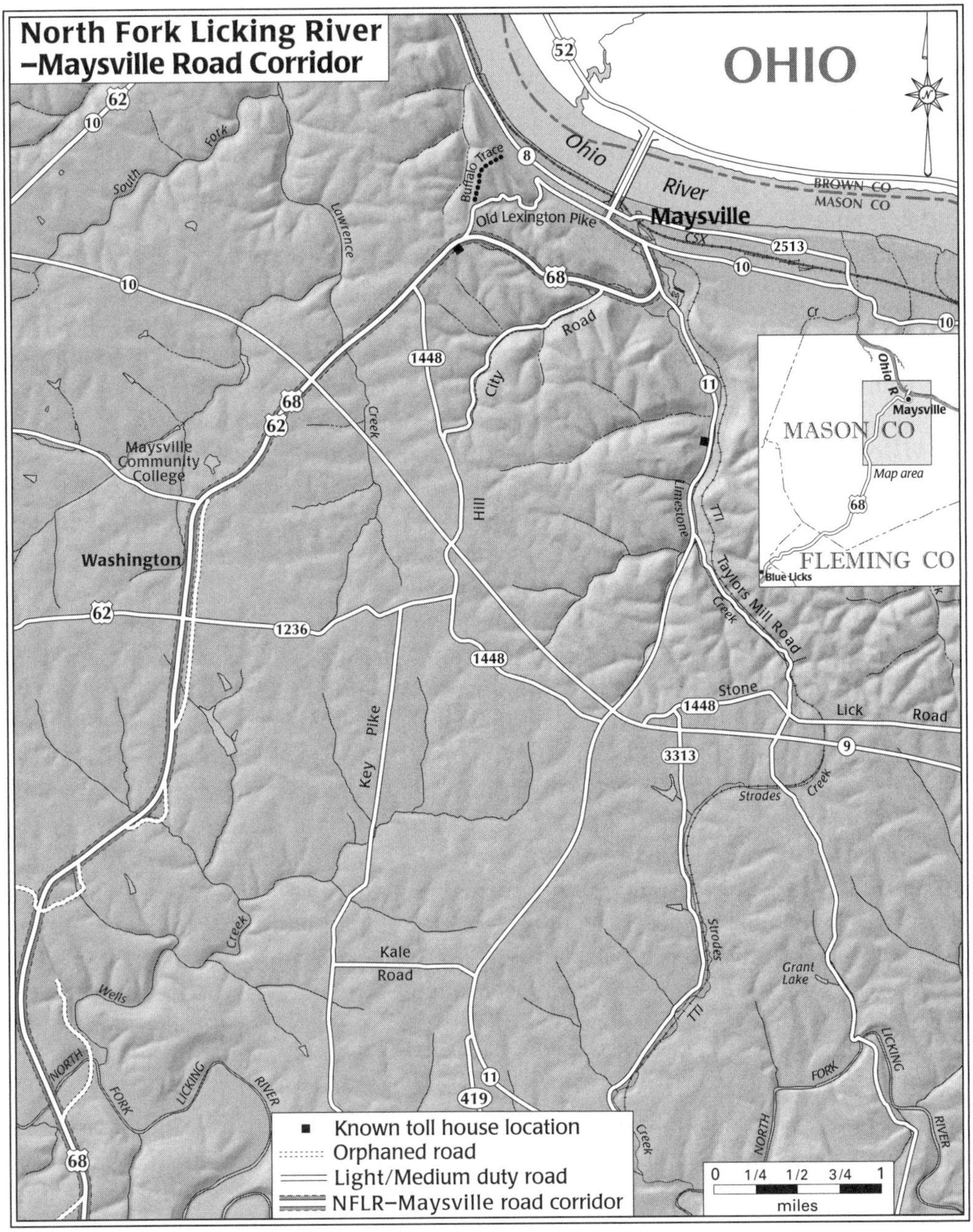

Mile 9.6 On this broad upland, U.S. 68 crosses the drainage divide between Lees Creek and the North Fork of the Licking River before descending into the North Fork bottoms.

Mile 10.3 The old roadbed appears as SR 2514 on the left. Before 1937 the old road crossed the present right-of-way here to run near the crest of the hill paralleling the present highway on the right. The old road disappears in the pasture on the right but some traces of the alignment can be seen as a bench or rut near the crest of the paralleling hill. The James Pyles family farmstead spreads across the hill spur just ahead on the right. The old road probably passed beside the farm buildings and is coincident with the present farm driveway. A dry-laid rock fence paralleled the old road on the right, or east, side, beginning along the farm driveway and then following the road's curve around the base of the hill before running out onto the North Fork floodplain for nearly one-quarter mile, where it ended just short of the river. In 1937 State Highway Department engineers drew up plans to straighten the Maysville Road between the hillcrest to the south and Washington.[27] The old road followed a winding four-curve route from the hillcrest on the south to the river bottom. The new route employed deep hill cuts and embankment fills to straighten the road's downhill grade into the valley, and it substituted two long sweeping curves for the old four-curve route.

Mile 10.4 Near the bottom of the hill, the new highway alignment continues straight ahead, crossing the North Fork of the Licking floodplain on an embanked causeway and a new concrete and steel bridge. In 1937, when state engineers undertook the first major road realignment here, the farm property on the right was owned by William Pyles, the person who organized the effort to build the state's first consolidated school in Mayslick in 1910. His son, James Pyles, was a large landowner here during the second half of the twentieth century. The farm included a dairy herd that produced Grade A milk for the Maysville market, a large poultry barn with a flock of laying hens, and burley tobacco fields. Many of the original farm buildings still stand.

Near the bottom of the hill, old U.S. 68 curved around the north side of the hill to the right. A 1950s concrete-block gas station—now converted to a residence—stands at the corner. One quarter mile farther on, a house stands at the roadside on the right that in the 1930s was the Eugene Pyles & Son Texaco service station and grocery; rental tourist cabins and trailer camp spaces were a secondary business. The original service station has been replaced by a concrete-block apartment building, but the original oval concrete gas pump island remains.

The 1937 U.S. 68 alignment continues in a long, sweeping curve toward the North Fork, flanking the broad floodplain to the left, where traces of the first-generation turnpike road are visible in the pasture. About three hundred feet to the left, the stone foundation piers that carried the original wooden covered bridge still stand on the North Fork's north and south banks. Originally built with a clear span of seventy-nine feet, the covered bridge collapsed under the weight of a heavy truck in 1936. Engineers subsequently realigned the road well to the right, placing it above the floodplain, atop an embanked roadbed. This segment included a new concrete bridge, which still stands in good condition just ahead. By repositioning the road to the right, engineers eliminated two tight-radius turns where the old turnpike track jutted into the base of the north bluff and aligned the road directly with the Wells Creek valley, a low-angle tributary of the North Fork, which carried the road north to the crest of a broad ridge. The 1937 concrete road ends about a quarter mile ahead at a large roadside quarry where someone has built a small house. The road now serves as a parking lot for old vehicles and machinery. Return to the intersection of new U.S. 68 and the 1937 road.

Mile 10.7 As U.S. 68 climbs out of the North Fork valley, a small, one-story house stands near the road on the left at the site of the historic Redd's Tavern. A Maysville Road tollhouse also stood somewhere near here.

Mile 11.8 East Parry Lane on the right is probably named for the Parry family, which had a farm in the area in the 1870s.

Mile 12.2 The north end of Parry Lane reconnects to U.S. 68.

Mile 12.5 A short, unnamed cutoff to the right represents the old road alignment here.

Mile 12.9 The cutoff, undrivable, rejoins U.S. 68.

Mile 13.0 Just south of Washington, U.S. 68 crosses the Maysville corporate boundary. Political leaders in many American cities recognize that the costs of maintaining city services such as police and fire protection and freshwater, sewerage, and storm-drain systems increase over time, whereas a city may lose a portion of its tax base through out-migration of both the population and traditional businesses to suburban locations beyond the city's political boundary. Annexing adjoining land into the old central city through corporate boundary extensions permits the city to enclose new suburban properties that will broaden a central city's tax base. Maysville officials elected to extend the corporate boundary some eight and one-half miles along the Ohio River front from near Kennedy Creek on the east to Lawrence Creek on the west, and about seven miles south from the river to this point near Washington. The net effect has been to draw onto the Maysville tax rolls the suburban development along U.S. 68 and the Alexandria-to-Ashland Highway (KY 9). Maysville also effectively ended a long-standing rivalry with Washington by politically absorbing the proud former county seat.

29

Old Washington

Washington, now called Old Washington, was a prosperous place in the early decades of this area's frontier development. Nineteenth-century affluence, however, gave way to economic decline; recently the town has been revitalized through its reinvention as a popular tourist destination. Early settlers entering Kentucky by the Ohio River route disembarked at the Limestone landing but rarely stayed the night there because of its exposed position and inadequate accommodations. Four miles inland, Washington welcomed travelers with shelter for them and their horses. Travelers' trip narratives invariably included comments on Washington. The Baptist preacher William Wood and Arthur Fox, a young Virginia surveyor, established the town in 1785 on land purchased from Simon Kenton.[1] Anticipating the deed transfer, early settlers built a few crude cabins in 1784, which merited notice from Ned Darnaby, who reached Washington in October of that year and saw "several houses commenced but not finished—bodies not covered. I don't know whether there were any persons living there."[2]

Building gained momentum, however, and by October 27, 1786, the petition submitted to the Virginia Assembly for the town's charter stated that "there are now upwards of Fifty families among who are Mechanics of divers kinds."[3] One hundred thirty-six individuals signed the petition, which the Virginia Assembly approved the same year by passing An Act for Establishing a Town in the County of Bourbon. The act acknowledged that the town contained about seven hundred acres following an in-lot and out-lot plat similar to that used in Lexington, Paris, and Millersburg, "with convenient streets." The first town trustees included nine "gentlemen," Daniel Boone among them. Arthur Fox, a town proprietor, was also named a town trustee. Boone, Fox, and the other trustees were authorized to make rules for building and to settle lot boundary disputes. One directive required that lot holders build a dwelling measuring at least sixteen by sixteen feet with a brick or stone chimney before they could "enjoy the same privileges and immunities which the freeholders and inhabitants of other towns, not incorporated, hold and enjoy."[4] By November 1788 Samuel Potts Pointer noted that there was only one hewn log house, but "a heap of cabins," crafted by rough-and-ready construction techniques that produced crude shelters suitable only for temporary habitation. The following month, Asa Farrar added a horse mill and a tavern to Washington's structure inventory.[5]

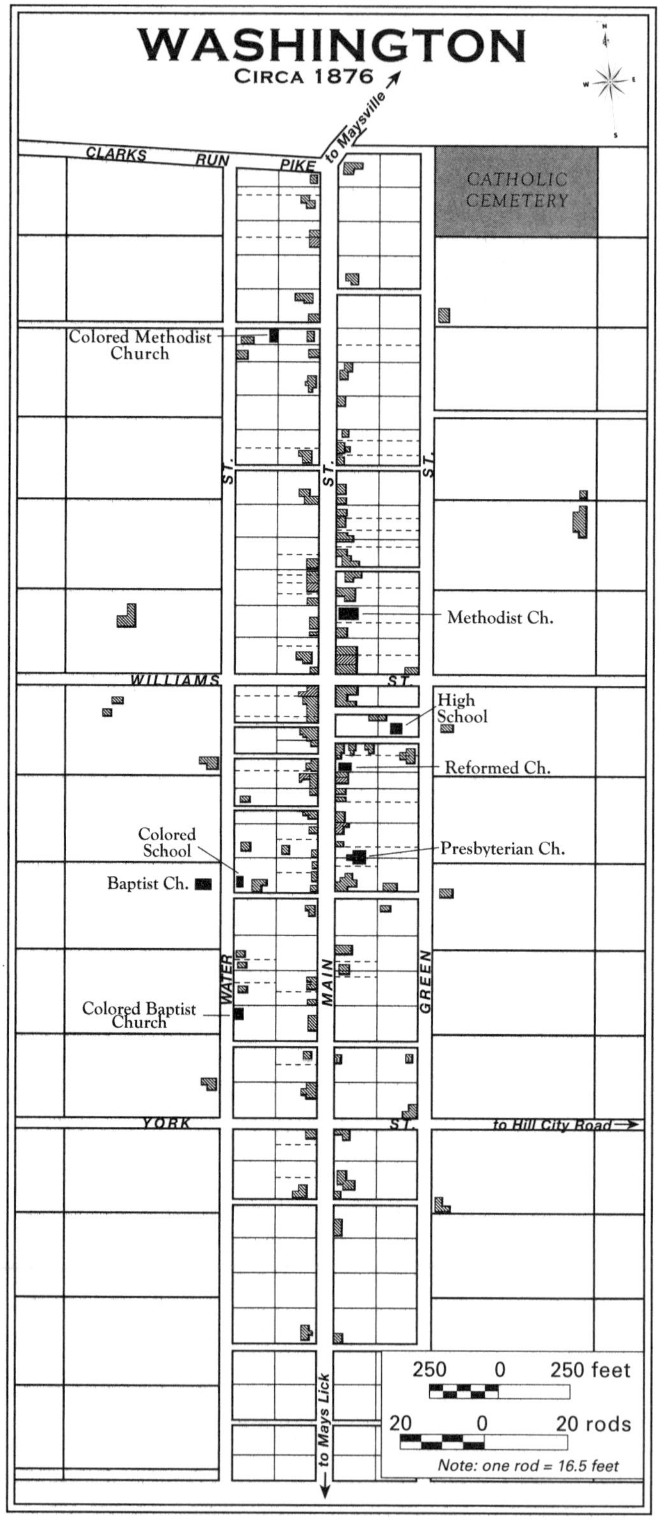
WASHINGTON
Circa 1876
to Maysville
Clarks Run Pike
Catholic Cemetery
Colored Methodist Church
Methodist Ch.
Williams St.
High School
Reformed Ch.
Colored School
Presbyterian Ch.
Baptist Ch.
Colored Baptist Church
Water St.
Main St.
Green St.
York St.
to Hill City Road
to Mays Lick
250 0 250 feet
20 0 20 rods
Note: one rod = 16.5 feet

By 1790 Washington was assiduously evolving from a rude straggle of cabins into a thriving roadside village; substantial new buildings replaced small cabins and in-filled vacant lots. One Washington resident, William Goforth, counted 119 cabins housing 462 inhabitants.[6] The town's population at the occasion of the first federal census, in 1790, was second only to Lexington's, an alacritous growth and development that is all the more noteworthy given that Mason County was still relatively exposed and vulnerable to occasional Indian raids and predations, so much so that the inhabitants built a stockade in the center of town for protection, "just in case."[7] Residents never had reason to use it, but the precaution was fueled by the knowledge that the frontier was still a potentially dangerous place and preparation was more admirable than retreat. The 1790 population included 163 adult white males over the age of sixteen, 95 white males under the age of sixteen, 183 white females of all ages, and 21 slaves.[8] Although the census enumerator did not tabulate the number of young females, conventional birthrate demographics suggest that they and the males were probably similar in number; if so, the ratio of adult males to adult females was very much skewed toward male predominance. The lower numbers of women may be due to the married men's practice of heading to the frontier to prepare adequate living arrangements before bringing their families and to a higher frequency of single young men emigrating in search of greater economic opportunity.

After several failed petitions, Mason County finally separated from Bourbon, its mother county, in September 1787.[9] The county court held its first meeting in the house of one of the trustees, Robert Rankin, on May 26 and 27, 1789, during which a sheriff, deputy sheriff, and county clerk were appointed; a surveyor and coroner were recommended for appointment by the professors of William and Mary College and the governor of Virginia, respectively; and two lawyers were admitted as counsel to the court. During what must have been an extended meeting, militia officers were appointed, as was a committee to "view and fix upon the most proper, and convenient place within the bounds of Washington for fixing the public buildings on." The court also issued to David Broderick and Robert Rankin the newly fledged county's first tavern licenses. Truncating any tendency toward price gouging, the court established rates for tavern meals, lodging, and liquor, and set prices for livestock fodder and stablage as well. The court heard and granted twelve motions for stock marks so that farmers could distinguish their livestock from those of their neighbors at this time of free and open range. On the second day the court named a committee to view a route for a road leading to Charlestown from the most convenient part of the Limestone Road. In addition, court officers appointed more militia officers and constables. The sheriff protested that he could not be held liable for escapes without an adequate jail in which to incarcerate criminals, and the clerk duly recorded his protest. Lawyers initiated the first estate settlement, and the clerk recorded the first deed, heralding what constituted the most common responsibilities of the county court—the legal transfer of land and the disposition of a deceased person's property.[10]

At the court's June meeting, the committee for the placement of public buildings brought a recommendation that the courthouse be built on vacant ground between Miles W. Conway and John Williams. This site was at the town center on Main Street between the two alleys connecting to Green (also colloquially called Back) Street south of Williams Street. Here Lewis Craig completed a beautiful stone courthouse in 1794. The neoclassical building was fifty feet long, twenty-three feet wide, two stories high, with a rooftop cupola capped by a weathervane graced by a spear and gilded ball. An eight-columned porch formalized the front facade.[11] In time county officials erected a whipping post, stocks, and a slave auction block on the public grounds. Thomas Williams offered his storehouse for use as a jail, over the objections of Sheriff Thomas Waring. The court accepted Williams's offer but ordered that a new jail be built immediately. The two-story stone jail, measuring sixteen by sixteen feet, was not completed until February 1790. One of the most important tasks accomplished by this court was the division of the county into three areas for recording tithables and tax collections.[12] Thus did the residents put the county's governing machinery into operational order.

In the meantime, Washington's town trustees attended to their own civic responsibilities. Minutes from the earliest trustees' meetings are lost, but minute books that begin in 1794 have been preserved. The first entry concerned the appointment of new trustees in compliance with an act passed by the Kentucky General Assembly on December 19, 1793, that established new rules and regulations regarding town governance. The trustees devoted their first meeting to electing a chairman and clerk, voting that a moderator be selected every six months, agreeing to meet on the first Friday of each month at 4:00 P.M., and recommending that the law that prohibited running horses and shooting in the streets be enforced.[13] This last directive grew out of a clause in the 1793 act that suggested that Washington's quietude was sometimes disturbed by rowdy behavior that endangered the residents. Not only did enforcement encourage peace in the streets, but the fines levied on offenders added to the town's coffers.[14] At subsequent meetings the trustees devoted time to improving the town's streets and establishing boundaries. The issue of county and town self-governance as illustrated by these early meetings suggests that Washington residents were as concerned with creating and embracing a legal framework for community life as they were with establishing habitable structures and clear farmland. Legal and political geographies developed in tandem with social, economic, and cultural institutions, and day-to-day experiences provided context for mutual and reciprocal adjustments and adaptations.

Washington's survey—lot lines, street routes, and other regularities of the town's layout—imposed an organizing geometric grid of irregular rectangular blocks on an existing settlement that was free-form if not chaotic. In some instances, the survey aligned streets where buildings already stood. The town establishment act failed to vest the appointed trustees with the power to convey lots, accordingly, the act passed by the Kentucky Assembly in 1793 authorized the trustees to settle and determine the limits of all lots. The town plan was an elongated linear grid: Main Street (the Limestone Road) formed the seventy-foot-wide main thoroughfare. The grid included two cross streets, Williams Street in the center of town and York Street on the south end (both forty feet wide). Two back streets, fifty feet wide and named Water and Green streets, paralleled Main Street. The trustees ordered a new town survey, which began with the installation of a standard or monument at the corner of William and Main streets, which served to align the town grid's principal meridian. Using the meridian as a baseline, the surveyors were to confirm in-lot and out-lot boundaries. Any surplus land was to be left in the alleys as they were shown on the earlier plat. As the survey got under way, the trustees ordered that a proper form be prepared before deeds were formally issued. Once the form was adopted, claimants came forward to receive legal title to their lots, a process that took a number of years.[15]

During the late 1790s the trustees applied themselves to questions of town infrastructure. In accordance with the 1793 act, they turned their attention to the town streets, which needed repairing. One of the first tasks was to build a bridge across Main Street, financed by taxes and fines. Although the board encountered difficulties with the bridge contractor, Eli Metcalfe, who failed to meet their schedule for finishing the bridge, they ordered a second bridge be built. This structure was forty feet wide and spanned one of the town's alleys. Natural drains ran across Main Street and, rather than obligate pedestrians to wade across muddy streets, the bridges allowed foot traffic to remain above the mire. Eventually, contractors built four foot bridges, one on Main Street, two on alleys, and one on East Back Street (another name for Green Street).[16]

When the need for a market house became apparent, town trustees appointed committees to procure permission from the county court to build on part of the public ground and sell subscriptions to underwrite the cost. The structure was built "four pannels below the pound" (an impoundment area for stray animals) on the west corner of the public ground. The building was small, twenty by thirty feet, with four thick brick pillars front and back supporting the roof. Inside, the brick-paved floor was divided into stalls for sellers.[17] The market opened in August 1806, and Wednesday and Saturday were assigned as market days; selling hours began at sunrise and ended at 10:00 P.M. All produce was subject to inspection by the market master. Fish, presumably caught in the Ohio River, were also for sale. In 1813 the market house was enclosed with a post and rail fence with a gate at each end. The first market house served the community for many years, but by 1825 it was in disrepair and the trustees contracted to reinforce the structure with five brick pillars on each side.[18]

Early in the nineteenth century Washington's trustees instituted regulations that held lot holders accountable for actions that created a public hazard or nuisance and directed them to manage their property to the benefit of the public. Such regulations suggest that basic urbanity was not within the realm of experience of Washington's early residents; town structure and life was, rather, the product of experiential evolution, not a template developed elsewhere that was simply dropped into place. For example, one regulation required lot holders to lay a six-foot-wide wood or stone pavement in front of their lots and keep it repaired for the benefit of foot traffic. Another required them to erect and maintain division fences between their lots. A short-lived law limited to one the number of dogs a householder could own; exceptions were made only for the tanner and the jailor. A regulation prohibited the discarding of dead animals in the town streets, for fear that they would become carrion. Pigs were not allowed to run in the streets—as they were in Cincinnati and many other cities. Horses were prohibited on Main Street footways that were railed in or paved. Laws prohibited residents from polluting the town wells and butchers from slaughtering animals on Main Street.[19] Outdoor toilets could not be built on or within any street or alley. The trustees ordered Benjamin Bayless to fill up the hole in Main Street where he had quarried stone, and they further directed that one McCullough tear down an old log house because it had become dilapidated and was frequented by stray hogs and other animals.[20] Town streets, it seemed, were initially deemed free or common spaces in the sense that residents used them for all manner of activities as well as places of public disposal—until the trustees considered such activity unacceptable. The movement of horse-drawn wagons and coaches, it seems, had not yet emerged as the primary use for streets. Enforced legal codes, not folk logic or practice, would finally gain for transport conveyances an exclusive right to the road's right-of-way.

By 1813 town trustees turned their attention to fire protection. Fire was a constant danger in Kentucky's early towns. Log and frame structures were highly flammable, water supplies were often inadequate, and minor fires frequently developed into disastrous conflagrations. A 1798 act of the Kentucky Assembly provided funds for a Washington water system that residents initiated by digging twenty-two wells at strategic points throughout the town. The Kentucky Assembly also authorized a tax levy of $750 on the town's real property, the purpose being to procure a fire engine. Property owners were required to pay 55¼ cents per $100 property value. Residents organized a fire company, complete with ranked officers, and all adult males were ordered to report when fires occurred. Policy required each firefighter to keep a fire bucket in good repair and bring it to each fire. Despite these precautions, a fire erupted on April 30, 1825, in Colonel Key's stone tavern, then occupied by a Mr. Hord. The fire quickly spread to buildings owned by members of the Craig family and occupied by a Mr. Artus, who operated a tavern there. The fire completely consumed these buildings together with stables, outhouses, and other subsidiary structures. Although some twenty buildings were ablaze during the conflagration, firefighters saved many from being destroyed.[21]

In the late 1790s Washington supported fifteen to twenty mercantile establishments, two taverns, ten mechanics' shops, three ropewalks, and three churches.[22] Residents established the Washington Emigrant Society to attract settlers. Several prestigious private schools, including the Franklin Academy, which opened in 1795, offered educational opportunities. Washington's citizens had the benefit of an early bank that provided the basis for a cash rather than a barter economy and processed the various currencies in circulation. The town erected Mason County's first post office and was the best or only place providing medical treatment and legal aid. Despite this early business base, Washington's population growth followed a boom-and-decline cycle that many frontier settlements experienced. From an estimated 462 inhabitants in 1790 the town's population increased steadily and more than doubled in the next two decades to a high of 1,001 citizens in 1810. Thereafter, locational advantages began to accrue to other places along the road, and decline set in. By 1820 Washington's population had dropped to 809, and a decade later had nearly been halved in a precipitous decline to 454; the population was halved again to 215 by 1840. Nevertheless, the town remained an important Mason County economic and social center, partly because Maysville's initial growth was slow and did not begin to accelerate until steamboat-borne river trade increased to a level that spurred development and growth at the river's edge.

The 1810 federal population census uncharacteristically listed occupations for some of Washington's inhabitants, thereby offering a glimpse of the town's available services and businesses. As the seat of county government and judicial systems, Washington was home to the county and circuit court clerks, jailor, and postmaster. The Franklin Academy preceptor and a minister were in residence, and they, in addition to two attorneys and three physicians, formed the town's professional class. Residents practiced nearly thirty other service- or commodities-oriented occupations, including various general storekeepers and innkeepers, hatters, boot- and shoemakers, tailors and a blue dyer (one who dyed wool or linen), blacksmiths and a coppersmith, tanners and saddle makers, manufacturers of hemp and cabinetry, wool carders, building tradesmen, a Windsor chair maker, a barber, a mill merchant, a brewer, and men who either made wagons or transported commodities in them. Washington residents capitalized on their location astride the Maysville Road, and the breadth of their professions suggests that they also served constituents in Mason County and the surrounding countryside.

Maysville's growing importance as an economic engine eventually resulted in the relocation of the county seat from inland Washington to the river's edge in 1848. Washington's citizens hotly contested losing the courthouse and its affiliations to minatory Maysville, but to no avail. As Maysville's riverfront business activity grew and profits mounted, Washington merchants, manufacturers, lawyers, and others followed the money and moved their businesses to the thriving river port in the 1820s and 1830s; that the seat of government would follow must have seemed inevitable to those left behind in locationally disadvantaged Washington. The county seat's formal move from Washington to Maysville in 1848 was a belated acknowledgment of an economic and social exodus that had already occurred. So precipitous was Washington's actual and perceived decline that the 1850 census did not acknowledge Washington as being a separate place but blended it in with the rest of the county, although a separate enumeration was reinstated in 1860.[23] From 1860 through 1880 Washington experienced yet another demographic shift. The aggregate population increased by about a third to 307 in 1860, but the variety of occupations declined and the workforce was dominated by day and farm laborers. The town's residents still received medical care from two physicians, and others such as two merchants and their clerks, two grocers, the postmaster at the post office, a hotel keeper, a tailor, and two shoemakers provided other needed services. But the town's prosperity and prospects had been abridged. Among Washington's residents in 1860 were thirty-five people born in Ireland. These émigrés presumably fled the Emerald Isle in the wake of "the Great Hunger," the famine that devastated Ireland during the 1840s; the postfamine exodus continued from 1850 to century's end.[24] Few Irishmen were employed in skilled trades, though Washington's group included a blacksmith and a clerk. Most others worked primarily as day laborers on farms and in towns in addition to working in the stone-related occupations—quarrying and road and fence building. The large Saint Patrick's Cemetery on

Washington's north side is primarily an Irish burial ground and contains many headstones whose epitaphs include the statement "Born in Ireland."

Before the Civil War most of Washington's African American inhabitants were enslaved; there were very few free black residents. Slaves accounted for over one-third of the town's population in 1810; free blacks numbered only ten. By 1820 the slave population remained at slightly more than one-third of the town's residents; free blacks numbered only five. Washington's population declined precipitously after 1820 and remained low until 1870. The slave population, however, spiked to two-thirds in 1830. Moreover, the percentage of white households that owned slaves ranged from forty-eight to sixty-five between 1810 and 1840. By the eve of the Civil War the town's population had doubled from its 1840 numbers, maintaining the same percentage of slaves as earlier, but the percentage of slave-owning families dropped to just over one-third. Significantly, Irish emigrants were not slave owners.

After the Civil War Washington's population continued to decline, although the proportion of black citizens increased dramatically, so that by 1870 they accounted for more than one-half of the population. Upon emancipation, many rural freed slaves either moved out of state altogether or moved to urban communities; their increased numbers in Washington mirrored a relocation process that was repeated across the Bluegrass Region. The number of Ireland-born residents declined by 1870 and continued to decrease through the remainder of the century. Beyond 1870, Washington's population gradually increased, and blacks continued to comprise over one-half of the town's citizenry. This trend continued through the next ten decades, until the 1960s, when local white citizens began buying and restoring historic buildings in Washington and Mason County.

From about 1910 to the 1960s people built few new buildings in Washington, and the remaining historic building stock weathered and aged. The U.S. 68 highway bypass constructed in the 1980s diverted through traffic and attention from Washington's Main Street, which, when paired with a quiescent local economy, meant that the town's appearance changed very little, other than selective deterioration of some properties, the by-product of inattention. In the 1960s the historic preservation movement prompted local activists to launch initiatives to save Mason County's significant historic places. As residents purchased and restored historic buildings for use as residences or businesses that catered to tourists, Washington's character became that of a picturesque, historic town whose log and brick buildings and stone walkways harkened back to the late eighteenth and early nineteenth centuries. A booster organization, Old Washington, Inc., took on the challenge of revitalizing the town by making it a desirable and popular tourist destination. Antiques and gift shops, restaurants, museums, and interesting historic architecture combine with annual festivals and events to draw tourists and entice travelers to veer off modern U.S. 68 and experience Old Washington.

Mile 0.0 The south end of Old Washington's Main Street, the old Maysville Road, has been realigned; to engage Main Street, one must turn right off of the new bypass; Washington Park is on the right.

Mile 0.3 Behind Minton's Garage, on the right, a large quarry has been excavated into the Upper Ordovician limestone, probably the Grant Lake member, which outcrops on the low hillside. The Grant Lake is widely excavated for construction stone, and it forms the ridge crest here that U.S. 68 will follow north to the Maysville Country Club. A 1902 state law provided counties the legal basis to acquire title to one acre of land per mile adjacent to any public macadamized road from which rock could be obtained for use in road repair. If potential quarry sites could not be obtained by private agreement with the landowner, the law permitted the county to condemn the land.[25] This roadside quarry is large and was already of landmark proportions in 1876.[26] Given its age, size, and proximity to the road, it is very likely that this quarry was used by nineteenth-century turnpikers as a source of road-building and surfacing material, and could have supplied a considerable amount of macadam stone for the Maysville Turnpike as well as construction stone for building foundations and the like.

Mile 0.6 The Main Street and Duke of York Street intersection. One can access the old Hill City Road wagon and truck route into Maysville by taking this street to the right. Passing straight ahead through the intersection, one enters Old Washington's historic district. Although the historic town plat included a large number of out-lots flanking four rows of smaller in-lots on each side of Main Street, out-lot development was limited and most of the surviving historic buildings are concentrated along Main Street and the cross streets and alleys.

Mile 0.7 The town's Visitor's Center occupies two hewn-log houses on Main Street's west side that are among the earliest log structures still standing in town. Both buildings stand on lot 92, which William Flemming of Fayette County bought in 1791. Flemming sold the lot to Benjamin Bayless, a prominent Washington resident and early town trustee, in 1803.[27] The buildings' construction dates are not known, but Lee, Lashbrook & Company (Henry Lee, Peter Lee, and John Lashbrook) operated a general store in the south building, whereas the north house became a residence. "Mr. Lee" was the "polite and obliging" merchant who made it possible in 1807 for the traveler Fortescue Cuming to hire two horses so that he and his companion could continue their journey to Lexington.[28] Peter Lee may have been the only merchant among the three proprietors living in Washington in 1810.[29] Henry Lee signed the petition to establish the town in 1786 and served with the first town trustees. Both Henry and Peter served in the county militia from 1789, as county lieutenant and captain, respectively. Henry Lee's involvement in managing the store was probably minimal because he became president of the Washington Branch Bank of Kentucky after its establishment in 1809.[30] He was also an assistant judge in 1810.[31] Lashbrook and the Lees were slave owners; Henry Lee owned forty-one, Lashbrook seventeen, and Peter Lee four slaves. The store may have continued in business as late as 1876, when a surviving partner or one of his Henry Lee's heirs sold the property.

The Bayless family owned the neighboring log house and probably rented it to tenants until 1855, when a free African American man named Frank Lee bought the property.[32] Lee's acquisition paralleled the accelerated growth in Washington's black population after the Civil War. The State of Kentucky eventually acquired the two log buildings in the 1970s and leased them to Old Washington, Inc.

Part of the Visitors' Center lot is planted in native cane (*Arundinaria gigantea*), the

Benjamin Bayless, an early Washington settler listed as a hatter in 1810, built this substantial brick house in the early nineteenth century at the corner of Main and E streets. Bayless served as an early town trustee and as a captain in the War of 1812. He moved to Maysville to run a ferry in 1823. The Forman family, originally from New Jersey, occupied the house after they purchased it from Bayless. Forman family members were involved in Washington civic affairs and were supporters of the Presbyterian church that still stands next door. In 1831 Thomas S. Forman, George Forman, and Charles A. Marshall received authority to "graduate and turnpike" an alley from Main Street to East Back Street and to grade East Back Street by filling the low ground in the vicinity of the "Golden Well." They deemed this construction necessary so that they could build a steam mill.

only bamboo species native to North America. Canebrakes constituted a significant place in the native vegetation, as it covered large acreages in some sections of Kentucky's Bluegrass Region before Anglo settlement. Cane grew so thickly in places that it was nearly impenetrable, and it often grew as an understory among mature trees. Settlers assiduously cleared cane so that they could cultivate the fertile land on which it grew; within a generation the impressive canebrakes of the early settlement period were largely gone. Small patches of cane did survive, however, and recent botanical research has brought about a resurgence of interest in the plant.[33]

The log structures at the corner of Main and E streets are not original to the town but were moved and reassembled here for use as a post office and a bank. Across E Street on the same side of Main Street stands the two-story brick house built in 1802 by Benjamin

Bayless, who married Elizabeth Wood, daughter of George Wood, a cofounder of Washington. The house was later occupied by the Forman and Taylor families.[34]

2126 Old Main Street

Parishioners built Grace Church here in 1870 as a replacement for the second Presbyterian Church, then located across the street. The frame building has architectural features in both Gothic and Classic Revival styles, represented in its columned porch and lancet windows on the front and side walls. Adjacent to Grace Church at 2128 Main Street is a vibrantly painted late Victorian house that once served as the parsonage for the Presbyterian Church next door.[35]

2123 Old Main Street

Although the stone house on the left is the last surviving late eighteenth-century stone building in Washington, stone structures were once quite common here. Built of native limestone, the house is plain but has handsome proportions. John Pickett bought the lot from town trustees in 1790 and sold the south half of the lot (where the house now stands) in 1799 to Daniel Carroll. Dr. William Goforth apparently started the house's construction but may have never lived there; he moved his practice to Cincinnati in 1799. Goforth, a prominent early physician, served as a mentor to Dr. Daniel Drake, who settled as a boy at Mayslick.[36]

2124 Old Main Street

The Harriet Beecher Stowe Slavery to Freedom Museum is housed within a two-story brick house originally built in 1807 as a residence for Colonel Marshall Key, a Virginian who came from Fauquier County to Kentucky in 1795. Colonel Key married Harriet Sellman, whose father was a doctor in Cincinnati. Before her marriage, Harriet Beecher Stowe taught at the Western Female Institute in Cincinnati, and one of her students was Elizabeth Key, Marshall and Harriet Key's daughter. Local oral tradition claims that Harriet Beecher visited the Keys in 1833 and witnessed a slave auction on the courthouse lawn. That experience inspired her to write the famous antislavery manifesto in novel form, *Uncle Tom's Cabin.* A brick outbuilding with distinctive beveled vertical slits in the second story was probably used as a smokehouse, although local folklore fancifully identifies the slits as "rifle ports." Concern about Indian attack was long forgotten by the time the Key house and outbuilding were built, however, and the architecture of the outbuilding is identical to that of smokehouses elsewhere in the county.[37]

2117–2121 Old Main Street

The three connected houses on the left give the impression of row houses, although they were not all built at the same time. They stand on the south half of in-lot 39 and

Construction over several decades eventually transformed two original buildings separated by an open lot into a continuous line of connected structures. The two end buildings were both built in the late eighteenth or early nineteenth centuries, whereas the middle building did not unite the two ends until the mid-nineteenth century. Given the buildings' central location in Washington's main business area, their contiguous construction suggests a concern with optimizing use of valuable urban land.

the north half of in-lot 37. The north house may have been built between 1800, when John Machir first purchased the south half of in-lot 39, and 1817, when he died. The house on the south end may have been built between 1790, when John Pickett bought in-lot 37 from the town trustees, and 1807, when he sold the north half of it to Joseph Canby. The middle house was built by attaching the front and rear walls to the existing side walls of the two neighboring houses. It stands on in-lot 39, and its deed history is closely tied to that of the north house. James Parry bought the north house and lot in 1840, and this deed mentioned only one house. Parry was involved in commerce in 1840 and may have used the building for his business, but by 1850 he was a farmer. Parry may have built the middle house for rental purposes between 1840 and 1860. The north house and the lot where the middle house now stands have a complicated history involving lawsuits and various deed irregularities. An Irish family headed by Frances Ryan bought the north house in 1860 and lived here for many years. One of Ryan's sons was a grocer when he lived here in 1880.

In 1866 John Taylor, a black laborer, purchased the middle house and lot. Taylor, his wife, Bettie, and son, Spencer, are listed in Frances Ryan's household in 1870, suggesting that the census taker considered the two connected houses a single residence. By 1880 Taylor had become a preacher and was still living in the house, but without his wife and son. Maria Gibbs and her four sons and three daughters were living with him, probably as boarders. Samuel Ames, a manufacturer, acquired the south house and lot before 1841. This property was also the subject of a lawsuit against John Machir's heirs. A free black man, Robert Langhorn, acquired the south house in 1864. He worked first as a laborer but later became an undertaker. The properties were part of the general restoration effort in Washington that began in the 1960s.[38]

2127 Old Main Street

A solid, two-story brick house on the west side of Main Street was Washington's first bank, a branch of the Bank of Kentucky. It is now a private residence. The act enabling the bank was approved December 27, 1806, and charged John Machir, Basil Duke, and Daniel Vertner—or any two of theme—with selling two hundred shares to local investors. Henry Lee, an early Washington settler, served as the bank's first president. The building was constructed on the north half of in-lot 39, purchased by John Machir from the trustees in 1795 and sold to the Bank of Kentucky in 1815.[39] Bank deposits were ensconced within sixteen-inch brick exterior walls and a vault protected by barred, solid metal doors. The bank moved as part of the general business exodus to Maysville in 1835, and its owners converted the building to a residence.[40]

2114 Old Main Street

The First Reformed Christian Church stands directly opposite the branch bank building and is now used as a public meeting place. One of two church buildings in town with similar design features, the former Christian Church has a distinctive corbelled parapet on the facade that steps down in a style reminiscent of Dutch architecture.[41]

Lewis Craig built the courthouse in the center of town by 1794. A lightning strike in 1909 ignited a fire that destroyed the building, which had served as a school after its original court function was discontinued in 1848, when the county seat moved to Maysville. A house was later built on the lot.

2110 Old Main Street

The Washington Hall hotel was built around 1844 in a vain attempt to convince officials to retain the seat of county government in Washington. The rationale for the building's construction was that a hotel would house the many county visitors who came to Washington on court-related business.[42] Its placement very close to the street is typical of commercial buildings of its time, as businesspeople tried to crowd their buildings as close to the principal thoroughfares as possible, often encroaching well into the right-of-way. The hotel featured drawing rooms and a grand ballroom in addition to sleeping accommodations. The building hosts several antiques shops today.

2100 Old Main Street

Taylor's Corner stands at the intersection of Paxton and Old Main Street. Ezekiel and Dolly (Wood) Forman built the house about 1830 for their daughter, Elizabeth Forman Taylor, and her husband, Robert Taylor Jr. The building functioned as a residence and a general store for many years. The Taylors made annual trips to Philadelphia to purchase a wide array of merchandise to stock the store. Before their trips the Taylors usually placed an advertisement in the local paper asking their credit customers to settle accounts so they could accumulate enough money to purchase additional goods from Philadelphia merchants.[43]

2030 Old Main Street

The Paxton Inn stands on the corner opposite the Taylor house and store. Built around 1810 by James A. Paxton, an attorney, the building was a favorite gathering spot where local lawyers and politicians debated the day's issues. Paxton moved to Ohio in 1823 because of his strong opposition to slavery. During a visit to the Blue Licks spa the following year, Paxton fell from his buggy, suffering injuries of sufficient severity to cause his death. Willis D. Lee operated the inn until 1838, when Paxton's heirs sold it. After passing among several owners, the building became the home of the Mason County Telephone Company. The distinctive Federal-style structure was nearly demolished when the telephone company converted to the dial system and sold out to the Kentucky Telephone Company, which planned to raze the structure to create a parking lot. Members of the Limestone Chapter of the Daughters of the American Revolution led a preservation campaign in 1966 to save the structure; they not only convinced the telephone company to donate the building but also persuaded it to make a cash gift toward its restoration. The Paxton Inn currently serves as a chapter house for the DAR as well as a tourist attraction.[44]

2028 Old Main Street

The house that James Paxton and his family occupied stands adjacent to the Paxton Inn. Although this house, the house north of it, and the Paxton Inn appear as three attached units, they were built at different times. David Davis, an early town trustee, built the Paxton House on an in-lot purchased in 1793 from Arthur Fox and William Wood. Davis sold the house to James Paxton in 1810. The Paxton heirs sold it in 1838 and after it passed through the hands of numerous owners, trustees of the Methodist Episcopal Church South purchased the structure for use as a parsonage. The house has since been acquired by Old Washington, Inc.[45]

2026 Old Main Street

The northernmost unit of the three-building cluster at the corner of Paxton and Old Main streets is known locally as the "Doctor's House" because physicians lived there for more than a century. Drs. James Taylor, Elijah O. Dimmitt, Joshua Barnes, and Alexander Hunter all were associated with the house. The house's simple federal design resembles that of its neighbors; its corner porch is a later addition.[46]

Corner of D and Old Main Streets

A second example of a corbelled parapet can be seen on the Methodist Episcopal Church South, built in 1848, when disagreements over slavery divided the congregation and its members formed two separate churches, North and South. The building now serves as a nondenominational church museum featuring religious artifacts and four panels depicting symbols of the four gospels of Matthew, Mark, Luke, and John. The church's affiliation with proslavery sentiments is indicated in its stonework, which reads, "Methodist Church South."[47]

2027 Old Main Street

The three gables on this frame house are distinctive and unusual architectural features in Old Washington. The house, formerly with a smaller porch than it currently has, was the residence of C. S. Collins in 1876.[48]

Broderick's Tavern

This generously proportioned frame house stands on the in-lot purchased by David Broderick, who received a tavern license at the first Mason County Court meeting. The building has undergone extensive remodeling, but some of the original frame-with-brick-nogging construction remains on the north side. Thomas Sloe, Washington's first postmaster, and David Broderick are thought to have built the tavern in 1794, Broderick serving as tavern keeper. The Stevenson family occupied the house as a private residence from the 1840s well into the twentieth century. Margaret Stevenson willed the house to the Mason County Historical Society in 1973. The society renovated the building for use as a restaurant, and it has served in this capacity under several different proprietors.[49]

2014 Old Main Street

William Murphy, Washington's third postmaster, built this brick mansion around 1805. The building's design combines Federal-style elements in the basic structure, Georgian characteristics in its one-story gabled addition with shed dormers, and a classicist-style porch. An early post office that predated the house once stood in the front yard. It was torn down and a hewn-log house reconstructed in its place. Washington was the distribution point for mail to the entire Northwest Territory—that area north of the Ohio River extending from present-day Ohio west and north through Illinois and beyond. Thomas Sloe became postmaster in 1794; Edward Harris succeeded him in 1797. Harris's strong Presbyterian beliefs caused him to oppose mail delivery on Sunday, and he offered to resign as a result of his views. His resignation was not accepted, and he continued as postmaster until 1802, when William Murphy took the job. An early newspaper, the *Washington Mirror*, was printed on this site in 1787 by William Hunter and William Beaumont.[50]

Mefford's Station

The floors of this diminutive log house were originally built from the logs used in an Ohio River flatboat that brought the Mefford family to Kentucky in 1785. George Mefford and his wife, Malinda, had thirteen children.[51] In 1810 the census listed a George Mefford as a blacksmith with eight children living with him. Another George Mefford headed a family with eleven children. Both men owned four slaves each. The relationship between the two Georges may have been father and son; in any event, either of their large families would have experienced close quarters living in this small house. Two younger Meffords, Nathan and Samuel, each headed their own young families and were probably George's grown sons. The structure was originally built elsewhere in the county but was moved to Washington to preserve it in 1969. The massive chimney seems oversized in proportion to the rest of the house, but large fireplaces were the norm in early houses, where cooking over an open hearth was customary.

1934 Old Main Street

An early log structure is concealed beneath the clapboard siding of this two-story frame house that sits on one of the highest elevations in town. Arthur Fox, cofounder of Washington, owned in-lot 7, on which the house stands, and built his own house on the adjoining in-lot 5. His son-in-law, Dr. William Goforth, bought in-lots 7 and 8 in 1790 and may have been responsible for the early log structure that forms the core of the house. The house and lot passed through several owners from 1792 to 1836. Julia Crookshanks bought the house and lot in 1836 and established a female academy here. Upon her death, a group of men serving as school trustees bought the property and a school continued to operate here until 1853. Thereafter, the building was used as a residence, first by Nancy Lane for many years, and then by the Bickley family, who owned the property until it was purchased by a local preservation group. Nancy Lane was born in Ireland and lived in the house with her blacksmith son, John, in 1860. Her real property was worth $250, but her personal property was valued at $1,300, a fairly high value for a woman who was not employed. In contrast, her son, John, did not own any real property and had only $100 worth of personal property. His financial situation improved considerably when he inherited his mother's estate. Angeline Bickley, the wife of William Bickley Jr., acquired the house in 1871. Angeline's father-in-law, William Bickley Sr., ran a hotel for many years with his wife, Julia, who continued as a hotel keeper after her husband's death sometime before 1880. Angeline's husband worked as a laborer in 1880, but by 1900 he was making a living as a fisherman. Their son, Dave Bickley, was responsible for the expansion of the original log house: he added a second floor and increased the number of rooms.[52]

Mile 1.3 Washington's Main Street reenters U.S. 68–62 at the town's north end. Slack Pike intersects the highway from the left. In 1945 state highway engineers realigned the old road as it exited Washington by replacing an angled intersection with a long radius curve from here past the north entrance to St. Patrick's Cemetery on the right.[53] That change was later modified further by the construction of the Washington bypass. The cemetery is the resting place of many Irish immigrants and their descendants. The singer-actress Rosemary Clooney was born in Maysville in 1928 and enjoyed a successful career in films and as a musical performer. After her death in 2002 she was interred here at St. Patrick's Cemetery.

30

Slavery, the Underground Railroad, and Hemp Production

Before the Civil War Kentucky's enslaved population was concentrated in the prime agricultural counties—the limestone lands of the Bluegrass and central and western Pennyroyal, and the alluvial river plains along the Ohio River near Owensboro.[1] In 1790 Kentucky counted 11,830 slaves, who accounted for about 16 percent of the state's total population. Only 114 free African Americans lived in the state at that time. By 1860, the eve of the Civil War, the state's enslaved population had increased to 225,483, or 19.5 percent, while the free black population was 10,684, or less than 1 percent of the total population.[2]

Large Bluegrass farms, often settled and operated by migrants from Virginia or Maryland, produced tobacco and hemp as commercial cash crops, together with corn, wheat, oats, and market-garden crops as well as beef cattle, horses, and mules. The labor requirements for tobacco and hemp were seasonal, and although their production was punctuated by concentrated periods of work, such as the harvest, they were not as labor-intensive as rice, cotton, and sugar cane, the traditional lowland South plantation crops. Some Bluegrass farmers with surplus slaves rented them to neighbors to work as laborers by the day or the season. Periodically, slave dealers collected slaves from several owners and then marched them as a group, or coffle, to area slave markets. Buyers or dealers then transported slaves into the South for resale to the sugar cane plantations of south Louisiana or the cotton plantations on the fertile chalk

Kentucky's Population, 1790–1860

Year	White	African American Free	African American Slave	Free as Percentage of African American	Slave as Percentage of Total Population	Total Population
1790	61,133	114	11,830	0.95	16.19	73,077
1800	179,871	741	40,343	1.80	18.26	220,955
1810	324,237	1,713	80,561	2.08	19.82	406,511
1820	434,644	2,759	126,732	2.13	22.46	564,135
1830	517,787	4,917	165,213	2.89	24.02	687,917
1840	590,253	7,317	182,258	3.86	23.37	779,828
1850	761,413	10,011	210,981	4.53	21.48	982,405
1860	919,484	10,684	225,483	4.52	19.51	1,155,651

The Reverend James Dickey witnessed a slave coffle passing through Paris in Bourbon County. About forty men chained together led the procession, followed by thirty women who were tied hand to hand. As though in mockery, the leading two men were forced to play violins, the second two had to wear cockaded hats, and "near the centre waved the 'Star-Spangled Banner!—the Flag of the 'Model Republic,' carried literally in chains!" (*The Coffle Gang,* from Anon., *The Suppressed Book about Slavery* [New York: Carleton, 1864], 164–65, plate between 96 and 97)

lands of Alabama and Mississippi, where the Black Belt plantation district developed in the 1830s and 1840s.[3] The Reverend Elisha W. Green, a slave in Mayslick in the 1820s, witnessed slaves being moved in this manner. "I saw in Mayslick another company of forty or fifty men, chained. . . . There were some five or six wagons loaded with women and children. The foremost man looked to be about seventy years old, and he was singing: 'Hark from the tomb.' Mrs. Ann Anderson, a white woman who was sitting at the window, could not help crying. Indeed it was enough to have moved a heart of stone. It was a scene upon which I looked with horror."[4] A two-story log building thought to have been used as a slave holding pen was discovered on a farm west of Maysville in Mason County in the 1990s. A slave market operated at Cheapside on the courthouse square in Lexington, and slaves were also sold in other area towns.

Encouraged by a largely anonymous group of abolitionist activists living in Kentucky and north of the Ohio River in Illinois, Indiana, and Ohio, slaves from Kentucky and other southern states sometimes attempted escape. The Fugitive Slave Law of 1793 permitted slaveholders to reclaim their human property in any state—slave or free. The law also prohibited anyone from aiding fleeing slaves.[5] Despite the law and concerted efforts by slave owners to prevent or deter slaves from trying to escape to the north, thousands of slaves from across the South, especially in the border states, fled their owners' control and tried to reach Canada by way of the northern states. Those slaves who successfully escaped were often aided by abolitionists. Escapees traveled by many routes, some of them no doubt paralleling the major roads. The routes, the modes of movement, and the individuals who actively provided assistance and places where slaves could be hidden while avoiding those that hunted them were collectively referred to as the Underground Railroad. The Maysville Road corridor was an especially active route in part because it was heavily traveled and because many abolitionists lived in southern Ohio and were active in assisting slaves to find their way north.[6] John Rankin of Ripley, Ohio, across the Ohio River near Maysville, was a notable example of the local activists who assisted slaves, and his home on a hill overlooking the town became what some have called the most famous landmark on the Underground Railroad.[7]

A law passed by the Kentucky General Assembly in 1835 established a recovery fee, or bounty schedule, to pay any person, state resident or not, who arrested and delivered runaway slaves to their owners. The slave hunter who caught and arrested a slave within the county of the owner's residence received payment of ten dollars. Arrests and returns from any other county were worth twenty dollars, while slave arrests made out of state were worth not less than thirty dollars. The General Assembly moved in 1840 to curtail unauthorized slave movements by enacting a law authorizing the courts in those counties bordering the Ohio River to appoint "strong and active patrolls" whose duty was to guard the river, report all "delinquents," and punish any slave caught off the master's premises without a permit with up to ten lashes. Patrols were also authorized to apprehend those intending to assist slaves in escaping. The 1840 law also increased the reward schedule for the return of runaway slaves. Upon receipt of captured slaves, owners were now obligated to pay a bounty to the patrol of twenty-five dollars, fifty dollars if the slave had been captured in an adjacent county.[8] Undeterred by the patrols, slaves continued to flee north toward the Ohio River.

So successful was the Underground Railroad that the ongoing loss of slaves forced southern slaveholders to press Congress for stronger prohibitions on escaping slaves, which resulted in the Fugitive Slave Law of 1850, a component of the Compromise of 1850. The 1850 law did not provide the desired deterrent, and underground agents continued to assist escaping slaves to flee Kentucky until the Civil War.[9] In May 1851 the *Maysville Post Boy* reported: "During the past week, a leave-taking fever has prevailed among the slaves in this section. On Sunday night, a woman and three children, the property of F. M. Weedon of our city left. On Wednesday night, nineteen in one gang left their owners, in Lewis [County]—eight belonging to Mrs. Eliza Shepperd, two to Chas. Wood. . . . From Nicholas [County] several have also departed for freedom during the past few days."[10] Information collected by Wilbur Siebert in the nineteenth century suggests that more than forty thousand slaves fled the South through Ohio alone, aided by more than one thousand Ohio residents.[11] The Underground Railroad movement is commemorated at a museum at 115 East Third Street in Maysville. And in 2004 the National Underground Railroad Freedom Center, operated by the National Park Service, opened on the Ohio Riverfront in Cincinnati.

RETURN TO THE WASHINGTON BYPASS

Mile 13.2 The route here makes a junction with CR 2515. The old turnpike continued straight north here, a link to Washington's Main Street. This route will remain on the bypass, completed in the 1980s. The bypass reveals how modern businesses have attached themselves to Old Washington's south and north gateways. On the south a modern gas station and machinery and recreational vehicle sales cluster at the connector road intersection. On the north developers have erected several frame business buildings with access to both Main Street and the bypass.

Mile 13.8 U.S. 68 intersects CR 1236, also known as Mt. Olivet Road.

Mile 13.9 The old Washington Cemetery is on the left.

Mile 14.6 The junction with CR 2515 at the north end of Washington. Main Street reconnects to the new bypass at this point.

KENTUCKY HEMP

Mile 14.9 As the historic marker on the left suggests, Mason County, together with the Inner Bluegrass counties, was a major nineteenth-century hemp producer; production was revived briefly, for strategic reasons, during World Wars I and II. Fiber-producing crops such as flax and hemp were in demand on the Kentucky frontier for locally woven yard goods, bagging, cordage, and rope. By the beginning of the nineteenth century, Inner Bluegrass farmers in the counties surrounding Lexington were producing hemp, together with corn, rye, oats, and tobacco.[12] Local manufacturers converted the fiber into twine, cotton bale cloth, sailboat cordage, and oakum.[13] James Hall described the central Kentucky farm landscape in 1838: "The ground [between the trees] is then sown with grass and extensive tracts . . . are thus converted into spacious lawns, studded with noble trees. These are so numerous . . . as to form a prominent feature in the scenery, and it is hardly possible to imagine anything more beautiful, than the alternations of woodland and meadow, with hemp and cornfields, and orchards, which the eye here meets in every direction."[14] Though Hall describes the farming countryside as a picturesque rural idyll, hemp production was hardly a romantic undertaking; rather, hemp demanded extended periods of heavy work that fell primarily to slaves before the Civil War, and freedmen farm laborers thereafter.[15]

The hemp-production calendar began in the fall, when farmers plowed or broke sod for hemp planting the following spring. If they replanted hemp in an old hemp field, farmers practiced spring plowing as part of an intensive soil-preparation program. On limestone lands hemp could be produced for several years in succession without fertilization. When the soil would no longer produce a profitable crop, farmers moved production to another field.[16]

Depending on weather and soil conditions, hemp planting began in April or May, when seed was broadcast across the field's surface. The best hemp fields contained a high plant density, each plant six to ten feet tall at maturity. Tall plants with lengthy spacing between leaf nodes produced the longest, most desirable fiber. During the growing season, the crop shaded the ground, preventing weed growth. At harvest, 100

The serene, pastoral quality of this historic hemp field scene belies the strenuous, backbreaking work that hemp processing required. Pre–Civil War hemp production was accomplished largely if not entirely by enslaved labor; farmers acted on the belief that blacks were better at understanding hemp's eccentricities and were experts in handling the crop. The slaves' expertise was gained through many years of enforced practice since, as a white Lexingtonian commented in 1836, the process was "very dirty, and so laborious that scarcely any white man would work at it." (Courtesy of the University of Louisville Library Special Collections, Eckstrom Library)

to 120 days after planting, laborers moved through the field cutting the standing hemp plants with a special hook knife, laying the stalks on the ground in a long row.[17] Special hemp mowers were available for hemp harvest before the Civil War; these mechanized the process to some extent. Though machinery use did increase the number of acres that could be harvested in a day, the tough plant stems caused frequent mechanical breakdowns, and many farmers elected to continue to harvest the crop by hand.

After a ripe hemp field had been cut, the stalks were allowed to lie out on the field until dry, or cured. After a few days of dry weather, laborers would again enter the field, gather the stalks into bundles that they then stacked, butt ends on the ground, in large conical stacks that remained in the field until early winter.

To free hemp fiber from the plant stalk, farm laborers opened the stacks in November and spread the stalks on the ground so that dew and cold winter rains could "rot" the stalks. Some farmers rotted their hemp directly in water, in creeks or ponds, but this practice was not common in Kentucky. After four to six weeks on the ground, when the fiber separated readily from the woody stalks, the hemp was again gathered and stacked in shocks, or stacks, to dry and await the next step, breaking.[18] Using a simple "hand break" constructed of two wooden A-frames suspended on short legs and held together by mortise and tenon joints, laborers crushed or broke the hemp stalks to separate the fiber, a dirty and fatiguing job. Breaking began after Christmas and continued until completed, usually in time for spring plowing. Laborers tied hemp fiber into bundles for weighing and storage in a hemp house or barn until it could be sold.[19]

Although hemp was widely used in home spinning and weaving, nineteenth-century hemp farmers also moved their product to centrally located inspection stations for grading, sale, and shipment to manufacturers. Increasing availability of local hemp prompted rope makers to establish ropewalks in Lexington and surrounding county seat towns by the late 1790s. By the early 1800s surplus hemp fiber moved from Kentucky farms through Ohio River ports such as Louisville, bound for East Coast manufacturers. The state had become a major center for hemp production, manufacturing, and export by the 1830s, and during that decade Lexington produced about 1 million yards of bagging and 2 million pounds of hemp cordage. Louisville processed about 1.2 million pounds of hemp each year. Mills and ropewalks in Maysville manufactured between 200,000 and 400,000 pounds of hemp annually, and Newport, Covington, Frankfort, and Georgetown all produced hemp products in large volume.[20] Hemp prices declined in the early 1840s as buyers sought higher-quality hemp and fiber products from foreign sources, especially India and Europe. Nevertheless, Kentucky's mills and looms, some of them steam- or horse-powered, continued to process large tonnages each year. By the eve of the Civil War in 1860, Kentucky had 159 bagging, rope, and cordage factories, though the number had declined by more than 40 percent since 1850 as many small-scale operations stopped production. The state's hemp processing plants employed over 2,000 workers, produced $2.3 million worth of hemp goods annually, and made up over one-third of the hemp-related factories in the nation.[21] Between 1870 and the turn of the twentieth century, hemp demand and pricing fluctuated so dramatically that many farmers dropped production. By 1900 the state's production area had retreated into the Inner Bluegrass counties, Fayette County being the largest producer.[22]

During World War I, Kentucky hemp production increased in response to strategic demand, but thereafter farmers largely abandoned the crop, so that by the eve of the Great Depression only five farms in the entire state still produced hemp. Again, during World War II, in response to the loss of imported rope and cordage fiber from the Philippines, the national demand for hemp increased, but Kentucky's production was limited and split between seed and fiber. Production ended after the war.[23]

Mile 15.0 The 118-acre Maysville Community and Technical College campus stands back from the highway on the left. In 1968 the Maysville Community College opened here as a unit of the University of Kentucky Community College System. The state legislature in 1997 passed a postsecondary education act that placed the school within the Kentucky Community and Technical College System. The MCTC campus includes four major buildings with 145,000 square feet of classroom and office space. Its twenty programs enroll some 1,800 students per semester. The school operates classroom and distance-learning courses at branch campuses in Cynthiana, Morehead, and the Eastern Kentucky Correctional Complex in West Liberty.[24]

31

Intersections and Commercial Roadside Development

Mile 15.2 U.S. 68 enters the south edge of the Maysville suburban commercial strip.

Mile 15.5 Kentucky SR 9, also popularly known as the AA Highway because it links Alexandria in Campbell County to Ashland in Boyd County, intersects U.S. 68. A Maysville-Lexington Turnpike tollhouse stood along the old road in this vicinity. Though this intersection is relatively new—this section of SR 9 was completed in the 1990s—highway-oriented businesses have already colonized the adjoining lots and a new, dispersed business district is beginning to emerge, strung out at relatively low density along both highways.

Commercial and retail businesses prefer business locations with the highest accessibility and, especially in the automobile era, visibility. Urban land values, therefore, tend to be highest at those sites that enjoy the greatest access, which is often the intersection of two major highways, be they interstate, federal, or state roads. The result is that the land adjacent to this primary intersection carries the highest demand and is the highest valued. Land values tend to decline in a linear fashion as distance from the intersection increases. If one highway has a greater traffic flow than the other, the highest land values will tend to follow the high-traffic corridor. In the absence of zoning regulations, landowners will differentiate their land use in accordance with the amount of land that their businesses require and land or rent costs. Lots adjacent to the high-access crossroads will therefore be the highest valued and will attract those businesses that can generate the highest profit per square foot. Along important transport corridors at the edge of a city, these are usually automobile-oriented businesses such as fast food outlets and shopping centers. Businesses such as automobile and truck dealerships, which require extensive space for vehicle parking and service garages, tend to be located farther from the primary high-value intersection where access and visibility remain good but land costs are lower. Businesses that require significant acreage of low-value land, such as mobile home or manufactured housing sales, cannot afford land near the primary high-value node and will generally resign themselves to a roadside site some distance away.

At the U.S. 68 and AA Highway intersection, fast food franchises, large gas stations, drive-in banks, and a shopping center occupy the peak-value lots. New development is extending east along the AA Highway, not south along U.S. 68 toward Washington. The 2007 traffic count on the AA Highway to the east is more than 16,500 vehicles per day, whereas the count on U.S. 68 south to Washington is about one third that number, at about 5,300 vehicles. This dramatic difference probably reflects both the volume of through traffic and the local traffic attracted to the new Wal-Mart and strip shopping center about one-half mile east on SR 9—high-traffic flow begets retail outlets that beget more traffic . . .[1] North toward Maysville, land uses segue into an unusual mix of old roadside businesses that have been in place since the 1960s, or even earlier, commingled with newer commercial establishments that opened here after the AA Highway opened.

Mile 15.9 The Mason County High School is on the right.

Mile 16.4 U.S. 68 intersects with SR 1448, or Maple Leaf Drive, across from the Maysville County Club. The country club opened in 1927 and includes an eighteen-hole golf course designed by William Newcomb. Newcomb's background includes a degree in landscape architecture from the University of Michigan. He has designed a number of prominent American golf courses, including Boyne Mountain, Thornapple Pointe, Calderone Farms, and Concord Hills, all in Michigan.

Mile 16.7 Jersey Ridge Road turns left off U.S. 68 and follows the Ohio River bluff crest to the northwest.

Mile 16.8 The modern rendition of U.S. 68 here dates to 1950, when highway engineers completed the bypass that swings off to the right and plunges downhill toward the Ohio River, following the shoulder of a small valley cut by a Limestone Creek tributary. At the bottom of the hill the highway curves back to the left, or west, to enter downtown Maysville. In 2000 engineers widened this hillside road section to four lanes and in the process cut a deep slice into the hillside, leaving behind a crumbling, bare bedrock wall. To reduce erosion on the steep new cut, engineers erected retaining walls made from woven wire gabion baskets filled with broken stone, an economical and resilient slope-stabilization solution though an eyesore for the traveling public.

Continuing straight ahead on old U.S. 68, and just beyond the Jersey Ridge Road intersection, CR 2516 splits off from the left side of U.S. 68. This place marks the top of the Ohio River bluff and the beginning of the steep descent down into Maysville and the riverfront. The county road is the old Lexington-Maysville Turnpike, and the stone house at the top of the hill on the right was a nineteenth-century tavern and stagecoach stop. The turnpike's Number 1 Tollhouse stood just to the north on the adjacent lot. The old pike negotiates the hillside by way of several switchback curves and arrives at Bank Street and the Maysville street grid near the bottom.

The old turnpike that linked Maysville and Lexington serves as a reminder that both cities were, and continue to be, local or regional transport hubs. Lexington, though landlocked, was linked via overland roads and turnpikes to distant port cities—west to Louisville on the Ohio, north to Covington-Newport on the Ohio, east to Ashland on the Ohio–Big Sandy, and southwest to Nashville on the Cumberland River.

Inner Bluegrass county seats were linked to Lexington by way of short turnpikes that, in the twentieth century, were upgraded to state or federal highways. Compared to Lexington, Maysville is the more dramatic transport focus. The state's first macadam turnpike opened to traffic here in 1830, connecting Maysville and Washington. That road was linked north via the river ferry to Zane's Trace—today Ohio 41, 32, and other highways—the early frontier track that connected Kentucky and south-central Ohio to the National Road at Zanesville. Riverside roads followed the Ohio Valley up- and downstream from here—today those roads are Kentucky 8 and U.S. 52 on the Ohio side. A web of smaller roads, many of them local-scale nineteenth-century neighborhood turnpikes, connected Maysville to adjoining county seats, to Upper Blue Licks, the eastern Kentucky iron furnaces, and other important destinations.

If these overland routes are transport arterials, the Ohio River is the potamic aorta that primes the arterial network by way of economical, high-capacity water transportation. Most of America's eighteenth- and nineteenth-century cities—certainly most urban settlements that grew into major metropolitan centers—were founded at waterfront harbor sites and thereafter remained oriented to water transportation. Not until the post–Civil War railroad era, when the settlement frontier reached the semiarid and arid West, did town founders readily accept alternatives to ocean, lake, river, or canal frontage sites.[2]

When transport costs are measured by ton-miles traveled, water-borne freight movement is exceptionally efficient, especially for large loads of bulky, low-value materials such as grain or coal. During the first two decades of the nineteenth century, overland wagon freight charges could exceed fifteen cents per ton-mile on the best roads. By comparison, freight rates charged by boats bound downriver were less than two cents per ton-mile. Dray wagon companies contracted to transport farm-produced commodities, such as flour or cured meats, could not move very far overland toward a distant market before freight costs totaled more than any profit that a farmer might realize. For example, farm products from the upper Ohio Valley could be shipped 1,700 miles downstream on the Ohio and Mississippi rivers to New Orleans, and then transported by sailboat several thousand miles through the Gulf of Mexico and up the Atlantic Coast to Philadelphia *more cheaply* than those same commodities could be shipped via wagon—also to Philadelphia—an overland distance of about 300 miles.[3] Until the steam-powered riverboat was perfected, upstream traffic costs were much more problematic.

32

Maysville

The Maysville town site had special qualities that made it an attractive place to establish a settlement. The Ohio River, in its present engineered configuration, lies at an elevation of about 460 feet at Maysville. South of the river, Limestone Creek rises at an origin point near the 900-foot elevation. From there the creek and its short tributaries flow about three miles north, cutting a low-angle valley down to the Ohio River at a rate of about 146 feet per mile, or a gradient of about one in forty. Though of comparatively low gradient, this potential route was complicated by the need to cross Limestone Creek at least once, which could have been a difficult undertaking before bridge construction. Were road surveyors and construction crews to confront the 440-foot-high river bluff directly, as they did in creating this section of the Lexington-Maysville Road, the overall gradient from river's edge to bluff top would be about one in ten, much steeper than the route along the Limestone Creek valley.

In addition to offering the option of different routes out of the Ohio River valley, the Maysville site possesses two other compelling characteristics. First, considering the Ohio's rather narrow valley and floodplain in this section—relative to its flow volume—the site offers a comparatively wide bench on which to build a settlement, and sections of the bench stand at fifty feet or higher above the river. Second, the site lies conveniently on the outside of a long river bend or meander curve. Across the eastern United States, where people founded towns at rivers' edges, they often chose locations on the outside of river bends for pragmatic reasons. Along the lower Mississippi River, for example, river-bend town sites include Memphis, Greenville, Vicksburg, and Natchez. Because a river's channel flow tends to be faster on the outside of a meander curve, the channel there is scoured deeper, and the adjoining riverbank tends to offer a relatively firm, well-drained surface. Should river water levels drop during a summer drought, river craft would seek the deepest navigational channel that would unavoidably be adjacent to the firm, well-drained bank. Across the channel, on the curve's inside radius, water flow is slower, so much so that the river deposits silt and sand, thereby creating an extended point bar and slack water shallows. The adjacent riverbank is often low, soft, and muddy. Given the elementary technology of eighteenth- and nineteenth-century river and overland transportation, the preferred landing site for riverboats was that point where the river was deep enough to permit anchorage adjacent to a dry, solid bank where heavily loaded wagons could approach the riverfront directly without risking the mire of extended mudflats common to the inside of a meander curve.[1]

From the Outer Bluegrass upland above the Ohio's south bank, there are four traditional routes into the valley at Maysville; three follow relatively gentle gradients along valleys incised into the upland by Limestone Creek and other small streams. These are the Hill City Road, which follows the west branch of Limestone Creek; Taylor Mill Pike on the east branch of Limestone Creek, also known as Flemingsburg Road, and State Highway 11. Only the old Lexington-Maysville Turnpike made a direct frontal assault on the high bluff above Maysville, gaining the upland by way of a series of steep switchbacks, an exceptionally difficult climb to negotiate with horses and heavily loaded wagons, and the bane of immigrants seeking access to the Bluegrass plain that began atop the looming bluffs behind the river landing.

Descending the bluff face along the modern rendition of the old Lexington-Maysville Road, now SR 2516, at the first switchback Edgemont Drive leads to the right, following the bluff crest about one-half mile before ending in a cul-de-sac. The bluff-top homes along Edgemont represent several building eras; a few Colonial Revival–style houses date from the late nineteenth century, others are 1960s ranch houses, some are nearly new modern or postmodern designs. Perched at bluff's edge, the homes on the road's north side enjoy a supernal view of Maysville and the valley.

As the Lexington-Maysville Road switchbacks downhill, it drops into the city's west-end residential district, where it segues into Fourth Street at the intersection of Lexington Pike and Fourth. The old pike curls sharply left and downhill, continuing the road's switchback pattern to Third. The houses here are a mix of nonstandard vernacular forms; most date from the late nineteenth century, and their unusual placements suggest that this residential section was pike-oriented, and its ad hoc lot sizes and orientations were probably caused, in part, by the subdividing of larger lots as the road developed and its alignment changed.

The steep lower bluff here is coterminous with the Kope formation of shales and limestones that form the core of the Eden Shale country to the south. From the crest of the Cincinnati Arch near Lexington to this point, the gently dipping Ordovician limestone and shale rock layers have changed character repeatedly but have nevertheless become progressively younger—albeit more than 425 million years old. Here that concomitant trend ends abruptly on the river terraces below Fourth Street. A backyard gardener wielding spade or tiller will encounter Pleistocene glacial outwash material here, as much as fifty feet deep, deposited during the Illinoian glacial period some 130,000 to 300,000 years ago. As the thick Illinoian ice pack to the north melted, the meltwater runoff carried vast amounts of crushed and broken bedrock material from far to the north, perhaps as far as present-day Michigan and Ontario. That material included clays, silts, sands, and gravels that were derived from parent rock formations to the north, including siltstone and sandstone, carbonate and crystalline rocks, chert, shale, quartz, and coal. This detritus washed into the area's streams, including the Ohio, that formed near the ice pack's southern terminus, and it often fashioned terraces that today stand well above the river.[2] Upriver, beyond Limestone Creek in

East Maysville, the glacial deposition story is even more fascinating. Here, too, Illinoian meltwater runoff deposited a thick terrace, which extends from near East Third Street north to the Ohio River. But south of Third rises a much higher terrace, this one comprising younger glacial materials deposited during the comparatively recent Wisconsin-era glacial period that was active from 10,000 to 110,000 years ago. The Wisconsin-age deposits extend south to the base of the bluff and are up to one hundred feet thick, well above potential river flood level and a likely place for residential and industrial development.[3]

As the old road drops onto the Illinoian-era terrace from the lower bluff along Fourth Street, one can see, in bird's-eye view, the towered and steepled city skyline that extends downhill to the river's edge. Upriver to the east, the Roebling-esque 1932 Simon Kenton suspension bridge towers soar in all their art deco majesty above the ranks of nineteenth-century redbrick commercial buildings and gabled residential rooftops. Multiple church steeples punctuate the Third Street corridor, suggesting the Ohio River valley's religious diversity, long known to readers of religious atlases.[4] The bridge's south tower and entrance ramp mark the business district's east edge and the original river-landing site, the place where early residents erected the town's first buildings. Josiah Espy, an English traveler, arrived here in mid-October 1805. The site, he wrote, was "the greatest landing place on the river. All the merchandise for Lexington and the neighboring towns leave the river at this place. The town itself contains only about fifty dwelling houses, and it does not appear to be rapidly growing."[5] Nearly four decades later, the dour James Silk Buckingham offered a perspective on the Maysville site and waterfront that was less sanguine. Upon arriving by steamboat from Cincinnati, he found Maysville "less conveniently situated than almost any of the small towns we had passed on the river, having only a breadth of less than half a mile between the water's edge and the steep hills that rise at the back of the town, . . . and instead of the fine sloping beach for a landing-place . . . it has a bluff and broken bank of soil, in front of the town, with an inconvenient and disagreeable landing, narrow, steep, ill-paved, and in every way defective. The town itself has nothing remarkable in it."[6] Espy's commentary was simply a gauge of the flow of commodities and people through the Maysville port; Buckingham's judgment was more attuned to the port's physical attributes and the demands of steamboat configuration and evolving on-load–off-load techniques.

Whether one views the town from the high-angle vantage point provided by the bluff road, or on city plats and maps, two general observations can immediately be made. First, Maysville today is not a large urban center—at 9,011 people in 2010, it is slightly larger than Paris (8,553).[7] Second, Maysville is not a single urban place but, rather, a composite of discrete parts or sections. A primary division occurs along the corridor occupied by Limestone Creek, the modern federal highways U.S. 62 and 68—including the Kenton bridge, and the Chesapeake & Ohio (now CSX) and Louisville & Nashville (now the TTI line, a subsidiary of CSX) railroad tracks. West of that topographic break lie the city's original river port and historic commercial and residential district, which once extended from Front Street at the river's edge uphill to Fourth Street. The Front Street alignment is now largely occupied by a levee and

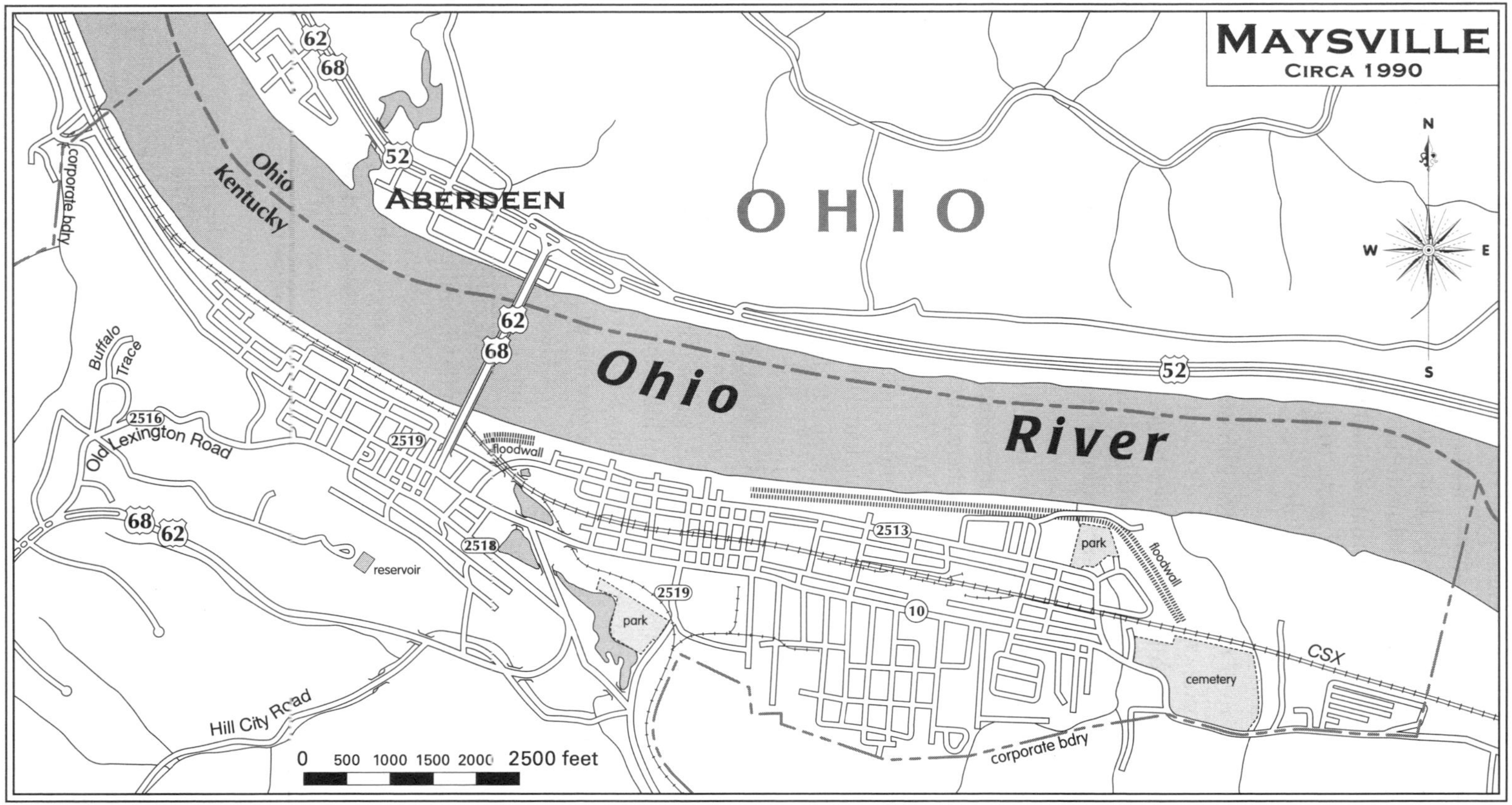

MAYSVILLE
CIRCA 1990
OHIO
ABERDEEN
Ohio
Kentucky
Ohio River
N
S
W
E
floodwall
park
cemetery
CSX
corporate bdry
reservoir
Buffalo Trace
Old Lexington Road
Hill City Road
0 500 1000 1500 2000 2500 feet

floodwall, the product of hard lessons learned in the great floods of 1913 and 1937. Railroad tracks fill much of the remaining land between the wall and the river. The traditional retail business section centers on Second, Market, and Court streets. It is flanked on the west and south by the city's old residential core, which comprises tightly packed small lots, almost European in scale, wedged into the sloping sliver of land at the bluff's base.

East Maysville lies east of Limestone Creek and is more than four times as large as the old port-oriented section to the west. The east side is primarily a railroad-era industrial and residential area bifurcated by a double-track rail line. East Maysville has no traditional business area per se but, rather, consists of a small collection of post–Civil War homes, 1920s to 1950s residential neighborhoods, and the city's tobacco-warehouse and industrial section. The Ohio River floodplain—in large part the Illinoian-age terrace—is much broader here, almost three times as wide as in the west section. East Maysville's backbone is Forest Avenue (SR 10), which runs for one and one-half miles along the crest of the Wisconsin-age terrace from Limestone Creek to the Goose Creek valley on the city's east side. South of Forest, the terrace again falls away into a low swale that probably marks an old river channel now occupied by tobacco warehouses and residential subdivisions. The city's west and east sections are radically different, and each, in turn, has its own subsections or neighborhoods.

The state's General Assembly authorized a town at the Limestone landing site in 1787, when the town trustees approved a plan drawn by the surveyor James Stevenson for streets and one-half-acre lots.[8] The earliest extant Maysville street plat is from 1822. Downriver, or below the Limestone Creek debouchment, the surveyor laid out a grid of fourteen rectangular blocks parallel to the riverfront, each divided by a central alley and each subdivided into eight long, narrow lots, all oriented toward the river. Limestone Creek's lower section followed a tight, L-shaped curve just above its junction with the river, as though it followed a very irregular topographic surface. The creek-river junction provided the starting point for the survey, as Limestone Pike became the easternmost street. Rerouting the creek produced a new channel configuration, a gentle, truncated-S curve that lay several hundred feet east of Limestone Pike.[9] The now-bypassed lower creek section remained largely low and marshy, though it was gradually filled in. The channel change and fill projects permitted development to expand east from Limestone Pike, including an extension of Second Street and construction of new streets such as Vine, Lee, and the aptly named Bridge Street, which crossed the creek and linked Maysville to East Maysville by way of East Second Street. Not until 1867 did Maysville annex East Maysville to knit the two places into a single political unit, although each town section maintained its own distinct character.[10]

Initially, a waterfront distillery occupied this new angle of reclaimed land.[11] By the 1890s bituminous coal barges and coal trains from eastern Kentucky arrived at the river's edge immediately east of Lexington Street, where they unloaded their cargo via a short incline elevator onto a coal dump that the C & O developed into a large, eight-bay coal bin. Delivery vehicles could enter a bay under the bin where coal filled wagon and truck boxes via gravity flow. Southward toward Second Street, a tobacco-leaf auction warehouse fronted Limestone, followed by the Ball plow manufacturing works at the Second and Limestone corner.[12] Over the next three decades development and redevelopment on this former marshland continued, so that by 1926 the incline, coal dump, and tobacco warehouse were all removed. By the eve of the Great Depression, the riverfront fill site was given over to the Maysville stockyards and a Chesapeake & Ohio switching yard and railroad tracks. The plow manufacturing plant site transmogrified into an automobile repair garage, and two other large garages, a lumberyard, and a wholesale poultry and produce company lined this eastern extension of Second Street. Vine Street was renamed Castro Alley, and a new street, Government Street, connected Second and Third east of Lee.[13]

The Virginia legislature authorized in 1787 a Maysville tobacco inspection station; this was one of the city's first buildings erected below, or downstream of, the intersection of Limestone Creek and the Ohio.[14] Within two years Ohio River flatboats were landing at the site at the rate of thirty per day.[15] Maysville grew slowly despite the rapid increase in river landings and the enhancement of cross-river traffic in 1797 by the first of five ferryboats established to connect with Aberdeen, Ohio, on the river's north side.

The Sutton Street market house that stood between Second and Third streets, near the west end, was the town's early economic and social focus. A new two-story market building on Market Street replaced it in 1829. On the market house's ground floor, farmers, fishermen, and merchant vendors occupied individual market stalls. The second floor, as was typical of large market houses in other cities, was reserved for city offices, which occupied the space until the city hall was completed in 1838.[16]

Mile 17.9 One of Maysville's westernmost cross streets, Bank Street, intersects Third Street on the left.

Mile 18.1 Proceed east on Third Street. As Maysville evolved from a scruffy frontier river landing into a regional mercantile center that coupled port and overland transport services, residents began to sort businesses and other town functions one from another and group them into districts on the basis of an embryonic capitalist logic that operated within the context of freehold land ownership. The nineteenth-century waterfront, perforce, included shipping and warehousing functions. Bankers and insurance companies established offices nearby and uphill from the river, together with newspaper offices, taverns, and hotels. Retail stores and businesses offering personal services such as barbershops were farther from the waterfront. Political functions such as city hall, the courthouse, and sheriff's office were well away from the river and shared a district with legal offices and churches. Though two centuries separate the modern-day city from the frontier site, this basic functional differentiation is still evident in Maysville's central business area. The city's land-use transition uphill from the river's edge is profound. Front Street was the historic riverfront, which, until some sections were removed to make space for a levee and flood wall, entertained two- and three-story brick taverns, business buildings, and warehouses. This space has been radically modified by a railroad right-of-way and a flood wall, but remnants of nineteenth-century structures still stand. Some space here is now given over to new public and commercial buildings and a French Quarter Inn motel, and, near the west end at Wall Street, a Victorian residence still stands cheek-by-jowl with the floodwall. Dockage and warehouse space along the town's waterfront expanded, and floods periodically inundated Front Street, prompting merchants to evacuate and move uphill and south to Second Street. Third Street lies at a substantially higher elevation than Second and offered choice properties for churches, a Masonic Temple, the courthouse, and high-value residences. Still farther up the slope, Fourth Street, now some distance from the active waterfront, was almost exclusively middle-class residential, as were Fifth and Sixth streets at the bluff's base.

Along Third, at Sutton Street, the Mason County Justice Building stands at the southwest corner. On the northeast corner, a nineteenth-century Federal-style hall-and-parlor house now serves as the county sheriff's office. The courthouse, built as a city hall in 1844 and designated the county court building in 1848, stands facing south, its tall Tuscan columns supporting a two-story portico. Although of modest scale by modern standards, the courthouse stands podium-like on a raised basement foundation, not unlike the famous Maison Carrée Roman temple in Nîmes, France, which Thomas Jefferson much admired. Raising the structure in this manner forces the visitor to climb a flight of steps to gain the front door, symbolically elevating the place of court-administered justice above the common jurisprudence of the street. The classical columns, portico with wall-front pilasters, and rooftop cupola together form a grand architectural gesture that reflects Jefferson's keen interest in public building design and was intended to remind passersby of ancient Roman virtues: Americans could control their destinies and mold the New World to fulfill their vision of a new republic. Perhaps the building also came to represent the city's success in winning the county seat from upstart Washington, a steep bluff and four miles to the south.[17]

Across the Midwest and upland South, many courthouses reside authoritatively alone in a central town square—the Bourbon County Courthouse in Paris is an example. The Mason County Courthouse does not enjoy a dedicated square but stands auspiciously on a large lot directly fronting the street, adjacent to an alley, a familiar position that suggests the building's origin as a city hall.[18] Stanley Reed Court, a mid-block alley, separates the courthouse and the First Presbyterian Church as though it is enforcing a distinction between secular and sacred. After Maysville became the county seat in 1848, lawyers built small office buildings along this alley to enhance their proximity to the courthouse and sheriff's office. The alley was originally named Armstrong Street after a Maysville merchant, John Armstrong, but city officials renamed it for Reed, who was born in Mason County in 1884 and became U.S. solicitor general. In 1938 Franklin D. Roosevelt appointed Reed a Supreme Court associate justice.[19]

Two state highways, 10 and 11, merge with Third Street. (See the map "North Fork Licking River–Maysville Road Corridor" in chapter 28.) SR 11 follows Third across the south Limestone Creek bridge into East Maysville. Just beyond the bridge, the road splits off to follow the Limestone Creek valley south, where it is also known as Flemingsburg Road. SR 10 also crosses the Limestone Creek bridge but continues into East Maysville, where it becomes Forest Avenue. SR 10 exits town on the east side and continues southeast into Lewis County, where it merges with the AA Highway,

Governmental and religious institutions are interspersed among residential buildings on Third Street. The hall-and-parlor houses of Mechanics Row adjoin the First Presbyterian Church, whose facade and bell tower partially mask the courthouse next door.

the 1990s two-lane expressway that intersects the Ohio River again in Greenup County north of Ashland.

Just beyond the First Presbyterian Church, Patton Alley divides this block north to south. Facing Third Street and beginning at the alley's edge is a row of seven adjoining three-story town houses whose collective design heritage includes Federal and Italianate, while the mansard-roofed units exude Second Empire influences. The structures date to the 1850s, and several follow a familiar hall-and-parlor floor plan, or what some architectural historians refer to as a one and one-half. That is, in cross section the house is a room and one-half wide, the room being a front parlor or living room, the half being an entry hall and stairway to the second floor. Sometimes referred to as Mechanics Row, the houses all have porches and small front yards. The cast- and wrought-iron yard fences and porch railings have been attributed to nineteenth-century river linkages between Maysville and the Hanging Rock Iron District, upriver to the east, and New Orleans, downriver to the south.

Mile 18.4 The Third and Market Street intersection is one of the city's important commercial focal points. A two-story city market house was built here in 1829. To provide access to the market stalls, the southernmost ten lots on both sides of Market Street between Second and Third were shortened about ten feet. After the market house was torn down, Market Street retained its distinctive flaring open space in mid-block, a feature that Pennsylvanians might have termed a "diamond" and others called a market square. Perhaps because of its early association with the market house, this block of Market became the city's grocery and dry goods center. By 1890, for example, the buildings fronting this block housed twenty-six businesses; five were grocery stores. Other Market Street merchants sold fresh meats, garden produce, dry goods, boots and shoes, clothing, stoves and tinwork, and harnesses.[20] The tallest building on the block stands at the Third Street intersection, a four-story, redbrick wholesale grocery store built in 1892 for $25,000 by Crapsey & Brown architects of Cincinnati and operated by M. C. Russell. Though the building is a functional rectangular box in plan and form, it exhibits Romanesque style cues, including large, arched second-story windows and rusticated stone pilasters that divide the first floor window bays. The building remains in good condition and includes, on the corner of Third and Market, a ceramic heraldry plaque that reads "MCR." Russell's son, James B. Russell, ran the wholesale grocery business after his father died and built the Russell Theater, farther along Third, in 1930. Though closed for many years, the theater recently underwent major renovation and is again open for performances. Most building facades on Market retain their nineteenth-century texture—including some with cast-iron fronts—minimally corrupted by modern material overlays.

Given the overall context of architectural styles exhibited on Third Street—modern county government and commercial buildings standing among nineteenth-century structures—how can one explain the apparent demise of Victorian building forms and finishes? The facade ornamentation influenced by pre–Civil War Federal- or Greek Revival–style or postwar Victorian preferences, in its varied "neo-style" configurations, has disappeared in favor of plain, even austere, structures that employ little more outward embellishment than the advancing and retreating planes created

M. C. Russell's wholesale grocery building still stands at the corner of Third and Market streets. The Russell Theater, with fanciful Spanish-Moorish design overtones, was built next door in 1930. Warner Bros.' 1927 film *The Jazz Singer*, featuring Al Jolson, was the first feature-length film with synchronized dialogue, and it marked the beginning of the end of the silent film era. By 1930 the American film industry was selling more than 90 million theater tickets per week nationwide. Maysville's Russell Theater was a very popular place for Depression-era entertainment, but attendance declined with the advent of television. Though the theater stood empty and in disrepair for years, it has been undergoing restoration.

by rows of metal window frames, sharp corners, and flat roof lines. Why? The answer is multifaceted. Tastes in building design changed, in part at the hands of architects seeking a refined philosophical rationale for their structures, in part in the minds of wealthy business owners who wanted to acknowledge new or revival designs that they encountered in Europe or in larger American cities, or for a host of other reasons. Building technology also changed. Except for their public street-facing facades, nineteenth-century business buildings followed basic construction configurations: four external brick or stone walls outlined the building perimeter and supported joist ends that in turn supported the building's floors. If buildings were much wider than eighteen feet, internal pillars might be used to support the joists. That such simple construction was relatively cheap allowed builders so disposed to allocate extra funds to decorating the building's facade. And when metal fabrication and brick and tile manufacturing became more efficient, builders could more readily afford to attach to their structures any number of mass-produced decorations: large, elaborate cornices, purpose-molded brick, precut stone, tile and precast ceramics, or entire building fronts cast in iron. Business building facades were not innocent conceptions of architects or builders; they served as monuments to the industriousness of the people who commissioned them and as advertisements for the businesses within.[21] The result was city business centers consisting of what the architectural historian Richard Longstreth terms two-part commercial buildings, the most common business building form in the country.[22] The two-part building is divided horizontally into a bottom zone, usually the ground floor, and an upper zone. The bottom zone includes the public business space. In retail stores, this space usually includes large plate-glass windows for merchandise display. The upper zone is private space and may include each of the upper stories, which serve variously as an owner's residence, rental apartments, professional office space, fraternal meeting rooms, or secure storage for the first-floor business.

But evolving building technologies radically altered construction priorities and costs. Economical structural steel, available by the 1880s, allowed builders to erect buildings without thick, load-bearing exterior walls. Engineers built the first steel-reinforced concrete high-rise building in the nation in Cincinnati, just downriver from Maysville, in 1903. Electricity, hydraulic pumps, glass-making technology, the Otis safety elevator, and forced-air heating and cooling systems all had direct application to commercial buildings but were comparatively expensive and consumed an increasing portion of the building exterior and interior space.[23] Some nineteenth-century buildings, if stoutly built and sound, could be retrofit with electricity, elevators, and air-handling systems.

By the early 1900s, commercial business–building design began to change. Facades became simpler, although the streamlined exuberance of the art deco and art moderne styles of the 1920s and 1930s—echoed in 1930s auto and train locomotive design—postponed the full transition to rather severe functionality until the 1950s and 1960s. Builders increasingly diverted construction funds into new materials, fixtures, and technology, sometimes visible in internal details such as marble floors and exotic lighting in lobbies or atriums—as though they had simply reversed the building facade and brought it inside the building. The expensive support equipment now resided in the basement or attic, in chases within the walls, or on the roof—mostly out of sight unless one had access to the roof of a taller building next door.

The pedestrian-oriented, walking-scale American city of the early 1800s gave way to the riding city of the pre–Civil War period when the horse-drawn omnibus and trolley came into use. After the 1880s electric trolleys replaced or augmented the earlier systems. Travel by electric trolley car allowed city expansion outward along the tracks as developers followed the rails to the city's fringe in search of cheaper land. The Maysville Street Railroad & Transfer Company received permission in 1890 to install an electric streetcar system in the city.[24] The demand for high-density central city business and living space stagnated and then began to decline. Increasingly, architects and designers built large commercial buildings as stand-alone structures not connected to adjoining buildings by party walls. Instead of being concerned with designing only the front facade—the sidewalls were hidden from view, after all—builders now built free-standing buildings "in the round," as it were, intended to be seen from any side. The rich heritage of Maysville's commercial building stock exhibits all three segments of this evolution—the original nineteenth-century shell-and-facade building with brick load-bearing walls, the transitional structures of the 1890s to the 1950s with internal skeletons of wood beams, concrete, or steel, and the simplified modern geometric forms.

The Maysville Street Railroad and Transfer Company began operations in 1883 as a horse-car system. In 1890 the line was electrified and extended to include four miles of track across the city from its western limits to the brickyard on its east side. Beginning on West Second Street near Beasley's Run, the trolley track followed Second Street east to Market; there was a double-track passing turnout between Wall and Sutton streets. At Market, the track turned south, or uphill, following Market one block to Third Street. At Third, the track again turned east, past the Russell and Cox buildings, and followed Third east to Plum, where it turned north, crossing Limestone Creek at east Second Street. In East Maysville, the route included a double-track passing turnout near Poplar Street and a carbarn at Beechwood Park. The entire trip across the city from the west end to Beechwood Park took only fifteen minutes and cost a nickel.[25] A replica of the old track is embedded in Market Street's brick surface. Trolleys might seem quaint to modern suburbanites, but the electrified street railroad allowed cities to expand by adding low-density suburban appendages. At the turn of the twentieth century, the trolley car already represented, in symbolic form, progress and technological achievement. A town risked being thought of as backward and unpromising if its residents eschewed the trolley. A new trolley system was a source of city pride; it came to be viewed as the very essence of what it meant to be urban. In 1910 men in fedoras rode the trolley car to work; white-gloved housewives rode the trolley downtown to shop and have tea with friends; children with book bags might even ride the trolley to school. In the era before the availability of inexpensive private automobiles, merchants sent parcels from their stores by trolley directly to their customers' homes.[26] No thriving community the size of Maysville could function without a trolley car system—it offered new economical mobility to those not yet dependent on the automobile.

Across the Market and Third Street intersection from Russell's wholesale grocery store stands the perdurable Romanesque Cox Building, which builders completed for William H. Cox Jr. in February 1887 at a cost exceeding $100,000. Designed by the Cincinnati architect W. R. Brown of the Crapsey & Brown firm to occupy the site of a former tanyard, the robust Richardsonian edifice incorporated rather florid redbrick and sandstone in a facade that enclosed three large business spaces on the ground level, professional office space on the second floor, and a York Rite Knights Templar Masonic Temple on the upper floors. A conical-roofed tower rises from the roof above the Market and Third Street corner. Along the roof parapet line below the tower, inverted arches accommodate two Green Man faces. The round stained-glass window in the Third Street wall includes Masonic symbols such as a cross in a crown, a gavel, an hourglass, the compass and square, and the all-seeing eye. Cox was a Maysville native, born here in 1856. He served as lieutenant governor from 1907 to 1911 during the governorship of Augustus E. Willson, who was also born in Maysville. From the building's completion until the 1950s, the ground-floor commercial spaces were occupied by pedestrian-oriented retail shops, including a sequence of drugstores, a confectionary, dry cleaners, and grocers. As businesses began to vacate downtown Maysville in favor of suburban locations, the demand for shop space here declined and a different set of businesses occupied the space, including a dance studio, chiropractor, bicycle repair shop, and secondhand store. In November 2010 a fire gutted the upper floors and destroyed much of the building's roof. Within a few months, construction crews had succeeded in installing a new roof and interior restoration was under way.

South on Market and uphill from Third, William Cox built a row of seven matching Queen Anne–style town-house apartments in 1886. Cox's Row still stands, stepped into the hillside in vertical echelon. The buildings wear cross-front staircases, their porches enclosed by delicately spindled railings; the first stories are brick and the second stories are covered in fish-scale shingles, the whole a feast of Victorian exuberance.

Two doors east on Third Street at number 14 is the home of William Cox's grandfather George Cox. The two-and-one-half-story redbrick and stone Romanesque structure, also designed by the Crapsey & Brown firm, cost $37,000 when built in 1886. Either the owner or the architect exhibited a sufficiently pliable and eclectic temperament to insist on adding a Queen Anne tower.[27] The substantial wrought-iron fence along the sidewalk is an exemplary composition that combines the mason's and blacksmith's arts. Each fence panel is mounted in limestone sleepers and bollardlike corner posts, now deeply weathered. Ebullient iron whorls and curls give the illusion of movement while combining to provide horizontal and vertical enclosure and containment.

Born in London, England, in 1791, George Cox died in Maysville nine decades later.[28] Cox and his wife, Ann, had several children, among them Horatio Nelson Cox, whose birth date was October 21, 1837. In England October 21 is celebrated as Trafalgar Day, commemorating the date in 1805 when the heroic Admiral Lord Horatio Nelson, commander of England's navy, defeated Napoleon's navy in the Battle of Trafalgar off the Spanish coast. It seems that Cox and his family, active in their Maysville dry goods business, remained Anglophiles, as did many Bluegrass Kentuckians.

This section of Third Street might have been named Church Street, given the concentration of churches here and on adjoining streets. At Third and Sutton Street stands the 1955 Trinity Methodist Church. The original church, built in 1847 with funds donated by John Armstrong, a successful Maysville merchant, stood on this site. Armstrong was born at Rosa-Hill near Enniskillen in the county of Fermanough, Ireland, in 1779, and was thus an early Scots-Irish immigrant to Maysville. His investments included Armstrong Row, the business buildings that lined West Second Street between numbers 207 and 227. The Baptist Church stands between Third and Fourth on Market, the third church to stand on that site. The aforementioned Presbyterian Church at Stanley Reed Court and Third was built in 1850. The 1877 redbrick First Christian Church follows, positioned in the middle of the block on Third. Farther along, on the corner of Third and Limestone, is the Episcopal Church of the Nativity, marked, like many Episcopal churches, by a red gothic-arched front door. Across the Third and Limestone intersection is St. Patrick Catholic Church. Completed in 1909, across the street from the original church building, St. Patrick is a large structure; its twin bell towers rise over a French Gothic facade; the cavernous interior seats 1,200.[29]

Mile 18.6 At the corner of Bridge Street and Third stands the old Louisville & Nashville Railroad passenger depot, its low-angle roof and extended eaves hinting of Prairie Style relatives farther west in Frank Lloyd Wright's Illinois prairie country. Built circa 1873, it was superseded by a new station in 1913. The city of Maysville bought the building in the 1930s and recycled it into Fire Station no. 1. In 1933 the fire department vacated the building for a more modern facility. The building is currently occupied by Maysville Police Department offices. In part to defend the river-borne trade moving along the Ohio River at Louisville from predation by railroad companies operating out of Nashville, on the Cumberland River, the Kentucky legislature in 1850 chartered the Louisville & Nashville Railroad to link the two cities but also to ensure that Kentucky's river city controlled the line. Over the next four decades, the L & N built or bought rail lines that completed connections between Louisville and the Gulf Coast by way of Birmingham, Pensacola, Mobile, and New Orleans. The line ran west to the Mississippi at Memphis and St. Louis, and east to the rim of the Appalachian coalfields, Knoxville, and Atlanta. In 1892 the L & N acquired the Kentucky Central Railway, which included the line from Lexington to Maysville.[30]

The fate of passenger and freight traffic on the Maysville Road was intimately linked to the establishment of a parallel railroad track, although the railroad was not generally viewed as an imminent threat. In 1842, for example, the *American Agriculturalist*, in an article on Kentucky farming, offered the opinion that "the great thoroughfares of the State are well McAdamized, making it a pleasure to travel over them at all seasons of the year." "Some railroads have been attempted," the editor continued, "but we believe all, except the one leading from Frankfort to Lexington, are now abandoned. We rejoice at this, for they are totally unsuited to any country, except to link large populous places, between which there is an immense travel. A railroad only accommodates a particular set, while a McAdam benefits all within its reach, and is especially to be preferred in an agricultural district."[31] When workers completed the first section of the Kentucky Central line between Lexington and Paris in the 1850s, crews were also completing bed work on the sections from Paris to Maysville. Though three thousand laborers were at work digging cuts through hills, filling in valleys with immense embankments, and boring two tunnels, the heavily dissected Eden Shale topography through which this northern railroad section necessarily had to pass exacted heavy costs. As financial failure loomed, banks withdrew their support from the project and construction stopped in 1854, not to resume until the 1870s. Maysville citizens were not compliant when bankers interdicted railroad construction. Nor did Maysville's business elite hold any particular allegiance to the Maysville Road, their traditional economic lifeline with the interior. Rather, they petitioned the railroad's directors to finish the railroad as promptly as possible. Maysville's boosters were business-oriented, and their rationale for strongly advocating for a resumption of railroad construction is revealing. They pleaded, "Our property must depreciate, our business leave us, and our prosperity have an end, if we postpone longer to complete the said road."[32] The railroad directors countered in a lengthy disquisition, explaining in detail construction and building material costs and suggesting that if the people living along the rail line would subscribe funds, the line could be finished promptly. They offered the further opinion that "no hope is now entertained of a county subscription from Nicholas or Fleming [counties]," where some of the most expensive construction was required.[33] To Maysville's business interests of the 1850s, their venerable road, their hard-won link to Lexington and Kentucky's fecund interior, seemed hoary, even archaic, compared to the iron and brass mechanical marvel on rails and the modernity and efficiency it promised, never mind what the luddite editors of the *American Agriculturalist* might think. Enticed by the enrapturing vision of the rail as a kind of magic carpet that entrepreneurs could direct from one pot of money to another, many communities grasped at any opportunity to gain access to train service. A century later, however, as the evolution of transport-related technologies produced high-speed highways, large-capacity trucks, and safe, comfortable automobiles, fickle consumer allegiance to the railroad faded. Accelerating federal support for highway construction and maintenance prompted railroad executives to grouse about unfair competition.[34] Eventually, passenger train service stopped and freight service declined to a point where the pragmatic railroaders carried only those goods that offered a profit, primarily bulky, low-value cargos that they moved over long distances.

The first Maysville railroad passenger depot was in service from 1873 to 1913, when it was replaced by a new structure. The recently refurbished freight depot still stands just to the east of the junction of SR 10 and U.S. 68 on the edge of a small rail yard that included a large railroad machine shop. The depots no longer serve trains, just as the old taverns along the Maysville Road no longer entertain overnight guests.

Mile 18.8 Bridge Street runs north to Second Street, a one-way street going west, or downriver. Just beyond Castro Street, Second Street runs beneath the south approach to the Simon Kenton Bridge, the two-lane cable-suspension bridge completed in 1932, and the first bridge to link Maysville to the Ohio towns across the river.[35]

The heaviest load that any bridge will carry is its own weight. Long-span bridges, such as those on the Ohio River, are best designed as suspension bridges, which are the lowest in aggregate self-weight. As John Roebling demonstrated in 1866 with his one-thousand-foot clear-span suspension bridge across the Ohio at Cincinnati, suspension bridges can be designed to surmount substantial barriers because of their comparatively light weight. The idea of a suspension bridge is straightforward. Two-legged towers, one on either side of the river, provide the vertical support members. Iron- or steel-wire rope spun together into heavy cable is strung back and forth across the tower tops to create two main suspension cables, which drape in a great parabola from tower to tower. Small vertical cables drop from the main suspension cable to support the bridge deck. The finished bridge looks rather like a giant's harp. In 2000 engineers completed a new cable-stayed suspension bridge west of Maysville that became part of a new U.S. 68 bypass around the city. The cable-stayed design is lighter than the classic suspension bridge because the massive suspension cables are eliminated, replaced

A diesel-powered tow guides chemical barges down the Ohio and between the Simon Kenton Bridge support towers. The two-lane suspension bridge was completed in 1931, the first bridge on this section of the river, effectively ending the ferry service that had been in place since 1794.

by thick stay cables that link the bridge deck and the suspension tower directly.[36] Seen from a distance in the morning sunshine, the cable-stayed bridge shimmers silver and gray and brings to mind a postmodern ship stripped of its sails to reveal the repeating geometry of sharply angled rigging. Engineers redecked the old Kenton Bridge in 2006, and some 8,300 vehicles still use it to cross the Ohio each day, compared to the 8,600 vehicles that use the new cable-stayed bridge on the bypass.[37]

Mile 18.9 Maysville's elegant brick and stone high school at Second and Limestone Pike was dedicated in 1909; the structure was converted into apartments for seniors in the 1990s. Ahead on Second Street, from Limestone to Sutton, is the historic Maysville central business area. The street here is lined by the city's tallest commercial buildings, most three to five stories, which housed a variety of financial and retail businesses. As Maysville's commercial development expanded, especially with increasing steam traffic on the river and the arrival of the steam-powered train in the mid-nineteenth century, some river-facing Front Street commerce moved here to Second Street and was soon joined by many new businesses.

The Maysville Street Railroad and Transfer Company trolley's upper-route track followed Third Street; the lower route followed West Second. Direct access to the trolley track influenced the kinds of businesses that chose locations along Second. East of the trolley track, businesses in the block between Limestone and Market streets represented a transition from the industrial waterfront on Limestone Creek to retail business near Market. Commercial activity closer to Limestone Creek included transportation-related businesses such as hotels, livery stables, carriage manufacturers, and tobacco and grain warehouses. Metal-use or metal-processing businesses also located here, including a blacksmith, locksmith, and plumber; and the most difficult-to-locate business, the undertaker, was here too. These businesses found economic comfort in close proximity to the river or the railroad track. Some depended on shipments by heavy dray wagons; others were associated with the nexus of road, rail, and river transport. The area generally was replete with industrial noise, dust, and congestion.

The last six lots on Second before the Market Street intersection transitioned sharply to sellers of wholesale and retail household and personal goods, such as furniture, groceries, drugs, and jewelry. At Market, the trolley tracks turned into Second Street with a transformational effect; the trolley provided the key to business differentiation that initiated the creation of the town's center for retail household and personal goods, the quintessential Main Street America. Between the end of the Civil War and 1900, land developers and builders replaced old Federal–style gabled structures and any remaining one-story frame gable-end and false-fronted buildings and built in their place wall-to-wall, flat-front, flat-roofed buildings that still stand. Builders faced the Victorian facades in brick, stone, or cast iron; the buildings' fronts ranged from plain to heavily ornamented with large overhanging cornices, upper-story window hoods, Greek Revival or Italianate window treatments, or decorative brickwork.

The 1890s Second Street, from Market west to Sutton, was an exemplar of competition and included four dry goods stores, four boot and shoe stores, three millinery shops, three drugstores, two bakery-confectioners, two jewelry stores, two furniture stores, two hardware stores, two book and stationery shops, two banks, and stores selling carpet, wallpaper, and groceries. The furniture stores are tall buildings—one features a spectacular stack of curved-glass bay windows on the upper stories; the upper floors were given over to furniture displays and storage. Sidewalk clocks atop eight-foot pedestals marked the jewelry stores; one stood in front of the former Traxel Jewelry at 9 West Second Street.[38] Several buildings along Second Street have cast-iron fronts, and a few have decorative black glass–covered bulkheads and show-window surrounds. Of special interest are the paired fronts at the former Traxel Jewelry store. Here at 11 West Second black-glass panels cover the front bulkhead up to the show windows. The front door is deeply recessed into the store's commercial space, and a beautiful multicolor art deco design has been laid into the vestibule floor. The storefront at 9 West Second next door includes custom curved black-glass panels across the bulkhead space.

The Maysville street address numbering system changes at Sutton Street. East Second is east of Sutton, West Second lies west of the Sutton intersection. West of Sutton, the land uses along Second Street change again. By the 1890s the urban

Though subject to high water during spring floods, Second Street had become Maysville's commercial street by the 1870s. West of Market Street, Second was lined with three- and four-story specialty retail stores.

sorting process had progressed here, as elsewhere in the city. Along West Second Street home- and personal-oriented retail stores gave way to a mix of grocery stores, a farm implement store, a carriage manufacturer, two large livery stables, and a church, all interspersed with family dwellings. The Washington Opera House is an unexpected structure here. A fire station occupied the ground floor, the performance space relegated to the second story. Limestone facing decorates the first-story facade, and decorative carved-stone blocks surround the oversize central front door. The upper story draws light through tall arched windows; the entire facade is elaborately finished in yellow brick highlighted by ruddy brick latticework. The Opera House served as the city's movie theater, the first film shown here in 1908, until the Russell Theater opened on Third Street.

At Wall Street, the Second Street business district segues into the west-side residential area. Nineteenth-century brick homes, some of them pre–Civil War, line the sidewalk on narrow lots. Farther west, brick Victorian-era homes stood on larger lots. Some property owners subdivided their lots to permit infill by smaller, newer structures.

In 1950 engineers completed a new U.S. 68 highway approach into Maysville, bypassing the tortuous track followed by the old Lexington Pike. The new route offered an enticement for traditional downtown businesses either to move to the bluff top above the city or to open branch stores there as a suburban alternative to Second Street. As happened in many American cities, the new highway soon attracted restaurants and strip shopping centers. Some Maysville Second Street businesses moved to the new suburban strip, and others closed.

33

Living with the River

Maysville's riverfront continues to be its most dynamic landscape. The historic river landing area that extended from the mouth of Limestone Creek west to Wall Street has been transformed by the razing of buildings, the installation of railroad tracks, and, most recently, the wholesale removal of much of Front Street. The space is now filled by a concrete flood wall that defends a new street, McDonald Parkway, a motel, and associated parking lots and buildings. The riverfront transformation is so comprehensive that only through historic maps, photographs, and personal accounts from the period can one attempt to reconstruct the scene here during the nineteenth century's first five decades.

Initially, flatboats and keelboats pulled into Limestone Creek or tied up at the adjacent banks to load and unload cargo. The steamboat *Enterprise,* built at Brownsville on the lower Monongahela south of Pittsburgh, demonstrated successfully in 1815 that Ohio Valley steamboats could readily move freight upstream, thereby rendering flatboats and keelboats anachronistic, if not primitive. Thereafter, steamboat construction at river ports such as Pittsburgh, Cincinnati, and Louisville proceeded rapidly. In 1820 sixty-nine steamboats with a collective capacity of 13,890 tons operated on the Ohio River. By 1855, 727 boats with a capacity of 170,000 tons plied the river.[1] At riverfront landings steamboats shouldered out the nonpowered craft. To enhance the rather confined Maysville landing area for steam-powered craft, engineers constructed a wharf boat and anchored it a short distance offshore at the foot of Market Street, where it was connected by a dock to the bank. The wharf boat was of sufficient length to tie up one large steamboat or two intermediate-size vessels. Port improvements proceeded apace, but nagging navigational problems limited large-scale development of river-borne commerce.

The prevailing annual climatic cycle of wet winters and dry, hot summers limited the primary shipping season to the weeks of maximum river flow, usually late winter until midsummer. Low river flow from midsummer through late fall, the driest months, limited steamboat travel to the river channel's deepest section, or what hydrologists term the *thalweg.* In many years the river's flow was so low that water traffic stopped for weeks at a time. In 1838, for example, low water confined riverboats to their harbors from July to November.[2] Even when the river rose to a level sufficient to permit boat travel, navigation required great care to avoid shallow bars, rocky ledges such as the Falls of the Ohio at Louisville, or collision with the thousands of sunken or floating snags that studded the channel like dragon's teeth. A snag was a large tree growing on a bank that the river undermined and washed out into the channel. Such trees often embedded themselves in the river-bottom silts. A waterlogged trunk and branches presented a bristling threat, like a riverine abatis, that grasped at vulnerable ship hulls. Between 1825 and 1829 riverboats wrecked on Ohio River snags lost cargos valued at more than $1.3 million.[3]

The Allegheny and Monongahela rivers join at Pittsburgh's Golden Triangle, forming the Ohio, which flows southwest 981 miles to its junction with the Mississippi near Cairo, Illinois. The Ohio drains a 204,000-square-mile watershed that extends from western New York, Pennsylvania, Maryland, North Carolina, and Virginia south and west to include most of West Virginia, Kentucky, Ohio, Indiana, and a tier of counties in eastern Illinois. The main river and its hundreds of tributaries form a dendritic watershed drainage pattern; only about 5 percent of the river's flow comes from runoff that moves directly into the main channel. Tributary characteristics therefore strongly influence the speed and volume of runoff into the main channel.[4]

By the eighteenth century's latter decades, Ohio River watershed resources were already known, at least in rough outline: hardwood forest in seemingly unending expanses, high-quality iron ore deposits, extensive bituminous coal measures, salt-producing brine springs, fertile soils and accessible topography, and a temperate climate.[5] All this provided an impetus for alacritous settlement and development, rapid growth of industry and manufacturing, and a diverse and productive agriculture. The lands on the Ohio's north side became the cradle of the Corn Belt. To the south, in West Virginia and Kentucky, lay the central Appalachian coalfield and the rich farmlands of Kentucky's Bluegrass and Pennyroyal regions.[6] Today twenty navigational dams control the river's flow and provide a minimum nine-foot-deep channel for commercial navigation. Hundreds of mines extract the region's coal in West Virginia, eastern Kentucky, and southeastern Ohio, much of which is shipped via barge to forty-nine electrical power–generating plants operating at river's edge. Total cargo tonnage moved on the river by modern barges exceeds 230 million tons annually, 70 percent of which is coal and other energy-producing products.[7]

In Maysville the linear zone between the river's south bank and Second Street has been contentious ground for more than two centuries. From the early years of settlement, as people sought optimal access to the river-road nexus, they claimed what they thought were competitive business positions at water's edge, only to lose their investments to periodic floods. Indians warned eighteenth-century settlers along the upper Ohio that the river flooded frequently, and as settlements extended down the valley in the nineteenth century's early decades, those warnings proved accurate. Since modern record keeping began in 1831, the Ohio flooded more than fifty times; fifteen notable floods occurred on this river section. The great flood of 1832, for example, submerged houses in Maysville's lowest-lying neighborhoods, swept other houses from their foundations into the river, and piled an immense debris jam onto the riverfront.[8] Major floods followed in 1867, 1883, 1884, 1913, and 1937. The river's modern dam system places Maysville on the ninety-five-mile-long pool created by the Meldahl Dam at river mile marker 436, some twenty-eight miles below Maysville. Normal river pool level at Maysville is thirty-four feet. The river reaches flood stage at fifty feet. The great flood of 1913 reached nearly sixty-nine feet, high enough for water to pour over Front Street building windowsills. On Second Street floodwater covered businesses' ground floors. The L & N Railroad tracks near Limestone Creek were inundated, as were the low-lying residential districts in East Maysville. In January 1937 a record monthly rainfall of 14.47 inches combined with snowmelt on northern tributaries to bring the Ohio Valley its largest recorded flood to date when the river reached seventy-five feet. In Maysville the floodwaters reached the tops of first-floor windows in Second Street business buildings, and the low-lying west-end residential area was inundated. Limestone Creek flooded as far south as Lexington Road (Fourth Street). Most of East Maysville, from river's edge south to Elizabeth Street and Vine Street, was underwater. The Forest Avenue tobacco warehouses stood above the high-water mark and provided a dry space for city residents to store their household furnishings out of harm's way. Some sections of the Ohio Valley were underwater for six weeks, and the accrued flood damage totaled more than $400 million.

A Depression-weary Congress finally passed into law the national Flood Control Act in 1937, and cities along the river developed plans to request floodwall construction by the U.S. Army Corps of Engineers. The following year, 1938, the corps began construction of a 17,900-foot-long floodwall at Huntington, West Virginia.[9] Federal appropriations for a Maysville floodwall were not forthcoming until 1949. To garner federal support, initially set at $5.5 million, the city had to finance a bond of about $275,000 for sewer system changes, right-of-way, and other site costs.[10] The Army Corps of Engineers completed Maysville's 14,000-foot-long floodwall and levee system seven years later, in 1956. The finished wall stood three feet higher than the 1937 flood crest and cost more than $7 million. Ten openings through the wall provided street access to the river and the railroad tracks. The completed floodwall provided a reassuring seal between city and river during high water. If the wall was overtopped by an epic flood, however, or if heavy rain fell during a flood, water would accumulate behind the wall, threatening the city with a new peril—a flood from within. To neutralize this hazard, and to ensure a positive flow of stream runoff that would otherwise accumulate behind the closed floodwall doors, the corps installed five pumping stations with a 220,000 gallon-per-minute capacity inside the wall to lift runoff water up and across the wall into the river.[11]

The 1950s highway improvements and floodwall completion presented downtown merchants and businesses with conflicting influences. The new U.S. 68 highway approach enhanced traffic flow up and down the great hill above the city, and the floodwall promised protection for those who embraced their traditional business-area locations. Some businesses nevertheless moved to the new strip shopping centers along U.S. 68 atop the bluff. By the 1980s city leaders—the Downtown Merchants Association, the Main Street Program, and the Friends of Maysville—were concerned that the historic business area was in need of revitalization to ensure business location stability. The city obtained a $1 million federal grant in 1988 to build Limestone

The side-wheel steamboat *Majestic* operates out of Pittsburgh. In October 2006, on its way to the Tall Stacks steamboat festival in Cincinnati, the *Majestic* docked at Maysville to fill its holding tanks with water. The city's historic waterfront docking area and wharf boat would have been just beyond the *Majestic*'s position. The limestone riprap in the foreground stabilizes the riverbank against erosion during high water.

Landing along the riverfront. The project opened a foot passage through the floodwall and created a walkway and a fishing pier at the river's edge. Private developers removed old buildings to make room for a new French Quarter Inn motel.[12] And in 1998 the city contracted with Robert Dafford, a mural artist from Lafayette, Louisiana, to paint a series of murals on the floodwall's interior sides representing key aspects of the city's changing landscapes from the seventeenth through the twentieth centuries.

34

East Maysville

Before engineers redirected the Maysville Road (termed the Lexington Road in Maysville) in the 1950s from its steep and winding historic entrance into Maysville's west side to the bypass that led into the lower Limestone Creek valley, traffic and travelers focused on the city's western side. This geographically favored place included the original river-landing site at the mouth of Limestone Creek, a locational advantage that fostered the area's transformation into the city's retail, governmental, and service area. A traveler bound from southern Ohio to Lexington via the Kenton Bridge and the old Lexington Road might not be aware that east of Limestone Creek lay the expansive and industrial East Maysville. By the 1790s the Limestone settlement had two river landing sites; one at the mouth of Limestone Creek, the other about a mile upstream at Rittersville or Brook's Landing, where unloading cranes and warehouses awaited arriving riverboats. Though it was a considerable distance from the Limestone Creek landing, Brook's Landing promoters could boast of the site's extensive bottomland—the impinging south bluff was three-fourths of a mile distant from the river's edge.[1] Despite promoters' entreaties and the potential that a large parcel of open land might have for development, a rather substantial portion of the east side was low lying and flooded periodically. Substantive real estate development began not at the comparatively remote Brook's Landing but on the east side of Limestone Creek, just across from the favored landing that spawned the city's business district.

The north section of the Maysville & Lexington Railroad was linked to the Ohio River in 1853 and entered East Maysville by way of the Limestone Creek valley. The railroad extended a track west, across Limestone Creek into Maysville to the passenger depot at the corner of Third and Bridge streets. The Louisville & Nashville Railroad acquired this rail line in 1891.[2] On the creek's east side, rail sidings served railroad freight depots and machine shops. The city of Maysville annexed East Maysville in 1867.[3] A decade later East Maysville comprised a grid of streets and lots six blocks long and three blocks wide. Streets paralleling the river—Front, Second, Third, and Fourth—extended from Maysville into East Maysville. Union Street marked the eastern corporate boundary. Farther east, individuals held large lots of five acres or more, and land speculators platted subdivisions such as Woodville and Chester along East Third Street straddling the Kentucky & Great Eastern Railroad tracks, the low-lying route later acquired by the Chesapeake & Ohio Railroad as its main line. The Chester subdivision centered on Main and Broadway. Two large additions to Chester extended the residential lot plat across the entire floodplain from the river's edge to the base of the bluff. The Maysville Trotting Track conducted horse races on the south side of Third Street, then called Race Street. In 1891 Maysville extended its corporate boundary farther east to annex Chester and its neighboring developments.[4]

Industries and businesses that required large land parcels with links to river and rail transport found land to satisfy their predilections in East Maysville. In the block between Second and Third, Lexington and Walnut, for example, workers at the Eagle Plow Works used Ohio Valley iron and hardwoods to produce single-moldboard walking plows for the southern farm market. Eagle was one of a dozen plow and farm machinery manufacturers in Maysville. Along Front Street, a sawmill and the Kentucky Planing Mill cut regional hardwoods into dimensional lumber and finished millwork.[5] In 1886 local investors financed a pulley builder to create the Ohio Valley Pulley Works, which became the city's largest manufacturing plant. The factory was on Third Street, at the corner of Main, and was served by a dedicated C & O Railroad siding. The firm name changed to Browning Manufacturing, which eventually became part of the Emerson Power Transmission Company. The firm continues in business as a supplier of power transmission equipment.[6] In 1905 Ewald Pawsat, a manufacturer from Sheboygan, Michigan, and his brother Herman relocated their bicycle parts plant to Maysville to take advantage of river and rail access.[7] Their company, Wald Manufacturing, made parts for major American bicycle manufacturers. By the 1950s the plant at 800 East Fifth Street employed more than three hundred people. As bicycle parts manufacturing moved offshore—most parts are now made in China—the plant adjusted its employment structure and production. The firm now specializes in manufacturing bicycle baskets and replacement parts as well as automobile parts.

Maysville was a major hemp rope manufacturer in the nineteenth century's early decades. As increasing burley tobacco production displaced traditional dark tobaccos by the 1880s, Maysville became a major tobacco marketing and processing center. By 1890 two small tobacco warehouses stood along East Second Street in East Maysville.[8] In 1904 the American Tobacco Company completed two expansive storage warehouses and a large tobacco re-drying plant. Re-drying, a preliminary step in tobacco processing, reduces the moisture content of cured tobacco leaves to a level appropriate for manufacturing. The city's first loose-leaf tobacco auction warehouse, Farmers, was built at Forest Avenue and Union Street in 1909. Additional warehouse construction followed as burley tobacco production expanded across the Outer Bluegrass lands of Mason and adjoining counties. R. J. Reynolds in 1917 followed the earlier example of American Tobacco and built an expansive processing plant in East Maysville, the company's largest outside their main plant in Winston-Salem, North Carolina. Eventually Reynolds added a large stemming machine to the plant, which further prepared the tobacco for manufacture into smoking products.[9] By the 1920s sixteen auction warehouses and seven re-drying plants operated in East Maysville, clustering primarily along Forest Avenue but also extending north to Third and south to Sixth.[10]

Though tobacco warehouses are in active use for a relatively short time—generally

Different transportation eras and technologies converge along East Maysville's East Second Street. Only one row of house lots separated East Second from the Ohio River bank, so each nineteenth-century house on the street's north side had a river view. A trolley track ran along Second Street, and buildings at the trolley stop corners often included commercial space on the first floor, where grocery stores or other retail shops conducted business. Oversize windows with access doors help identify these stores, though their uses have changed. The building's remaining floor space was often owner-occupied or residential rental property. The sign on the pickup truck door announces the Crounse Corporation, which is one of the major river tow transportation companies in the nation. George P. Crounse Sr. developed the idea of propeller-driven river tows as a replacement for the traditional stern paddlewheel on river towboats. The first tow of Crounse's design was built in 1949. At present the company operates 27 towboats and 860 barges on the Ohio and its major tributaries. Their primary cargo is Appalachian bituminous coal, which they deliver to riverfront electrical power–generation plants. The Crounse Corporation is headquartered in Paducah, in western Kentucky, but the company opened a branch office on this corner of East Second Street in Maysville in 1969.

the tobacco sales season extended from late November through January—the pre-Depression auctions nevertheless sold nearly thirty million pounds of tobacco annually, so the warehouses were necessarily large structures. The Home Warehouse advertised itself as the largest in the world (as did the Penn Brothers Warehouse on South Broadway in Lexington). The Burley Tobacco Growers Co-Operative Association operated two warehouses on Forest Avenue in 1926. Both were two hundred feet wide. One was seven hundred feet long. The other exceeded nine hundred feet in length. Together, the two buildings provided the association more than seven acres of auction floor space.[11] The East Maysville tobacco auction and processing center is the product of road and rail access as well as its proximity to the historic birthplace of burley tobacco. The agglomeration of warehouses and large re-drying and stemming plants employed more than five hundred people and represented one of the largest concentrations of tobacco-related structures in the multistate burley-producing region. With the rapid decline in burley tobacco production after 2000 and the end of the tobacco auction system, warehouses here fell into disuse and by 2011 some had been demolished.

East Maysville's residential housing stock is eclectic, its variability related to proximity to and elevation above the river, the historic trolley-car route, the railroad tracks, and tobacco warehouses and processing plants. A few large two- or three-story Victorian-era brick homes stand on Second Street, but most neighborhoods, especially those near the tobacco warehouses and manufacturing plants, are modest clapboard T-plan cottages, bungalows, and small Tudor Revival homes that date from 1900 to the 1940s. The two east-west arterial streets, Second and Forest Avenue, exhibit very different land-use patterns. The trolley car led late nineteenth-century suburbanization along Second Street. Blocks of handsome Queen Anne and other revival-style suburban houses stand on large lots—albeit in the floodplain—along Second. Every few blocks, small commercial buildings occupy a corner lot at a street intersection that had once been a trolley car stop. First-floor grocery stores provided fresh bread, milk, and other basic household necessities to trolley car passengers returning from a day's work in the central business area, much as gasoline-station convenience stores do today. The stores' upper stories often functioned as rental apartments.

Conversely, Forest Avenue is a truck- and automobile-era street—warehouses and tobacco processing plants to the west segue into auto-oriented strip shopping centers, single-story 1960s commercial buildings, and defunct drive-in restaurants to the east.

East Maysville's residential district terminates at the Maysville Cemetery. Situated atop one of the highest points on the East Maysville floodplain, the cemetery reflects the development in America of rural picturesque burial grounds first exemplified at Mount Auburn Cemetery in Cambridge, Massachusetts, in the 1830s. Mount Auburn's founder, the physician Jacob Bigelow, believed that traditional burial grounds under and around city churches were unhealthy, and burial in a picturesque rural setting would help assuage survivors' grief.[12] By the 1850s nearly a dozen cities across America had established such burial grounds, including Spring Grove Cemetery in Cincinnati. Maysville Cemetery is a miniature version of Spring Grove; curvilinear access driveways wind across the hill among mature hardwood and evergreen trees. From the names on headstones, tablets, and family plot obelisks one can glean a historical roster of Maysville's founders, prominent businesspeople, and sundry politicians. The nineteenth-century merchants George Cox and John Armstrong are buried in large family plots here, as are U.S. Supreme Court Justice Stanley Reed and U.S. Representatives James Kehoe, Elija Phister, Richard Stanton, and William Wadsworth. From the center of the burial ground, looking downriver to the west, the view, just across SR 10, is dominated by the expansive roof of Duke Warehouse no. 2, which is wedged between the road's right-of-way and other buildings dedicated to burley tobacco.

Part IV

Reflecting on Roads and American Culture

The highway stands for unity. It is that installation which joins one part of the public landscape to another, which enables organized society to make its influence felt everywhere.

—J. B. Jackson,
Landscapes: Selected Writings of J. B. Jackson

35

The Changing Landscape of Mobility

Engineers completed reconstruction on the twelve-mile segment of the Maysville Road between Lexington and Paris in 2003. Reconfigured as the four-lane Paris Pike parkway, the new road was acclaimed as an aesthetic triumph and a splendid example of collaborative design work by professional engineers, landscape architects, and the public. Yet the new parkway has effectively expunged the old road. Local residents who travel the route routinely and knew intimately the old road's character recognize little of the original roadbed in the new corridor. That the new road is immeasurably safer than the old pike is laudatory—the ultimate purpose of a road, after all, is to provide safe, predictable, and punctual passage. But one cannot modify a road, be it Paris Pike, the northern sections of the Maysville Road, or any other road, for that matter, without also modifying the long-established landscape attendant to it. This is one reason that the study of old roadways is so endlessly fascinating: roads are windows into past aspirations, technologies, politics, and economies. Transportation, in turn, is the linchpin of America's economy and social life—freedom and ubiquity of movement lie at the very core of America's national culture. As technologies, political priorities, and social behaviors change through time, we in turn exact change on various elements of our built environment, especially our transportation networks.

Americans embrace mobility to a degree found in few other places in the world, and to enhance our mobility—whether for shipment of manufactured goods and farm products to market or personal movement to work or leisure—we eagerly adopted, over the last three centuries, each new transportation mode as it was invented and developed. Our enthusiasm was particularly piqued by transportation innovations that increased the speed of movement. Perambulatory mobility seemed ploddingly slow when new transport technologies that accelerated movement became available.[1] The form and function of those technologies were initially more strongly influenced by a desire for speed than by demands for improved reliability or increased capacity.[2] We replaced wind-powered sailing ships and current-directed river flatboats with steam-powered boats and railroads. Canals preceded overland roads in some favored regions. But canal routes were strongly controlled by river alignments and water availability, and the lower construction and maintenance costs and higher speed and reliability of roads and railroads led us to favor them over canals. With great relish and eagerness we elected to replace Pennsylvania-built Conestoga wagons and New Hampshire–made Concord stagecoaches with internal combustion engine–powered trucks and automobiles from Detroit, Lansing, and Hamtramck, Michigan. Eventually even the railroad engineer's prestigious status as mythic hero to youthful daydreamers was captured by drivers of over-the-road trucks and Greyhound buses.

As Americans adopted each new transportation mode in turn, they built new landscapes to accommodate it, only to abandon their work when the next innovation appeared.[3] Roads, canals, and railroads all spawned towns; some evolved organically at important crossroads; others were carefully planned and platted settlements. Yet, as one transport epoch gives way to the next, old railroad depots become police stations, community museums, or restaurants, and people convert old railroad track beds into hiking and biking trails. We choose to bypass crooked old roads or bury them below new asphalt strips that follow graceful, long-radius, super-elevated curves. Merchants in small towns bypassed by new highway construction try to attract travelers back to Main Street by converting vacant department stores into antiques malls and former specialty retail stores into curio shops.

The story of the Maysville Road is much more than a regional epic; it is really the story of how Americans embraced those tools that allowed them to make mobility a cornerstone of their cosmology—their fundamental philosophy of how they believe the world should work. A road's story is also a narrative about historic origins and change, an elucidation of how political actions and construction projects intertwine, and a chronicle of social processes and cultural change. A road and its companion roadside landscape are a kind of archive of their own geography and history. Reading that archive, or at least becoming aware of some of its content, helps illuminate the process of adaptation as new technologies replace old. Take as an example the manner in which political will, or lack of it, is manifest in how state officials or turnpike company commissioners embraced road construction, and the methods by which legal and technical codes for road finance, design and building, and use are created. In short, reading the road and its attendant roadside allows one to begin to unravel the complex process whereby we create and sustain places.[4]

Because Lexington is landlocked, its historic urban growth and development could not benefit directly from economical waterway transport. Rather, the city was dependent on overland road and railroad connections to the Ohio River. The federal census of 2010 recorded Lexington's combined city-county population at some 295,800, or more than thirty-two times the size of Maysville, the river town whose presence spawned the Maysville Road and whose historical port transshipped the commodities that fed the demands of Lexington's rapidly growing businesses.[5] The evolution of transportation technology gave the railroad and then the interstate highway certain advantages and economies over river transport, so that by the second half of the twentieth century Ohio River traffic was largely low-value bulk cargo such as sand and gravel or coal. High-value cargo such as manufactured goods traveled to Lexington by the more expeditious rail boxcar or highway-bound truck, and Maysville's role as life-giving economic umbilical faded. Maysville's modern-day port function is not as an importer of goods headed toward Lexington and other Bluegrass communities, but as an exporting link between the state's Appalachian bituminous coalfields and Ohio Valley electrical power–generation plants that are dependent on that coal.

Depending on one's perspective, the Maysville-to-Lexington Road ends or begins at the Ohio River's edge at the junction of four different but interlocked transport technologies—river, trace-and-pike, railroad, and state and federal highway. Whether the road is superimposed on a city street grid or following an old track across the open country, its geographical history is intricately layered. Once formally established, the route corridor has proven resilient, altered only in minor ways as engineers widened and straightened the road to accommodate vehicles capable of larger loads and higher speeds. Nowhere along its sixty-seven-mile length does the modern road diverge more than a mile or so from the oldest roadbed. The road enabled growth of urban places at both ends and along its right-of-way. Once it was established, vigorous town economies provided a purpose for continuing road use—be it wagon and stagecoach, or truck and automobile—thereby reinforcing the road's location and alignment. After 1926 transportation planners deemed the road of sufficient importance to include it in the new federal highway system as U.S. 68.

Our thinking about roads is directed by the scale of our questions and concerns. All roads are unique if one focuses on local geographies, specific characteristics, and historical incidents. All roads are familial if one seeks general themes in their genesis, subsequent use patterns, and role in interlinking the local scene and connecting that to a regional and national social, political, and economic milieu. Careful study of the Maysville Road yields an object lesson about road evolution in the historical trans-Appalachian west, a process shared with other important regional or national routeways. When one considers the Maysville Road within its local and regional context, its historical geography can be read as serially ordered tableaux, a narrative that illuminates how today's highway landscape emerged from the past.[6] The road's story is composed as is no other. The road is the theater of local settlement, an engine of regional economic development, an icon of regional and national political process. As a macadam turnpike, the Maysville Road demonstrated the practicality of rigorous road-engineering techniques to those nineteenth-century travelers who passed along its way. But the road has also proven vulnerable to competition from the railroad, especially during the half century that began in the 1870s, when the new railbed from Carlisle to Maysville diverted freight and passenger traffic away from the road, thereby stimulating the growth of small towns that grew up around depots that the railroad built at intervals along its right-of-way. In the late twentieth century engineers rebuilt some road segments, and in 2003 the road's Paris-to-Lexington section became a nationally recognized demonstration of collaborative road-reconstruction planning that blended the concerns and opinions of local landowners with state transportation priorities. The Paris Pike parkway represents an evolving perspective on American highway construction, the concern for the visual integrity of an internationally renowned landscape within the context of safe passage engineering.[7]

In the twentieth century engineers and law enforcement increasingly gained control over road construction and traffic flow, exacting new regulative and legal disciplines on what until then had been a linear space where people embraced the freedom of movement with few formal restrictions other than tolls. The roadside attendant to the Maysville Road is also a dynamic place where groups as varied as city planners, farmers, and national franchise restaurants engage the road as a conduit of legal jurisdiction, political policy, social interaction, and economic opportunity.[8]

Some towns and rural settlements have been bypassed by new road construction, and the new roadway attracts new roadside construction: houses, businesses, and institutions such as schools. Bypass buildings usually reflect national rather than local design trends, just as the bypass road itself conforms to state or federal standards, rather than reflecting local conditions a century ago when adjustments to local topographic vagaries yielded idiosyncratic road alignments. Merchants may erect signs on the tops or sides of their buildings large enough to be read from the bypass, reminding passersby that their places of business remain beside the old road. Town gateways attract national chain or franchised businesses housed in buildings replicated a thousand times across the country. Should road realignments bypass such locations, local people often reclaim and revernacularize old roadside businesses, turning former general stores into antiques shops, schools into auction barns, gas stations into used-car lots, motels into apartments. The road and the roadside landscape mirror the social and economic polarities that accompany America's changing transportation preferences.

The old road still bisects central Paris, Millersburg, Mayslick, and Washington, each town's eighteenth-century location contingent on the road, each town's nineteenth-century economy entwined with the road. These places retain much of their historic character as captured in the vernacular forms and styles of locally built structures. Active preservation groups and Chambers of Commerce seek to maintain their towns' venerable buildings in recognition that historic facades merit preservation and represent to a curious public a sense of community pride and a concern that although historical geography cannot be sealed in amber for perpetuity, its essence can be maintained in symbolic form.

Despite the regimentation that engineering and legal precepts bring to road construction, maintenance, and use, primary roads and their attendant roadsides rarely reach equilibrium or stasis. Road landscapes are, rather, dynamic and continually changing and evolving, although change occurs in unsystematic ways. A road's surface begins to degrade soon after construction is completed and the first traffic passes. Plants—both native and invasive—reclaim freshly graded drainage ways; bedrock exposed in raw road cuts weathers and may spall or slump. Roads are largely public entities—unlike corporately owned railroads—that are closely paralleled by private property. Changing the road surface requires considered coordination between governmental agencies and engineering and surveying firms. Building a structure on private land adjoining a road may require certain government-issued permits, but the building's design, materials, and purpose are largely at the landowner's discretion. Changing the public road surface is a regimented and circumscribed process, whereas changing the privately held roadside is idiosyncratic. Yet the road and its roadside form a singular landscape. The rate of road and roadside change is often predicated on road capacity. Roads linking large towns and cities may change quickly, often in energetic construction projects enabled by outsize earth-moving machinery and dump trucks that carve down hillsides and fill in valleys and articulated cranes that throw new bridges across steams. Backcountry roads may evolve slowly over a generation or more, yet they change. Assessing change along a road is complicated by its linearity. A road's landscape context cannot easily be delineated by a literal boundary, as can a farm, a building, or a town made up of many buildings. The roadway's linearity at the same time constrains and extends the kinds of change that occur. A road landscape is not a bounded, discrete areal unit, but a prescribed succession of segments, each a unique assembly of surfaces, intersections, attendant structures, and political jurisdictions.

Since the 1920s federal, state, county, and metropolitan laws and engineering directives have shaped the road's physical attributes more than local political or economic priorities. Roads often cross from one political jurisdiction to another and are therefore subject to not one jurisdiction but many. Official county boundary signs, mile markers, and Chamber of Commerce welcome signs mark the transition from county to county or state to state, just as a cross-highway splice between concrete and asphalt or old and new road surfaces is one obvious sign that a road has crossed a county or state boundary. The road's linearity, therefore, is perforce a cross section of variable political terrain, of different economic and cultural districts, just as it simultaneously transects a varied topographic, geologic, and hydrologic land surface.

Roads are unconventional landscape entities that reside at the nexus of complex surveying and engineering, pervasive political control, and social and economic experimentation. The road's way and structure are melded by evolving road-construction techniques, transportation mode technology, design aesthetics, political priorities and chicanery, ecological context, and land-use experiments conducted by people who take up residence or establish businesses at the road's edge. Roads therefore mirror larger technical, social, and political processes that operate at regional, national, and even international scales. Nineteenth-century road building marked a transition from medieval folk traditions to the application of science by trained engineers who introduced applied geometry and physics to roadway construction. By 1926 road building had become embedded in the nation's political ideology, the basis for economic growth within a state's boundaries, and the avenue to large-scale land and resource development, employment, and financial prosperity. Road engineering became institutionalized at the federal and state levels, and the gap between the technical requirements for road construction advocated by state and federal regulations and actual construction practices by road builders narrowed, thereby ushering in the modern highway era.

Control and management of road configurations and road usage by county, state, or national government agencies constrained the personal vagaries of driving while promoting the illusion that ease of movement equaled a form of personal freedom. Yet, simultaneously, regulating road construction and use also implied that travel would be reliable and predictable. All this now enables a consistent movement along the road: local people, travelers from distant places, and sundry commodities, all proximal yet all encapsulated in cars or trucks that meet and pass by one another in a kind of mobile entourage. With the exception of their license plates, they exist in anonymity one from another. To ensure safe passage and arrival at desired destinations, each driver must engage with the road, the roadside, and other travelers individually and in aggregate. Thus, the bromide "following the rules of the road" implies much more than simply obeying the speed limit and observing stop signs.

Travel on the roadway today offers the promise of movement so effortless that we measure it in terms of time rather than distance. We regard the territory we now cross with alacrity as scenery, not as farmland traversed by ruts through deep mud, steep hills and difficult grades, or dangerous, even life-threatening fords across swiftly flowing streams. The expedience that modern road travel has become should not deter us from contemplating a road's origins and evolution as we follow its track through towns and across the countryside. We should, rather, seek out those remaining markers of past geographies, of lost landscapes, and appreciate them as primary historical documents. If we do this, we will recognize the road as one of the salient generic places that give form and meaning to the American experience, and we will come to realize that the road has become, as J. B. Jackson has observed, the most powerful force for the destruction or creation of landscapes that we have.[9]

Acknowledgments

We wish to recognize the contributions of William Marshall, Terry Birdwhistell, and Gordon Hogg of the Margaret King Library Special Collections Department; Faith Harders of the College of Design Library; and Gwen Curtis of the Geological Sciences Library and Map Collection for their suggestions and access to important documents. We also convey our gratitude to the staff at the University of Kentucky W. T. Young Library Interlibrary Loan Department and the University Law Library for their contributions to the completion of this project. Richard Gilbreath, director of the Gyula Pauer Cartography and GIS Laboratory in the Department of Geography at the University of Kentucky, and Jeff Levy contributed elegant cartographic work and employed contemporary geographic information system technology to help bridge the analog-digital gap.

Thanks also to Thomas Owen, archivist for regional history at the University of Louisville's Ekstrom Library and University Archives, and to Charles Castner and Amy Purcell, also of the Ekstrom Library and University Archives; Cathy Schenck and her staff at the Keeneland Association Library; Lynn David at the Kentucky Gateway Museum Center in Maysville; Neal O. Hammon of Shelbyville, Kentucky; Jo Frederick, Bettye Hitch, and Nancy Donavan of Ewing, Kentucky, who participated in a focus-group discussion on the geographical history of Ewing. Gerald Griffith, also of Ewing, not only contributed to the focus group but also provided several rare and unpublished documents relating to Ewing and its association with the L & N Railroad. James Pyles of Mason County guided us on a tour of his farmstead and the old road from Maysville to Blue Licks. Donald Thompson, owner of the John Grant Station property in Bourbon County, provided access to the station site and useful information on historic road alignments and related properties. We also wish to acknowledge the contributions of the staff at the State Historic Preservation Office in Frankfort and thank them for their assistance and access to their files.

For their permission to publish images and photographs, we wish to acknowledge the following: the University of Louisville Ekstrom Library for their permission to reprint the hemp field photograph; the University Press of Kentucky for permission to reprint three Clay Lancaster drawings of Rose Hill House, photographs of Joyland, Elmendorf Farm's Green Hills house and interurban waiting room, an engraving of the Phoenix Hotel, and segments of John Filson's map of Kentucky; the Kentucky Historical Society for the use of the Blue Licks Hotel photograph from their Frank Dunn Collection; B. J. Gooch and the Transylvania Library Special Collections for permission to reproduce images from the J. Winston Coleman Jr. Photographic Collection; and the Hopewell Museum in Paris, Kentucky, for access to their collection of historical photography.

We wish to thank George Thompson, founder and director of the Center for American Places at Columbia College Chicago, for his invaluable contributions to this volume. George brought his enthusiasm for research, writing, and photography of the American landscape to this project through his encouragement and gifted editorial oversight.

Partial funding for this project has been provided by the Federal Highway Administration Transportation Enhancement Grants program as administered by the Kentucky Transportation Cabinet.

Notes

1. Reading America's Roads

1. Ronald Kline and Trevor Pinch, "Users as Agents of Technological Change: The Social Construction of the Automobile in the Rural United States," *Technology and Culture* 37, no. 4 (1996): 763–95, esp. 765.

2. Richard H. Schein, "The Place of Landscape: A Conceptual Framework for Interpreting an American Scene," *Annals of the Association of American Geographers* 87, no. 4 (1997): 660–80, esp. 662.

3. Ibid., 663.

4. Bruce E. Seely, "The Scientific Mystique in Engineering: Highway Research at the Bureau of Public Roads, 1918–1940," *Technology and Culture* 25, no. 4 (1984): 798–831, esp. 799–802.

5. Harwood Frost, *The Art of Roadmaking* (New York: McGraw-Hill, 1910), 137–53.

6. James E. Vance Jr., *Capturing the Horizon: The Historical Geography of Transportation since the Transportation Revolution of the Sixteenth Century* (New York: Harper & Row, 1986), 7.

7. Frost, *The Art of Roadmaking*, 323–25.

8. Ibid., 380.

9. M. D. Ross, "Progress in Looking Backward: History of the First Concrete Road in the State of Kentucky," *Kentucky Highways* 1, no. 9 (1927): 24–27.

10. See Henry Petroski, *Design Paradigms: Case Histories of Error and Judgment in Engineering* (New York: Cambridge University Press, 1994).

11. Reynold M. Wik, "Benjamin Holt and the Invention of the Track-Type Tractor," *Technology and Culture* 20, no. 1 (1979): 90–107.

12. Prevost Hubbard, "Efficiency of Bituminous Surfaces and Pavements under Motor Truck Traffic," *Public Roads* 1, no. 10 (1919): 25; and Seely, "The Scientific Mystique in Engineering," 803.

13. Merrill J. Roberts, "The Motor Transportation Revolution," *Business History Review* 30, no. 1 (1956): 56–95, esp. 59.

14. M. H. Crump, *Kentucky Highways: History of the Old and New Systems*, Bulletin no. 13, U.S. Department of Agriculture (Washington, D.C.: Government Printing Office, 1895), 7.

15. Karl Raitz and Nancy O'Malley, "Local-Scale Turnpike Roads in Nineteenth-Century Kentucky," *Journal of Historical Geography* 33 (2007): 1–23; see also John L. Larson, *Internal Improvement: National Public Works and the Promise of Popular Government in the Early United States* (Chapel Hill: University of North Carolina Press, 2001), 182–85.

16. Andrew Jackson, "Maysville Road: Message from the President of the United States," May 27, 1830, Doc. no. 113, 21st Cong., 1st sess., 5.

17. *Charter of the Maysville and Lexington Turnpike Road Company Including All Amendments to the Year 1865* (Maysville, Ky.: Eagle Printers, 1865).

18. Sylvester Welch, "Directions for the Construction of Turnpike Roads," in *Report of the Board of Internal Improvement* (Frankfort, Ky.: Board of Internal Improvement, 1837), 169–74.

19. Thomas P. Hughes, *Networks of Power: Electrification in Western Society, 1880–1930* (Baltimore: Johns Hopkins University Press, 1983), 79–80.

20. See John B. Rae, *The Road and the Car in American Life* (Cambridge: MIT Press, 1971), 31–35; Peter J. Hugill, "Good Roads and the Automobile in the United States, 1880–1929," *Geographical Review* 72, no. 3 (1982): 327–49; Howard L. Preston, *Dirt Roads to Dixie: Accessibility and Modernization in the South, 1885–1935* (Knoxville: University of Tennessee Press, 1991), 11–38; Karl Raitz, "American Roads, Roadside America," *Geographical Review* 88, no. 3 (1998): 363–87; William Wyckoff, *On the Road Again: Montana's Changing Landscape* (Seattle: University of Washington Press, 2006); John A. Jakle and Keith A. Sculle, *Motoring: The Highway Experience in America* (Athens: University of Georgia Press, 2008), 33–54.

21. J. T. Madison, "Which Are State Roads: A Question Which Most People Cannot Answer," *Kentucky Road Builder* 1, no. 4 (1922): 6–7.

22. "The Editorial Viewpoint," *Kentucky Road Builder* 1, no. 6 (1922): 10.

23. Ruth S. Cowan, *A Social History of American Technology* (New York: Oxford University Press, 1997), 233–34; and U.S. Department of Transportation, *America's Highways, 1776–1976: A History of the Federal-Aid Program* (Washington, D.C.: U.S. Government Printing Office, 1977), 113–15.

24. E. N. Todd, "Follow the Route Numbers: The Uniform Marking System for Kentucky's Main Highways," *Kentucky Highways* 1, no. 1 (1926): 9, 12–14; see also Tom Lewis, *Divided Highways: Building the Interstate Highways, Transforming American Life* (New York: Viking, 1997), 13–19.

25. U.S. Department of Transportation, *America's Highways,* 129–30.

26. Kline and Pinch, "Users as Agents of Technological Change," 770.

2. Traveling the Road

1. For an extended and detailed treatment of the relationship between historic road travel and taverns in New Hampshire, see Donna-Belle Garvin and James L. Garvin, *On the Road North of Boston: New Hampshire Taverns and Turnpikes, 1700–1900* (Hanover, N.H.: University Press of New England, 1988). See also Daniel B. Thorp, "Taverns and Tavern Culture on the Southern Colonial Frontier: Rowan County, North Carolina, 1753–1776," *Journal of Southern History* 62, no. 4 (1996): 661–88.

2. Joel Watkins, "Joel Watkins' Diary of 1789," ed. Virginia Smith Derold, *Register of the Kentucky Historical Society* 34, no. 108 (1936): 224.

3. Travel Narrative of Needham Parry (1794), Lyman Copeland Draper Manuscripts, the Wisconsin Historical Society, Madison, 14CC2.

4. Ned Darnaby, interview by John Dabney Shane (n.d.), Lyman Copeland Draper Manuscripts, 11CC165.

5. Thomas Chapman, "A Journal of a Journey through the United States, 1795–96, from the Original Manuscript," *Historical Magazine and Notes and Queries* 15 (1869): 357–68.

6. Ibid.

7. "Some Particulars Relative to the Soil, Situation, Productions &c. of Kentucky; Extracted from the Manuscript Journal of a Gentleman Not Long Since Returned from Those Parts," in

Eugene I. Schwab, ed., *Travels in the Old South,* 2 vols. (Lexington: University Press of Kentucky, 1973), 1:53–60.

8. "Travels in Hot Weather," *Western Monthly Magazine* 2 (October 1834): 528–39, reprinted in Schwab, *Travels in the Old South,* 266–85.

9. Ibid., 277.

10. Kentucky General Assembly, "An Act to Regulate Taverns and Restrain Tippling Houses, Approved December 19, 1793," chap. 40 (Frankfort: John Bradford, 1794), 47–51.

11. Kentucky General Assembly, "An Act to Repeal in Part, an Act Entitled, 'An Act to Amend an Act Regulating Taverns and Restraining Tippling Houses,'" approved December 29, 1823, chap. 639 (Frankfort: Jacob H. Holeman, 1824), 363.

12. Sharon V. Salinger, *Taverns and Drinking in Early America* (Baltimore: Johns Hopkins University Press, 2002), 245.

13. J. Winston Coleman, *Stage-Coach Days in the Bluegrass* (1935; repr., Lexington: University Press of Kentucky, 1996), 165.

14. Craig Thompson Friend, *Along the Maysville Road: The Early American Republic in the Trans-Appalachian West* (Knoxville: University of Tennessee Press, 2005).

15. Kincaid Herr, *The Louisville & Nashville Railroad, 1850–1963,* 5th ed. (1964; repr., Lexington: University Press of Kentucky, 2000), 115–16.

16. E. A. Hewitt and G. W. Hewitt, *Topographical Map of the Counties of Bourbon, Fayette, Clark, Jessamine and Woodford, Kentucky* (New York: Smith, Gallup, 1861).

17. *Kentucky State Gazetteer, Shipper's Guide and Business Directory for 1865 and 1866* (Louisville: Hodgman & Co., 1865).

18. *Kentucky State Gazetteer and Business Directory for 1879–80* (Louisville: R. L. Polk & Co. and A. C. Danser, 1879).

19. *Kentucky State Gazetteer and Business Directory, 1883–1884,* (Louisville: R. L. Polk and Co. and A. C. Danser, 1884).

20. *Kentucky State Gazetteer and Business Directory* (Detroit: R. L. Polk & Co., 1896).

21. Clerk of Court, Bourbon County, Bourbon County Deed Book 54, Paris, Ky., 340.

22. Raitz, "American Roads, Roadside America," 378–79. See also John A. Jakle, Keith A. Sculle, and Jefferson Rogers, *The Motel in America* (Baltimore: Johns Hopkins University Press, 1996), 23–31.

3. Coming to Kentucky

1. Harry Toulmin, *The Western Country in 1793: Reports on Kentucky and Virginia,* ed. Marion Tinling and Godfrey Davies (San Marino, Calif.: Castle Press, 1948), 132.

2. John Melish, *Travels in the United States of America, in the Years 1806 and 1807, and 1809, 1810, and 1811,* 2 vols. (Philadelphia: T. & G. Palmer, Printers, 1812), 2:189. See also Richard L. Troutman, "The Physical Setting of the Bluegrass Planter," *Register of the Kentucky Historical Society* 66, no. 4 (1968): 367–77; and Raymond F. Betts, "'Sweet Meditation through This Pleasant Country': Foreign Appraisals of the Landscape of Kentucky in the Early Years of the Commonwealth," *Register of the Kentucky Historical Society* 90, no. 1 (1992): 26–44.

3. Neal O. Hammon, "Settlers, Land Jobbers, and Outlyers: A Quantitative Analysis of Land Acquisition on the Kentucky Frontier," *Register of the Kentucky Historical Society* 84, no. 3 (1986): 241–62.

4. See C. F. J. Whebell, "Corridors: A Theory of Urban Systems," *Annals of the Association of American Geographers* 59, no. 1 (1969): 1–26.

5. Ralph H. Brown, *Historical Geography of the United States* (New York: Harcourt, Brace

& World, 1948), 197; and W. Wallace Carson, "Transportation and Traffic on the Ohio and the Mississippi before the Steamboat," *Mississippi Valley Historical Review* 7, no. 1 (1920): 26–38.

6. Mary Verhoff, *The Kentucky Mountains: Transportation and Commerce, 1750 to 1911* (Louisville: Filson Club, 1911), 101.

7. Lewis Collins, *History of Kentucky,* 2 vols. (orig. 1797; this ed. 1847, repr. Lexington, Ky.: Henry Clay Press, 1968), 1:39; and F. A. Michaux, "Travels to the West of the Alleghany Mountains in the States of Ohio, Kentucky, and Tennessee," in Reuben Gold Thwaites, ed., *Early Western Travels, 1748–1846,* 32 vols. (Cleveland: Arthur H. Clark, 1904–7), 3:202.

8. Thomas Metcalfe, *Annual Report of the Board of Internal Improvement* (Frankfort: Kentucky State Legislature, 1846), 474.

9. Julian P. Bretz, "Early Land Communication with the Lower Mississippi Valley," *Mississippi Valley Historical Review* 13, no. 1 (1926): 27–29. As a candidate for president in 1824, Henry Clay advocated an "American System" that included protective tariffs and internal improvements, a philosophy supported by most other Republicans of the time. For the twenty-first congressional election (1829–31), Kentucky was divided into twelve state congressional districts; the second congressional district comprised the Maysville Road corridor from Mason County southwest to Fayette County. Nicholas Coleman, a pro-Jackson representative, was elected to represent the district. Two years later, and after Jackson's veto of the Maysville-Washington Road project, the second congressional district changed allegiance and elected as their representative Thomas Marshall, who was a member of the Anti-Jackson Republican (Whig) party. The district remained Whig until the twenty-eighth congressional elections in 1843, which redrew district boundaries. See Kenneth C. Martis, *The Historical Atlas of the Political Parties in the United States Congress, 1789–1989* (New York: Macmillan, 1989), 29, 90–91.

4. Regional Context

1. Moses Austin, "The Journal," *American Historical Review* 5, no. 3 (1900): 525.

2. Lucien Beckner, ed., "John D. Shane's Copy of Needham Parry's Diary of Trip Westward in 1794," *Filson Club History Quarterly* 22, no. 4 (1948): 231.

3. Ibid., 232.

4. Ibid.

5. Ibid.

6. William Faux, "Memorable Days in America: Being a Journal of a Tour to the United States," in Thwaites, *Early Western Travels,* 1:186–87.

7. Ibid., 188.

8. Michaux, "Travels to the West of the Alleghany Mountains," 197. Michaux was probably describing the Point Pleasant Bed limestone of the Clays Ferry Formation, formerly known as the Cynthiana limestone. See L. C. Robinson, "Vein Deposits of Central Kentucky," *Kentucky Geological Survey,* ser. 6, vol. 41 (1931): 14–15, and G. W. Weir, W. L. Peterson, and W. C. Swadley, *Lithostratigraphy of Upper Ordovician Strata Exposed in Kentucky,* U.S. Geological Survey Professional Paper 1151-E (Washington, D.C.: U.S. Government Printing Office, 1984), E19, E24.

9. Michaux, "Travels to the West of the Alleghany Mountains," 199–200.

10. Weir, Peterson, and Swadley, *Lithostratigraphy of Upper Ordovician Strata,* E31–E34. Note that the term *Eden Shale* is part of an older nomenclature utilized by the Geological Survey for several strata units, one of which is now known as the Kope Formation. We will retain the earlier designation, which is the term used in earlier publications to identify the hills that surround the Inner Bluegrass, but we will also refer to specific formations in Part III because their particular characteristics are important to interpreting landscape and land use.

11. Edward Harris, "Letter by Edward Harris, 1797," ed. R. C. Ballard Thruston, *Historical Quarterly* 2, no. 4 (1928): 165–66.

12. Faux, "Memorable Days in America," 186; and Melish, *Travels in the United States of America,* 2:189.

6. Indian Paths and Buffalo Traces

1. Archaeological research demonstrates that deer and elk were present in Kentucky during the late Pleistocene, between 6,000 and 7,000 B.C., when they provided food for hunters and gatherers. See Richard W. Jefferies, "Hunters and Gatherers after the Ice Age," in R. Barry Lewis, ed., *Kentucky Archaeology* (Lexington: University Press of Kentucky, 1996), 45–77. Place names can serve as a rough surrogate for the importance of environmental features encountered by early settlers, such as drainage features, vegetation, and types of animals. Across Kentucky, for example, there are eighty-nine places named for elk, seventy places named for buffalo, and twenty-nine places named for deer. See Thomas P. Field's exhaustively researched *Guide to Kentucky Place Names,* ser. 10, special publication 5 (Lexington, Ky.: University of Kentucky, Kentucky Geological Survey, 1961).

2. Gwynn A. Henderson. "Dispelling the Myth: Seventeenth- and Eighteenth-Century Indian Life in Kentucky," *Register of the Kentucky Historical Society* 90, no. 1 (1992): 1–25.

3. Erhard Rostlund, "The Geographic Range of the Historic Bison in the Southeast," *Annals of the Association of American Geographers* 50, no. 4 (1960): 395.

4. John A. Jakle, "Salt on the Ohio Valley Frontier, 1770–1820," *Annals of the Association of American Geographers* 59, no. 4 (1969): 691; and Thomas D. Clark, "Salt, a Factor in the Settlement of Kentucky," *Filson Club Historical Quarterly* 12, no. 1 (1938): 42–52.

5. J. A. Allen, "The American Bisons, Living and Extinct," in N. S. Shaler, ed., *Memoirs of the Geological Survey of Kentucky* (Cambridge: University Press, 1876), 1:112.

6. James Smith, "Tours into Kentucky and the Northwest Territory," ed. Josiah Morrow, *Ohio Archaeological and Historical Publications* 16 (1907): 371–72.

7. John Filson, *The Discovery, Settlement, and Present State of Kentucke* (Wilmington, Del.: James Adams, 1784), 32–33.

8. Allen, "American Bisons," 116.

9. William Blane, *An Excursion through the United States and Canada during the Years 1822–23* (1824; repr., New York: Negro Universities Press, 1969), 106.

7. Pioneer Road

1. Bayrd Still, ed., "The Westward Migration of a Planter Pioneer in 1796," *William and Mary Quarterly,* 2nd ser., 21, no. 4 (1941): 318–20.

2. Ibid., 332.

3. Ibid.

4. Ibid., 333.

5. Ibid.

6. Ibid., 334.

7. Michaux, "Travels to the West of the Alleghany Mountains," 198.

8. Toulmin, *The Western Country in 1793,* 69.

9. Blane, *An Excursion through the United States and Canada,* 104–5.

10. Mary Dewees, "Mrs. Mary Dewees's Journal from Philadelphia to Kentucky," ed. Johon Blair, *Register of the Kentucky Historical Society* 63, no. 3 (1965): 205.

11. Anonymous, "Some Particulars Relative to Kentucky," in Schwab, *Travels in the Old South,* 1:56. The term *levels* was used in Virginia and West Virginia to describe expansive areas

of rolling land in otherwise hilly country. The Big Levels area of West Virginia is an expansive limestone plain in Greenbrier County, for example. See John P. Hale, *History of the Great Kanawha Valley, with Family History and Biographical Sketches* (Gauley Bridge, W.V.: Gauley & New River, 1994), 152.

12. George Flower, "The Mississippi Valley in 1816 through an Englishman's Diary," ed. Otto L. Schmidt, *Mississippi Valley Historical Review* 14, no. 2 (1927): 151.

13. Lowell H. Harrison, "A Virginian Moves to Kentucky, 1793," *William and Mary Quarterly* 15, no. 2 (1958): 213.

14. Otto A. Rothert, ed., "John D. Shane's Interview with Pioneer John Hedge, Bourbon County," *Filson Club Historical Quarterly* 14, no. 1 (1940): 178; and Lewis Condict, "Journal of a Trip to Kentucky in 1795," *Proceedings of the New Jersey Historical Society* 4 (1919): 119–20.

15. Toulmin, *The Western Country in 1793,* 69.

16. Ibid.

17. John Moylan, Ledger, University of Kentucky Library, Special Collections, Lexington, n.d.

18. Michaux, "Travels to the West of the Alleghany Mountains," 198.

19. Blane, *An Excursion through the United States and Canada,* 107; and *Niles Weekly Register* 7, no. 22 (January 28, 1815): 339–40.

20. Sam Bass Warner Jr., "If All the World Were Philadelphia: A Scaffolding for Urban History, 1774–1930," *American Historical Review* 74, no. 1 (1968): 26–43; Cynthia Shelton, "The Role of Labor in Early Industrialization: Philadelphia, 1787–1837," *Journal of the Early Republic* 4, no. 4 (1984): 365–94; Allen Pred, "Manufacturing in the American Mercantile City: 1800–1840," *Annals of the Association of American Geographers* 56, no. 2 (1966): 307–38; and J. Wreford Watson, *North America: Its Countries and Regions,* rev. ed. (New York: Frederick A. Praeger, 1967), 606–9.

21. Verhoff, *The Kentucky Mountains,* 44. For a discussion of the colonial tradition of road law as it concerned issues of compensation to private landowners through whose land new roads were established, see John F. Hart, "Takings and Compensation in Early America: The Colonial Highway Acts in Social Context," *American Journal of Legal History* 40, no. 3 (1996): 253–306.

22. Jackson, *A Sense of Place, a Sense of Time,* 6–7.

23. William Littell, *The Statute Law of Kentucky,* 5 vols. (Frankfort: William Hunter, 1809–19), 1:633.

24. Verhoff, *The Kentucky Mountains,* 44.

25. Littell, *The Statute Law of Kentucky,* 1:635–36.

26. Karl Raitz and Nancy O'Malley, "The Nineteenth-Century Evolution of Local-Scale Roads in Kentucky's Bluegrass," *Geographical Review* 94, no. 4 (2004): 424.

27. Louis Ward Kemp, "Putting Down Routes: Folk and Popular Perceptions of the Road," *Western Folklore* 42, no. 3 (1983): 157–78, esp. 178.

8. Turnpike Road

1. Andrew Ellicott, *The Journal of Andrew Ellicott* (Philadelphia: William Fry, 1814), 16.

2. Fortescue Cuming, *Sketches of a Tour to the Western Country* (Pittsburgh: Cramer, Spear & Eichbaum, 1810), 149.

3. Ibid., 151.

4. Ibid., 153.

5. Ibid., 154.

6. Ibid., 155.
7. Ibid., 158–59.
8. Ibid., 160.
9. Ibid., 161.
10. Ibid., 164–66, 406.
11. Theodore G. Gronert, "Trade in the Blue-Grass Region, 1810–1820," *Mississippi Valley Historical Review* 5, no. 3 (1918): 317.
12. Ibid., 318.
13. Ibid., 315.
14. Bernard Mayo, "Lexington: Frontier Metropolis," in Eric F. Goldman, ed., *Historiography and Urbanization* (Baltimore: Johns Hopkins Press, 1941), 31; and Gronert, "Trade in the Blue-Grass Region," 315.
15. Gronert, "Trade in the Blue-Grass Region," 316; and Mayo, "Lexington: Frontier Metropolis," 29–30.
16. Collins, *History of Kentucky,* 1:539.
17. William Darby, *The Emigrant's Guide to the Western and Southwestern States and Territories* (New York: Kirk & Mercein, 1818), 206.
18. Gronert, "Trade in the Blue-Grass Region," 319.
19. Ibid., 321.
20. Quoted in Mayo, "Lexington: Frontier Metropolis," 37.
21. Kentucky General Assembly, *Acts Passed at the First Session of the Twenty-Fifth General Assembly,* chap. 113, December 2, 1816 (Frankfort: Gerard & Kendall, 1817), 197–200.
22. Henry Clay, *The Life and Speeches of the Hon. Henry Clay,* ed. Daniel Mallory, 2 vols., 4th ed. (New York: Van Amringe and Bixby, 1844), 1:583–84.
23. Mayo, "Lexington: Frontier Metropolis," 40; and Richard C. Wade, "Urban Life in Western America, 1790–1830," *American Historical Review* 64, no. 1 (1958): 18, 26.
24. Collins, *History of Kentucky,* 1:538.
25. Similarly, Tennessee's early turnpike system focused on Nashville, central to the Nashville Basin, a geological sister to the Bluegrass country. See Stanley J. Folmsbee, "The Turnpike Phase of Tennessee's Internal Improvement System of 1836–1838," *Journal of Southern History* 3, no. 4 (1937): 453–77.
26. Charles Singer et al., eds., *A History of Technology,* 8 vols. (London: Oxford Clarendon Press, 1954–84), 4:536.
27. William M. Gillespie, *A Manual of the Principles and Practice of Road-Making,* 9th ed. (New York: A. S. Barnes, 1858), 194–216.
28. R. Higgins to Valentine Peers, September 30, 1826, Valentine Peers Papers, 1798–1837, Kentucky Historical Society Library, Frankfort; and Kentucky General Assembly, *Acts Passed at the First Session of the Twenty-Fifth General Assembly,* chap. 113, 197–200.
29. John S. Snead to Valentine Peers, November 13, 1826, Valentine Peers Papers, 1798–1837.
30. Basil Hobbs to John S. Snead, November 14, 1826, Valentine Peers Papers, 1798–1837.
31. Collins, *History of Kentucky,* 1:541.
32. Kentucky General Assembly, *Acts Passed at the First Session of the Twenty-Fifth General Assembly,* chap. 113, 198.
33. James Darnaby and William Ellis Jr., *A Platt and Survey of the Road from Lexington to Maysville Made under the Directions of the Commr's. Appointed by an Act of the General Assembly of the Co:wealth of Kentucky,* 1827, Special Collections, M. I. King Library, University of Kentucky, Lexington, map 301. This map is reproduced at reduced scale in Cecil Harp

and J. Winston Coleman Jr., "The Old Lexington and Maysville Turnpike," *Kentucky Engineer* 4, no. 2 (1941): 13–16.

34. Harp and Coleman, "The Old Lexington and Maysville Turnpike," 13.

35. Kentucky General Assembly, *Acts Passed at the First Session of the Forty-Second General Assembly,* chap. 517, December 31, 1833 (Frankfort: Albert Hodges, 1834), 734–35.

36. Kentucky General Assembly, *Acts Passed at the First Session of the Twenty-Fifth General Assembly,* chap. 113, December 2, 1816, 190.

37. Clerk of Court Office, Bourbon County Courthouse, Paris, Ky., Road Book A, 442–43.

38. Raitz and O'Malley, "Local-Scale Turnpike Roads in Nineteenth-Century Kentucky."

39. Kerby A. Miller, *Emigrants and Exiles: Ireland and the Irish Exodus to North America* (New York: Oxford University Press, 1985), 53–56.

40. John W. Jones, Diaries, entry for October 4, 1870, John W. Jones Papers, Special Collections, M. I. King Library, University of Kentucky, Lexington; and Coleman, *Stage-Coach Days in the Bluegrass,* 236.

41. Coleman, *Stage-Coach Days in the Bluegrass,* 240.

42. Ibid., 79.

43. Ibid., 80.

44. Ibid., 82.

45. James S. Buckingham, *The Eastern and Western States of America,* 3 vols. (London: Fisher, Son, & Co., 1842), 2:439, 447–48.

46. A. B. Allen and R. L. Allen, eds., "Kentucky Farming," *American Agriculturalist* 1, no. 5 (1842): 139.

47. Raitz and O'Malley, "The Nineteenth-Century Evolution of Local-Scale Roads in Kentucky's Bluegrass," 426–27.

48. A. B. Allen, "Plantation of Mr. James E. Letton," *American Agriculturalist* 3, no. 8 (1844): 231.

49. N. S. Shaler, *American Highways* (New York: Century, 1896), 95.

50. Coleman, *Stage-Coach Days in the Bluegrass,* 242–46.

51. William Owsley, Samuel Daviess, and Manlius Thompson, *Report of the Board of Internal Improvement* (Frankfort, Ky.: Board of Internal Improvement, 1836), 71.

52. Ibid., 72.

53. Welch, "Directions for the Construction of Turnpike Roads," 169–74.

54. Roy Stone, *Kentucky Highways: History of the Old and New Systems,* U.S. Department of Agriculture, Bulletin no. 13 (Washington, D.C.: Government Printing Office, 1895), 12–17.

55. Sylvester Welch, "Maysville, Washington, Paris and Lexington Turnpike Road," in *Report of the Board of Internal Improvement of the State of Kentucky* (Frankfort: Board of Internal Improvement, 1838), 93–98; and Sylvester Welch, "Directions for Repairing Turnpike Roads," in *Report of the Board of Internal Improvement of the State of Kentucky* (Frankfort: Board of Internal Improvement, 1838), 99–104.

56. Welch, "Maysville, Washington, Paris, and Lexington Turnpike Road," 268; and Will Huston, Treasurer, Maysville, Washington, Paris, and Lexington Turnpike Road Company, "Treasurer's Statement," June 2, 1845, Kentucky State Archives, Frankfort.

57. Will Huston, Treasurer, Maysville, Washington, Paris, and Lexington Turnpike Road Company, "Report to Harry Bodley, State Auditor," December 1, 1845, Kentucky State Archives, Frankfort.

58. Verhoff, *The Kentucky Mountains,* 51.

59. Thomas Metcalfe, *Annual Report of the Board of Internal Improvement of the State of Kentucky* (Frankfort: Board of Internal Improvement, 1844), 480.

60. Thomas Metcalfe, *Annual Report of the Board of Internal Improvement of the State of Kentucky* (Frankfort: Board of Internal Improvement, 1845), 557; Thomas Metcalfe, *Annual Report of the Board of Internal Improvement of the State of Kentucky* (Frankfort: Board of Internal Improvement, 1846), 481; and Thomas Metcalfe, *Annual Report of the Board of Internal Improvement of the State of Kentucky* (Frankfort: Board of Internal Improvement, 1847), 597–98.

61. Kentucky General Assembly, *Reports of the Legislature of Kentucky*, December 1848 sess., 503–4; and O. G. Cates, *Annual Report of the Board of Internal Improvement* (Frankfort: Board of Internal Improvement, 1850), 524–25. To review the process whereby local roads in Bourbon County were built, see Raitz and O'Malley, "The Nineteenth-Century Evolution of Local-Scale Roads in Kentucky's Bluegrass," 415–39.

62. Turner W. Allen, "The Turnpike System in Kentucky: A Review of State Road Policy in the Nineteenth Century," *Filson Club Historical Quarterly* 28, no. 3 (1954): 253–55.

63. Ibid., 256.

9. State and Federal Highway

1. Kentucky Department of Public Roads, *First Biennial Report* (Frankfort: Department of Public Roads, 1913), 5–6; and Kentucky General Assembly, *Acts of the General Assembly of the Commonwealth of Kentucky* (Frankfort, 1912), 96.

2. Kentucky Department of Public Roads, *First Biennial Report*, 8.

3. Ibid., 14.

4. Ibid., 16–26.

5. Kentucky Department of Public Roads, *Third and Fourth Biennial Reports* (Frankfort, 1919), map "Kentucky Inter-County Seat System of Highways also Federal Aid Schemes," 21.

6. Ibid., 11–24.

7. Ibid., 185; see also the map "Kentucky Roads Constructed under State Aid," between pp. 48 and 49; W. M. Jarvis, "Building a Water-Bound Macadam Road," *Kentucky Road Builder* 1, no. 6 (1922): 6.

8. Kentucky Department of Public Roads, *Third and Fourth Biennial Reports*, map "Kentucky Inter-County Seat System of Highways also Federal Aid Schemes."

9. Department of State Roads and Highways, *Fifth Biennial Report* (Frankfort, 1921), 21–22; J. T. Madison, "Our State Highway Commission, Its Powers and Duties," *Kentucky Road Builder* 1, no. 7 (1922): 6, 23.

10. Madison, "Our State Highway Commission," 29, 95.

11. *Kentucky Road Builder* 2, no. 12 (1923): map insert "Road Conditions Map."

12. Ibid., 51.

13. State Highway Commission, *Seventh Biennial Report* (Frankfort, 1925), 25.

14. "Completing the Dixie Hiway," *Kentucky Road Builder* 3, no. 10 (1924): 7; "Closing the Gaps," *Kentucky Highways* 1, no. 4 (1926): 14.

15. "Speeders Are Becoming Readers," *Kentucky Road Builder* 4, no. 1 (1925): 14.

16. J. Stacy Hill, "The Eastern Dixie Highway," *Kentucky Road Builder* 2, no. 11 (1923): 7.

17. Ibid., 23.

18. E. N. Todd, "Follow the Route Numbers: The Uniform Marking System for Kentucky's Main Highways," *Kentucky Highways* 1, no. 1 (1926): 12.

19. "Highways and Byways in 'Arcady,'" *Kentucky Highways* 2, no. 1 (1927): 4.

20. "Tourists Compliment Kentucky Highways," *Kentucky Progress Magazine* 1, no. 2 (1928): 26.

21. "Roads That Carry Millions Annually," *Kentucky Highways*, 4, no. 6 (1929): 24–25.

22. State Highway Commission, *Seventh Biennial Report,* 25, map "Kentucky Showing Condition of Highways," appended.

23. State Highway Commission, *Eighth Biennial Report* (Frankfort, 1927), 135, 137, 141, 143.

24. G. Glenn Clift, *History of Maysville and Mason County* (Lexington: Transylvania Printing, 1936), 261.

25. Also in 2000 the Kentucky Legislature approved a resolution to designate the section of U.S. 68 from Maysville to Lexington the Simon Kenton Highway. Virginia born, Kenton moved to the Kentucky frontier in 1775 and established a settlement in Mason County. He became a scout and was a contemporary of Daniel Boone, George Rogers Clark, and Anthony Wayne.

26. State Highway Department, "Plan and Profile of Proposed State Highway F.A. 234 D-GS," State Project no. 20, sheets 1–4, Mason County, 1937.

27. State Highway Department, "Plan and Profile of Proposed State Highway F 234 G," State Project no. 91-139-1, sheets 1, 13, Nicholas County, 1948.

28. State Highway Commission, *Ninth Biennial Report* (Frankfort, 1929), 11, 13.

29. Department of Highways, *Biennial Report* (Frankfort, 1942), 80–81, 86–87.

30. Vance, *Capturing the Horizon,* 19.

31. Julius H. Parmelee and Earl R. Feldman, "The Relation of the Highway to Rail Transportation," in Jean Labatut and Wheaton J. Lane, eds., *Highways in Our National Life* (Princeton: Princeton University Press, 1950), 227–39; Herr, *The Louisville & Nashville Railroad,* 214–29.

32. Herr, *The Louisville & Nashville Railroad,* 248.

33. *Maysville, Kentucky, City Directory,* master ed., ABCD no. 422 (Chillicothe, Ohio: Mullin-Kille, 1950), 1:41.

10. From Turnpike to Parkway

1. Darnaby and Ellis, *A Platt and Survey of the Road from Lexington to Maysville,* map 301.

2. See, for example, Clerk of Court Office, Bourbon County Courthouse, Road Book A. An 1844 petition requested that the court consider diverting the new road or establishing a new connector road near Bethlehem Road in Bourbon County (Road Book A, 453–54).

3. Kentucky Department of Public Roads, *Third and Fourth Biennial Reports,* 149.

4. See Krista L. Schneider, *The Paris-Lexington Road: Community-Based Planning and Context Sensitive Highway Design* (Washington, D.C.: Island Press, 2003).

11. The Road as a Corridor of Complexity

1. See Mark Twain, *Roughing It* (1872; repr., New York: Harper & Brothers, 1913).

2. Richard H. Schein, "Normative Dimensions of Landscape," in Chris Wilson and Paul Groth, eds., *Everyday America: Cultural Landscape Studies after J. B. Jackson* (Berkeley: University of California Press, 2003), 199–203.

12. Lexington

1. Abijah Hunt and John Wesley Hunt, Day Book, July 2, 1796–October 1, 1796, Special Collections, M. I. King Library, University of Kentucky, Lexington. The Hunts' inventory included Queen's Ware from England's Staffordshire potteries. They also displayed on their store's shelves Irish sheeting, buckram (a stiff cloth), brown sugar, indigo, green tea, coffee, and cloves. In 1790 the nation had only twenty-four urban places. Philadelphia was the country's largest city, with a population of 42,452.

2. Duncan Hines, *Adventures in Good Eating,* 46th ed. (Bowling Green, Ky.: Adventures in Good Eating, 1955), 127.

3. "Lexington, Kentucky, 1886," map (New York: Sanborn-Perris Map Co., 1886), sheets 9, 10.

4. For a summary of the works commissioned by the Treasury Department's Section on Painting and Sculpture—later known as the Section of Fine Arts—see Patricia Raynor, "Off the Wall: New Deal Post Office Murals," *EnRoute* 6, no. 4 (1997), at www.postalmuseum.si.edu/resources/6a2q_postalmurals.html. The post office–courthouse art deco facade includes brass and steel door surrounds. Above the doors on either end of the building are two Greek Revival Doric order fluted columns. According to tradition, the Doric order represented strength. Attached to the frieze above the columns are six triglyphs that comprise three vertical bars standing atop a small horizontal tablet, under which are suspended six small round balls, all executed in limestone. The symbolism of the triglyphs—as well as many other aspects of Greek architecture—is thought to extend to pre-archaic Greek animistic cult practices that included animal sacrifice. The triglyph, for example, is thought to represent the thighbone of an animal that was cut three times (hence the Greek word *triglyphos*), wrapped in layers of fat, and placed on a hot altar represented by the horizontal tablet. The melted fat formed liquid drops that are represented by the small round balls. Clearly, the deeply historical symbolic meaning associated with Greek Revival design was lost before Thomas Jefferson and other architects brought the style to America, for it is unlikely that a knowledgeable architect would have included such details in a post office–courthouse building had he known the original meaning of these elements. See John Hersey, *The Lost Meaning of Classical Architecture* (Cambridge: MIT Press, 1988), and Daniel Barbiero, "Rereading the Classics," *Diacritics* 20, no. 2 (1990): 40–53.

5. J. Winston Coleman Jr., *The Squire's Sketches of Lexington,* 2nd ed. (Lexington, Ky.: Henry Clay Press, 1972), 68.

6. John Kellogg, "The Formation of Black Residential Areas in Lexington, Kentucky, 1867–1887," *Journal of Southern History* 48, no. 1 (1982): 24.

7. James E. Vance Jr., *This Scene of Man: The Role and Structure of the City in the Geography of Western Civilization* (New York: Harper's College Press, 1977), 168–69.

8. Michael J. Doucet and John C. Weaver, "Material Culture and the North American House: The Era of the Common Man, 1870–1920," *Journal of American History* 72, no. 3 (1985): 560–87, esp. 565–68.

9. Coleman, *Stage-Coach Days in the Bluegrass,* 78–79; and Coleman, *The Squire's Sketches of Lexington,* 39.

10. Bettie L. Kerr and John D. Wright Jr., *Lexington: A Century in Photographs* (Lexington, Ky.: Lexington-Fayette County Historic Commission, 1984), 214.

11. Ibid., 45–46.

12. Lexington, Ky., City Planning and Zoning Commission and L. Segoe, Consulting Engineer, *Comprehensive Plan for Lexington and Its Environs* (Cincinnati: L. Segoe, 1931), 35.

13. Clay Lancaster, *Vestiges of the Venerable City: A Chronicle of Lexington, Kentucky* (Lexington: Lexington-Fayette County Historic Commission, 1978), 57–59.

14. See, for example, www.transysports.com/sports/2011/4/27/GEN_0427113825.aspx?id=45.

15. John E. Kleber, ed., *Kentucky Encyclopedia* (Lexington: University Press of Kentucky, 1992), 894–96.

16. *Lexington Herald-Leader,* Community Section, July 17, 1996, 17.

17. Clay Lancaster, *Antebellum Architecture of Kentucky* (Lexington: University Press of Kentucky, 1991), 145–47.

18. Clay Lancaster, *Ante Bellum Houses of the Bluegrass* (Lexington: University of Kentucky Press, 1961), 61–62; Boyd L. Shearer, "The Daily Aesthetic: A Multimedia Exploration of Leisure and Recreation in Lexington's Segregated Urban Park System" (master's thesis, University of Kentucky, 1999); Julius P. Bolivar MacCabe, *Directory of the City of Lexington and County of Fayette for 1838 and 1839* (Lexington, Ky.: J. C. Noble, 1838), 3; and John D. Wright Jr., *Lexington, Heart of the Bluegrass* (Lexington, Ky.: Lexington-Fayette County Historic Commission, 1982), 77–79.

19. Kellogg, "The Formation of Black Residential Areas in Lexington, Kentucky," 30.

20. Ibid., 34.

21. Ibid., 38–40.

22. See, for example, Beverly Fortune, "Renovation Projects Bring Optimism to North Limestone," *Lexington Herald-Leader,* July 27, 2010, B1, and Cheryl Truman, "North Limestone Making a Turn," *Lexington Herald-Leader,* March 11, 2012, B1.

13. The Original Limestone Trace

1. John A. Jakle and Keith A. Sculle, *Signs in America's Auto Age: Signatures of Landscape and Place* (Iowa City: University of Iowa Press, 2004), 8.

2. Clay Lancaster, *Ante Bellum Houses of the Bluegrass,* attached map. Lancaster's map illustrates estate-scale homes still standing in 1961.

3. James A. Ramage, *John Wesley Hunt: Pioneer Merchant, Manufacturer, and Financier* (Lexington: University Press of Kentucky, 1974), 21, 24–25.

4. Ibid., 26–27.

5. Ibid., 37.

6. Ibid., 48–51.

7. Ibid., 54, 60–61.

8. Ray Allen Billington, *Westward Expansion: A History of the American Frontier,* 4th ed. (New York: Macmillan, 1974), 258–59.

9. Ramage, *John Wesley Hunt,* 66–67.

10. Ibid., 79–89.

11. Ibid., 88–89.

12. Ibid., 100.

13. See, for example, "Blandwood: Alexander Jackson Davis," www.blandwood.org/history/ajdavis.html.

14. Lancaster, *Antebellum Architecture of Kentucky,* 270–73; and "History of Loudoun House," www.lexingtonartleague.org/historyofloudoun.htm.

15. Kentucky Transportation Cabinet, Division of Planning, "Traffic Station Counts, Fayette County, Kentucky" (2008), map.

16. Richard Ulack, "Manufacturing," in Richard Ulack, Karl Raitz, and Gyula Pauer, eds., *Atlas of Kentucky* (Lexington: University Press of Kentucky, 1998), 186–90.

17. See Tracy Heath, "Interstate 75: North America's Industrial Corridor," *Site Selection,* May 2000, 1–2, www.siteselection.com/features/2000may/i75/.

18. Interview with Daniel Bryan, and Daniel Bryan to Lyman C. Draper, letters, Lyman Copeland Draper Manuscripts, 22C9–19.

19. Ibid.

20. Bob Sehlinger and Johnny Molloy, *A Canoeing & Kayaking Guide to Kentucky,* rev. ed. (Birmingham, Ala.: Menasha Ridge Press, 1994). For details on North Elkhorn Creek's water quality, see the University of Kentucky Water Resources Research Institute at www.uky.edu/WaterResources/Watershed/KRB_AR/PDF_Files/Tables/T_5280.PDF.

21. Karl Raitz, *The Kentucky Bluegrass: A Regional Profile and Guide,* Studies in Geography no. 14 (Chapel Hill: UNCH Department of Geography, 1980), 140–41.

22. Clerk of Court, Bourbon County, Bourbon County Deed Book B, Paris, Ky., 88.

14. The City-to-Country Transition

1. State Highway Department, Commonwealth of Kentucky, "Plan and Profile of Proposed State Highway, State Project No. F.A. 296 C-G, Fayette County" (1937), sheet 1.

2. See Kentucky Transportation Cabinet, Division of Planning, "Traffic Station Counts, Fayette County, Kentucky" (2004).

3. Lexington-Fayette Urban County Planning Commission, *1980 Comprehensive Plan, Growth Planning System* (Lexington: LFUCG, 1980), 26–29.

4. See, for example, "William A. Marquard Field," www.transy.edu/about/building.htm?stop=marquard; "Kentucky Breeder/Owner William A. Marquard Dead," Bloodhorse.com, October 25, 2006, www.bloodhorse.com/horse-racing/articles/35984/kentucky.

5. *Lexington Herald-Leader,* May 16, 2001, and June 16, 2004; *Lexington Herald,* June 22, 1965; Lafayette Studio Collection, M. I. King Library, University of Kentucky, Lexington, photo nos. 694, 2120, 669.

6. Raitz and O'Malley, "The Nineteenth-Century Evolution of Local-Scale Roads in Kentucky's Bluegrass," 415–16; Schneider, *The Paris-Lexington Road,* 9–13; Greg Kocher, "Parkway Result of 37-Year Struggle," *Lexington Herald-Leader,* November 30, 2003, A1, A16–A17.

15. Gentleman Farms and the Inner Bluegrass Landscape

1. *Racing Times,* December 2, 1991, n.p.

2. *Daily Racing Form,* June 12, 1986, 5.

3. *Lexington Herald-Leader,* May 16, 1993, K1.

4. Frank T. Phelps, "The Whitney Tradition," *Lexington Herald-Leader,* April 14, 1975, n.p.

5. Stephen Birmingham, "Keep on the Sonny Side," *Special Report,* February–April 1989, 45, in clipping file in Keeneland Library Collection.

6. Thoroughbred Racing Associations, Inc., "C. V. Whitney, One Title Cinched, Aims at Three Championships," New York, August 15, 1960, n.p., on file in Keeneland Library Collection.

7. "C. V. Whitney's Will Leaves Estate to Widow," *Lexington Herald-Leader,* December 24, 1992.

8. Karl Raitz, "Rock Fences and Preadaptation," *Geographical Review* 85, no. 1 (1995): 50–62; and Carolyn Murray-Wooley and Karl Raitz, *Rock Fences of the Bluegrass* (Lexington: University Press of Kentucky, 1992).

9. Murray-Wooley and Raitz, *Rock Fences of the Bluegrass,* 95–96.

10. Schneider, *The Paris-Lexington Road,* 23–55.

11. "John Gaines Is One of a Few 'Two-Way Horsemen,'" *Lexington Herald-Leader,* January 15, 1967; and Cathy Schenck, comp., "John R. Gaines" (1991), in Keeneland Library Collection.

12. Jobie Arnold, "Gainesway Patriarch Inspects Progress at Old Keene Place," *Lexington Herald-Leader,* May 31, 1963.

13. "Congratulations Gainesway Farm," *Lexington Herald-Leader,* July 1, 1984, C20.

14. Sandra Duerr and Jennie Rees, "South African Horseman Buys Gainesway Farm," *Louisville Courier Journal,* February 20, 1989, A1, A8.

15. Jim Jordan, "S. African to Buy Most of Whitney Farm," *Lexington Herald-Leader,* October 24, 1997.

16. Oliver Rackham, *The History of the Countryside* (London: J. M. Dent, 1986), 119–39.

17. James F. Hopkins, ed., "Henry Clay, Farmer and Stockman," *Journal of Southern History* 15, no. 1 (1949): 89–96.

18.Henry Clay, *The Private Correspondence of Henry Clay,* ed. Calvin Colton (New York: A. S. Barnes, 1856), 361.

19. Raitz, *The Kentucky Bluegrass,* 76–79; and Karl B. Raitz, "Gentleman Farms in Kentucky's Inner Bluegrass: A Problem in Mapping," *Southeastern Geographer* 15 (1975): 33–46.

20. "Daniel Swigert, Owner of Elmendorf Stud Farm, Sold 'Splendid Estate' to C. J. Enright of Louisville," *Livestock Record* 34, no. 19 (1891): 347.

21. "Elmendorf at Auction," *Thoroughbred Record* 46, no. 13 (September 25, 1897): 149.

22. "Elmendorf Sold," *Thoroughbred Record* 46, no. 18 (October 30, 1897): 210.

23. Philip Ardery, "The Fabulous James Ben Ali Haggin," *Louisville Courier-Journal Magazine,* May 8, 1983, 34–41; and "Mansion at Elmendorf Will Cost $350,000—Mr. Haggin and Architects Here," *Lexington Morning Herald,* January 27, 1902.

24. "Haggin, the Millionaire Turfman and Mine Owner, Weds Miss Pearl Voorhies in Versailles Today," *Lexington Daily Leader,* December 30, 1897, 1.

25. "Elmendorf," *Lexington Morning Herald,* September 29, 1901, 9.

26. Sue Wahlgren, "Famous Blue Grass Thoroughbred Farm," *Lexington Herald-Leader,* February 6, 1972, F-2.

27. Clerk of Court, Fayette County, General Index to Deeds, Mortgages, etc., Fayette County, Ky., 1794–1903, 215, 222–24, and General Index to Deed, Mortgages, etc., Fayette County, Ky., 1914–1918, 183.

28. "Elmendorf Sold," *Thoroughbred Record* 46 (October 1897): 210.

29. Ardery, "The Fabulous James Ben Ali Haggin," 39–40.

30. J. E. Crosland, *Industrial and Freight Shippers Directory, 1914–1915* (Louisville: Louisville & Nashville Railroad Co., 1915), 97.

31. Obituary, *Thoroughbred Record* 80 (September 1914): 136.

32. "Elmendorf," *Lexington Morning Herald,* September 29, 1901, 9.

33. Wahlgren, "Famous Blue Grass Thoroughbred Farm," F-3.

34. Christine Amos, "Haggin Quarry," *Historic American Engineering Record,* no. KY-35 (2001): 1–2.

35. Andrew G. Leonard, "J. B. Haggin's Beautiful Kentucky Estate," *Illustrated Sporting News,* December 12, 1903, 28–29.

36. Cherie Suchy, "Legacy of the Land," *Thoroughbred Record* 213, no. 1 (January 7, 1981): 48–51.

37. John H. Clark, "James Ben Ali Haggin and Elmendorf," *Thoroughbred Times,* June 7, 1991, 27.

38. P. A. B. Widener, *Without Drums* (New York: G. P. Putnam's Sons, 1940), 231.

39. Karl Raitz and Dorn Van Dommelen, "Creating the Landscape Symbol Vocabulary for a Regional Image: The Case of the Kentucky Bluegrass," *Landscape Journal* 9, no. 2 (1990): 109–21.

40. "Elmendorf Owner Max Gluck Dies," *Daily Racing Form,* November 24, 1984.

41. Frank Mitchell, "Multimillionaire Sportsman Jack Kent Cooke Dead at 84," *Daily Racing Form,* April 9, 1997.

42. Lancaster, *Ante Bellum Houses of the Bluegrass,* 96.

43. Raitz, *The Kentucky Bluegrass,* 138.

44. "History and Past Coverage," http://horseracing.about.com/od/history/l/blderbywin.htm.

45. Lancaster, *Ante Bellum Houses of the Bluegrass,* 33.

46. Barney Nagler, "Racing Still Real . . . ," *Daily Racing Form,* April 1, 1983.

47. Rick Bailey, "Normandy Farm Pace Doesn't Slow When Summer Yearling Sales End," *Lexington Herald-Leader,* August 6, 1972, 36.

48. Raitz, *The Kentucky Bluegrass,* 136–37.

49. See http://gluedideas.com/content-collection/national-cyclopedia/Alderney-Cattle.html.

50. Raitz, *The Kentucky Bluegrass,* 133–35.

51. "Thoroughbred Owner Plans to Purchase Eaton Ridge," *Lexington Leader,* February 11, 1965, 15.

52. "Kentucky Equine Economy," www.horseswork.com/index.php?option=com_content&view=article&id=64:industry-facts&catid=40:learn&Itemid=82.

53. Raitz and Van Dommelen, "Creating the Landscape Symbol Vocabulary for a Regional Image."

54. Hewitt and Hewitt, *Topographical Map.*

55. Jennifer L. Barber, "Phase II and III Archaeological Excavations at the Armstrong Farmstead (15FA185), Fayette County, Kentucky" (Item no. 7–163.00), Contract Publication Series 03-62 (Lexington: Cultural Resource Analysts, 2005).

56. Hewitt and Hewitt, *Topographical Map*; D. G. Beers and J. Lanagan, *Map of Fayette County, Kentucky from New and Actual Surveys* (Philadelphia: Beers & Lanagan, 1877); Clerk of Court, Fayette County, Kentucky Deed Book, 113, 535; J. P. Mullin and J. M. Corbin, *Map of Fayette County, Kentucky* (Lexington: J. P. Mullin and J. M. Corbin, 1904).

57. Edwina Ann Doyle, Ruby Layson, and Anne Armstrong Thompson, eds., *From the Fort to the Future: Educating the Children of Kentucky* (Lexington: Kentucky Images, 1987).

58. Walter E. Langsam and William G. Johnson, *Historic Architecture of Bourbon County, Kentucky* (Paris: Historic Paris–Bourbon County, 1985).

59. Darnaby and Ellis, *A Platt and Survey of the Road from Lexington to Maysville,* map 301.

60. Coleman, *Stage-Coach Days in the Bluegrass,* 107.

61. U.S. Census Bureau, 1850 census, Bourbon County.

62. Coleman, *Stage-Coach Days in the Bluegrass,* 103.

63. Clerk of Court, Bourbon County, Kentucky Mortgage Book 2, Paris, Ky., 445.

64. Clerk of Court, Bourbon County, Kentucky Deed Book 46, Paris, Ky., 231–32.

65. Coleman, *Stage-Coach Days in the Bluegrass,* 107.

66. James Hall, *Notes on the Western States: Containing Descriptive Sketches of Their Soil, Climate, Resources and Scenery* (Philadelphia: H. Hall, 1838), 65–66.

67. National Register of Historic Places, "Nomination for Hopewell Presbyterian Church," Kentucky Heritage Council, Frankfort.

68. Clerk of Court, Bourbon County, Kentucky Deed Book 51, Paris, Ky., 467; Don R. Smith and Wayne Roberts, *The Three Link Fraternity—Odd Fellowship in California* (Linden, Calif.: Linden Publications, 1993).

69. Kentucky Transportation Cabinet, Division of Planning, "Traffic Station Counts, Bourbon County, Kentucky" (2005), map.

70. Glenye Cain, "Idle Hour Farm Diversifies," *Daily Racing Form,* November 9, 2003, 17.

71. Paul Daley, "Iron Deficient," *Blood Horse,* April 19, 2003, 2222–24.

72. Grant Day and R. Berle Clay, "Phase III Excavations at McConnell's Homestead Site (15Bb75), Bourbon County, Kentucky," Contract Publication Series 00-117 (Lexington: Cultural Resource Analysts, 2002).

73. Lewis C. Gray, *History of Agriculture in the Southern United States to 1860,* 2 vols. (1933; repr., Gloucester, Mass.: Peter Smith, 1941), 2:877.

74. Bettye Lee Mastin, "Antiques Add Charm to Bourbon House," *Lexington Herald-Leader,* May 11, 1985, D1.

75. Ibid.

76. Dan Liebman, "Breeder of Timeless Nature Tells of Colt's $1 Heritage," *Daily Racing Form,* August 6, 1984.

77. Hewitt and Hewitt, "Topographical Map," 1:63, 360.

78. Ibid.

79. Jennifer Barber et al., "Phase III Excavations at the Hamlet of Monterey, Site 15Bb112, Bourbon County, Kentucky," Item no. 7–163.22, Contract Publication Series 04011 (Lexington: Cultural Resource Analysts, 2005).

80. Diaries kept by John W. Jones, a Bourbon County farmer who lived near North Middletown, suggest that during the construction of the North Middletown–Cane Ridge Road Turnpike in the 1860s, Jones, as a major shareholder and the turnpike company's treasurer, constructed wood-frame shanties for the Irish laborers who built the turnpike. Though he did not describe the buildings' design, his account makes clear that providing temporary housing for itinerant turnpike laborers was common. John W. Jones, Diaries, entry for May 1868, Catalogue no. M-147. See Raitz and O'Malley, "Local-Scale Turnpike Roads in Nineteenth-Century Kentucky."

81. Herr, *The Louisville & Nashville Railroad,* 115–16.

82. Langsam and Johnson, *Historic Architecture of Bourbon County,* 201.

83. See "Course Info," www.houstonoaksgc.com/course/course-info.html; "Hunt Remembered in Coverage of America's Richest," www.bloodhorse.com/horse-racing/articles/6137/hunt-remembered-in-coverage-of-americas-richest; "Milestones: Hunt Relishes Past Successes, Aims for More in Future," *Thoroughbred Times,* July 10, 2004, www.thoroughbredtimes.com/weekly-feature-articles/2004/july/10/mileposts-hunt-relishes-past-successes-aims-for-more-in-future.aspx; and Mark Tatge, "Happy Returns," www.forbes.com/forbes/2001/1008/224.html.

84. See Richard F. Weingroff, "Blue Star Memorial Highways," www.fhwa.dot.gov/infrastructure/blue01.cfm.

85. Hewitt and Hewitt, "Topographical Map," 1:63, 360.

86. Kentucky Transportation Cabinet, "Bourbon County F296 (19), Paris-Lexington Road," sheet 15 of 69 (1973). See also Kentucky Transportation Cabinet, "KYTC Traffic Counts," http://maps.kytc.ky.gov/trafficcounts/.

16. Siting Paris

1. U.S. Census Bureau, 2010 census.

2. Mrs. William Breckinridge Ardery, *Paris (Hopewell) Sesquicentennial: A Record of the One Hundred and Fiftieth Anniversary of the Founding of Bourbon's County Seat* (Paris: Paris Sesquicentennial Committee, 1939); Survey no. 3920 #2, Virginia Survey Book 5, 53; Virginia Grant Book 5, 14–15, Special Collections, M. I. King Library, University of Kentucky, Lexington.

3. Clerk of Court, Bourbon County, Bourbon County Deed Book A, Paris, Ky., 335.

4. Ardery, *Paris (Hopewell) Sesquicentennial,* 20.

5. The Paris street plan is distinctive. Richard Pillsbury identified more than forty such towns in Pennsylvania that were established before 1815, and he termed the plan the Linear-R; the term *linear* referred to the longitudinal orientation of in-lots to a road frontage, and

the letter *R* referred to the overall rectilinear form. See Richard Pillsbury, "The Urban Street Pattern as a Culture Indicator: Pennsylvania, 1682–1815," *Annals of the Association of American Geographers* 60, no. 3 (1970): 439–41. Hugh Wilhelm and Artimus Keiffer identified the same linear town plan in National Road towns in southeast Ohio, where the back streets that ran parallel to the main street served as alternative routes that allowed drovers to divert from the center of town large herds of livestock being driven to eastern market cities. See Hubert G. H. Wilhelm and Artimus Keiffer, "From Wheeling to Columbus, Ohio," in Karl Raitz, ed., *A Guide to the National Road* (Baltimore: Johns Hopkins University Press, 1996), 130–32.

6. Langsam and Johnson, *Historic Architecture of Bourbon County,* 242.

7. Ibid., 240–41.

8. Richard V. Francaviglia, *Main Street Revisited: Time, Space, and Image Building in Small-Town America* (Iowa City: University of Iowa Press, 1996), 29–30.

9. Richard Mattson, "Storefront Remodeling on Main Street," *Journal of Cultural Geography* 3, no. 2 (1983): 42.

10. Ibid., 45–47.

11. Langsam and Johnson, *Historic Architecture of Bourbon County,* 222.

17. Side Trip: High Street from the Bourbon County Courthouse

1. "Moore's Inn," *Kentucky Gazette,* August 18, 1806, 1. See also "Paris, Kentucky," map (New York: Sanborn-Perris Map Co., 1896).

18. Nineteenth-Century Paris

1. Advertisement in *Western Citizen,* July 12, 1839.

2. H. E. Everman, *The History of Bourbon County* (Paris, Ky.: Bourbon Press, 1977), 77.

3. Ibid., 80.

4. "Pay for Slaves in the Army," *Western Citizen,* April 14, 1865, 3.

19. Paris toward Blue Licks

1. Edward K. Muller and Paul A. Groves, "The Emergence of Industrial Districts in Mid-Nineteenth Century Baltimore," *Geographical Review* 69, no. 2 (1979): 159–78, esp. 160.

2. Harriet Kerslake, "Map of Paris as It Appeared in 1809," in Ardery, *Paris (Hopewell) Sesquicentennial.*

3. Russell E. Teague, "Hospital Construction under the Hill-Burton Act in Kentucky," *Journal of the Kentucky State Medical Association* 56 (December 1958): 1190, 1284.

4. Louis S. Reed and Edward T. Blomquist, "Tuberculosis Facilities and Planning under the Hospital Survey and Construction Act," *Public Health Reports* 65, no. 5 (1950): 146–54. In per capita income, Kentucky ranked forty-fourth of forty-eight states, and therefore the adjusted Hill-Burton allotment to the state for hospital construction was set at $1.12 per capita, or the second-highest rate in the nation; Mississippi received the highest per capita allotment at $1.16. See Paul A. Brinker and Burley Walker, "The Hill-Burton Act: 1948–1954," *Review of Economics and Statistics* 44, no. 2 (1962): 208–12.

5. Kentucky Transportation Cabinet, "Bourbon County F296 (19), Paris-Lexington Road," sheet 15. See also Kentucky Transportation Cabinet, "KYTC Traffic Counts," http://maps.kytc.ky.gov/trafficcounts/.

6. See Kentucky Transportation Cabinet, "Six Year Highway Plan," at http://transportation.ky.gov/program-management/highway%20plan/2012recommendedprojectlisting.pdf.

7. Raitz and O'Malley, "The Nineteenth-Century Evolution of Local-Scale Roads in Kentucky's Bluegrass," 431–33.

8. Karl Raitz, "The Agricultural Landscape," in Ulack et al., *Atlas of Kentucky*, 164.

9. See "American Saddle Horse, Saddlebred, Originally Kentucky Saddle Horse," http://horsehints.org/Breeds/AmericanSaddlebred.htm.

10. See "About the Farm," www.hillcroftfarm.net/about.html; and American Hackney Horse Society, http://hackneysociety.com; www.american-saddlebred.com (you will be redirected to an archived version of the site; click on "History of the Breed").

11. Department of Highways, Commonwealth of Kentucky, "Plan and Profile of Proposed State Highway, State Project F 234 (13)," sheets 1, 3, 4, and 5, Bourbon County, (1956).

12. Kentucky Transportation Cabinet, Division of Planning, "Traffic Station Counts, Bourbon County, Kentucky" (2005), map.

13. See Kentucky Transportation Cabinet, "Kentucky's FY 2010-FY 2012 Enacted Biennial Highway Plan," July 2010, http://transportation.ky.gov/program-management/Highway%20plan/2010projectlisting.pdf, and http://transportation.ky.gov/program-management/Highway%20plan/2010ProjectMaps.pdf.

20. Millersburg

1. Department of Highways, Commonwealth of Kentucky, "Plan and Profile of Proposed State Highway, State Project 9-59-3," sheets 1, 2, and 3, Bourbon County (1950).

2. Clerk of Court, Bourbon County, Bourbon County Order Book A, Paris, Ky., 150, 163, 181.

3. Travel Narrative of Needham Parry.

4. A hide is an old English measure of land equal to 120 acres. Hans Blumenfield, "Form and Function in Urban Communities," *Journal of the American Society of Architectural Historians* 3, nos. 1–2 (1943): 11–21, esp. 14.

5. Michael P. Conzen, "The Non-Pennsylvania Town: Diffusion of Urban Plan Forms in the American West," *Geographical Review* 96, no. 2 (2006): 183–211, esp. 194; Edmund H. Chapman, "City Planning under Mercantile Expansion: The Case of Cleveland, Ohio," *Journal of Architectural Historians* 10, no. 4 (1951): 10–17; and Alexander Garvin, "Helping Adam Smith's Invisible Hand," *Bulletin of the Association for Preservation Technology* 13, no. 2 (1981): 27–30.

6. Pillsbury, "The Urban Street Pattern as a Culture Indicator," 439–41.

7. Clerk of Court, Bourbon County, Bourbon County Deed Book F, Paris, Ky., 250.

8. U.S. Census Bureau, *Population and Slave Censuses for 1850 and 1860, Bourbon County, Kentucky*.

9. U.S. Census Bureau, *Population Census for Bourbon County, Kentucky*, 1870.

10. Ibid.

11. U.S. House of Representatives, *Narrative of the Cholera Epidemic of 1873 in the United States*, 43rd Congress, 2d sess., House of Representatives, Executive Document no. 95 (1875).

12. U.S. Census Bureau, *Population Census for Bourbon County, Kentucky*, 1880.

13. *Narrative of the Cholera Epidemic*.

14. Peter C. Smith and Karl B. Raitz, "Negro Hamlets and Agricultural Estates in Kentucky's Inner Bluegrass," *Geographical Review* 64, no. 2 (1974): 217–34.

15. Elmer G. Sulzer, "Shuttle 'Cocks o' The Walk': Nos.137 and 138 Are Just Local Freights, but They Have the Right-of-Way along That 50-Mile Stretch of Track from Paris to Maysville," *Louisville & Nashville Employes' Magazine* 24, no. 2 (1948): 14–15, 34–35.

16. U.S. Census Bureau, 2010 census.

17. Langsam and Johnson, *Historic Architecture of Bourbon County*, 294–95.

18. Ibid., 291.

19. Sulzer, "Shuttle 'Cocks o' The Walk,'" 15.

20. "MMI to Boot Out Boot Camp Image," *Lexington Herald-Leader,* April 5, 2006, A1, and "Millersburg Military School to Stay Closed," *Lexington Herald-Leader,* August 19, 2006, A1.

21. See Kentucky Transportation Cabinet, Division of Planning, "Traffic Station Counts, Nicholas County, Kentucky" (2005), map; Kentucky Transportation Cabinet, "US 68 Reconstruction: Bourbon-Nicholas Counties," item no. 7-310.00, at http://pmtoolbox.kytc.ky.gov/sypmaps/d_7/Bourbon.html#.

22. State Highway Department, Commonwealth of Kentucky, "Plan and Profile of Proposed State Highway, State Project No. 91-139, Sec. F 234," sheets 12, 13, and 14, Nicholas County (1948).

23. See for example, http://breederscup.com/bio.aspx?id=15503.

21. The Eden Shale Hills

1. Lyman C. Draper's notes on Ready Money Jack (n.d.), Lyman Copeman Draper Manuscripts, 11CC19; 11CC45.

2. Kentucky Transportation Cabinet, Division of Planning, "Traffic Station Counts, Nicholas County, Kentucky" (2005), map.

3. Roberts M. Wallace, *Geologic Map of the Piqua Quadrangle, Northeastern Kentucky* (Reston, Va.,: U.S. Geological Survey, 1978).

4. See Artcroft's website at www.artcroft.org/.

5. Collins, *History of Kentucky,* 1:538.

6. J. T. Morehead, Samuel Daviess, Thomas Metcalfe, and Finis E. McLean, *Annual Report of the Board of Internal Improvement of the State of Kentucky* (Frankfort: A. G. Hodges, 1840), 240–43.

7. Metcalfe, *Annual Report of the Board of Internal Improvement* (1847), 593–98.

8. Joan Weissinger Conley, comp. and ed., *History of Nicholas County* (Carlisle, Ky.: Nicholas County Historical Society, 1976), 73.

9. State Highway Department, Commonwealth of Kentucky, "Plan and Profile of Proposed State Highway, State Project No. 234, Sec. A2, B–G, Nicholas County" (1932), sheet 1.

10. Department of Highways, Commonwealth of Kentucky, "Plan and Profile of Proposed State Highway, State Project No. FN 234 (32), Nicholas, Robertson, and Fleming Counties" (1967), sheets 3 and 4.

22. Blue Licks

1. Daniel Drake, *Pioneer Life in Kentucky, 1785–1800* (New York: Henry Schuman, 1948), 61.

2. David E. Buchele, Jerry M. Baskin, and Carol C. Baskin, "Ecology of the Endangered Species *Solidago shortii.* I. Geography, Populations, and Physical Habitat," *Bulletin of the Torrey Botanical Club* 116 (1989): 344–55.

3. Willard Rouse Jillson, *The Discovery of Pleistocene Vertebrates at Lower Blue Licks, 1785–1946* (Frankfort, Ky.: Roberts Printing Co., 1949).

4. Neal O. Hammon and Richard Taylor, *Virginia's Western War, 1775–1786* (Mechanicsburg, Pa.: Stackpole Books, 2002).

5. Roseann R. Hogan, "Buffaloes in the Corn: James Wade's Account of Pioneer Kentucky," *Register of the Kentucky Historical Society* 89 (1991): 5.

6. Ben Guthrie interview by John Dabney Shane (n.d.), Lyman Copeland Draper Manuscripts, 11CC253–257.

7. Jakle, "Salt on the Ohio Valley Frontier," 700; Clark, "Salt, a Factor in the Settlement of Kentucky," 42–52; and Ellicott, *The Journal of Andrew Ellicott,* 13–15. When Ellicott visited the Ohio Salt Lick in November 1796, he found workers tending 170 iron boiling kettles that produced thirty bushels of salt per day, at fifty pounds per bushel. The salt sold for two dollars per bushel or three dollars in trade. See also Arthur C. McFarlan, *Geology of Kentucky* (Lexington: University of Kentucky Press, 1943), 429.

8. Federal Writers' Project, *Kentucky: A Guide to the Bluegrass State* (New York: Harcourt, Brace, 1939), 235.

9. Samuel M. Wilson, *Battle of Blue Licks, August 19, 1782* (Lexington: privately printed, 1927); Neal O. Hammon, *Daniel Boone and the Defeat at Blue Licks* (North Oaks, Minn.: Boone Society, 2005).

10. Wendell McChord, personal communication, 2006.

11. Clerk of Court, Nicholas County, Nicholas County Order Book C, Carlisle, Ky., 412; Clerk of Court, Nicholas County, Nicholas County Survey Book, Carlisle, Ky.

12. Cuming, *Sketches of a Tour to the Western Country,* 153–55.

13. Coleman, *Stage-Coach Days in the Bluegrass;* Conley, *History of Nicholas County;* Darnaby and Ellis, *A Platt and Survey of the Road from Lexington to Maysville.*

14. Collins, *History of Kentucky; Covington Daily Commonwealth,* June 24, 1884.

15. Mabel Alstetter and Gladys Watson, "Western Military Institute, 1847–1861," *Filson Club History Quarterly* 10 (1936): 100–115.

23. Commemoration, Heritage, and a Battlefield Park

1. Charles Hay, "History of Pioneer National Monument Association and the Fort Boonesborough State Park Association," unpublished manuscript (n.d.), 1, Eastern Kentucky University Archives, Richmond, Ky.; see also Charles Hay, comp., "Guide to the Records of the Pioneer National Monument Association and the Fort Boonesborough State Park Association, www.library-old.eku.edu/new/content/archives/findingaids/boonesborough.htm.

2. Kenneth E. Foote, *Shadowed Ground: America's Landscapes of Violence and Tragedy* (Austin: University of Texas Press, 1997), 111.

3. David Lowenthal, *Possessed by the Past: The Heritage Crusade and the Spoils of History* (New York: Free Press, 1996), 94.

4. Paul A. Shackel, ed., *Myth, Memory, and the Making of the American Landscape* (Gainesville: University Press of Florida, 2001), 9–10; Schein, "The Place of Landscape," 672–74. A concise history of the Mount Vernon Ladies' Association is at www.mountvernon.org/educational-resources/library/mount-vernon-ladies-association. Similarly, http://tennesseeencyclopedia.net//entry.php?rec=758 chronicles the origin of the Ladies' Hermitage Association.

5. Hay, "History of Pioneer National Monument Association and the Fort Boonesborough State Park Association," 1–6.

6. Lowenthal, *Possessed by the Past,* ix–xi.

7. See James M. Mayo, *War Memorials as Political Landscape: The American Experience and Beyond* (New York: Praeger, 1988), 144–54; G. Kurt Piehler, *Remembering War the American Way* (Washington, D.C.: Smithsonian Institution Press, 1995), 10–46.

24. Blue Licks toward Maysville

1. Lawrence V. Blade, *Geologic Map of the Cowan Quadrangle, Northeastern Kentucky* (GQ 1466) (Lexington, Ky.: U.S. Geological Survey, 1978). These ancient stream deposits probably date from the Pleistocene geological period (some 2.6 million to 11,700 years ago) or even from the earlier Pliocene period (5.3 to 2.6 million years ago). See, for example, James T.

Teller and Richard P. Goldthwait, "The Old Kentucky River: A Major Tributary to the Teays River," in Wilton N. Melhorn and John P. Kempton, eds., *Geology and Hydrology of the Teays-Mahomet Bedrock Valley System,* Special Paper 258 (Boulder, Colo.: Geological Society of America, 1991), 29–42.

2. State Highway Department, Commonwealth of Kentucky, "Plan and Profile of Proposed State Highway," State Project no. 48, sec. A–G, Robertson County (1928).

3. See the USGS "Cowan, Kentucky," topographic quadrangle map published in 1952, and photorevised in 1978, which records the buffalo trace–county boundary relationship.

25. Fairview and Ewing

1. Lake, Griffing & Stevenson, *An Illustrated Atlas of Mason County, Kentucky* (Philadelphia, 1876); and *An Atlas of Bath & Fleming Counties, Ky., from Actual Surveys by J. M. Lathrop and J. H. Summers* (Philadelphia: J. D. Lake & Co., 1884).

2. M. V. Clark, "The Dynasties of the Maysville Branch," *Louisville & Nashville Employes' Magazine* 8, no. 2 (1932): 13–14.

3. Crosland, *Industrial and Freight Shippers Directory, 1914–1915,* 97. The Powell Hotel was torn down in March 2009.

4. Thomas Worthington, "Ewing as I Saw It from the Early 1900's," unpublished manuscript, n.d.; Thomas Worthington, "Ewing Structures—March 1998," unpublished manuscript, n.d.; Thomas Worthington, "Map of Ewing," unpublished document, n.d.

5. Bonnie Barton, "The Creation of Centrality," *Annals of the Association of American Geographers* 68, no. 1 (1978): 34–44.

6. Focus group interview with Nancy Donavan, Jo Frederick, Gerald Griffith, and Bettye Hitch, Ewing, Ky., Community Center, November 1, 2006.

7. Sulzer, "Shuttle 'Cocks o' The Walk,'" 15.

8. Worthington, "Ewing as I Saw It," 13, 16.

9. Sulzer, "Shuttle 'Cocks o' The Walk,'" 15.

10. Kentucky Transportation Cabinet, Division of Planning, "Traffic Station Counts, Fleming County, Kentucky" (2007), map.

11. Bruce Poundstone and Walter J. Roth, "Types of Farming in Kentucky," Bulletin no. 357 (Kentucky Agricultural Experiment Station, 1935), 84–85.

26. Fairview toward Mason County

1. State Highway Department, Commonwealth of Kentucky, "Plan and Profile of Proposed State Highway," State Project no. 32-250 and 81-175, sheet 1, Fleming-Mason Counties (1947).

2. Frost, *The Art of Roadmaking,* 243.

3. Ibid., 357–58.

4. Ibid., 169–79.

27. The Outer Bluegrass

1. W. F. Axton, *Tobacco and Kentucky* (Lexington: University Press of Kentucky, 1975), 24–26.

2. Ulack et al., *Atlas of Kentucky,* 65–66.

3. Axton, *Tobacco and Kentucky,* 50.

4. Maysville, Ky., Public Ledger, November 29, 1956, Mason County Museum Research Library, clipping file.

28. Mayslick—"The Asparagus Bed of Mason County"

1. Jakle, "Salt on the Ohio Valley Frontier," 687–709.
2. Drake, *Pioneer Life in Kentucky,* 13–14.
3. Ibid., 34–35.
4. Clift, *History of Maysville and Mason County,* 74–76.
5. Drake, *Pioneer Life in Kentucky,* 179.
6. Ibid., 179–80.
7. Ibid., 187.
8. Ibid., 188.
9. F. A. Michaux, "Travels to the West of the Alleghany Mountains," 195–97.
10. U.S. Bureau of the Census, Agricultural Census, 2002.
11. Lynn David and Liz Comer, "May's Lick: Asparagus Bed of Mason County," *Northern Kentucky Heritage* 12, no. 2 (2005): 43.
12. Rudy Forsythe and Steve E. Jacobs, *Soil Survey of Mason County, Kentucky* (Washington, D.C.: U.S. Department of Agriculture and Soil Conservation Service, 1986), 26–30, 55–59, and attached maps.
13. Drake, *Pioneer Life in Kentucky,* 188.
14. David and Comer, "May's Lick: Asparagus Bed of Mason County," 39.
15. Drake, *Pioneer Life in Kentucky,* 193–94.
16. "St. Rose of Lima," *Catholic Encyclopedia,* www.newadvent.org/cathen/13192c.htm.
17. Alicestyne Turley-Adams, *Rosenwald Schools in Kentucky, 1917–1932* (Frankfort: Kentucky Heritage Council and the Kentucky African American Heritage Commission, 1997), 4–8.
18. Ibid., 21.
19. Ibid., 61.
20. See, for example, "The Rosenwald School Initiative, 2009," http://nationalregister.sc.gov/2009landmark/nthpresenwald.pdf, and www.rosenwaldschools.com; and "National Rosenwald Schools Conference," www.rosenwaldschools.com/architecture.html.
21. Kentucky General Assembly, *Acts of the General Assembly of the Commonwealth of Kentucky,* chap. 56, "An Act for the Government and Regulation of the Common Schools of the State" (Louisville: Globe Printing Co., 1908), 133–43, esp. 138–39.
22. R. F. Gaither, "The Mays Lick Consolidated School, Mays Lick, Kentucky," *Atlantic Educational Journal* 9, no. 6 (1914): 217–20.
23. James L. Pyles, "Kentucky Hasn't Always Been Last in Education," *Lexington Herald-Leader,* January 20, 1984. See also David and Comer, "May's Lick: Asparagus Bed of Mason County," 37–49.
24. David and Comer, "May's Lick: Asparagus Bed of Mason County," 44.
25. Drake, *Pioneer Life in Kentucky,* 59.
26. Kentucky Historical Society, *Guide to Kentucky Historical Highway Markers* (Frankfort: Kentucky Historical Society, 1969); Kentucky Historical Society, *Supplement to Guide to Kentucky Historical Highway Markers* (Frankfort: Kentucky Historical Society, 1973); Christopher S. Dwyer, "Raiding Strategy: As Applied by the Western Confederate Cavalry in the American Civil War," *Journal of Military History* 63, no. 2 (1999): 268–70; Thomas D. Clark, *The Kentucky,* Bicentennial ed. (Lexington: University Press of Kentucky, 1992), 299–309; and Lowell H. Harrison and James C. Klotter, *A New History of Kentucky* (Lexington: University Press of Kentucky, 1997), 198–203.
27. State Highway Department, Commonwealth of Kentucky, "Plan and Profile of Proposed State Highway, Mason County," F.A. 234-D-GS, State Project no. 20 (1937).

29. Old Washington

1. Clerk of Court, Mason County, Mason County Deed Book A (n.d.), 1–2.

2. Ned Darnaby, interview by John Dabney Shane (n.d.), Lyman Copeland Draper Manuscripts, 11CC165.

3.Clift, *History of Maysville and Mason County,* 56.

4. Ibid., 57.

5. Samuel Potts Pointer, interview by John Dabney Shane (n.d.), Lyman Copeland Draper Manuscripts, 12CC247, and Asa Farrar, interview by John Dabney Shane (n.d.), ibid., 13CC37.

6. Clift, *History of Maysville and Mason County*, 57.

7. Ibid., 60.

8. Ibid., 100–101.

9. J. R. Robertson, *Petitions of the Early Inhabitants of Kentucky* (Louisville: Filson Club Publications, 1914); Clift, *History of Maysville and Mason County*, 101.

10. Clift, *History of Maysville and Mason County*, 79–84.

11. Edna Hunter Best, *The Historic Past of Washington* (Maysville, Ky.: privately printed, 1944), 16–17.

12. Clift, *History of Maysville and Mason County*, 85.

13. Trustees' Minutes for the Town of Washington, microfilm on file, Mason County Genealogical-Historical Research Library, Maysville, Ky.

14. Clift, *History of Maysville and Mason County*, 120.

15. Ibid., 119.

16. Nancy O'Malley, *A New Village Called Washington* (Maysville: Old Washington, Inc., Kentucky Heritage Council, 1987), 13–14.

17. Ibid., 14.

18. Ibid., 17.

19. Martin V. Melosi, *The Sanitary City: Urban Infrastructure in America from Colonial Times to the Present* (Baltimore: Johns Hopkins University Press, 2000), 19.

20. O'Malley, *A New Village Called Washington,* 15–16.

21. Clift, *History of Maysville and Mason County*, 160.

22. Best, *The Historic Past of Washington,* 25.

23. An analysis of District 3 of the 1850 federal population census of Mason County reveals names of people who were living in Washington in either 1840 or 1860. Their names occurred on five contiguous pages that also included typical urban occupations. This section of the census probably was the enumeration for the town, but no internal notation by the census taker was included to confirm this assumption.

24. Timothy J. Hatton and Jeffrey G. Williamson, "After the Famine: Emigration from Ireland, 1850–1913," *Journal of Economic History* 53, no. 3 (1993): 575–600; Patrick L. Blessing, "Irish Emigration to the United States, 1800–1920: An Overview," in P. J. Drudy, ed., *The Irish in America: Emigration, Assimilation, and Impact* (Cambridge: Cambridge University Press, 1985), 11–37.

25. Lev Russell, comp., *Statutes of Kentucky, Systematized and Annotated* (Lexington: James E. Hughes, 1909), 1326–27.

26. Lake, Griffing & Stevenson, *An Illustrated Atlas of Mason County, Kentucky* (1876; repr., Maysville, Ky., Mason County Historical Society, 1970), 41.

27. Clerk of Court, Mason County, Mason County Deed Book A, Maysville, Ky., 77; Deed Book G, 318.

28. Clift, *History of Maysville and Mason County*, 149.

29. U.S. Census Bureau, "1810 Population Returns for Mason County," town of Washington.

30. Frances Goggin Maltby, "Washington Celebrates Its Sesquicentennial," *Kentucky Progress Magazine* 7, no. 3 (1936): 132–33.

31. U.S. Census Bureau, 1810 census.

32. O'Malley, *A New Village Called Washington,* 71.

33. Julian J. N. Campbell, *The Land of Cane and Clover: Presettlement Vegetation in the So-Called Bluegrass Region of Kentucky* (Lexington: Herbarium Report, University of Kentucky, 1985).

34. John D. Walden, and Vogt, Sage, & Pflum, *Washington, Kentucky Preservation Development* (Washington, Ky.: Old Washington, Inc., and Washington, Kentucky, Historic Township Commission, 1975), Appendix A.

35. Jean Calvert and John Klee, *The Towns of Mason County—Their Past in Pictures* (Maysville, Ky.: Maysville and Mason County Library Historical and Scientific Association, 1986), 26; Walden et al., *Washington, Kentucky Preservation Development,* Appendix A.

36. O'Malley, *A New Village Called Washington,* 67–68.

37. Calvert and Klee, *The Towns of Mason County,* 24–25; Walden et al., *Washington, Kentucky Preservation Development,* Appendix A.

38. O'Malley, *A New Village Called Washington,* 59–66.

39. Clerk of Court, Mason County, Mason County Deed Book B-1, Maysville, Ky., 509; and Deed Book P, Maysville, Ky., 40.

40. Walden et al., *Washington, Kentucky Preservation Development,* Appendix B.

41. Ibid., Appendix A.

42. Calvert and Klee, *The Towns of Mason County,* 27.

43. Ibid., 23.

44. Ibid., 20–21. For further examples of the role of women in the historic preservation movement in the South, see W. Fitzhugh Brundage, *The Southern Past: A Clash of Race and Memory* (Cambridge: Belknap Press of Harvard University Press, 2005), 183–226.

45. Walden et al., *Washington, Kentucky Preservation Development,* Appendix A.

46. Ibid.

47. Calvert and Klee, *The Towns of Mason County,* 21.

48. Lake, Griffing, and Stevenson, *An Illustrated Atlas of Mason County,* 37.

49. Calvert and Klee, *The Towns of Mason County,* 18.

50. Walden et al., *Washington, Kentucky Preservation Development,* Appendix A; Calvert and Klee, *The Towns of Mason County,* 13.

51. Calvert and Klee, *The Towns of Mason County,* 17.

52. O'Malley, *A New Village Called Washington,* 52–53; U.S. Bureau of the Census, population figures for Mason County, various years.

53. State Highway Department, Commonwealth of Kentucky, "Plan and Profile of Proposed State Highway, Mason County," State Project no. 81-195-1, Rural Part-3 (1945).

30. Slavery, the Underground Railroad, and Hemp Production

1. Sam B. Hilliard, *Atlas of Antebellum Southern Agriculture* (Baton Rouge: Louisiana State University Press, 1984), 29–34.

2. United States Federal Census of Population, 1790–1860. See also J. Blaine Hudson, *Fugitive Slaves and the Underground Railroad in the Kentucky Borderland* (Jefferson, N.C.: McFarland, 2002), 14, 20.

3. A. E. Perkins, *The South: Its Economic-Geographic Development* (New York: John Wiley & Sons, 1938), 203–7; John C. Hudson, *Across This Land: A Regional Geography of the United States and Canada* (Baltimore: Johns Hopkins University Press, 2002), 124, 178; and

Merle Prunty Jr., "The Renaissance of the Southern Plantation," *Geographical Review* 45, no. 4 (1955): 459–91.

4. Elisha W. Green, *Life of the Rev. Elisha W. Green* (Maysville, Ky.: Republican Printing Office, 1888), 2–3.

5. Keith P. Griffler, *Frontline of Freedom: African Americans and the Forging of the Underground Railroad in the Ohio Valley* (Lexington: University Press of Kentucky, 2004), 16–17.

6. Hudson, *Fugitive Slaves and the Underground Railroad,* 123–24.

7. Ibid., 61.

8. Kentucky General Assembly, *Acts of the General Assembly of the Commonwealth of Kentucky,* chap. 835, "An Act to secure to persons taking up Slaves that escape from their Masters, compensation for their services" (Frankfort: A. G. Hodges State Printer, 1835), 282, and *Acts of the General Assembly of the Commonwealth of Kentucky,* chap. 409, "An Act further to provide for the appointment of Patrolles in this Commonwealth" (Frankfort: A. G. Hodges State Printer, 1841), 76–77.

9. Wilbur H. Siebert, "Light on the Underground Railroad," *American Historical Review* 1, no. 3 (1896): 461–62.

10. *Louisville Courier,* May 15, 1851, quoted in Hudson, *Fugitive Slaves and the Underground Railroad,* 48.

11. Hudson, *Fugitive Slaves and the Underground Railroad,* 463.

12. François A. Michaux, *Travels to the Westward of the Allegany Mountains* (London: L. Mawman Publisher, 1805), 74–75.

13. John H. Garland, "Hemp, a Minor American Fiber Crop," *Economic Geography* 22, no. 2 (1946): 126–27.

14. Hall, *Notes on the Western States,* 65–66.

15. James F. Hopkins, *A History of the Hemp Industry in Kentucky* (Lexington: University of Kentucky Press, 1951), 25.

16. Ibid., 44.

17. Ibid., 50.

18. Ibid., 54.

19. Ibid., 61.

20. Ibid., 130–31.

21. Ibid., 147–49.

22. Karl Raitz, Richard Schein, Berle Clay, and Nancy O'Malley, "Historical and Cultural Landscapes," in Ulack et al., *Atlas of Kentucky,* 67.

23. Hopkins, *A History of the Hemp Industry in Kentucky,* 210–13.

24. See the MCTC web page at www.maysville.kctcs.edu.

31. Intersections and Commercial Roadside Development

1. See Kentucky Transportation Cabinet, Division of Planning, "Traffic Station Counts, Mason County, Kentucky" (2006).

2. James E. Vance, "The Oregon Trail and Union Pacific Railroad: A Contrast of Purpose," *Annals of the Association of American Geographers* 51, no. 4 (1961): 357–79.

3. Carville Earle, "Regional Economic Development West of the Appalachians, 1815–1860," in Robert D. Mitchell and Paul A. Groves, eds., *North America: The Historical Geography of a Changing Continent* (Totowa, N.J.: Rowman & Littlefield, 1987), 175.

32. Maysville

1. Karl B. Raitz, "Rivers, Towns, and Topographic Maps," *Journal of Geography* 86, no. 2 (1987): 68–76.

2. A. B. Gibbons and Malcolm P. Weiss, *Geologic Map of the Maysville West Quadrangle, Kentucky-Ohio* (GQ 1005) (Lexington, Ky.: Kentucky Geological Survey, 1972).

3. Malcolm P. Weiss, F. A. Shilling Jr., K. L. Pierce, and S. A. Ali, *Geologic Map of the Maysville East Quadrangle, Ohio-Kentucky* (GQ 1006) (Lexington, Ky.: Kentucky Geological Survey, 1972).

4. Edwin S. Gaustad, *Historical Atlas of Religion in America* (New York: Harper & Row, 1962).

5. Josiah Espy, *Memorandums of a Tour Made by Josiah Espy in the States of Ohio and Kentucky and Indiana Territory in 1805* (Cincinnati: Robert Clarke, 1870), 17.

6. Buckingham, *The Eastern and Western States of America,* 2:437.

7. U.S. Census Bureau, 2010 census.

8. Littell, *The Statute Law of Kentucky,* 3:565–66. See also Clerk of Court, Mason County, Mason County Deed Book D, 42.

9. Eli L. Hayes, *Illustrated Atlas of the Upper Ohio River and Valley from Pittsburgh, Penn., to Cincinnati, Ohio* (Philadelphia: Titus, Simmons & Titus, 1877), 210–11 (map).

10. Martha P. Comer, ed., *As We Look Back, Maysville, 1833–1933* (Maysville, Ky.: Maysville Centennial Exposition Commission, 1933), n.p.

11. Ibid.

12. "Maysville, Kentucky," map (New York: Sanborn-Perris Map Co., 1890), sheet 6.

13. Ibid., sheet 4.

14. Clift, *History of Maysville and Mason County,* 73.

15. Ibid., 78.

16. Comer, *As We Look Back.*

17. Alan Gowans, *Images of American Living: Four Centuries of Architecture and Furniture as Cultural Expression* (Philadelphia: J. B. Lippincott, 1964), 242–55; and Michael Kammen, "Temples of Justice: The Iconography of Judgment and American Culture," in Maeva Marcus, ed., *Origins of the Federal Judiciary: Essays on the Judiciary Act of 1789* (New York: Oxford University Press, 1992), 248–80.

18. Edward T. Price, "The Central Courthouse Square in the American County Seat," *Geographical Review* 58, no. 1 (1968): 29–60.

19. F. William O'Brien, *Justice Reed and the First Amendment* (Washington, D.C.: Georgetown University Press, 1958), 3. Two of Stanley Reed's clients were the Chesapeake & Ohio Railroad and the Burley Tobacco Grower's Co-operative Association. Both organizations played a central role in the Mason County and Maysville economy. See ibid., 208.

20. "Maysville, Kentucky," map, sheet 5.

21. Richard Longstreth, *The Buildings of Main Street* (Washington, D.C.: Preservation Press, 1987), 13. In this way a building facade is related in purpose to the donor's tablet on the stained-glass window in a church sanctuary and the grand tombstone in the community cemetery.

22. Ibid., 24–53.

23. Thomas J. Misa, *A Nation of Steel: The Making of Modern America, 1865–1925* (Baltimore: Johns Hopkins University Press, 1995), 45–90; and Peirce Lewis, "America between the Wars: The Engineering of a New Geography," in Thomas F. McIlwraith and Edward K. Muller, eds., *North America: The Historical Geography of a Changing Continent,* 2nd ed. (Lanham, Md.: Rowman & Littlefield, 2001), 381–408.

24. Comer, *As We Look Back.*

25. Larue Tuggle, "Maysville Is Aggressive," *Louisville & Nashville Employes' Magazine* 4 (March 1928): 45–46, 52.

26. *Northern Kentucky Heritage: A Periodical of Regional History and Genealogy* 3, no. 2 (1954): 16–17.

27. U.S. Bureau of the Census, census manuscripts for 1850, 1870, 1880, 1900, and 1910.

28. George Cox's birthplace is listed on his gravestone in the Maysville Cemetery on East Forest Avenue.

29. See Jim Reis, "A Pair of St. Patrick's" in *Cincinnati Post,* March 17, 1997, at www.kypost.com/opinion/reis31797.html.

30. George Drury, *The Historical Guide to North American Railroads* (Waukesha, Wisc.: Kalmbach, 1992), 178–81.

31. Allen and Allen, "Kentucky Farming," 139.

32. John Shackleford, "Correspondence to the President and Directors of the Maysville and Lexington Rail Road," in *Exhibit of the Maysville and Lexington Railroad Company* (Maysville, Ky.: Maysville Eagle Office, 1854), 3.

33. H. Waller, C. Shultz, A. M. January, William Nunn, and Francis Hord to John Shackleford, July 25, 1854, in *Exhibit of the Maysville and Lexington Railroad Company,* 20.

34. "Maysville Celebrates Hundredth Year as a City," *Louisville & Nashville Employes' Magazine* 9 (October 1933): 11.

35. Clift, *History of Maysville and Mason County,* 1:261.

36. Brian Hayes, *Infrastructure: A Field Guide to the Industrial Landscape* (New York: W. W. Norton, 2005), 405–12.

37. Kentucky Transportation Cabinet, Division of Planning, "Traffic Station Counts, Maysville, KY" (map), rev. 2005; see http://transportation.ky.gov/planning/pages/count-maps.aspx.

38. "Maysville, Kentucky," map, sheets 4, 5, and 6.

33. Living with the River

1. George R. Taylor, *The Transportation Revolution: 1815–1860* (New York: Holt, Rinehart and Winston, 1964), 63–64.

2. Leland Johnson, *Men, Mountains, and Rivers: An Illustrated History of the Huntington District, U.S. Army Corps of Engineers, 1754–1974* (Washington, D.C.: U.S. Government Printing Office, 1977), 38–39.

3. Ibid., 36. The current value of this lost cargo would be about $30 million.

4. See "Ohio River Basin," www.waterwayscouncil.org/WWSystem/State%20profiles/OhioBasin.pdf.

5. R. E. Banta, *The Ohio* (New York: Rinehart, 1949), 485–507.

6. David E. Bigham, "River of Opportunity: Economic Consequences of the Ohio," in Robert L. Reid, ed., *Always a River: The Ohio River and the American Experience* (Bloomington: Indiana University Press, 1991), 142.

7. "Ohio River Basin," www.waterwayscouncil.org/WWSystem/State%20profiles/OhioBasin.pdf.

8. Johnson, *Men, Mountains, and Rivers,* 141.

9. Ibid., 169–76.

10. *Maysville Daily Independent,* July 13, 1949.

11. *Maysville Daily Independent,* November 27, 1956, 1.

12. Nick Comer, "Development Projects Seen as Key to Revitalization," *Maysville Daily Independent,* February 17, 1993, 1–2.

34. East Maysville

1. Lewis Collins, *History of Kentucky* (1877; repr., Frankfort: Kentucky Historical Society, 1966), 558.

2. Herr, *The Louisville & Nashville Railroad,* 114.

3. Comer, *As We Look Back.*

4. Ibid.

5. Hayes, *Illustrated Atlas of the Upper Ohio River and Valley,* 210–11.

6. Jean Calvert and John Klee, *Maysville, Kentucky: From Past to Present in Pictures* (Maysville: Mason County Museum, 1983), 183.

7. Ibid., 185.

8. "Maysville, Kentucky," map, sheet 9.

9. H. S. Ellis, "The Burley Tobacco Industry at Maysville, Ky.," *Louisville & Nashville Employes' Magazine* 2 (July 1926): 16, 24.

10. "Maysville, Kentucky," map (New York: Sanborn-Perris Map Co., 1926), sheets 9, 13; and Clift, *History of Maysville and Mason County,* 258–60.

11. "Maysville, Kentucky" map, 1926, sheet 13. For context, an acre is 43,560 square feet, or approximately the size of a football field minus one end zone.

12. Margaretta J. Darnall, "The American Cemetery as Picturesque Landscape: Bellefontaine Cemetery, St. Louis," *Winterthur Portfolio* 8, no. 4 (1983): 249–69, esp. 252.

35. The Changing Landscape of Mobility

1. Stephen Kern, *The Culture of Time and Space: 1880–1918* (Cambridge: Harvard University Press, 1983), 129–30.

2. Daniel J. Boorstin, *The Americans: The National Experience* (New York: Random House, 1965), 97.

3. Peirce Lewis, "The Landscapes of Mobility," in Karl Raitz, ed., *The National Road* (Baltimore: Johns Hopkins University Press, 1996), 11.

4. See Robert Z. Melnick, "Rural Surveys: Tools and Techniques," *Public Historian* 9, no. 1 (1987): 20–30, esp. 23; and May Theilgaard Watts, *Reading the Landscape of America,* rev. ed. (New York: Macmillan, 1975).

5. U.S. Census Bureau, 2010 census.

6. Gabrielle M. Spiegel, *The Past as Text: The Theory and Practice of Medieval Historiography* (Baltimore: Johns Hopkins University Press, 1997), xiv, 185–87.

7. For a thorough review of early efforts by highway engineers to acknowledge unique landscape aesthetics in roadway construction in national parks, see Timothy Davis, Todd A. Croteau, and Christopher H. Marston, eds., *America's National Park Roads and Parkways* (Baltimore: Johns Hopkins University Press, 2004).

8. Raymond Williams, *The Country and the City* (New York: Oxford University Press, 1973), 2–5.

9. J. B. Jackson, "By Way of Conclusion: How to Study the Landscape," in Helen L. Horowitz, ed., *Landscape in Sight: Looking at America* (New Haven: Yale University Press, 1997), 307–21, esp. 315. See also Barry Lopez, "Losing Our Sense of Place," *Teacher* 1 (February 1990): 38–44.

Bibliography

Books, Articles, Documents

"About the Farm." www.hillcroftfarm.net/about.html; American Hackney Horse Society, www.hackneysociety.com.

"Advertisement of Executor's Sale of William Moreland's Estate." *Western Citizen,* September 17, 1852.

Allen, A. B. "Plantation of Mr. James E. Letton." *American Agriculturalist* 3, no. 8 (1844).

Allen, A. B., and R. L. Allen, eds. "Kentucky Farming." *American Agriculturalist* 1, no. 5 (1842).

Allen, J. A. "The American Bisons, Living and Extinct." In N. S. Shaler, ed., *Memoirs of the Geological Survey of Kentucky,* vol. 1. Cambridge: University Press, 1876.

Allen, Turner W. "The Turnpike System in Kentucky: A Review of State Road Policy in the Nineteenth Century." *Filson Club Historical Quarterly* 28, no. 3 (1954).

Alstetter, Mabel, and Gladys Watson. "Western Military Institute, 1847–1861." *Filson Club History Quarterly* 10 (1936).

"American Saddle Horse, Saddlebred, Originally Kentucky Saddle Horse." http://horsehints.org/Breeds/AmericanSaddlebred.htm.

Amos, Christine. "Haggin Quarry." *Historic American Engineering Record,* no. KY-35 (2001).

Anonymous. "Some Particulars Relative to Kentucky." In Eugene L. Schwab, ed., *Travels in the Old South,* 2 vols. Lexington: University Press of Kentucky, 1973.

Ardery, Mrs. William Breckinridge. *Paris (Hopewell) Sesquicentennial: A Record of the One Hundred and Fiftieth Anniversary of the Founding of Bourbon's County Seat.* Paris, Ky.: Paris Sesquicentennial Committee, 1939.

Ardery, Philip. "The Fabulous James Ben Ali Haggin." *Louisville Courier-Journal Magazine,* May 8, 1983.

Arnold, Jobie. "Gainesway Patriarch Inspects Progress at Old Keene Place." *Lexington Herald-Leader,* May 31, 1963.

An Atlas of Bath & Fleming Counties, Ky., from Actual Surveys by J. M. Lathrop and J. H. Summers. Philadelphia: D. J. Lake & Co., 1884.

Austin, M. "The Journal." *American Historical Review* 5, no. 3 (1900).

Axton, W. F. *Tobacco and Kentucky.* Lexington: University Press of Kentucky, 1975.

Bailey, Rick. "Normandy Farm Pace Doesn't Slow When Summer Yearling Sales End." *Lexington Herald-Leader,* August 6, 1972.

Banta, R. E. *The Ohio.* New York: Rinehart, 1949.

Barber, Jennifer L. "Phase II and III Archaeological Excavations at the Armstrong Farmstead (15FA185), Fayette County, Kentucky." Item no. 7-163.00. Contract Publication Series 03-62. Lexington, Ky.: Cultural Resource Analysts, 2005.

Barber, Jennifer, Jessica L. Allgood, R. Berle Clay, Grant L. Day, William B. Lees, Trina C. Maples, Lori O'Connor, and Michael W. Tuma. "Phase III Excavations at the Hamlet of Monterey, Site 15Bb112, Bourbon County, Kentucky." Item no. 7–163.22. Contract Publication Series 04011. Lexington, Ky.: Cultural Resource Analysts, 2006.

Barbiero, Daniel. "Rereading the Classics." *Diacritics* 20, no. 2 (1990).

Barton, Bonnie. "The Creation of Centrality." *Annals of the Association of American Geographers* 68, no. 1 (1978).

Beckner, Lucien, ed. "John D. Shane's Copy of Needham Parry's Diary of Trip Westward in 1794." *Filson Club History Quarterly* 22, no. 4 (1948).

Beers, D. G., and J. Lanagan. *Map of Fayette County, Kentucky from New and Actual Surveys.* Philadelphia: Beers & Lanagan, 1877.

Best, Edna Hunter. *The Historic Past of Washington.* Maysville, Ky.: privately printed, 1944.

Betts, Raymond F. "'Sweet Meditation through This Pleasant Country': Foreign Appraisals of the Landscape of Kentucky in the Early Years of the Commonwealth." *Register of the Kentucky Historical Society* 90, no. 1 (1992).

Bigham, David E. "River of Opportunity: Economic Consequences of the Ohio." In Robert L. Reid, ed., *Always a River: The Ohio River and the American Experience.* Bloomington: Indiana University Press, 1991.

Billington, Ray Allen. *Westward Expansion: A History of the American Frontier.* 4th ed. New York: Macmillan, 1974.

Birmingham, Stephen. "Keep on the Sonny Side." *Special Report,* February–April 1989.

Blade, Lawrence V. *Geologic Map of the Cowan Quadrangle, Northeastern Kentucky* (GQ 1466). Lexington, Ky.: U.S. Geological Survey, 1978.

"Blandwood: Alexander Jackson Davis." www.blandwood.org/history/ajdavis.html.

Blane, William. *An Excursion through the United States and Canada during the Years 1822–23.* 1824. Reprint. New York: Negro Universities Press, 1969.

Blessing, Patrick L. "Irish Emigration to the United States, 1800–1920: An Overview." In P. J. Drudy, ed., *The Irish in America: Emigration Assimilation and Impact.* Cambridge: Cambridge University Press, 1985.

Blumenfield, Hans. "Form and Function in Urban Communities." *Journal of the American Society of Architectural Historians* 3, nos. 1–2 (1943).

Boorstin, Daniel J. *The Americans: The National Experience.* New York: Random House, 1965.

Bretz, Julian P. "Early Land Communication with the Lower Mississippi Valley." *Mississippi Valley Historical Review* 13, no. 1 (1926).

Brinker, Paul A., and Burley Walker. "The Hill-Burton Act: 1948–1954." *Review of Economics and Statistics* 44, no. 2 (1962).

Brown, Ralph H. *Historical Geography of the United States.* New York: Harcourt, Brace & World, 1948.

Brundage, W. Fitzhugh. *The Southern Past: A Clash of Race and Memory.* Cambridge: Belknap Press of Harvard University Press, 2005.

Buchele, David E., Jerry M. Baskin, and Carol C. Baskin. "Ecology of the Endangered Species *Solidago shortii.* I. Geography, Populations, and Physical Habitat." *Bulletin of the Torrey Botanical Club* 116 (1989).

Buckingham, James S. *The Eastern and Western States of America.* 3 vols. London: Fisher, Son, & Co., 1842.

Cain, Glenye. "Idle Hour Farm Diversifies." *Daily Racing Form,* November 9, 2003, 17.

Calvert, Jean, and John Klee. *Maysville, Kentucky: From Past to Present in Pictures.* Maysville, Ky.: Mason County Museum, 1983.

———. *The Towns of Mason County—Their Past in Pictures.* Maysville, Ky.: Maysville and Mason County Library Historical and Scientific Association, 1986.

Campbell, Julian J. N. *The Land of Cane and Clover: Presettlement Vegetation in the So-Called Bluegrass Region of Kentucky.* Lexington: Herbarium Report, University of Kentucky, 1985.

Carson, W. Wallace. "Transportation and Traffic on the Ohio and the Mississippi before the Steamboat." *Mississippi Valley Historical Review* 7, no. 1 (1920).

Cates, O. G. *Annual Report of the Board of Internal Improvement.* Frankfort, Ky.: Board of Internal Improvement, 1850.

Chapman, Edmund H. "City Planning under Mercantile Expansion: The Case of Cleveland, Ohio." *Journal of Architectural Historians* 10, no. 4 (1951).

Chapman, Thomas. "A Journal of a Journey through the United States, 1795–96, from the Original Manuscript." *Historical Magazine and Notes and Queries* 15 (1869).

Charter of the Maysville and Lexington Turnpike Road Company Including All Amendments to the Year 1865. Maysville, Ky.: Eagle Printers, 1865.

Clark, John H. "James Ben Ali Haggin and Elmendorf." *Thoroughbred Times,* June 7, 1991.

Clark, M. V. "The Dynasties of the Maysville Branch." *Louisville & Nashville Employes' Magazine* 8, no. 2 (1932).

Clark, Thomas D. *The Kentucky.* Bicentennial Edition. Lexington: University Press of Kentucky, 1992.

———. "Salt, a Factor in the Settlement of Kentucky." *Filson Club Historical Quarterly* 12, no. 1 (1938).

Clay, Henry. *The Life and Speeches of the Hon. Henry Clay.* Ed. Daniel Mallory. 2 vols. 4th ed. New York: Van Amringe and Bixby, 1844.

———. *The Private Correspondence of Henry Clay.* Ed. Calvin Collins. New York: A. S. Barnes, 1856.

Clift, G. Glenn. *History of Maysville and Mason County.* Lexington, Ky.: Transylvania Printing, 1936.

"Closing the Gaps." *Kentucky Highways* 1, no. 4 (1926).

Coleman, J. Winston, Jr. *The Squire's Sketches of Lexington.* Lexington, Ky.: Henry Clay Press, 1972.

———. *Stage-Coach Days in the Bluegrass.* 1935. Reprint. Lexington: University Press of Kentucky, 1996.

Collins, Lewis. *History of Kentucky.* 2 vols. Original publication 1797. This edition 1847. Reprint. Frankfort: Kentucky Historical Society, 1966.

Comer, Martha P., ed. *As We Look Back, Maysville, 1833–1933.* Maysville, Ky.: Maysville Centennial Exposition Commission, 1933.

Comer, Nick. "Development Projects Seen as Key to Revitalization." *Maysville Daily Independent,* February 17, 1993.

"Completing the Dixie Hiway." *Kentucky Road Builder* 3 (1924).

Condict, Lewis. "Journal of a Trip to Kentucky in 1795." *Proceedings of the New Jersey Historical Society* 4 (1919).

"Congratulations Gainesway Farm." *Lexington Herald-Leader,* July 1, 1984, C20.

Conley, Joan Weissinger, ed. and comp. *History of Nicholas County.* Carlisle, Ky.: Nicholas County Historical Society, 1976.

Conzen, Michael P. "The Non-Pennsylvania Town: Diffusion of Urban Plan Forms in the American West." *Geographical Review* 96, no. 2 (2006).

Cowan, Ruth S. *A Social History of American Technology.* New York: Oxford University Press, 1997.

Crosland, J. E. *Industrial and Freight Shippers Directory, 1914–1915.* Louisville, Ky.: Louisville & Nashville Railroad Company, 1915.

Crump, M. H. *Kentucky Highways: History of the Old and New Systems.* Bulletin no. 13, U.S. Department of Agriculture. Washington, D.C.: Government Printing Office, 1895.

Cuming, Fortescue. *Sketches of a Tour to the Western Country.* Pittsburgh: Cramer, Spear & Eichbaum, 1810.

"C. V. Whitney's Will Leaves Estate to Widow." *Lexington Herald-Leader,* December 24, 1992.

Daley, Paul. "Iron Deficient." *Blood Horse,* April 19, 2003, 2222–24.

Darby, William. *The Emigrant's Guide to the Western and Southwestern States and Territories.* New York: Kirk & Mercein, 1818.

Darnaby, James, and William Ellis Jr. *A Platt and Survey of the Road from Lexington to Maysville Made under the Directions of the Commr's. Appointed by an Act of the General Assembly of the Co:wealth of Kentucky.* Map 301. 1827. Special Collections, M. I. King Library, University of Kentucky, Lexington.

Darnall, Margaretta J. "The American Cemetery as Picturesque Landscape: Bellefontaine Cemetery, St. Louis." *Winterthur Portfolio* 8, no. 4 (1983).

David, Lynn, and Liz Comer. "May's Lick: Asparagus Bed of Mason County." *Northern Kentucky Heritage* 12, no. 2 (2005).

Davis, Timothy, Todd A. Croteau, and Christopher H. Marston, eds. *America's National Park Roads and Parkways.* Baltimore: Johns Hopkins University Press, 2004.

Day, Grant, and R. Berle Clay. "Phase III Excavations at McConnell's Homestead Site (15Bb75), Bourbon County, Kentucky." Contract Publication Series 00-117. Lexington, Ky.: Cultural Resource Analysts, 2002.

Department of Highways. Commonwealth of Kentucky. "Plan and Profile of Proposed State Highway, State Project 9-59-3," sheets 1, 2, and 3, Bourbon County. 1950.

———. "Plan and Profile of Proposed State Highway, State Project F 234 (13)," sheets 1, 3, 4, and 5, Bourbon County. 1956.

———. "Plan and Profile of Proposed State Highway, State Project No. FN 234 (32)," Nicholas, Robertson, and Fleming Counties. 1967.

Dewees, Mary. "Mrs. Mary Dewees's Journal from Philadelphia to Kentucky." Ed. John L. Blair. *Register of the Kentucky Historical Society* 63, no. 3 (1965).

Donavan, Nancy, Jo Frederick, Gerald Griffith, and Bettye Hitch. Group interview by Karl Raitz, Ewing, Ky. November 1, 2006.

Doucet, Michael J., and John C. Weaver. "Material Culture and the North American House: The Era of the Common Man, 1870–1920." *Journal of American History* 72, no. 3 (1985).

Doyle, Edwina Ann, Ruby Layson, and Anne Armstrong Thompson, eds. *From the Fort to the Future: Educating the Children of Kentucky.* Lexington: Kentucky Images, 1987.

Drake, Daniel. *Pioneer Life in Kentucky, 1785–1800.* New York: Henry Schuman, 1948.

Draper, Lyman Copeland. Manuscripts. Wisconsin Historical Society, Madison.

Drury, George. *The Historical Guide to North American Railroads.* Waukesha, Wisc.: Kalmbach, 1992.

Dwyer, Christopher S. "Raiding Strategy: As Applied by the Western Confederate Cavalry in the American Civil War." *Journal of Military History* 63, no. 2 (1999).

Earle, Carville. "Regional Economic Development West of the Appalachians, 1815–1860." In Robert D. Mitchell and Paul A. Groves, ed., *North America: The Historical Geography of a Changing Continent.* Totowa, N.J.: Rowman & Littlefield, 1987.

"The Editorial Viewpoint." *Kentucky Road Builder* 1, no. 6 (1922).

Ellicott, Andrew. *The Journal of Andrew Ellicott.* Philadelphia: William Fry, 1814.

Ellis, H. S. "The Burley Tobacco Industry at Maysville, Ky." *Louisville & Nashville Employes' Magazine,* July 2, 1926.

"Elmendorf Owner Max Gluck Dies." *Daily Racing Form,* November 24, 1984.

Esperdy, Gabrielle. *Modernizing Main Street: Architecture and Consumer Culture in the New Deal.* Chicago: University of Chicago Press, 2008.

Espy, Josiah. *Memorandums of a Tour Made by Josiah Espy in the States of Ohio and Kentucky and Indiana Territory in 1805.* Cincinnati: Robert Clarke, 1870.

Everman, H. E. *The History of Bourbon County*. Paris, Ky.: Bourbon Press, 1977.

Faux, W. "Memorable Days in America: Being a Journal of a Tour to the United States." In Reuben Gold Thwaites, ed., *Early Western Travels, 1748–1846.* 32 vols. Cleveland: Arthur H. Clark, 1904–7. Vol. 3.

Federal Writers' Project. *Kentucky: A Guide to the Bluegrass State.* New York: Harcourt, Brace, 1939.

Field, Thomas P. *A Guide to Kentucky Place Names.* Series 10, special publication 5. Lexington: University of Kentucky, Kentucky Geological Survey, 1961.

Filson, John. *The Discovery, Settlement, and Present State of Kentucke.* Wilmington, Del.: James Adams, 1784.

Flower, George. "The Mississippi Valley in 1816 through an Englishman's Diary." Ed. Otto L. Schmidt. *Mississippi Valley Historical Review* 14, no. 2 (1927): 151.

Folmsbee, Stanley J. "The Turnpike Phase of Tennessee's Internal Improvement System of 1836–1838." *Journal of Southern History* 3, no. 4 (1937).

Foote, Kenneth E. *Shadowed Ground: America's Landscapes of Violence and Tragedy.* Austin: University of Texas Press, 1997.

Forsythe, Rudy, and Steve E. Jacobs. *Soil Survey of Mason County, Kentucky.* Washington, D.C.: U.S. Department of Agriculture and Soil Conservation Service, 1986.

Francaviglia, Richard V. *Main Street Revisited: Time, Space, and Image Building in Small-Town America.* Iowa City: University of Iowa Press, 1996.

Friend, Craig Thompson. *Along the Maysville Road: The Early American Republic in the Trans-Appalachian West.* Knoxville: University of Tennessee Press, 2005.

Frost, Harwood. *The Art of Roadmaking.* New York: McGraw-Hill, 1910.

Gaither, R. F. "The Mays Lick Consolidated School, Mays Lick, Kentucky." *Atlantic Educational Journal* 9, no. 6 (1914).

Garland, John H. "Hemp, a Minor American Fiber Crop." *Economic Geography* 22, no. 2 (1946).

Garvin, Alexander. "Helping Adam Smith's Invisible Hand." *Bulletin of the Association for Preservation Technology* 13, no. 2 (1981).

Garvin, Donna-Belle, and James L. Garvin. *On the Road North of Boston: New Hampshire Taverns and Turnpikes, 1700–1900.* Hanover, N.H.: University Press of New England, 1988.

Gaustad, Edwin S. *Historical Atlas of Religion in America.* New York: Harper & Row, 1962.

Gibbons, A. B., and Malcolm P. Weiss. *Geologic Map of the Maysville West Quadrangle, Kentucky-Ohio* (GQ 1005). Lexington: Kentucky Geological Survey, 1972.

Gillespie, William M. *A Manual of the Principles and Practice of Road-Making.* 9th ed. New York: A. S. Barnes, 1858.

Gowans, Alan. *Images of American Living: Four Centuries of Architecture and Furniture as Cultural Expression.* Philadelphia: J. B. Lippincott, 1964.

Gray, Lewis C. *History of Agriculture in the Southern United States to 1860.* 2 vols. 1933. Reprint. Gloucester, Mass.: Peter Smith, 1941.

Green, Elisha W. *Life of the Rev. Elisha W. Green* Maysville, Ky.: Republican Printing Office, 1888.

Griffler, Keith P. *Frontline of Freedom: African Americans and the Forging of the Underground Railroad in the Ohio Valley.* Lexington: University Press of Kentucky, 2004.

Gronert, Theodore G. "Trade in the Blue-Grass Region, 1810–1820." *Mississippi Valley Historical Review* 5, no. 3 (1918).

Hale, John P. *History of the Great Kanawha Valley, with Family History and Biographical Sketches.* Gauley Bridge, W.V.: Gauley & New River, 1994.

Hall, James. *Notes on the Western States; Containing Descriptive Sketches of Their Soil, Climate, Resources and Scenery.* Philadelphia: H. Hall, 1838.

Hammon, Neal O. *Daniel Boone and the Defeat at Blue Licks.* North Oaks, Minn.: Boone Society, 2005.

———. "Settlers, Land Jobbers, and Outlyers: A Quantitative Analysis of Land Acquisition on the Kentucky Frontier." *Register of the Kentucky Historical Society* 84, no. 3 (1986).

Hammon, Neal O., and Richard Taylor. *Virginia's Western War, 1775–1786.* Mechanicsburg, Pa.: Stackpole Books, 2002.

Harp, Cecil, and J. Winston Coleman Jr. "The Old Lexington and Maysville Turnpike." *Kentucky Engineer* 4, no. 2 (1941).

Harrison, Lowell H. "A Virginian Moves to Kentucky, 1793." *William and Mary Quarterly* 15, no. 2 (1958).

Harrison, Lowell H., and James C. Klotter. *A New History of Kentucky.* Lexington: University Press of Kentucky, 1997.

Hart, John F. "Takings and Compensation in Early America: The Colonial Highway Acts in Social Context." *American Journal of Legal History* 40, no. 3 (1996).

Hatton, Timothy J., and Jeffrey G. Williamson. "After the Famine: Emigration from Ireland, 1850–1913." *Journal of Economic History* 53, no. 3 (1993).

Hay, Charles. "History of Pioneer National Monument Association and the Fort Boonesborough State Park Association." Unpublished manuscript (n.d.). Eastern Kentucky University Archives, Richmond, Ky.

Hayes, Brian. *Infrastructure: A Field Guide to the Industrial Landscape.* New York: W. W. Norton, 2005.

Hayes, Eli L. "City of Maysville." In *Illustrated Atlas of the Upper Ohio River and Valley from Pittsburgh, Penn., to Cincinnati, Ohio.* Philadelphia: Titus, Simmons & Titus, 1877.

Heath, Tracy. "Interstate 75: North America's Industrial Corridor." *Site Selection,* May 2000. www.siteselection.com/features/2000may/i75/.

Henderson, Gwynn A. "Dispelling the Myth: Seventeenth- and Eighteenth-Century Indian Life in Kentucky." *Register of the Kentucky Historical Society* 90, no. 1 (1992).

Herr, Kincaid. *The Louisville & Nashville Railroad, 1850–1963.* Rev. ed. Lexington: University Press of Kentucky, 2000.

Hersey, John. *The Lost Meaning of Classical Architecture.* Cambridge: MIT Press, 1988.

Hewitt, E. A., and G. W. Hewitt. *Topographical Map of the Counties of Bourbon, Fayette, Clark, Jessamine and Woodford, Kentucky.* New York: Smith, Gallup, 1861.

Higgins, R., to Valentine Peers, September 30, 1826. Valentine Peers Papers, 1798–1837. Kentucky Historical Society Library, Frankfort.

"Highways and Byways in 'Arcady.'" *Kentucky Highways* 2, no. 1 (1927).

Hill, J. Stacy. "The Eastern Dixie Highway." *Kentucky Road Builder,* November 1923.

Hilliard, Sam B. *Atlas of Antebellum Southern Agriculture.* Baton Rouge: Louisiana State University Press, 1984.

"History and Past Coverage." http://horseracing.about.com/od/history/l/blderbywin.htm.
"History of Loudoun House." www.lexingtonartleague.org/historyofloudoun.htm.
Hobbs, Basil, to John S. Snead, November 14, 1826. Valentine Peers Papers, 1798–1837. Kentucky Historical Society Library, Frankfort.
Hogan, Roseann R. "Buffaloes in the Corn: James Wade's Account of Pioneer Kentucky." *Register of the Kentucky Historical Society* 89 (1991).
Hopkins, James F., ed. "Henry Clay, Farmer and Stockman." *Journal of Southern History* 15, no. 1 (1949).
———. *A History of the Hemp Industry in Kentucky*. Lexington: University of Kentucky Press, 1951.
Hubbard, Prevost. "Efficiency of Bituminous Surfaces and Pavements under Motor Truck Traffic." *Public Roads* 1, no. 10 (1919).
Hudson, J. Blaine. *Fugitive Slaves and the Underground Railroad in the Kentucky Borderland*. Jefferson, N.C.: McFarland, 2002.
Hudson, John C. *Across This Land: A Regional Geography of the United States and Canada*. Baltimore: Johns Hopkins University Press, 2002.
Hughes, Thomas P. *Networks of Power: Electrification in Western Society, 1880–1930*. Baltimore: Johns Hopkins University Press, 1983.
Hugill, Peter J. "Good Roads and the Automobile in the United States, 1880–1929." *Geographical Review* 72, no. 3 (1982).
Hunt, Abijah, and John Wesley Hunt. Day Book, July 2–October 1, 1796. Special Collections, M. I. King Library, University of Kentucky, Lexington.
Huston, Will. "Report to Harry Bodley, State Auditor." December 1, 1845. Kentucky State Archives, Frankfort.
———. "Treasurer's Statement." June 2, 1845. Kentucky State Archives, Frankfort.
Jackson, Andrew. "Maysville Road: Message from the President of the United States." May 27, 1830. Doc. no. 113, 21st Congress, 1st sess.
Jackson, John B. "By Way of Conclusion: How to Study the Landscape." In Helen L. Horowitz, ed., *Landscape in Sight: Looking at America*. New Haven: Yale University Press, 1997.
———. *A Sense of Place, a Sense of Time*. New Haven: Yale University Press, 1994.
Jakle, John A. "Salt on the Ohio Valley Frontier, 1770–1820." *Annals of the Association of American Geographers* 59, no. 4 (1969).
Jakle, John A., and Keith A. Sculle. *Motoring: The Highway Experience in America*. Athens: University of Georgia Press, 2008.
———. *Signs in America's Auto Age: Signatures of Landscape and Place*. Iowa City: University of Iowa Press, 2004.
Jakle, John A., Keith A. Sculle, and Jefferson Rogers. *The Motel in America*. Baltimore: Johns Hopkins University Press, 1996.
Jarvis, W. M. "Building a Water-Bound Macadam Road." *Kentucky Road Builder* 1, no. 6 (1922).
Jefferies, Richard W. "Hunters and Gatherers after the Ice Age." In R. Barry Lewis, ed., *Kentucky Archaeology*. Lexington: University Press of Kentucky, 1996.
Jillson, Willard Rouse. *The Discovery of Pleistocene Vertebrates at Lower Blue Licks, 1785–1946*. Frankfort, Ky.: Roberts Printing Co., 1949.
"John Gaines Is One of a Few 'Two-Way Horsemen.'" *Lexington Herald-Leader*, January 15, 1967.
Johnson, Leland R. *Men, Mountains, and Rivers: An Illustrated History of the Huntington*

District, U.S. Army Corps of Engineers, 1754–1974. Washington, D.C.: U.S. Government Printing Office, 1977.

Jones, John W. Diaries. John W. Jones Papers. Special Collections, M. I. King Library, University of Kentucky, Lexington.

Jordan, Jim. "S. African to Buy Most of Whitney Farm." *Lexington Herald-Leader,* October 24, 1997.

Kammen, Michael. "Temples of Justice: The Iconography of Judgment and American Culture." In Maeva Marcus, ed., *Origins of the Federal Judiciary, Essays on the Judiciary Act of 1789.* New York: Oxford University Press, 1992.

Kellogg, John. "The Formation of Black Residential Areas in Lexington, Kentucky, 1867–1887." *Journal of Southern History* 48, no. 1 (1982).

Kemp, Louis Ward. "Putting Down Routes: Folk and Popular Perceptions of the Road." *Western Folklore* 2, no. 3 (1983).

Kentucky Department of Highways. *Biennial Report.* 1942.

Kentucky Department of Public Roads. *First Biennial Report.* December 1913.

———. *Third and Fourth Biennial Reports.* December 1919.

Kentucky Department of State Roads and Highways. *Fifth Biennial Report.* 1921.

Kentucky General Assembly. *Acts of the General Assembly of the Commonwealth of Kentucky.* Frankfort: 1912.

———. *Acts of the General Assembly of the Commonwealth of Kentucky.* Chap 40, "An Act to Regulate Taverns and Restrain Tippling Houses, Approved December 19, 1793." Frankfort: John Bradford Publisher, 1794.

———. *Acts of the General Assembly of the Commonwealth of Kentucky.* Chap. 56, "An Act for the Government and Regulation of the Common Schools of the State." Louisville: Globe Printing Company, 1908.

———. *Acts of the General Assembly of the Commonwealth of Kentucky.* Chap. 409, "An Act further to provide for the appointment of Patrolles in this Commonwealth." Frankfort: A. G. Hodges State Printer, 1841.

———. *Acts of the General Assembly of the Commonwealth of Kentucky.* Chap. 639, "An Act to Repeal in Part, an Act Entitled, 'An Act to Amend an Act Regulating Taverns and Restraining Tippling Houses.'" Approved December 29, 1823. Frankfort: Jacob H. Holeman, 1824).

———. *Acts Passed at the First Session of the Twenty-Fifth General Assembly.* Chap. 113. December 2, 1816. Frankfort: Gerard & Kendall, 1817.

———. *Acts Passed at the First Session of the Forty-Second General Assembly.* Chap. 517. December 31, 1833. Frankfort: Albert Hodges, 1834.

———. *Reports of the Legislature of Kentucky.* December sess. Frankfort, 1848.

Kentucky Historical Society. *Guide to Kentucky Historical Highway Markers.* Frankfort: Kentucky Historical Society, 1969.

———. *Supplement to Guide to Kentucky Historical Highway Markers.* Frankfort: Kentucky Historical Society, 1973.

Kentucky State Gazetteer and Business Directory for 1879–80. Louisville: R. L. Polk & Co. and A. C. Danser, 1880.

Kentucky State Gazetteer and Business Directory, 1883–1884. Louisville: R. L. Polk & Co. and A. C. Danser, 1884.

Kentucky State Gazetteer and Business Directory. Detroit: R. L. Polk & Co., 1896.

Kentucky State Gazetteer Shipper's Guide and Business Directory for 1865 and 1866. Louisville: Hodgman & Co., 1866.

Kentucky State Highway Commission. *Seventh Biennial Report.* Frankfort, 1925.

———. *Eighth Biennial Report.* Frankfort, 1927.

———. *Ninth Biennial Report.* Frankfort, 1929.

Kentucky State Highway Department. "Plan and Profile of Proposed State Highway." State Project no. F.A. 296 C-G, Fayette County. 1937.

———. "Plan and Profile of Proposed State Highway F 234 G." State Project no. 91-139-1, sheets 1, 13, Nicholas County. 1948.

———. "Plan and Profile of Proposed State Highway F.A. 234 D-GS." State Project no. 20, sheets 1–4, Mason County. 1937.

Kentucky Transportation Cabinet. "Bourbon County F296 (19), Paris-Lexington Road." Frankfort,.1973.

———. "US 68 Reconstruction: Bourbon-Nicholas Counties." Item no. 7-310.00. http://pmtoolbox.kytc.ky.gov/sypmaps/d_7/Bourbon.html#.

———. Division of Planning. "Traffic Station Counts, Bourbon County, Kentucky." 2005.

———. "Traffic Station Counts, Fayette County, Kentucky." 2004.

———. "Traffic Station Counts, Fleming County, Kentucky." 2005.

———. "Traffic Station Counts, Mason County, Kentucky." 2006.

———. "Traffic Station Counts, Maysville, Ky." (map). 2005. Revised. http://maps.kytc.ky.gov/trafficcounts/.

———. "Traffic Station Counts, Nicholas County, Kentucky" (map). 2005.

Kern, Stephen. *The Culture of Time and Space: 1880–1918.* Cambridge: Harvard University Press, 1983.

Kerr, Bettie L., and John D. Wright Jr. *Lexington: A Century in Photographs.* Lexington, Ky.: Lexington-Fayette County Historic Commission, 1984.

Kerslake, Harriet. "Map of Paris as It Appeared in 1809." In Mrs. William Breckenridge Ardery, ed., *Paris (Hopewell) Sesquicentennial: A Record of the One Hundred and Fiftieth Anniversary of the Founding of Bourbon's County Seat.* Paris, Ky.: Paris Sesquicentennial Committee, 1939.

Kleber, John E., ed. *Kentucky Encyclopedia.* Lexington: University Press of Kentucky, 1992.

Kline, Ronald, and Trevor Pinch. "Users as Agents of Technological Change: The Social Construction of the Automobile in the Rural United States." *Technology and Culture* 37, no. 4 (1996).

Kocher, Greg. "Parkway Result of 37-Year Struggle." *Lexington Herald-Leader,* November 30, 2003.

Lafayette Studio Collection (photographs). M. I. King Library, University of Kentucky, Lexington.

Lake, Griffing & Stevenson. *An Illustrated Atlas of Mason County, Kentucky.* 1876. Reprint. Maysville: Mason County Historical Society, 1970.

Lancaster, Clay. *Ante Bellum Houses of the Bluegrass.* Lexington: University of Kentucky Press, 1961.

———. *Antebellum Architecture of Kentucky.* Lexington: University Press of Kentucky, 1991.

———. *Vestiges of the Venerable City: A Chronicle of Lexington, Kentucky.* Lexington: Lexington-Fayette County Historic Commission, 1978.

Langsam, Walter E., and William G. Johnson. *Historic Architecture of Bourbon County, Kentucky.* Paris: Historic Paris-Bourbon County, 1985.

Larson, John L. *Internal Improvement: National Public Works and the Promise of Popular Government in the Early United States.* Chapel Hill: University of North Carolina Press, 2001.

Leonard, Andrew G. "J. B. Haggin's Beautiful Kentucky Estate." *Illustrated Sporting News,* December 12, 1903, 28–29.

Lewis, Peirce. "America between the Wars: The Engineering of a New Geography." In Thomas F. McIlwraith and Edward K. Muller, eds., *North America: The Historical Geography of a Changing Continent.* 2nd ed. Lanham, Md.: Rowman & Littlefield, 2001.

———. "The Landscapes of Mobility." In Karl Raitz, ed., *The National Road.* Baltimore: Johns Hopkins University Press, 1996.

Lewis, Tom. *Divided Highways: Building the Interstate Highways, Transforming American Life.* New York: Viking, 1997.

"Lexington, Kentucky, 1886." New York: Sanborn-Perris Map Company, 1886.

Lexington, Ky., City Planning and Zoning Commission and L. Segoe, Consulting Engineer. *Comprehensive Plan for Lexington and Its Environs.* Cincinnati: L. Segoe, 1931.

Lexington-Fayette Urban County Planning Commission. *1980 Comprehensive Plan, Growth Planning System.* Lexington, Ky.: Lexington Fayette Urban County Government, 1980.

Liebman, Dan. "Breeder of Timeless Nature Tells of Colt's $1 Heritage." *Daily Racing Form,* August 6, 1984.

Littell, William. *The Statute Law of Kentucky.* 5 vols. Frankfort: William Hunter, 1809–19.

Longstreth, Richard. *The Buildings of Main Street.* Washington, D.C.: Preservation Press, 1987.

Lopez, Barry. "Losing Our Sense of Place." *Teacher* 1 (February 1990).

Lowenthal, David. *Possessed by the Past: The Heritage Crusade and the Spoils of History.* New York: Free Press, 1996.

MacCabe, Julius P. Bolivar. *Directory of the City of Lexington and County of Fayette for 1838 and 1839.* Lexington, Ky.: J. C. Noble, 1938.

Madison, J. T. "Our State Highway Commission, Its Powers and Duties." *Kentucky Road Builder* 1, no. 7 (1922).

———. "Which Are State Roads: A Question Which Most People Cannot Answer." *Kentucky Road Builder* 1, no. 4 (1922).

Maltby, Frances Goggin. "Washington Celebrates Its Sesquicentennial." *Kentucky Progress Magazine* 7, no. 3 (1936).

Martis, Kenneth C. *The Historical Atlas of the Political Parties in the United States Congress, 1789–1989.* New York: Macmillan, 1989.

Mastin, Bettye Lee. "Antiques Add Charm to Bourbon House." *Lexington Herald-Leader,* May 11, 1985.

Mattson, Richard. "Storefront Remodeling on Main Street." *Journal of Cultural Geography* 3, no. 2 (1983).

Mayo, Bernard. "Lexington: Frontier Metropolis." In Eric F. Goldman, ed., *Historiography and Urbanization.* Baltimore: Johns Hopkins University Press, 1941.

Mayo, James M. *War Memorials as Political Landscape: The American Experience and Beyond* New York: Praeger, 1988.

"Maysville Celebrates Hundredth Year as a City." *Louisville & Nashville Employes' Magazine,* October 9, 1933.

"Maysville, Kentucky" (map). New York: Sanborn-Perris Map Company, 1890.

"Maysville, Kentucky" (map). New York: Sanborn-Perris Map Company, 1926.

Maysville, Kentucky, City Directory. Master ed., vol. 1, ABCD no. 422. Chillicothe, Ohio: Mullin-Kille Co., 1950.

McFarlan, Arthur C. *Geology of Kentucky.* Lexington: University of Kentucky Press, 1943.

Melish, John. *Travels in the United States of America, in the Years 1806 and 1807, and 1809, 1810, and 1811.* 2 vols. Philadelphia: T. & G. Palmer, Printers, 1812.

Melnick, Robert Z. "Rural Surveys: Tools and Techniques." *Public Historian* 9, no. 1 (1987).

Melosi, Martin V. *The Sanitary City: Urban Infrastructure in America from Colonial Times to the Present.* Baltimore: Johns Hopkins University Press, 2000.

Metcalfe, Thomas. *Annual Report of the Board of Internal Improvement of the State of Kentucky.* Frankfort: Board of Internal Improvement, 1844.

———. *Annual Report of the Board of Internal Improvement of the State of Kentucky.* Frankfort: Board of Internal Improvement, 1845.

———. *Annual Report of the Board of Internal Improvement of the State of Kentucky.* Frankfort: Board of Internal Improvement, 1846.

———. *Annual Report of the Board of Internal Improvement of the State of Kentucky.* Frankfort: Board of Internal Improvement, 1847.

Michaux, François A. "Travels to the West of the Alleghany Mountains in the States of Ohio, Kentucky, and Tennessee." In Reuben Gold Thwaites, ed., *Early Western Travels, 1748–1846.* 32 vols. Cleveland: Arthur H. Clark, Co., 1904. Vol. 3.

———. *Travels to the Westward of the Allegany Mountains.* London: L. Mawman Publisher, 1805.

Miller, Kerby A. *Emigrants and Exiles: Ireland and the Irish Exodus to North America.* New York: Oxford University Press, 1985.

Misa, Thomas J. *A Nation of Steel: The Making of Modern America, 1865–1925.* Baltimore: Johns Hopkins University Press, 1995.

Mitchell, Frank. "Multimillionaire Sportsman Jack Kent Cooke Dead at 84." *Daily Racing Form,* April 9, 1997.

Morehead, J. T., Samuel Daviess, Thomas Metcalfe, and Finis E. McLean. *Annual Report of the Board of Internal Improvement of the State of Kentucky.* Frankfort: A. G. Hodges, 1840.

Moylan, John. Ledger. Special Collections, M. I. King Library, University of Kentucky, Lexington.

Muller, Edward K., and Paul A. Groves. "The Emergence of Industrial Districts in Mid-Nineteenth Century Baltimore." *Geographical Review* 69, no. 2 (1979).

Mullin, P., and J. M. Corbin. *Map of Fayette County, Kentucky.* Lexington: J. P. Mullin and J. M. Corbin, Associate Engineers, 1904.

Murray-Wooley, Carolyn, and Karl Raitz. *Rock Fences of the Bluegrass.* Lexington: University Press of Kentucky, 1992.

Nagler, Barney. "Racing Still Real . . ." *Daily Racing Form,* April 1, 1983.

National Register of Historic Places. "Nomination for Hopewell Presbyterian Church." Frankfort: Kentucky Heritage Council, n.d.

O'Brien, F. William. *Justice Reed and the First Amendment.* Washington, D.C.: Georgetown University Press, 1958.

O'Malley, Nancy. *A New Village Called Washington.* Maysville, Ky.: Old Washington, Inc., Kentucky Heritage Council, 1987.

Owsley, William, Samuel Daviess, and Manlius Thompson. *Report of the Board of Internal Improvement.* Frankfort, Ky.: Board of Internal Improvement, 1836.

"Paris, Kentucky, 1896." New York: Sanborn-Perris Map Company, 1896.

Parmelee, Julius H., and Earl R. Feldman. "The Relation of the Highway to Rail Transportation." In Jean Labatut and Wheaton J. Lane, eds., *Highways in Our National Life.* Princeton: Princeton University Press, 1950.

Perkins, A. E. *The South: Its Economic-Geographic Development.* New York: John Wiley & Sons, 1938.

Petroski, Henry. *Design Paradigms: Case Histories of Error and Judgment in Engineering.* New York: Cambridge University Press, 1994.
Phelps, Frank T. "The Whitney Tradition." *Lexington Herald-Leader,* April 14, 1975.
Piehler, G. Kurt. *Remembering War the American Way.* Washington, D.C.: Smithsonian Institution Press, 1995.
Pillsbury, Richard. "The Urban Street Pattern as a Culture Indicator: Pennsylvania, 1682–1815." *Annals of the Association of American Geographers* 60, no. 3 (1970).
Poundstone, Bruce, and Walter J. Roth. "Types of Farming in Kentucky." Bulletin no. 357. Kentucky Agricultural Experiment Station. University of Kentucky, Lexington, 1935.
Pred, Allen. "Manufacturing in the American Mercantile City: 1800–1840." *Annals of the Association of American Geographers* 56, no. 2 (1966).
Preston, Howard L. *Dirt Roads to Dixie: Accessibility and Modernization in the South, 1885–1935.* Knoxville: University of Tennessee Press, 1991.
Price, Edward T. "The Central Courthouse Square in the American County Seat." *Geographical Review* 58, no. 1 (1968).
Prunty, Merle, Jr. "The Renaissance of the Southern Plantation." *Geographical Review* 45, no. 4 (1955).
Pyles, James L. "Kentucky Hasn't Always Been Last in Education." *Lexington Herald-Leader,* January 20, 1984.
Rackham, Oliver. *The History of the Countryside.* London: J. M. Dent, 1986.
Rae, John B. *The Road and the Car in American Life.* Cambridge: MIT Press, 1971.
Raitz, Karl. "The Agricultural Landscape." In Richard Ulack, Karl Raitz, and Gyula Pauer, eds., *Atlas of Kentucky.* Lexington: University Press of Kentucky, 1998.
———. "American Roads, Roadside America." *Geographical Review* 88, no. 3 (1998).
———. "Gentleman Farms in Kentucky's Inner Bluegrass: A Problem in Mapping." *Southeastern Geographer* 15 (1975).
———. *The Kentucky Bluegrass: A Regional Profile and Guide.* Studies in Geography no. 14. Chapel Hill: University of North Carolina, Chapel Hill, Department of Geography, 1980.
———. "Rivers, Towns, and Topographic Maps." *Journal of Geography* 86, no. 2 (1987).
———. "Rock Fences and Preadaptation." *Geographical Review* 85, no. 1 (1995).
Raitz, Karl, and Nancy O'Malley. "Local-Scale Turnpike Roads in Nineteenth-Century Kentucky." *Journal of Historical Geography* 33, no. 1 (2007).
———. "The Nineteenth-Century Evolution of Local-Scale Roads in Kentucky's Bluegrass." *Geographical Review* 94, no. 4 (2004).
Raitz, Karl, Richard Schein, Berle Clay, and Nancy O'Malley. "Historical and Cultural Landscapes." In Richard Ulack, Karl Raitz, and Gyula Pauer, eds., *Atlas of Kentucky.* Lexington: University Press of Kentucky, 1998.
Raitz, Karl, and Dorn Van Dommelen. "Creating the Landscape Symbol Vocabulary for a Regional Image: The Case of the Kentucky Bluegrass." *Landscape Journal* 9, no. 2 (1990).
Ramage, James A. *John Wesley Hunt: Pioneer Merchant, Manufacturer, and Financier.* Lexington: University Press of Kentucky, 1974.
Raynor, Patricia. "Off the Wall: New Deal Post Office Murals." *EnRoute* 6, no. 4 (1997). www.postalmuseum.si.edu/resources/6a2q_postalmurals.html.
Reed, Louis S., and Edward T. Blomquist. "Tuberculosis Facilities and Planning under the Hospital Survey and Construction Act." *Public Health Reports* 65, no. 5 (1950).
Reis, Jim. "A Pair of St. Patrick's." *Cincinnati Post,* March 17, 1997.
"Road Conditions Map" (map insert). *Kentucky Road Builder* 2 (1923).
"Roads That Carry Millions Annually." *Kentucky Highways* 4, no. 6 (1929).

Roberts, Merrill J. "The Motor Transportation Revolution." *Business History Review* 30, no. 1 (1956).

Robertson, J. R. *Petitions of the Early Inhabitants of Kentucky.* Filson Club Publications 34. Louisville, Ky.: Filson Club, 1914.

Robinson, L. C. "Vein Deposits of Central Kentucky." *Kentucky Geological Survey,* ser. 6, vol. 41 (1931).

Ross, M. D. "Progress in Looking Backward: History of the First Concrete Road in the State Highway Department, Commonwealth of Kentucky." *Plan and Profile of Proposed State Highway, State Project No.91-139, Sec. F 234, Sheets 12, 13, and 14, Nicholas County.* Frankfort, 1948.

Rostlund, Erhard. "The Geographic Range of the Historic Bison in the Southeast." *Annals of the Association of American Geographers* 50, no. 4 (1960).

Rothert, Otto A., ed. "John D. Shane's Interview with Pioneer John Hedge, Bourbon County." *Filson Club Historical Quarterly* 14, no. 1 (1940).

Russell, Lev, comp. *Statutes of Kentucky, Systematized and Annotated.* Lexington: James E. Hughes, 1909.

Salinger, Sharon V. *Taverns and Drinking in Early America.* Baltimore: Johns Hopkins University Press, 2002.

Schein, Richard H. "Normative Dimensions of Landscape." In Chris Wilson and Paul Groth, eds., *Everyday America: Cultural Landscape Studies after J. B. Jackson.* Berkeley: University of California Press, 2003.

———. "The Place of Landscape: A Conceptual Framework for Interpreting an American Scene." *Annals of the Association of American Geographers* 87, no. 4 (1997).

Schenck, Cathy, comp. "John R. Gaines." 1991. Keeneland Library Collection.

Schneider, Krista L. *The Paris-Lexington Road: Community-Based Planning and Context Sensitive Highway Design.* Washington, D.C.: Island Press, 2003.

Schwab, Eugene I. *Travels in the Old South.* 2 vols. Lexington: University Press of Kentucky, 1973.

Seely, Bruce E. "The Scientific Mystique in Engineering: Highway Research at the Bureau of Public Roads, 1918–1940." *Technology and Culture* 25, no. 4 (1984).

Sehlinger, Bob, and Johnny Molloy. *A Canoeing & Kayaking Guide to Kentucky.* Rev. ed. Birmingham, Ala.: Menasha Ridge Press, 1994.

Shackel, Paul A., ed. *Myth, Memory, and the Making of the American Landscape.* Gainesville: University Press of Florida, 2001.

Shackleford, John. "Correspondence to the President and Directors of the Maysville and Lexington Rail Road." In *Exhibit of the Maysville and Lexington Railroad Company.* Maysville, Ky.: Maysville Eagle Office, 1854.

Shaler, N. S. *American Highways.* New York: Century Company, 1896.

Shearer, Boyd L. "The Daily Aesthetic: A Multimedia Exploration of Leisure and Recreation in Lexington's Segregated Urban Park System." Master's thesis, University of Kentucky, 1999.

Shelton, Cynthia. "The Role of Labor in Early Industrialization: Philadelphia, 1787–1837." *Journal of the Early Republic* 4, no. 4 (1984).

Siebert, Wilbur H. "Light on the Underground Railroad." *American Historical Review* 1, no. 3 (1896).

Simpson, Pamela H. "Cheap, Quick, and Easy: The Early History of Rockfaced Concrete Block Building." *Perspectives in Vernacular Architecture* 3 (1989).

Singer, Charles, E. J. Holmyard, A. R. Hall, and Trevor I. Williams, eds. *A History of Technology,* 8 vols. London: Oxford Clarendon Press, 1954–84.

Smith, Don R., and Wayne Roberts. *The Three Link Fraternity—Odd Fellowship in California.* Linden, Calif.: Linden Publications, 1993.

Smith, James. "Tours into Kentucky and the Northwest Territory." Ed. Josiah Morrow. *Ohio Archaeological and Historical Publications* 16 (1907).

Smith, Peter C., and Karl B. Raitz. "Negro Hamlets and Agricultural Estates in Kentucky's Inner Bluegrass." *Geographical Review* 64, no. 2 (1974).

Snead, John S., to Valentine Peers, November 13, 1826. Valentine Peers Papers, 1798–1837. Kentucky Historical Society Library, Frankfort.

"Speeders Are Becoming Readers." *Kentucky Road Builder* 4, no. 1 (1925).

State Highway Department, Commonwealth of Kentucky. "Plan and Profile of Proposed State Highway, Mason County, F.A. 234-D-GS, State Project no. 20." 1937.

———. "Plan and Profile of Proposed State Highway, Mason County, State Project No. 81-195-1, Rural Part-3." 1945.

———."Plan and Profile of Proposed State Highway, State Project No. 48, Sec. A–G, Robertson County." 1928.

———. "Plan and Profile of Proposed State Highway, State Project No. 234, Sec. A2, B–G, Nicholas County." 1932.

———. "Plan and Profile of Proposed State Highway, State Project No. 32-250, and 81-175, Sheet 1, Fleming-Mason Counties." 1947.

State of Kentucky. *Kentucky Highways* 1, no. 9, n.d.

Stewart, George R. *U.S. 40: Cross Section of the United States of America.* Boston: Houghton Mifflin, 1953.

Still, Bayrd, ed. "The Westward Migration of a Planter Pioneer in 1796." *William and Mary Quarterly,* 2nd ser., 21, no. 4 (1941).

Stone, Roy. *Kentucky Highways, History of the Old and New Systems.* U.S. Department of Agriculture, Bulletin no. 13. Washington, D.C.: Government Printing Office, 1895.

Suchy, Cherie. "Legacy of the Land." *Thoroughbred Record,* January 7, 1981.

Sulzer, Elmer G. "Shuttle 'Cocks o' The Walk': Nos. 137 and 138 Are Just Local Freights, but They Have the Right-of-Way along That 50-Mile Stretch of Track from Paris to Maysville." *Louisville & Nashville Employes' Magazine* 24, no. 2 (1948).

Tatge, Mark. "Happy Returns." www.forbes.com/forbes/2001/1008/224.html.

Taylor, George R. *The Transportation Revolution: 1815–1860.* New York: Holt, Rinehart and Winston, 1964.

Teague, Russell E. "Hospital Construction under the Hill-Burton Act in Kentucky." *Journal of the Kentucky State Medical Association* 56 (December 1958).

Teller, James T., and Richard P. Goldthwait. "The Old Kentucky River: A Major Tributary to the Teays River." In Wilton N. Melhorn and John P. Kempton, eds., *Geology and Hydrology of the Teays-Mahomet Bedrock Valley System.* Special paper 258. Boulder, Colo.: Geological Society of America, 1991.

Thoroughbred Racing Association. "C. V. Whitney, One Title Cinched, Aims at Three Championships." New York: 15 August (1960). On file in Keeneland Library Collection.

Thorp, Daniel B. "Taverns and Tavern Culture on the Southern Colonial Frontier: Rowan County, North Carolina, 1753–1776." *Journal of Southern History* 62, no. 4 (1996).

Thruston, R. C. Ballard, ed. "Letter by Edward Harris, 1797." *Historical Quarterly* 2, no. 4 (1928).

Todd, E. N. "Follow the Route Numbers: The Uniform Marking System for Kentucky's Main Highways." *Kentucky Highways* 1, no. 1 (1926).

Toulmin, Harry. *The Western Country in 1793: Reports on Kentucky and Virginia by Harry Toulmin.* Ed. Marion Tinling and Godfrey Davies. San Marino, Calif.: Castle Press, 1948.

"Tourists Compliment Kentucky Highways." *Kentucky Progress Magazine* 1, no. 2 (1928).

Troutman, Richard L. "The Physical Setting of the Bluegrass Planter." *Register of the Kentucky Historical Society* 66, no. 4 (1968).

"Trustees' Minutes for the Town of Washington." N.d. Microfilm. Mason County Genealogical-Historical Research Library, Maysville, Ky.

Tuggle, Larue. "Maysville Is Aggressive." *Louisville & Nashville Employes' Magazine*, March 4, 1928.

Turley-Adams, Alicestyne. *Rosenwald Schools in Kentucky, 1917–1932.* Frankfort: Kentucky Heritage Council and the Kentucky African American Heritage Commission, 1997.

Twain, Mark. *Roughing It.* 1872. Reprint. New York: Harper & Brothers, 1913.

Ulack, Richard. "Manufacturing." In Richard Ulack, Karl Raitz, and Gyula Pauer, eds., *Atlas of Kentucky.* Lexington: University Press of Kentucky, 1998.

Ulack, Richard, Karl Raitz, and Gyula Pauer, eds. *Atlas of Kentucky.* Lexington: University Press of Kentucky, 1998.

University of Kentucky Water Resources Research Institute. www.uky.edu/WaterResources/watershed/KRB_AR/PDF_Files/Tables/T_5280.PDF.

U.S. Department of Transportation. *America's Highways, 1776–1976: A History of the Federal-Aid Program.* Washington, D.C.: U.S. Government Printing Office, 1976.

U.S. House of Representatives. *Narrative of the Cholera Epidemic of 1873 in the United States.* Executive Document no. 95, 43rd Congress, 2d sess., Washington, D.C., 1875.

Vance, James E., Jr. *Capturing the Horizon: The Historical Geography of Transportation since the Transportation Revolution of the Sixteenth Century.* New York: Harper & Row, 1986.

———. "The Oregon Trail and Union Pacific Railroad: A Contrast of Purpose." *Annals of the Association of American Geographers* 51, no. 4 (1961).

———. *This Scene of Man: The Role and Structure of the City in the Geography of Western Civilization.* New York: Harper's College Press, 1977.

Verhoff, Mary. *The Kentucky Mountains: Transportation and Commerce, 1750 to 1911.* Louisville, Ky.: Filson Club, 1911.

Virginia Survey Book 5. Survey no. 3920 #2. Special Collections, M. I. King Library, University of Kentucky, Lexington.

Wade, Richard C. "Urban Life in Western America, 1790–1830." *American Historical Review* 64, no. 1 (1958).

Wahlgren, Sue. "Famous Blue Grass Thoroughbred Farm." *Lexington Herald-Leader*, February 6, 1972.

Walden, John D., and Vogt, Sage & Pflum. *Washington, Kentucky Preservation Development.* Washington: Old Washington, Inc., and Washington, Kentucky, Historic Township Commission, 1975.

Wallace, Roberts M. *Geologic Map of the Piqua Quadrangle, Northeastern Kentucky* (GQ 1978). Lexington, Ky.: Kentucky Geological Survey, 1978.

Waller, H., C. Shultz, A. M. January, William Nunn, and Francis Hord to John Shackleford, July 25, 1854. In *Exhibit of the Maysville and Lexington Railroad Company.* Maysville, Ky.: Maysville Eagle Office.

Warner, Sam Bass, Jr. "If All the World Were Philadelphia: A Scaffolding for Urban History, 1774–1930." *American Historical Review* 74, no. 1 (1968).

Watkins, Joel. "Joel Watkins' Diary of 1789." Ed. Virginia Smith Herold. *Register of the Kentucky Historical Society* 34, no. 108 (1936).

Watson, J. Wreford. *North America: Its Countries and Regions.* Rev. ed. New York: Frederick A. Praeger, 1967.

Watts, May Theilgaard. *Reading the Landscape of America.* Rev. ed. New York: Macmillan, 1975.

Weingroff, Richard F. "Blue Star Memorial Highways." www.fhwa.dot.gov/infrastructure/blue01.cfm.

Weir, G. W., W. L. Peterson, and W. C. Swadley. *Lithostratigraphy of Upper Ordovician Strata Exposed in Kentucky.* U.S. Geological Survey Professional Paper 1151-E. Washington, D.C.: U.S. Government Printing Office, 1984.

Weiss, Malcolm P., F. A. Shilling Jr., K. L. Pierce, and S. A. Ali. *Geologic Map of the Maysville East Quadrangle, Ohio-Kentucky* (GQ 1006). Lexington: Kentucky Geological Survey, 1972.

Welch, Sylvester. "Directions for Repairing Turnpike Roads." *Report of the Board of Internal Improvement of the State of Kentucky.* Frankfort, Ky.: Board of Internal Improvement, 1838.

———."Directions for the Construction of Turnpike Roads." *Report of the Board of Internal Improvement.* Frankfort, Ky.: Board of Internal Improvement, 1837.

———. "Maysville, Washington, Paris, and Lexington Turnpike Road." *Annual Report of the Board of Internal Improvement of the State of Kentucky.* Frankfort: Board of Internal Improvement, 1840.

———. "Maysville, Washington, Paris and Lexington Turnpike Road." *Report of the Board of Internal Improvement of the State of Kentucky.* Frankfort: Board of Internal Improvement, 1838.

Whebell, C. F. J. "Corridors: A Theory of Urban Systems." *Annals of the Association of American Geographers* 59, no. 1 (1969).

Widener, P. A. B. *Without Drums.* New York: G. P. Putnam's Sons, 1940.

Wik, Reynold M. "Benjamin Holt and the Invention of the Track-Type Tractor." *Technology and Culture* 20, no. 1 (1979).

Wilhelm, Hubert G. H., and Artimus Keiffer. "From Wheeling to Columbus, Ohio." In Karl Raitz, ed., *A Guide to the National Road.* Baltimore: Johns Hopkins University Press, 1996.

Williams, Raymond. *The Country and the City.* New York: Oxford University Press, 1973.

Wilson, Samuel M. *Battle of Blue Licks, August 19, 1782.* Lexington, Ky.: Privately printed, 1927.

Worthington, Thomas. "Ewing as I Saw It from the Early 1900's." Unpublished manuscript. N.d.

———. "Ewing Structures—March 1998." Unpublished manuscript. 1998.

Wright, John D., Jr. *Lexington, Heart of the Bluegrass.* Lexington, Ky.: Lexington-Fayette County Historic Commission, 1982.

Wyckoff, William. *On the Road Again: Montana's Changing Landscape.* Seattle: University of Washington Press, 2006.

Zube, Ervin H. *Landscapes: Selected Writings of J. B. Jackson.* Amherst: University of Massachusetts Press, 1970.

Periodicals

Covington Daily Commonwealth
Daily Racing Form
Illustrated Sporting News
Lexington Daily Leader
Lexington Herald
Lexington Herald-Leader

Lexington Morning Herald
Livestock Record
Louisville Courier Journal
Maysville Daily Independent
Maysville Public Ledger
Niles Weekly Register
Northern Kentucky Heritage: A Periodical of Regional History and Genealogy
Racing Times
Thoroughbred Record
Western Citizen

Web Pages

Alderney cattle. http://gluedideas.com/content-collection/national-cyclopedia/Alderney-Cattle.htmlAmerican.

American Saddle Horse. http://horsehints.org/Breeds/AmericanSaddlebred.htm.

Artcroft. http://artcroft.org.

Crounse Corporation. http://crounse.com/Aboutus.aspx.

Federal Highway Department. "Blue Star Memorial Highways." www.fhwa.dot.gov/infrastructure/blue01.cfm.

Houston Oaks Golf Course. www.houstonoaksgc.com/course/course-info.html.

"Hunt Remembered in Coverage of America's Richest." www.bloodhorse.com/horse-racing/articles/6137/hunt-remembered-in-coverage-of-americas-richest.

"Kentucky Breeder/Owner William A. Marquard Dead." Bloodhorse.com, October 25, 2006, www.bloodhorse.com/horse-racing/articles/35984/kentucky.

Kentucky Community and Technical College System. www.maysville.kctcs.edu.

Kentucky Derby winners. http://horseracing.about.com/od/history/l/blderbywin.htm.

Kentucky Equine Education Project. http://horseswork.com/index.php?option=com_content&view=article&id=64&Itemid=82.

Kentucky Transportation Cabinet. "Interactive Statewide Traffic Counts Map." http://transportation.ky.gov/planning/pages/count-maps.aspx.

———. "KYTC Traffic Counts." http://maps.kytc.ky.gov/trafficcounts/.

"Milestones: Hunt Relishes Past Successes, Aims for More in Future." *Thoroughbred Times*, July 10, 2004. www.thoroughbredtimes.com/weekly-feature-articles/2004/july/10/mileposts-hunt-relishes-past-successes-aims-for-more-in-future.aspx.

"National Rosenwald Schools Conference." www.rosenwaldschools.com.

"Ohio River Basin." www.waterwayscouncil.org/WWSystem/State%20profiles/OhioBasin.pdf.

"The Rosenwald Schools Initiative." http://nationalregister.sc.gov/2009landmark/nthpresenwald.pdf.

Tatge, Mark. "Happy Returns." www.forbes.com/forbes/2001/1008/224.html.

Transylvania University. "John R. Hall Athletic Field." www.transy.edu/about/building.htm?stop=hall.

"William A. Marquard Field." www.transy.edu/about/building.htm?stop=marquard.

Index

Bold page numbers refer to illustrations.

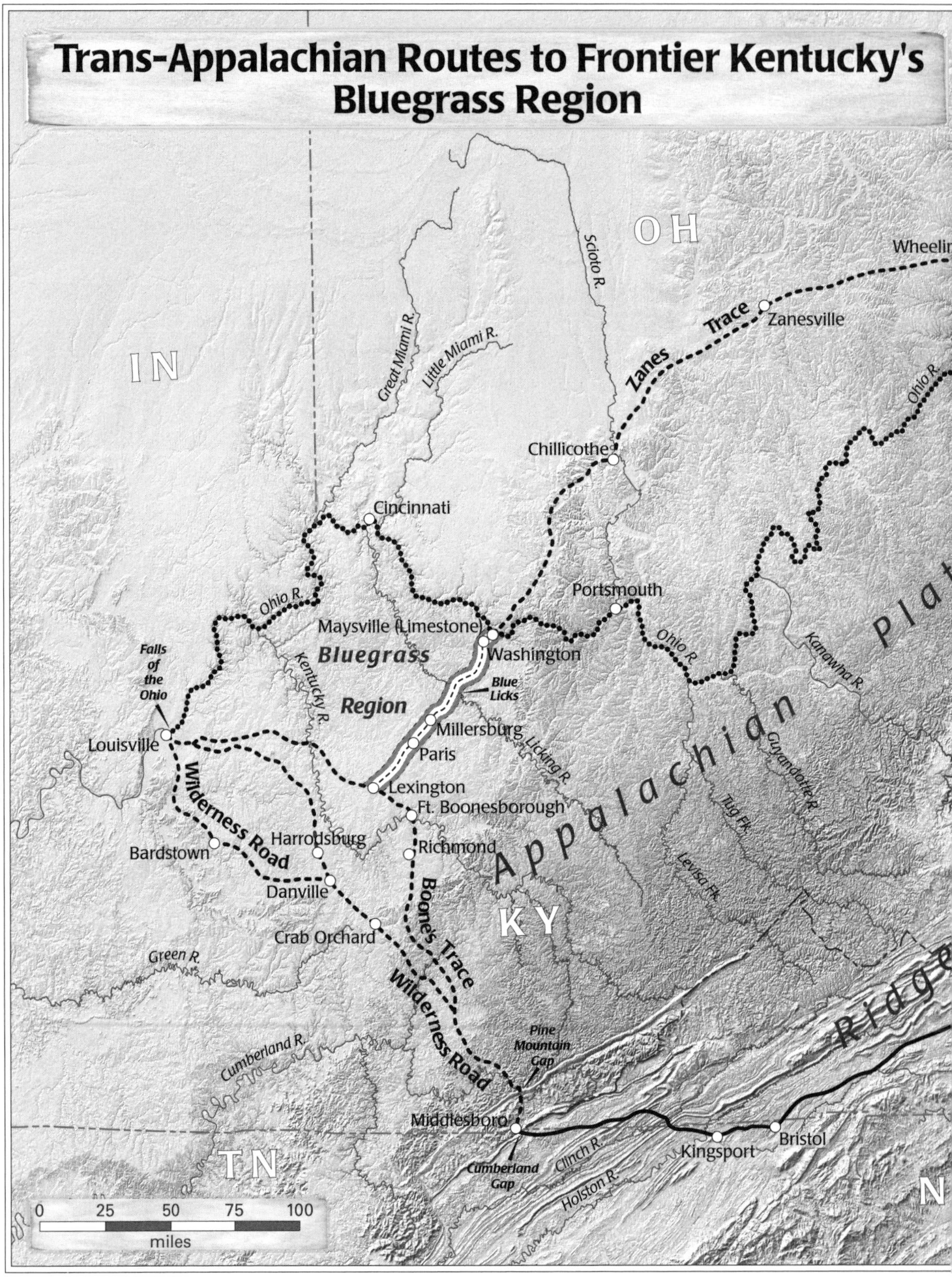
Trans-Appalachian Routes to Frontier Kentucky's Bluegrass Region
OH
IN
KY
TN
Scioto R.
Wheelin
Zanesville
Zanes Trace
Great Miami R.
Little Miami R.
Ohio R.
Chillicothe
Cincinnati
Portsmouth
Maysville (Limestone)
Washington
Bluegrass Region
Falls of the Ohio
Kentucky R.
Blue Licks
Kanawha R.
Appalachian Plat
Millersburg
Paris
Licking R.
Louisville
Lexington
Ft. Boonesborough
Guyandotte R.
Tug Fk.
Levisa Fk.
Wilderness Road
Harrodsburg
Richmond
Bardstown
Danville
Boone's Trace
Crab Orchard
Green R.
Ridge
Pine Mountain Gap
Cumberland R.
Middlesboro
Cumberland Gap
Clinch R.
Kingsport
Bristol
Holston R.
N
0 25 50 75 100
miles